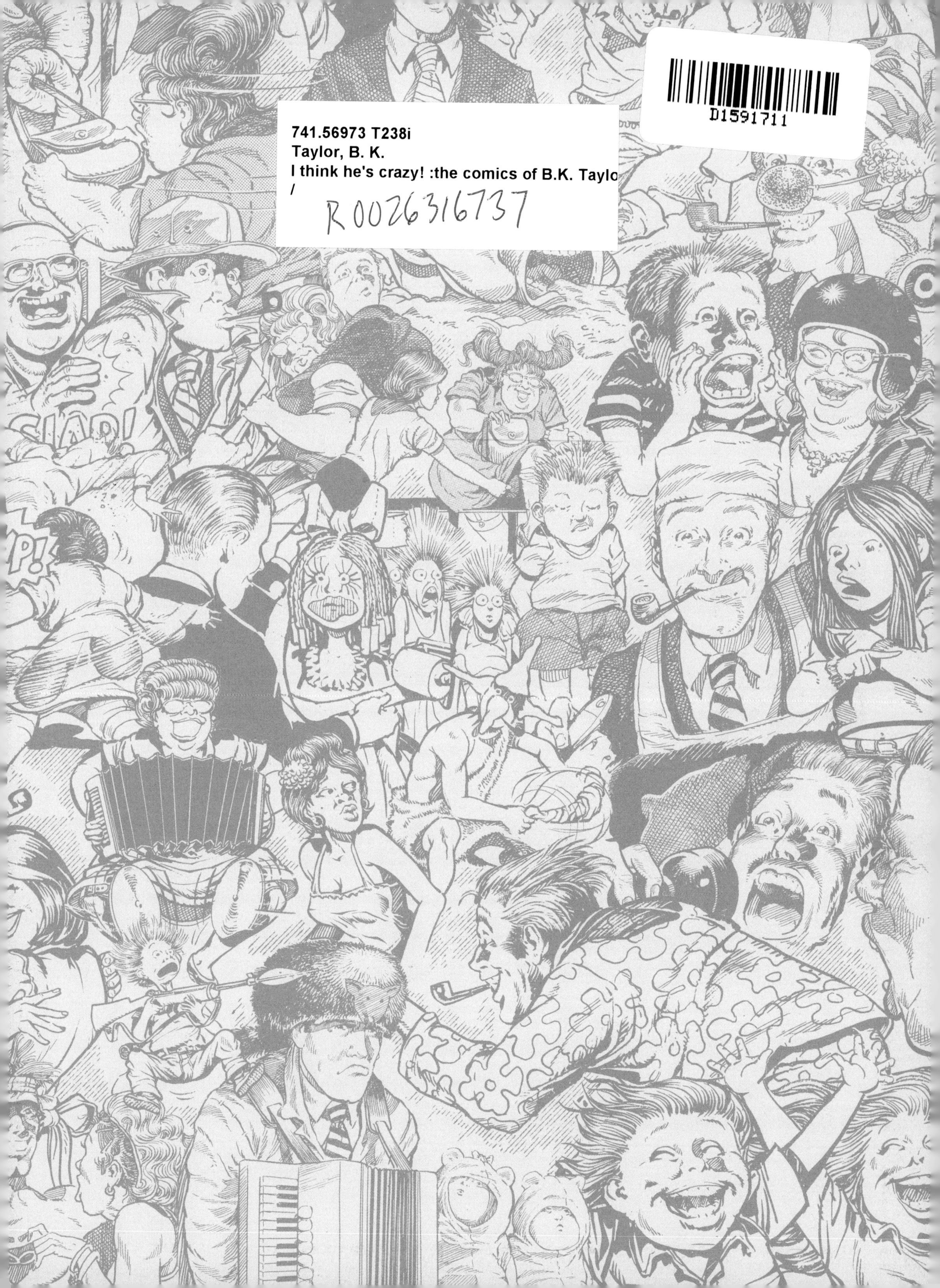

I THINK HE'S CRAZY

THE COMICS OF B.K. TAYLOR

SEATTLE

Publisher: GARY GROTH
Senior Editor: J. MICHAEL CATRON
Designer: JUSTIN ALLAN-SPENCER
Production: PAUL BARESH and CHRISTINA HWANG
Associate Publisher: ERIC REYNOLDS

Fantagraphics Books, Inc.
7563 Lake City Way NE
Seattle WA 98115
(800) 657-1100

Fantagraphics.com · Twitter: @fantagraphics · facebook.com/fantagraphics.

Note: There is no connection between the character Norm Appleton and
the Church of the SubGenius (although we think he would enjoy the title).
But Mr. Appleton, who made his debut in print before the Church did,
nonetheless wishes them all the best.

First Fantagraphics Books edition: June 2020
ISBN 978-1-68396-287-8
Library of Congress Control Number: 2019944875
Printed in Singapore

I THINK HE'S CRAZY

THE COMICS OF B.K. TAYLOR

Ripped from the pages of

NATIONAL LAMPOON®

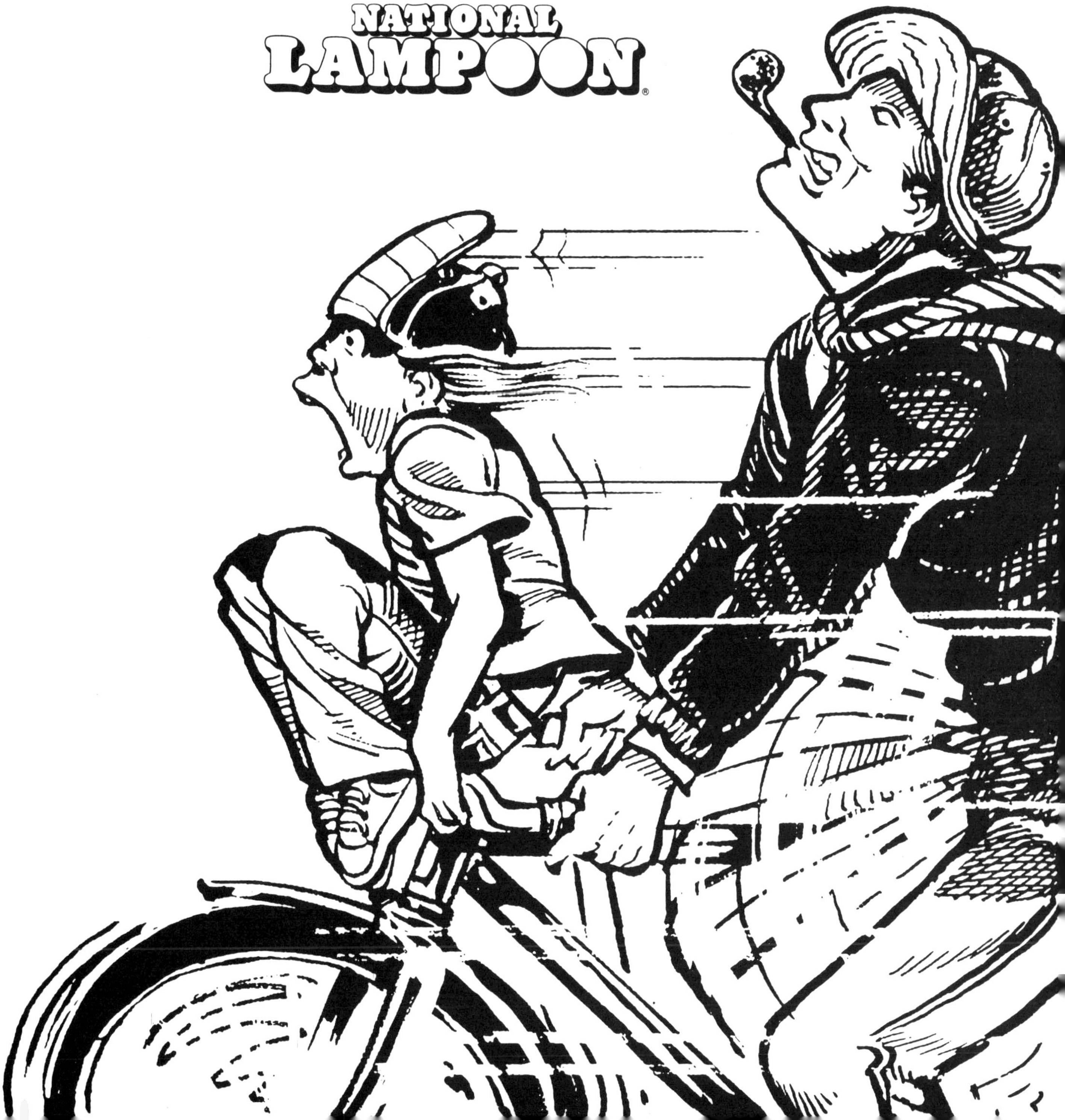

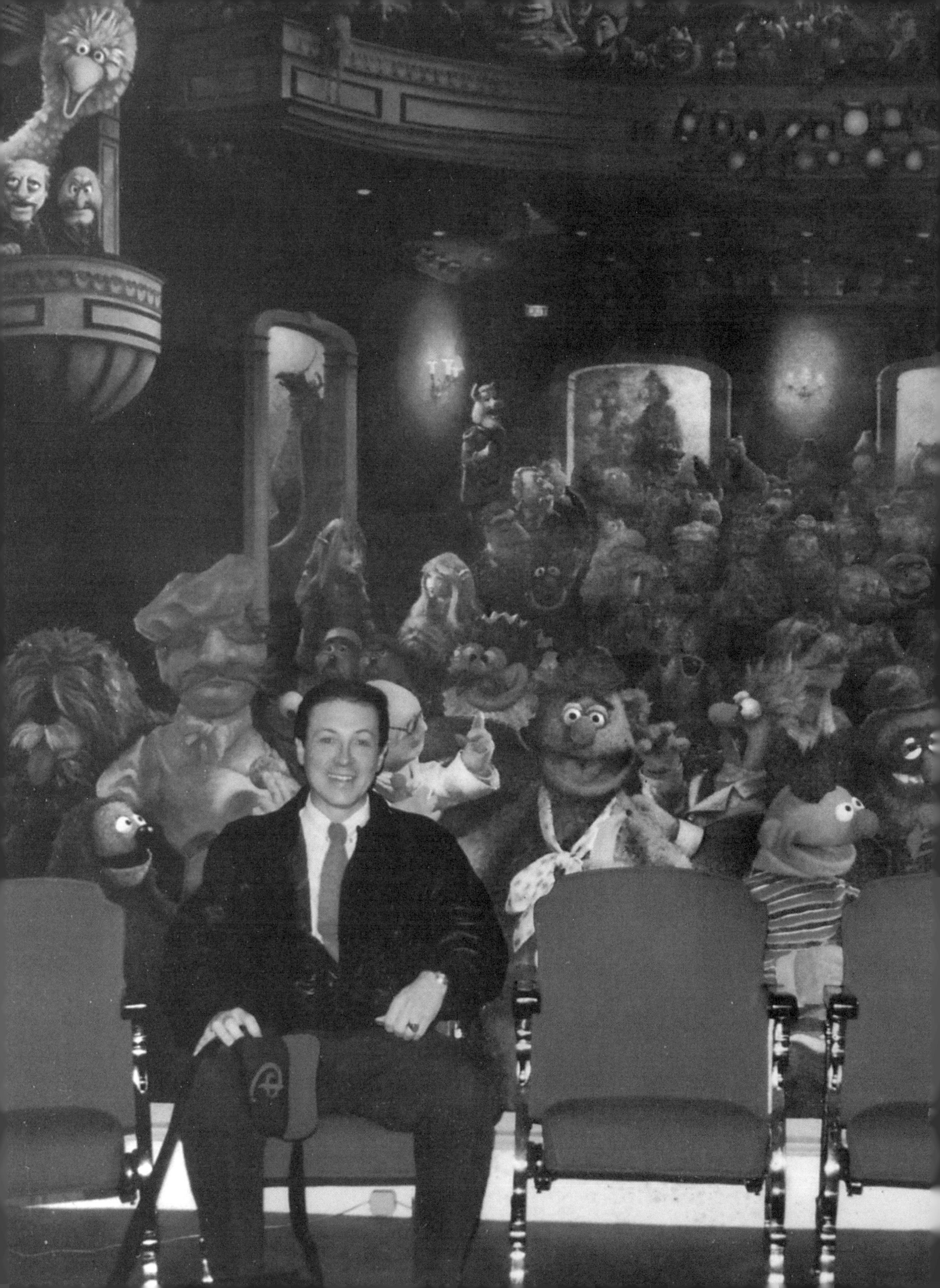

YOU THINK I'M CRAZY?

INTRODUCTION BY B.K. TAYLOR

IN A WORLD GONE SLIGHTLY MAD — WHERE saying anything publicly is a potential powder keg of online outrage from one group or another — in this atmosphere of ambush and accusation, we've decided to publish this book. Thus the title — *I Think He's Crazy!*

Now that you're past the title and reading this, I would guess that you're intrigued by what's to come in these pages, you're a former *National Lampoon* reader, or you're a psychoanalyst looking for new clientele. Whatever the case, what you hold in your hands is the collection of my cartoons, writings, and other nonsense from my years as a contributor to the *National Lampoon*.

The majority of this book is based on the three cartoon strips that the magazine alternated from issue to issue. The first strip, *The Appletons*, gives a friendly wink to the all-American family sitcoms from the early, more innocent days of American television — with the exception of the slightly deranged Mr. Appleton.

The second strip is *Timberland Tales*, a salute to our neighbors to the north, which portrays a group of isolated, slightly naïve and, of course, very friendly Canadians, who are constantly coming into contact with the harsh realities of the modern world.

And last, but certainly not least, *Uncle Kunta* — a strip that lightly satirizes the classic tales of Joel Chandler Harris's "Uncle Remus," giving each episode an African-American point of view, from history to creation to most anything else. This was the last of my strips to appear, and one of my favorites. Sadly, *National Lampoon* changed hands in the late '80s, thus ending the opportunity for further adventures with Uncle Kunta.

I hope you'll read this book in the spirit of the time when the *Lampoon* was at the vanguard of humor, with a large pool of talented writers and artists who consistently pushed the proverbial envelope to its limits. The material was new and fresh — sometimes successful, sometimes not.

The *Lampoon* contributors literally changed the course of American humor, with very few sacred cows left unscathed. The result is still evident today.

I'm afraid I tested those boundaries myself once or twice, which felt devilishly fun at the time — as you'll discover for yourself if you'll stop reading this in the store and buy the damn book, already!

The characters in the three strips are, for the most part, polar opposites. *The Appletons,* featuring Norm Appleton, was created to jar the reader with Norm's bizarre antics; whereas the cast in *Timberland Tales* approached most situations from a naïve, almost adolescent point of view — particularly the prepubescent, always curious Maurice and his loyal companion, Constable Tom. *Uncle Kunta*, on the other hand, had a devil-may-care attitude, told through his colorful stories with a more-than-slightly skewed point of view.

In closing, I want to share an observation with you that proved to be an epiphany for me. An artist friend of mine sent me an old book he'd found in a used bookstore with a note that read, "The enclosed book is very funny. I think you'll enjoy it."

The book was an anthology of the work of A.B. Frost, a cartoonist from the turn of the 20th century who was a pioneer in sequential art (the classic comic strip). I wasn't sure something that old would hold up after so many decades. I read it, and, to my amazement, I did laugh. Yet more than the wonderful art and humor, I was fascinated by the idea that here is a person I've never met — never even knew existed — and yet, a hundred years after his death, this cartoonist made me laugh out loud. I hope that you, dear reader, will laugh out loud at a few things in these pages. It may be a childish thrill for me, but, even though you and I have never met, I hope I make you laugh.

Many people ask where I came up with some of the ideas for the various strips. "Did you have a strange upbringing? Were you on drugs? Are you now?" No, I can't fall back on those old excuses. Actually, I'm just like everyone else — I put my pants on in the morning, one arm at a time.

— *B.K. Taylor*

OPPOSITE: B.K. Taylor in the Manhattan offices of Jim Henson Studios in the late '90s.

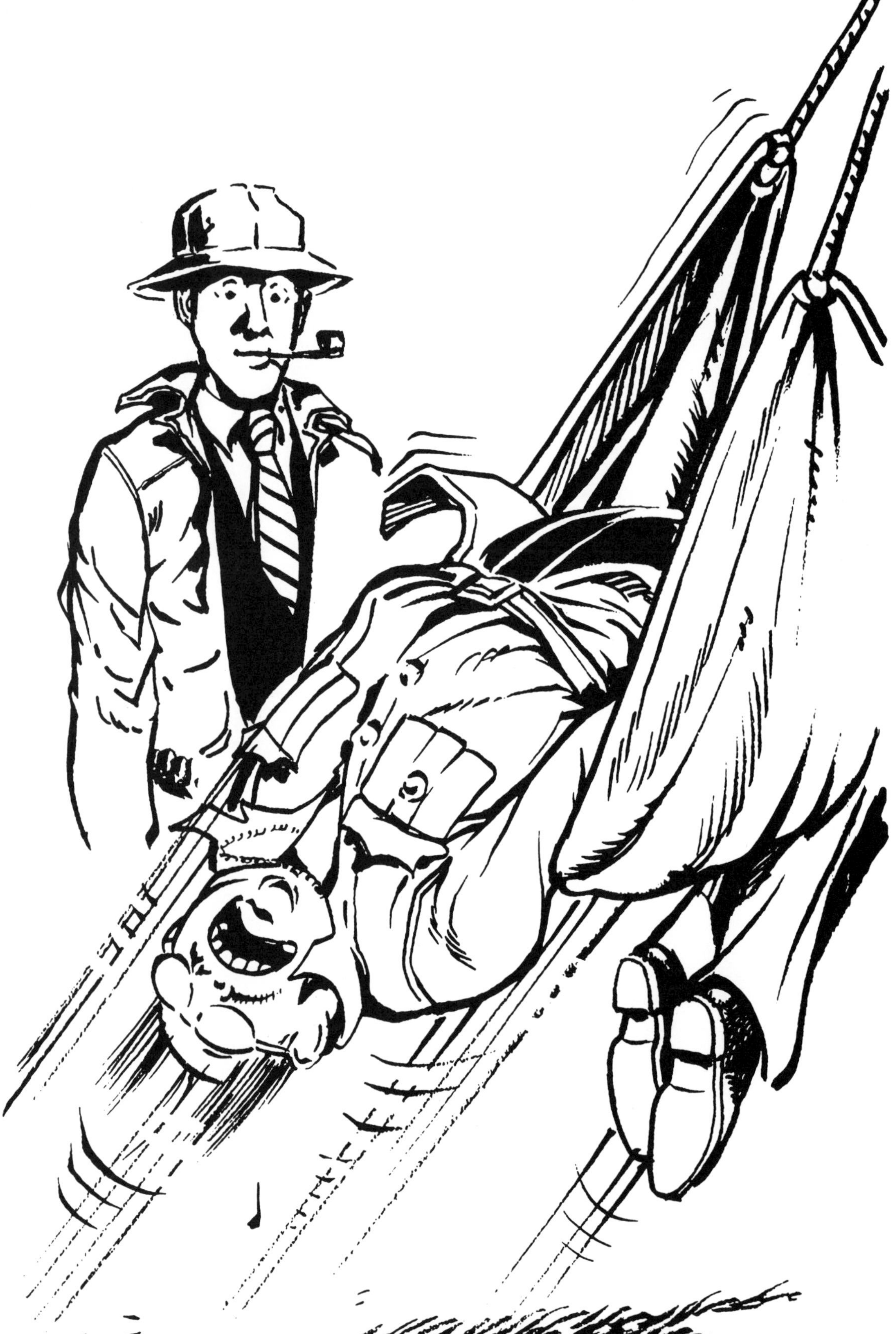

EXPLAINING THE UNEXPLAINABLE

—— FOREWORD BY TIM ALLEN ——

SOME THINGS IN LIFE ARE UNEXPLAINABLE: UFOs, Sasquatch, and, not least, B.K. Taylor and the collection of cartoon strips you're holding in your hand.

I discovered the *National Lampoon* during my first year in college. In the back of the magazine appeared a cartoon strip, *The Appletons*. I felt a kinship with Norm Appleton. He was doing things we all think about at one time or another but never dare act upon. Norm is the embodiment of an early TV sitcom dad — he combines a cardigan sweater, khaki pants, and loafers with the persona of a mentally deranged Mr. Brady.

There was definitely something uniquely different about B.K.'s strips that intrigued me. While *The Appletons* are all-American, *Timberland Tales* is pure Canadian and possibly even more bizarre. And Taylor's third strip, *Uncle Kunta*, poses a skewed view of creation, which certainly shakes up our preconceived notion of the original.

Years later, I brought up the cartoon strips at a hometown comedy club where I was appearing in my early standup days. I was shocked to discover, through a mutual friend, that Taylor actually lived in the same area! A meeting was arranged, and within a short time we found we have much in common, including a rather warped sense of humor.

We've shared various project ideas over the years, and B.K. even wrote on *Home Improvement* for the first three seasons. We've been good friends ever since — but I make it a practice never to turn my back on him.

— *Tim Allen, Los Angeles*

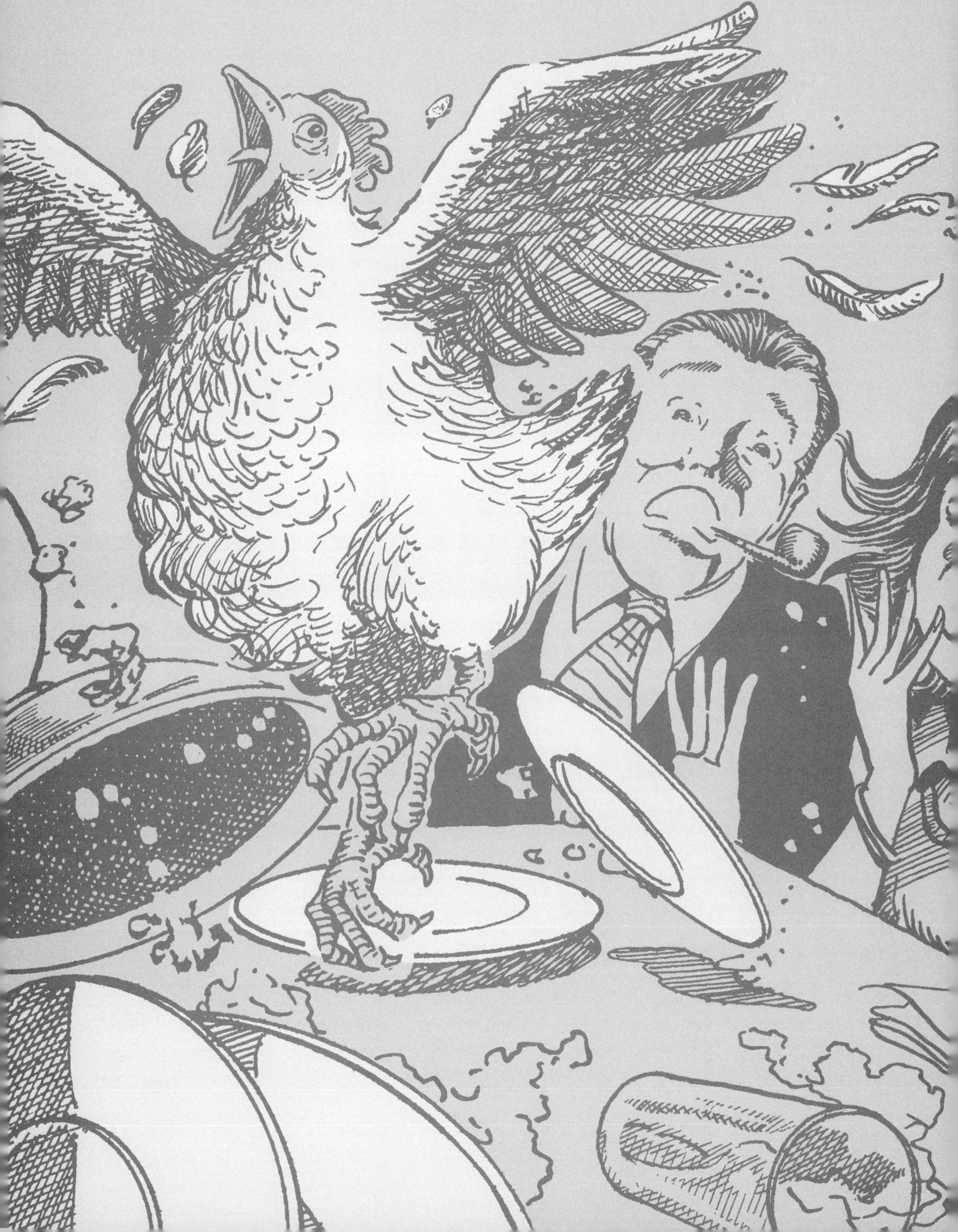

INTRODUCING

THE APPLETONS

NORM

HELEN

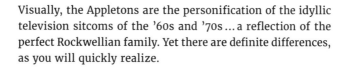

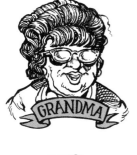

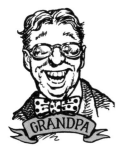

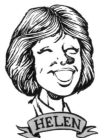

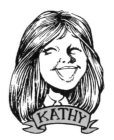

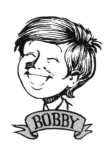

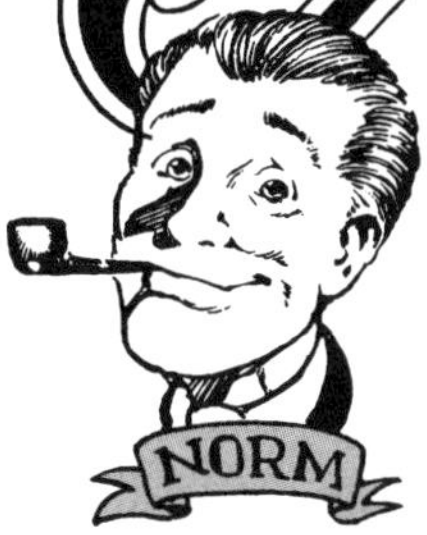

Visually, the Appletons are the personification of the idyllic television sitcoms of the ’60s and ’70s … a reflection of the perfect Rockwellian family. Yet there are definite differences, as you will quickly realize.

Our cast of characters includes:

GRANDMA

KATHY

> **Norm Appleton**, the image of Robert Reed’s Mike Brady or Hugh Beaumont’s Ward Cleaver, but with his own unique way of dealing with life. Though his parenting skills are, at best, unconventional, he usually ends the strip with a moral or slightly convoluted lesson.
>
> **Helen Appleton** and the children, **Kathy** and **Bobby**, who personify the all-American wholesome family unit and are oblivious to any imperfections in Norm.
>
> The **Grandparents**, Norm’s mother and father, who are unique in themselves — some would say colorful, others would say certifiable. When they visit, we can see where Norm gets his quirky personality.

GRANDPA

BOBBY

This all-American family may push the envelope a bit but, if we’re honest, there’s a little bit of Appleton in all of us.

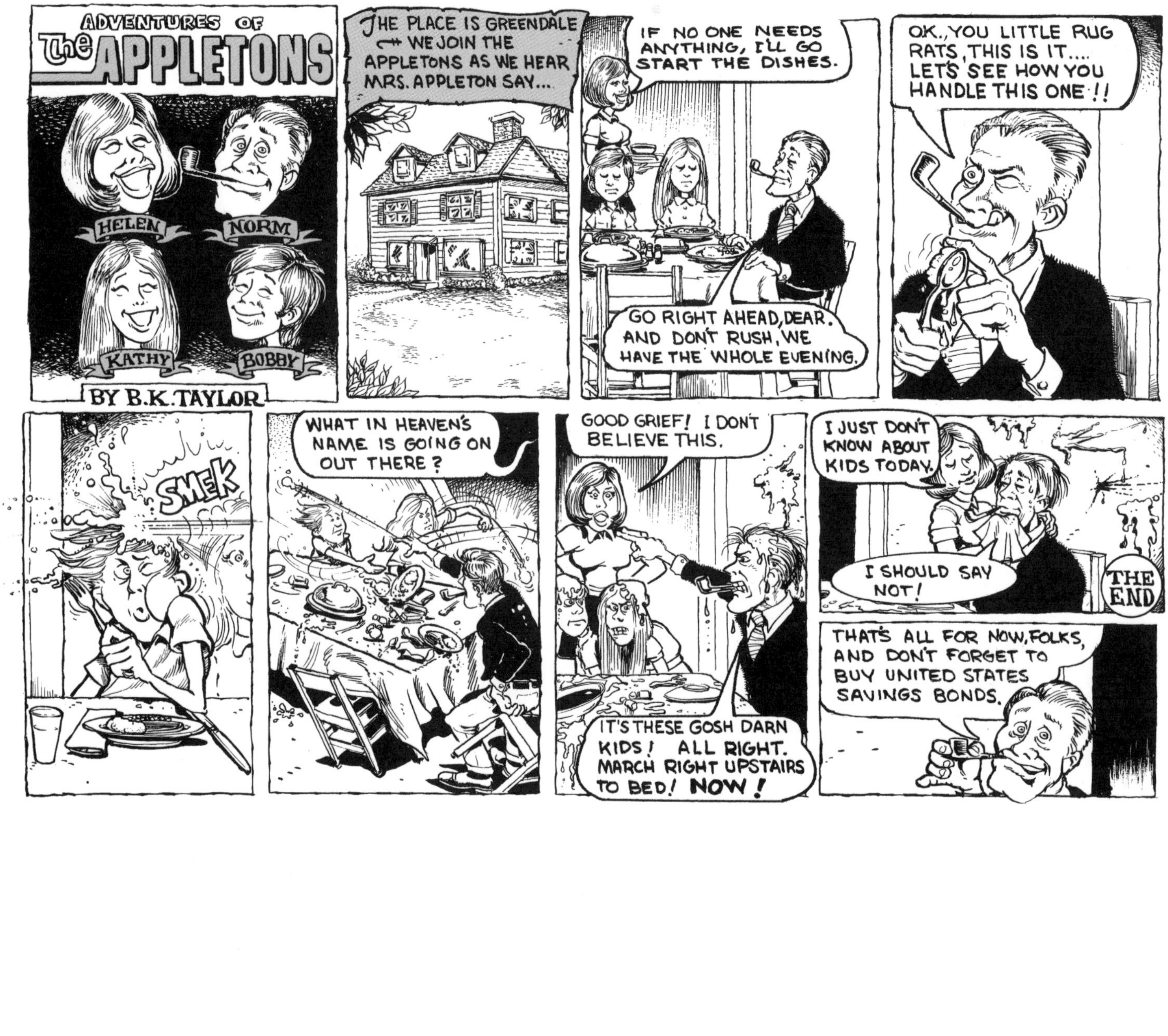
ADVENTURES OF
The APPLETONS
HELEN
NORM
KATHY
BOBBY
BY B.K. TAYLOR
THE PLACE IS GREENDALE — WE JOIN THE APPLETONS AS WE HEAR MRS. APPLETON SAY...
IF NO ONE NEEDS ANYTHING, I'LL GO START THE DISHES.
GO RIGHT AHEAD, DEAR. AND DON'T RUSH, WE HAVE THE WHOLE EVENING.
O.K., YOU LITTLE RUG RATS, THIS IS IT.... LET'S SEE HOW YOU HANDLE THIS ONE!!
SMEK
WHAT IN HEAVEN'S NAME IS GOING ON OUT THERE?
GOOD GRIEF! I DON'T BELIEVE THIS.
IT'S THESE GOSH DARN KIDS! ALL RIGHT. MARCH RIGHT UPSTAIRS TO BED! NOW!
I JUST DON'T KNOW ABOUT KIDS TODAY.
I SHOULD SAY NOT!
THE END
THAT'S ALL FOR NOW, FOLKS, AND DON'T FORGET TO BUY UNITED STATES SAVINGS BONDS.

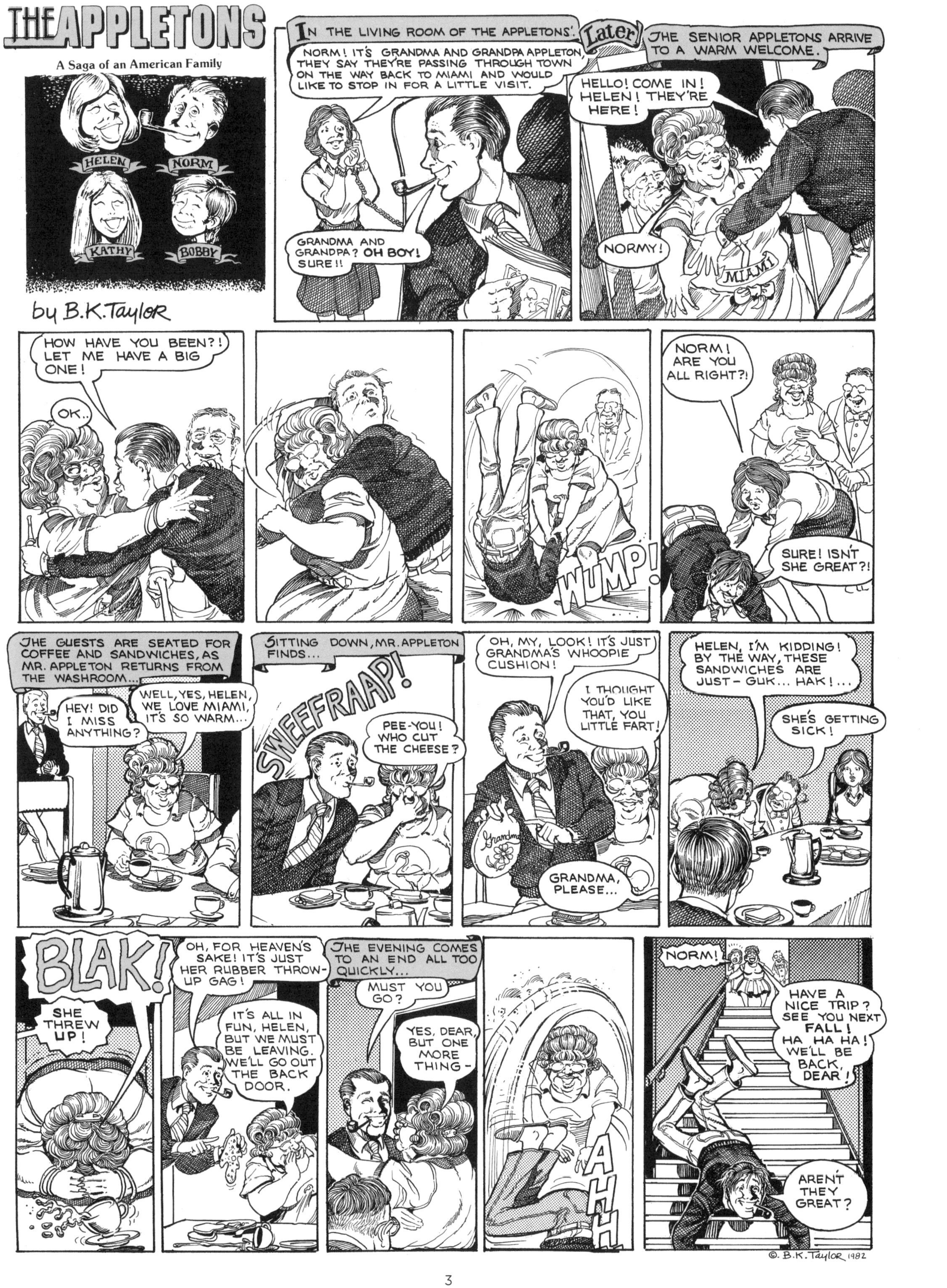
THE APPLETONS
A Saga of an American Family
HELEN
NORM
KATHY
BOBBY
by B.K.Taylor
IN THE LIVING ROOM OF THE APPLETONS'.
NORM! IT'S GRANDMA AND GRANDPA APPLETON, THEY SAY THEY'RE PASSING THROUGH TOWN ON THE WAY BACK TO MIAMI AND WOULD LIKE TO STOP IN FOR A LITTLE VISIT.
GRANDMA AND GRANDPA? OH BOY! SURE!!
Later!
THE SENIOR APPLETONS ARRIVE TO A WARM WELCOME.
HELLO! COME IN! HELEN! THEY'RE HERE!
NORMY!
MIAMI
HOW HAVE YOU BEEN?! LET ME HAVE A BIG ONE!
OK..
WUMP!
NORM! ARE YOU ALL RIGHT?!
SURE! ISN'T SHE GREAT?!
THE GUESTS ARE SEATED FOR COFFEE AND SANDWICHES, AS MR. APPLETON RETURNS FROM THE WASHROOM...
HEY! DID I MISS ANYTHING?
WELL, YES, HELEN, WE LOVE MIAMI, IT'S SO WARM...
SITTING DOWN, MR. APPLETON FINDS...
SWEEFRAAP!
PEE-YOU! WHO CUT THE CHEESE?
OH, MY, LOOK! IT'S JUST GRANDMA'S WHOOPIE CUSHION!
I THOUGHT YOU'D LIKE THAT, YOU LITTLE FART!
Grandma
GRANDMA, PLEASE...
HELEN, I'M KIDDING! BY THE WAY, THESE SANDWICHES ARE JUST- GUK... HAK!...
SHE'S GETTING SICK!
BLAK!
SHE THREW UP!
OH, FOR HEAVEN'S SAKE! IT'S JUST HER RUBBER THROW-UP GAG!
IT'S ALL IN FUN, HELEN, BUT WE MUST BE LEAVING. WE'LL GO OUT THE BACK DOOR.
THE EVENING COMES TO AN END ALL TOO QUICKLY...
MUST YOU GO?
YES, DEAR, BUT ONE MORE THING-
AHHH
NORM!
HAVE A NICE TRIP? SEE YOU NEXT FALL! HA HA HA! WE'LL BE BACK, DEAR!
AREN'T THEY GREAT?
©. B.K. Taylor 1982

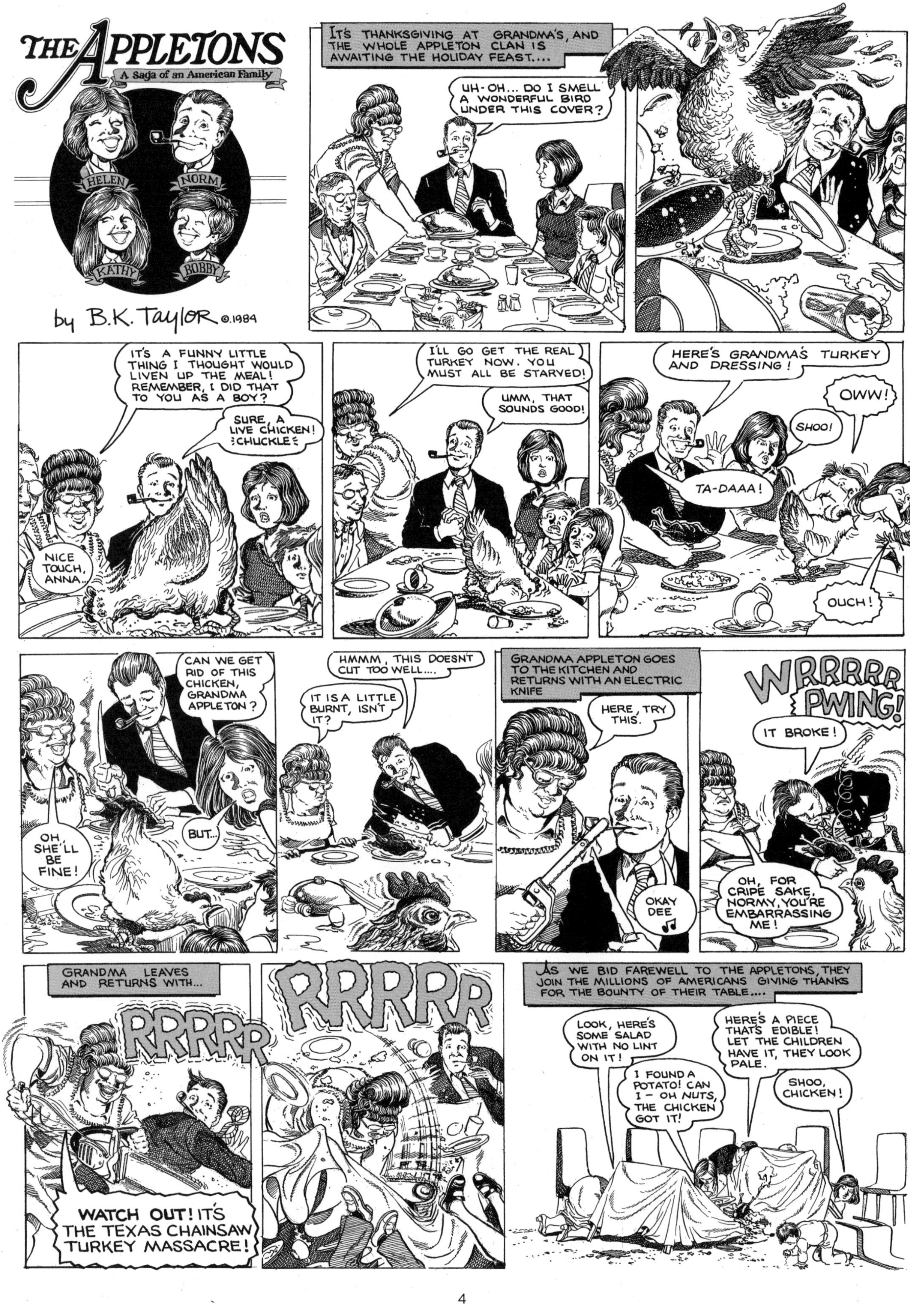
THE APPLETONS
A Saga of an American Family
HELEN
NORM
KATHY
BOBBY
by B.K. Taylor ©.1984
IT'S THANKSGIVING AT GRANDMA'S, AND THE WHOLE APPLETON CLAN IS AWAITING THE HOLIDAY FEAST....
UH-OH... DO I SMELL A WONDERFUL BIRD UNDER THIS COVER?
IT'S A FUNNY LITTLE THING I THOUGHT WOULD LIVEN UP THE MEAL! REMEMBER, I DID THAT TO YOU AS A BOY?
SURE, A LIVE CHICKEN! CHUCKLE
NICE TOUCH, ANNA...
I'LL GO GET THE REAL TURKEY NOW. YOU MUST ALL BE STARVED!
UMM, THAT SOUNDS GOOD!
HERE'S GRANDMA'S TURKEY AND DRESSING!
OWW!
SHOO!
TA-DAAA!
OUCH!
CAN WE GET RID OF THIS CHICKEN, GRANDMA APPLETON?
OH, SHE'LL BE FINE!
BUT...
HMMM, THIS DOESN'T CUT TOO WELL....
IT IS A LITTLE BURNT, ISN'T IT?
GRANDMA APPLETON GOES TO THE KITCHEN AND RETURNS WITH AN ELECTRIC KNIFE
HERE, TRY THIS.
OKAY DEE
WRRRRR
PWING!
IT BROKE!
OH, FOR CRIPE SAKE, NORMY, YOU'RE EMBARRASSING ME!
GRANDMA LEAVES AND RETURNS WITH...
RRRRR
WATCH OUT! IT'S THE TEXAS CHAINSAW TURKEY MASSACRE!
RRRRR
AS WE BID FAREWELL TO THE APPLETONS, THEY JOIN THE MILLIONS OF AMERICANS GIVING THANKS FOR THE BOUNTY OF THEIR TABLE....
LOOK, HERE'S SOME SALAD WITH NO LINT ON IT!
I FOUND A POTATO! CAN I - OH NUTS, THE CHICKEN GOT IT!
HERE'S A PIECE THAT'S EDIBLE! LET THE CHILDREN HAVE IT, THEY LOOK PALE.
SHOO, CHICKEN!

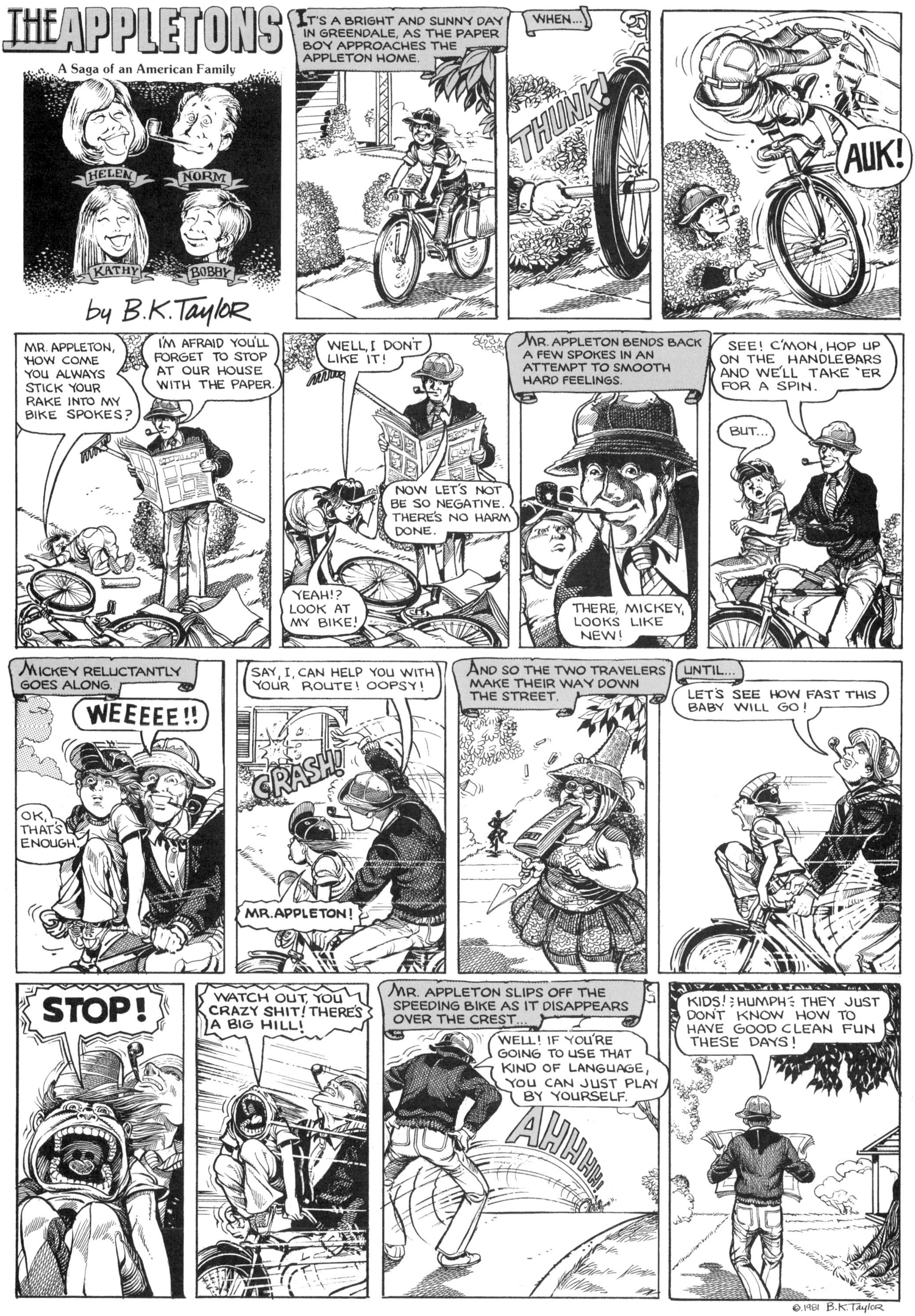
THE APPLETONS
A Saga of an American Family
HELEN
NORM
KATHY
BOBBY
by B.K. Taylor
IT'S A BRIGHT AND SUNNY DAY IN GREENDALE, AS THE PAPER BOY APPROACHES THE APPLETON HOME.
WHEN...
THUNK!
AUK!
MR. APPLETON, HOW COME YOU ALWAYS STICK YOUR RAKE INTO MY BIKE SPOKES?
I'M AFRAID YOU'LL FORGET TO STOP AT OUR HOUSE WITH THE PAPER.
WELL, I DON'T LIKE IT!
NOW LET'S NOT BE SO NEGATIVE. THERE'S NO HARM DONE.
YEAH!? LOOK AT MY BIKE!
MR. APPLETON BENDS BACK A FEW SPOKES IN AN ATTEMPT TO SMOOTH HARD FEELINGS.
THERE, MICKEY, LOOKS LIKE NEW!
SEE! C'MON, HOP UP ON THE HANDLEBARS AND WE'LL TAKE 'ER FOR A SPIN.
BUT...
MICKEY RELUCTANTLY GOES ALONG.
WEEEEE!!
OK, THAT'S ENOUGH.
SAY, I, CAN HELP YOU WITH YOUR ROUTE! OOPSY!
CRASH!
MR. APPLETON!
AND SO THE TWO TRAVELERS MAKE THEIR WAY DOWN THE STREET.
UNTIL...
LET'S SEE HOW FAST THIS BABY WILL GO!
STOP!
WATCH OUT, YOU CRAZY SHIT! THERE'S A BIG HILL!
MR. APPLETON SLIPS OFF THE SPEEDING BIKE AS IT DISAPPEARS OVER THE CREST...
WELL! IF YOU'RE GOING TO USE THAT KIND OF LANGUAGE, YOU CAN JUST PLAY BY YOURSELF.
AHHHH!
KIDS! HUMPH THEY JUST DON'T KNOW HOW TO HAVE GOOD CLEAN FUN THESE DAYS!
©.1981 B.K. Taylor

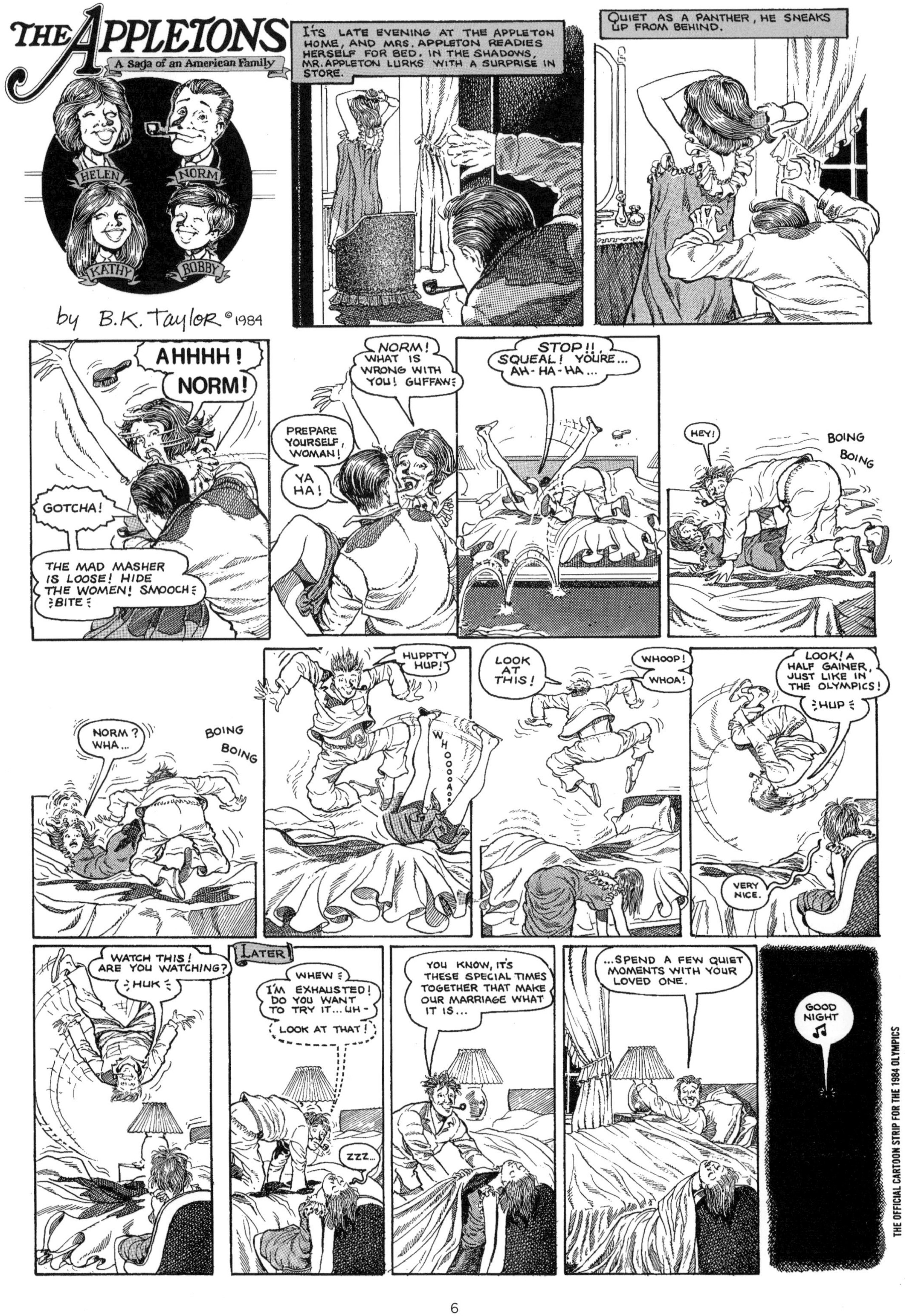
THE APPLETONS
A Saga of an American Family
HELEN
NORM
KATHY
BOBBY
by B.K. Taylor ©1984
IT'S LATE EVENING AT THE APPLETON HOME, AND MRS. APPLETON READIES HERSELF FOR BED. IN THE SHADOWS, MR. APPLETON LURKS WITH A SURPRISE IN STORE.
QUIET AS A PANTHER, HE SNEAKS UP FROM BEHIND.
AHHHH!
NORM!
GOTCHA!
THE MAD MASHER IS LOOSE! HIDE THE WOMEN! SMOOCH BITE
NORM! WHAT IS WRONG WITH YOU! GUFFAW
PREPARE YOURSELF, WOMAN!
YA HA!
STOP!! SQUEAL! YOU'RE... AH-HA-HA...
HEY!
BOING
BOING
NORM? WHA...
BOING
BOING
HUPPTY HUP!
WHOOOOAA...
LOOK AT THIS!
WHOOP!
WHOA!
LOOK! A HALF GAINER, JUST LIKE IN THE OLYMPICS!
HUP
VERY NICE.
WATCH THIS! ARE YOU WATCHING?
HUK
LATER
WHEW
I'M EXHAUSTED! DO YOU WANT TO TRY IT... UH -
LOOK AT THAT!
ZZZ...
YOU KNOW, IT'S THESE SPECIAL TIMES TOGETHER THAT MAKE OUR MARRIAGE WHAT IT IS...
...SPEND A FEW QUIET MOMENTS WITH YOUR LOVED ONE.
GOOD NIGHT
THE OFFICIAL CARTOON STRIP FOR THE 1984 OLYMPICS

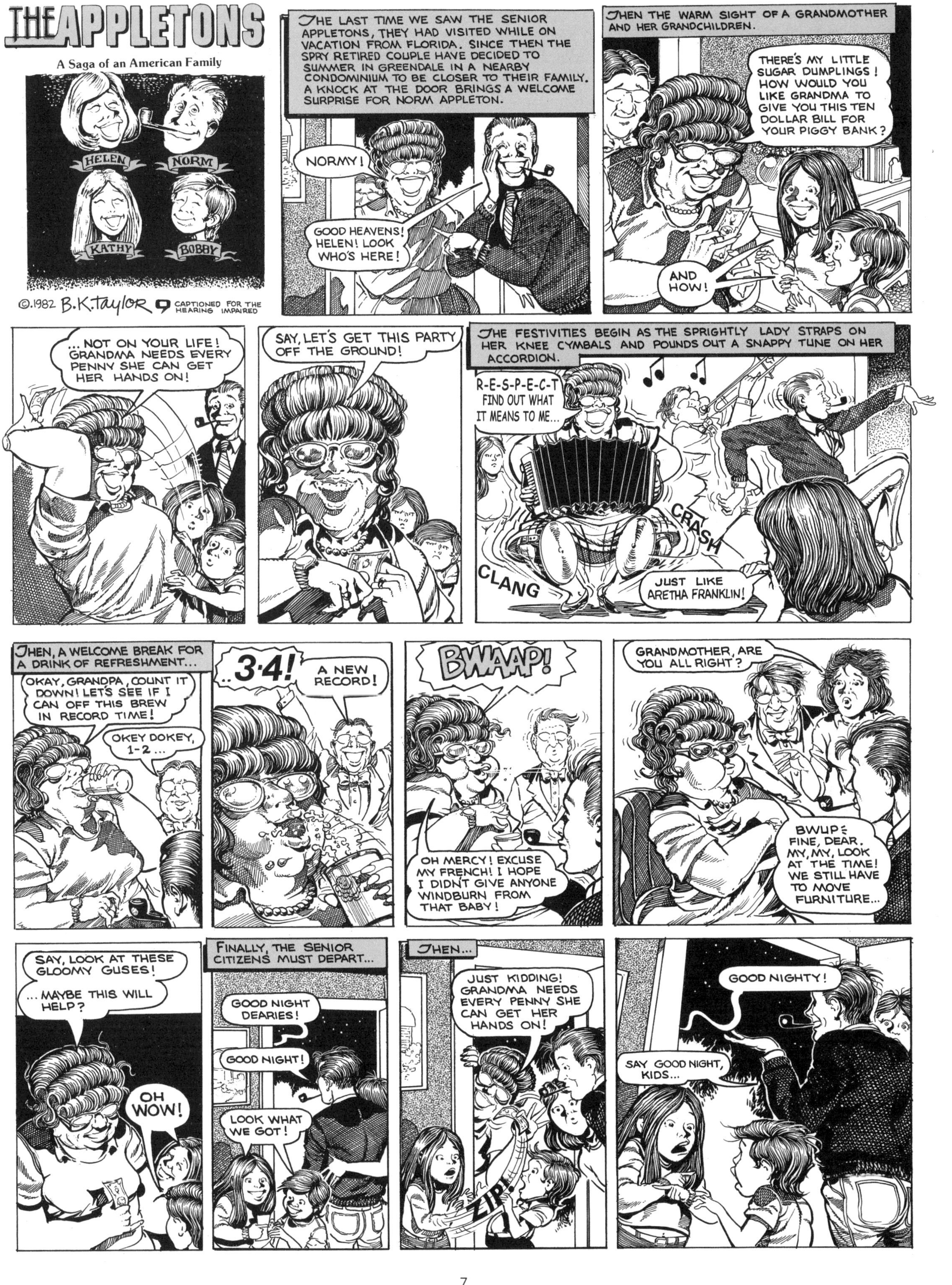
THE APPLETONS
A Saga of an American Family
HELEN
NORM
KATHY
BOBBY
©.1982 B.K.Taylor
CAPTIONED FOR THE HEARING IMPAIRED
THE LAST TIME WE SAW THE SENIOR APPLETONS, THEY HAD VISITED WHILE ON VACATION FROM FLORIDA. SINCE THEN THE SPRY RETIRED COUPLE HAVE DECIDED TO SUMMER IN GREENDALE IN A NEARBY CONDOMINIUM TO BE CLOSER TO THEIR FAMILY. A KNOCK AT THE DOOR BRINGS A WELCOME SURPRISE FOR NORM APPLETON.
NORMY!
GOOD HEAVENS! HELEN! LOOK WHO'S HERE!
THEN THE WARM SIGHT OF A GRANDMOTHER AND HER GRANDCHILDREN.
THERE'S MY LITTLE SUGAR DUMPLINGS! HOW WOULD YOU LIKE GRANDMA TO GIVE YOU THIS TEN DOLLAR BILL FOR YOUR PIGGY BANK?
AND HOW!
... NOT ON YOUR LIFE! GRANDMA NEEDS EVERY PENNY SHE CAN GET HER HANDS ON!
SAY, LET'S GET THIS PARTY OFF THE GROUND!
THE FESTIVITIES BEGIN AS THE SPRIGHTLY LADY STRAPS ON HER KNEE CYMBALS AND POUNDS OUT A SNAPPY TUNE ON HER ACCORDION.
R-E-S-P-E-C-T FIND OUT WHAT IT MEANS TO ME...
CRASH
CLANG
JUST LIKE ARETHA FRANKLIN!
THEN, A WELCOME BREAK FOR A DRINK OF REFRESHMENT...
OKAY, GRANDPA, COUNT IT DOWN! LET'S SEE IF I CAN OFF THIS BREW IN RECORD TIME!
OKEY DOKEY, 1-2...
..3·4!
A NEW RECORD!
BWAAP!
OH MERCY! EXCUSE MY FRENCH! I HOPE I DIDN'T GIVE ANYONE WINDBURN FROM THAT BABY!
GRANDMOTHER, ARE YOU ALL RIGHT?
BWUP FINE, DEAR. MY, MY, LOOK AT THE TIME! WE STILL HAVE TO MOVE FURNITURE...
SAY, LOOK AT THESE GLOOMY GUSES!
... MAYBE THIS WILL HELP?
OH WOW!
FINALLY, THE SENIOR CITIZENS MUST DEPART...
GOOD NIGHT DEARIES!
GOOD NIGHT!
LOOK WHAT WE GOT!
THEN...
JUST KIDDING! GRANDMA NEEDS EVERY PENNY SHE CAN GET HER HANDS ON!
ZIP!
GOOD NIGHTY!
SAY GOOD NIGHT, KIDS...

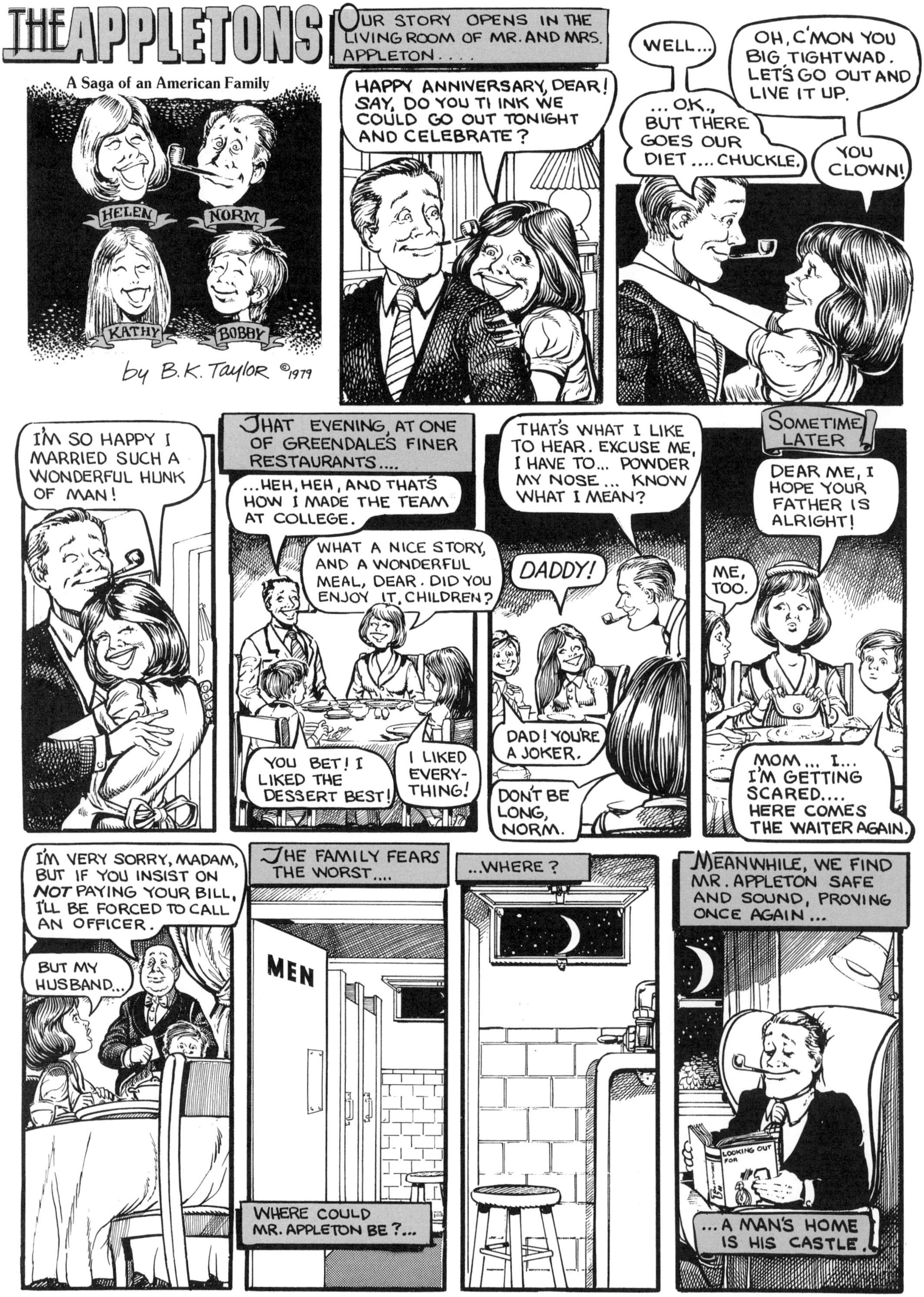

THE APPLETONS
A Saga of an American Family
HELEN
NORM
KATHY
BOBBY
by B.K. Taylor ©1979
OUR STORY OPENS IN THE LIVING ROOM OF MR. AND MRS. APPLETON....
HAPPY ANNIVERSARY, DEAR! SAY, DO YOU THINK WE COULD GO OUT TONIGHT AND CELEBRATE?
WELL...
... O.K., BUT THERE GOES OUR DIET.... CHUCKLE.
OH, C'MON YOU BIG TIGHTWAD. LET'S GO OUT AND LIVE IT UP.
YOU CLOWN!
I'M SO HAPPY I MARRIED SUCH A WONDERFUL HUNK OF MAN!
THAT EVENING, AT ONE OF GREENDALE'S FINER RESTAURANTS....
...HEH, HEH, AND THAT'S HOW I MADE THE TEAM AT COLLEGE.
WHAT A NICE STORY, AND A WONDERFUL MEAL, DEAR. DID YOU ENJOY IT, CHILDREN?
YOU BET! I LIKED THE DESSERT BEST!
I LIKED EVERYTHING!
THAT'S WHAT I LIKE TO HEAR. EXCUSE ME, I HAVE TO... POWDER MY NOSE... KNOW WHAT I MEAN?
DADDY!
DAD! YOU'RE A JOKER.
DON'T BE LONG, NORM.
SOMETIME LATER
DEAR ME, I HOPE YOUR FATHER IS ALRIGHT!
ME, TOO.
MOM... I... I'M GETTING SCARED.... HERE COMES THE WAITER AGAIN.
I'M VERY SORRY, MADAM, BUT IF YOU INSIST ON NOT PAYING YOUR BILL, I'LL BE FORCED TO CALL AN OFFICER.
BUT MY HUSBAND...
THE FAMILY FEARS THE WORST....
MEN
WHERE COULD MR. APPLETON BE?...
...WHERE?
MEANWHILE, WE FIND MR. APPLETON SAFE AND SOUND, PROVING ONCE AGAIN...
LOOKING OUT FOR
... A MAN'S HOME IS HIS CASTLE.

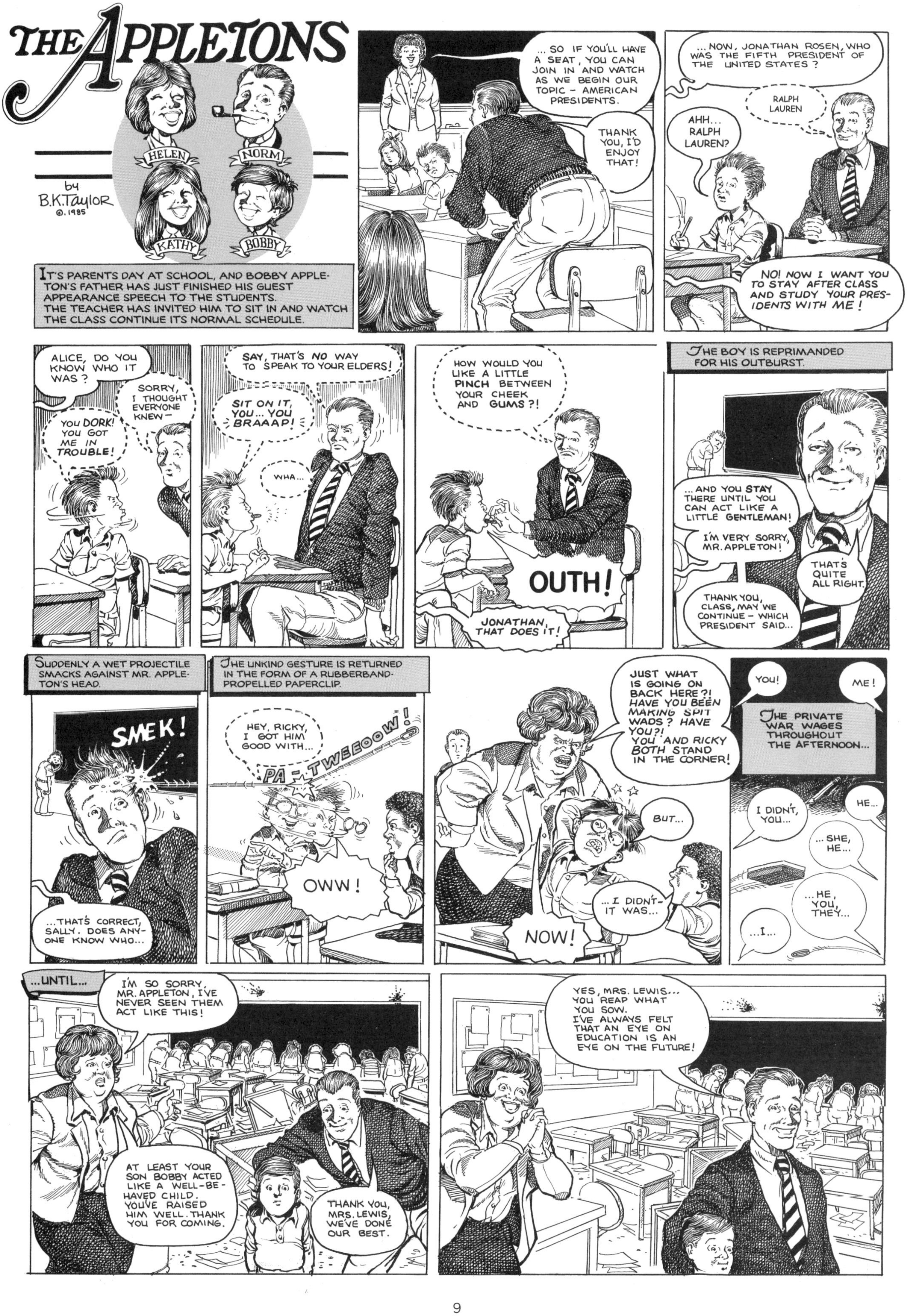
THE APPLETONS
HELEN
NORM
KATHY
BOBBY
by B.K.Taylor ©.1985
IT'S PARENTS DAY AT SCHOOL, AND BOBBY APPLETON'S FATHER HAS JUST FINISHED HIS GUEST APPEARANCE SPEECH TO THE STUDENTS. THE TEACHER HAS INVITED HIM TO SIT IN AND WATCH THE CLASS CONTINUE ITS NORMAL SCHEDULE.
... SO IF YOU'LL HAVE A SEAT, YOU CAN JOIN IN AND WATCH AS WE BEGIN OUR TOPIC - AMERICAN PRESIDENTS.
THANK YOU, I'D ENJOY THAT!
... NOW, JONATHAN ROSEN, WHO WAS THE FIFTH PRESIDENT OF THE UNITED STATES?
RALPH LAUREN
AHH... RALPH LAUREN?
NO! NOW I WANT YOU TO STAY AFTER CLASS AND STUDY YOUR PRESIDENTS WITH ME!
ALICE, DO YOU KNOW WHO IT WAS?
SORRY, I THOUGHT EVERYONE KNEW -
YOU DORK! YOU GOT ME IN TROUBLE!
SAY, THAT'S NO WAY TO SPEAK TO YOUR ELDERS!
SIT ON IT, YOU... YOU BRAAAP!
WHA...
HOW WOULD YOU LIKE A LITTLE PINCH BETWEEN YOUR CHEEK AND GUMS?!
OUTH!
JONATHAN, THAT DOES IT!
THE BOY IS REPRIMANDED FOR HIS OUTBURST.
... AND YOU STAY THERE UNTIL YOU CAN ACT LIKE A LITTLE GENTLEMAN!
I'M VERY SORRY, MR. APPLETON!
THAT'S QUITE ALL RIGHT.
THANK YOU, CLASS, MAY WE CONTINUE - WHICH PRESIDENT SAID...
SUDDENLY A WET PROJECTILE SMACKS AGAINST MR. APPLETON'S HEAD.
SMEK!
...THAT'S CORRECT, SALLY. DOES ANYONE KNOW WHO...
THE UNKIND GESTURE IS RETURNED IN THE FORM OF A RUBBERBAND-PROPELLED PAPERCLIP.
HEY, RICKY, I GOT HIM GOOD WITH...
PA-TWEEOOW!
OWW!
JUST WHAT IS GOING ON BACK HERE?! HAVE YOU BEEN MAKING SPIT WADS? HAVE YOU?! YOU AND RICKY BOTH STAND IN THE CORNER!
BUT...
... I DIDN'T IT WAS...
NOW!
YOU!
ME!
THE PRIVATE WAR WAGES THROUGHOUT THE AFTERNOON...
I DIDN'T YOU...
HE...
... SHE, HE...
... HE, YOU, THEY...
... I...
...UNTIL...
I'M SO SORRY, MR. APPLETON, I'VE NEVER SEEN THEM ACT LIKE THIS!
AT LEAST YOUR SON BOBBY ACTED LIKE A WELL-BEHAVED CHILD. YOU'VE RAISED HIM WELL. THANK YOU FOR COMING.
THANK YOU, MRS. LEWIS, WE'VE DONE OUR BEST.
YES, MRS. LEWIS... YOU REAP WHAT YOU SOW. I'VE ALWAYS FELT THAT AN EYE ON EDUCATION IS AN EYE ON THE FUTURE!

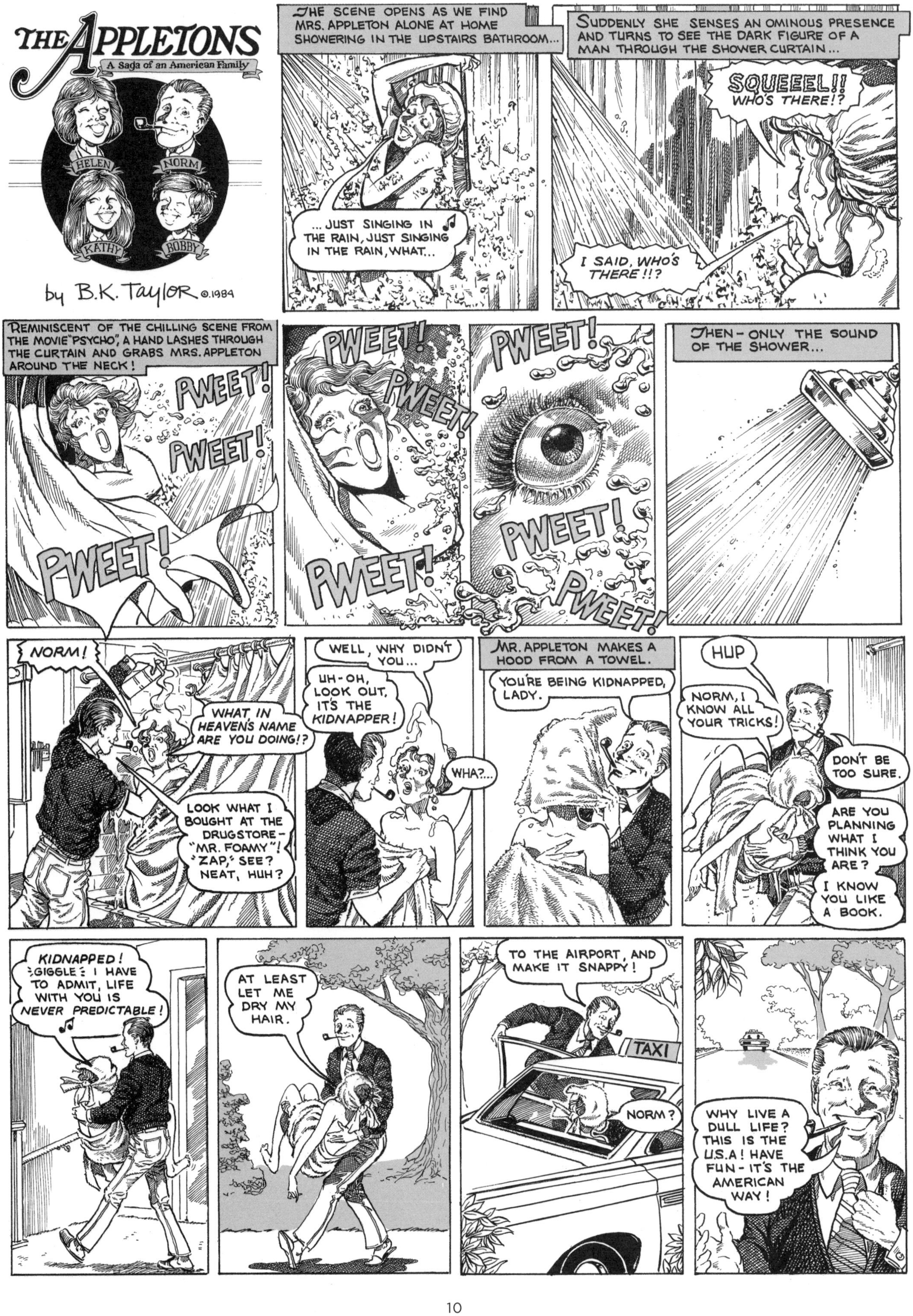
THE APPLETONS
A Saga of an American Family
HELEN
NORM
KATHY
BOBBY
by B.K. Taylor ©.1984
THE SCENE OPENS AS WE FIND MRS. APPLETON ALONE AT HOME SHOWERING IN THE UPSTAIRS BATHROOM...
... JUST SINGING IN THE RAIN, JUST SINGING IN THE RAIN, WHAT...
SUDDENLY SHE SENSES AN OMINOUS PRESENCE AND TURNS TO SEE THE DARK FIGURE OF A MAN THROUGH THE SHOWER CURTAIN...
SQUEEEL!! WHO'S THERE!?
I SAID, WHO'S THERE!!?
REMINISCENT OF THE CHILLING SCENE FROM THE MOVIE "PSYCHO", A HAND LASHES THROUGH THE CURTAIN AND GRABS MRS. APPLETON AROUND THE NECK!
PWEET!
PWEET!
PWEET!
PWEET!
PWEET!
PWEET!
PWEET!
PWEET!
PWEET!
THEN - ONLY THE SOUND OF THE SHOWER...
NORM!
WHAT, IN HEAVEN'S NAME ARE YOU DOING!?
LOOK WHAT I BOUGHT AT THE DRUGSTORE - "MR. FOAMY"! "ZAP," SEE? NEAT, HUH?
WELL, WHY DIDN'T YOU...
UH-OH, LOOK OUT, IT'S THE KIDNAPPER!
WHA?...
MR. APPLETON MAKES A HOOD FROM A TOWEL.
YOU'RE BEING KIDNAPPED, LADY.
HUP
NORM, I KNOW ALL YOUR TRICKS!
DON'T BE TOO SURE.
ARE YOU PLANNING WHAT I THINK YOU ARE?
I KNOW YOU LIKE A BOOK.
KIDNAPPED! :GIGGLE: I HAVE TO ADMIT, LIFE WITH YOU IS NEVER PREDICTABLE!
AT LEAST LET ME DRY MY HAIR.
TO THE AIRPORT, AND MAKE IT SNAPPY!
TAXI
NORM?
WHY LIVE A DULL LIFE? THIS IS THE U.S.A! HAVE FUN - IT'S THE AMERICAN WAY!

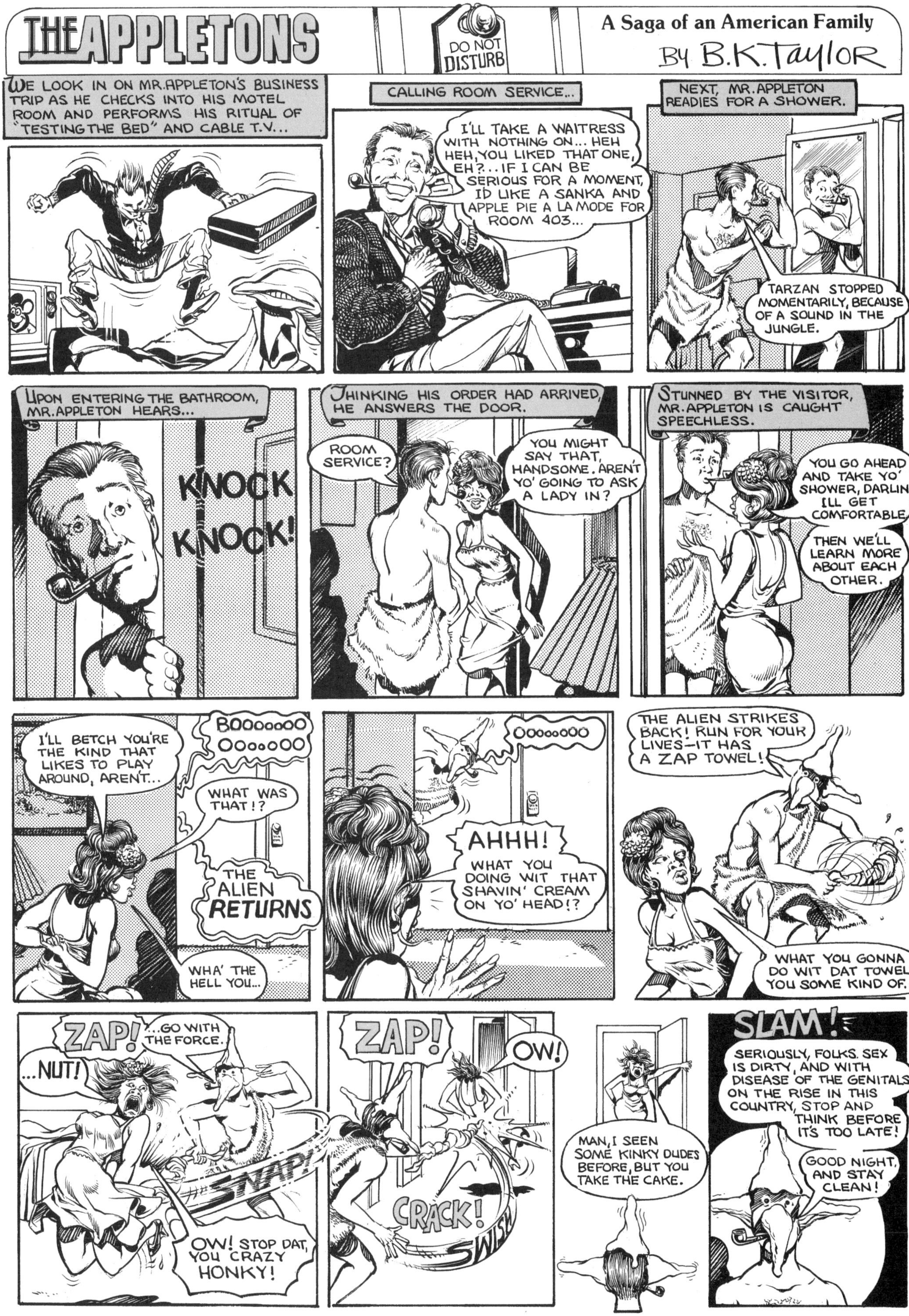
THE APPLETONS
DO NOT DISTURB
A Saga of an American Family
By B.K. Taylor
WE LOOK IN ON MR. APPLETON'S BUSINESS TRIP AS HE CHECKS INTO HIS MOTEL ROOM AND PERFORMS HIS RITUAL OF "TESTING THE BED" AND CABLE T.V...
CALLING ROOM SERVICE...
I'LL TAKE A WAITRESS WITH NOTHING ON... HEH HEH, YOU LIKED THAT ONE, EH?.. IF I CAN BE SERIOUS FOR A MOMENT, I'D LIKE A SANKA AND APPLE PIE A LA MODE FOR ROOM 403...
NEXT, MR. APPLETON READIES FOR A SHOWER.
TARZAN STOPPED MOMENTARILY, BECAUSE OF A SOUND IN THE JUNGLE.
UPON ENTERING THE BATHROOM, MR. APPLETON HEARS...
KNOCK KNOCK!
THINKING HIS ORDER HAD ARRIVED, HE ANSWERS THE DOOR.
ROOM SERVICE?
YOU MIGHT SAY THAT, HANDSOME. AREN'T YO' GOING TO ASK A LADY IN?
STUNNED BY THE VISITOR, MR. APPLETON IS CAUGHT SPEECHLESS.
YOU GO AHEAD AND TAKE YO' SHOWER, DARLIN'. I'LL GET COMFORTABLE.
THEN WE'LL LEARN MORE ABOUT EACH OTHER.
I'LL BETCH YOU'RE THE KIND THAT LIKES TO PLAY AROUND, AREN'T...
BOoooooo OOooOO
WHAT WAS THAT!?
THE ALIEN RETURNS
WHA' THE HELL YOU...
OOooooOO
AHHH! WHAT YOU DOING WIT THAT SHAVIN' CREAM ON YO' HEAD!?
THE ALIEN STRIKES BACK! RUN FOR YOUR LIVES—IT HAS A ZAP TOWEL!
WHAT YOU GONNA DO WIT DAT TOWEL? YOU SOME KIND OF...
ZAP!
...NUT!
...GO WITH THE FORCE.
SNAP!
OW! STOP DAT, YOU CRAZY HONKY!
ZAP!
OW!
CRACK!
SWISH
MAN, I SEEN SOME KINKY DUDES BEFORE, BUT YOU TAKE THE CAKE.
SLAM!
SERIOUSLY, FOLKS. SEX IS DIRTY, AND WITH DISEASE OF THE GENITALS ON THE RISE IN THIS COUNTRY, STOP AND THINK BEFORE IT'S TOO LATE!
GOOD NIGHT, AND STAY CLEAN!

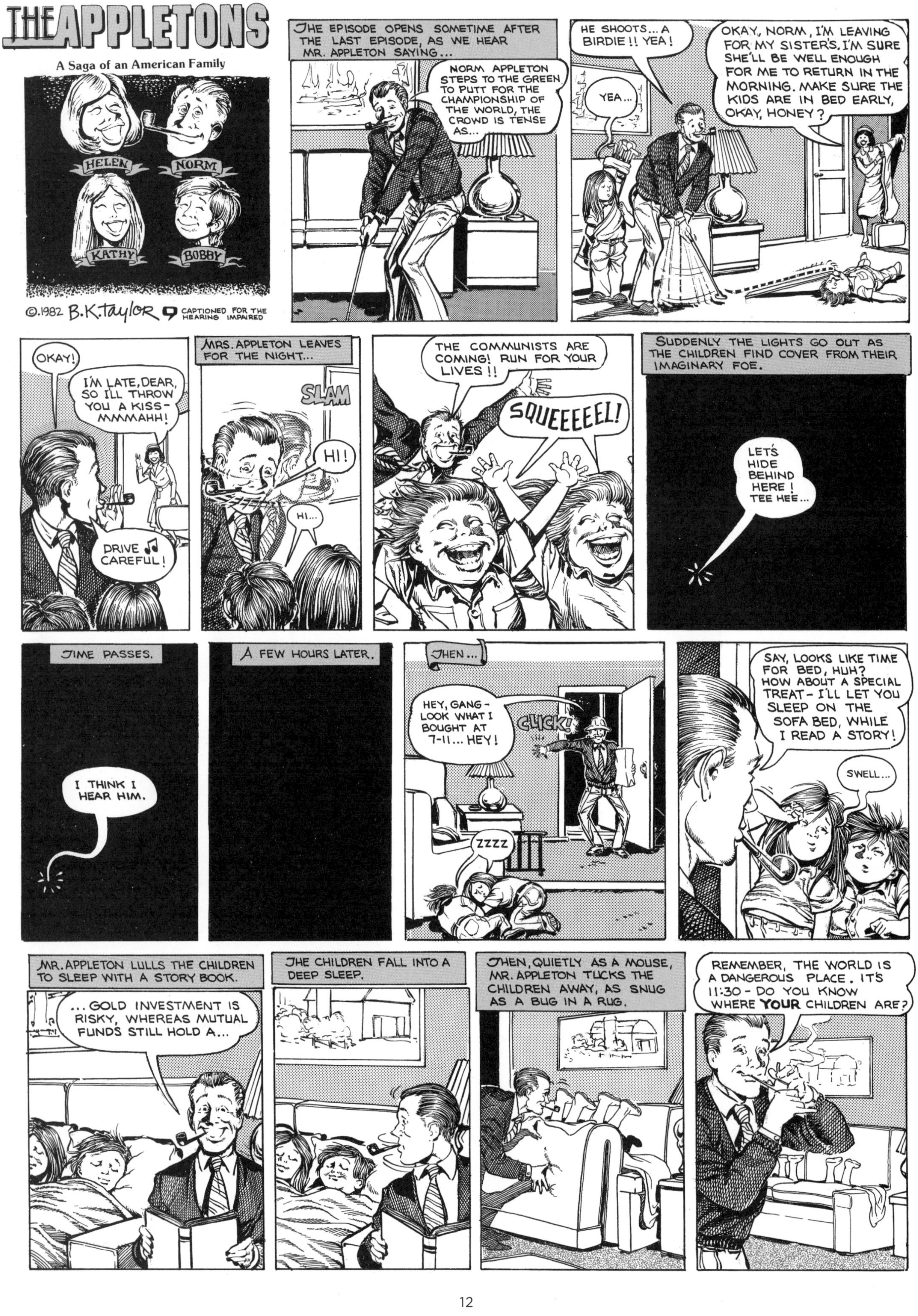
THE APPLETONS
A Saga of an American Family
HELEN
NORM
KATHY
BOBBY
©.1982 B.K.Taylor
CAPTIONED FOR THE HEARING IMPAIRED
THE EPISODE OPENS SOMETIME AFTER THE LAST EPISODE, AS WE HEAR MR. APPLETON SAYING...
NORM APPLETON STEPS TO THE GREEN TO PUTT FOR THE CHAMPIONSHIP OF THE WORLD, THE CROWD IS TENSE AS...
HE SHOOTS... A BIRDIE!! YEA!
YEA...
OKAY, NORM, I'M LEAVING FOR MY SISTER'S. I'M SURE SHE'LL BE WELL ENOUGH FOR ME TO RETURN IN THE MORNING. MAKE SURE THE KIDS ARE IN BED EARLY, OKAY, HONEY?
OKAY!
I'M LATE, DEAR, SO I'LL THROW YOU A KISS-MMMAHH!
DRIVE CAREFUL!
MRS. APPLETON LEAVES FOR THE NIGHT...
SLAM
HI!
HI...
THE COMMUNISTS ARE COMING! RUN FOR YOUR LIVES!!
SQUEEEEEL!
SUDDENLY THE LIGHTS GO OUT AS THE CHILDREN FIND COVER FROM THEIR IMAGINARY FOE.
LET'S HIDE BEHIND HERE! TEE HEE...
TIME PASSES.
I THINK I HEAR HIM.
A FEW HOURS LATER.
THEN...
HEY, GANG - LOOK WHAT I BOUGHT AT 7-11... HEY!
CLICK!
ZZZZ
SAY, LOOKS LIKE TIME FOR BED, HUH? HOW ABOUT A SPECIAL TREAT - I'LL LET YOU SLEEP ON THE SOFA BED, WHILE I READ A STORY!
SWELL...
MR. APPLETON LULLS THE CHILDREN TO SLEEP WITH A STORY BOOK.
...GOLD INVESTMENT IS RISKY, WHEREAS MUTUAL FUNDS STILL HOLD A...
THE CHILDREN FALL INTO A DEEP SLEEP.
THEN, QUIETLY AS A MOUSE, MR. APPLETON TUCKS THE CHILDREN AWAY, AS SNUG AS A BUG IN A RUG.
REMEMBER, THE WORLD IS A DANGEROUS PLACE. IT'S 11:30 - DO YOU KNOW WHERE YOUR CHILDREN ARE?

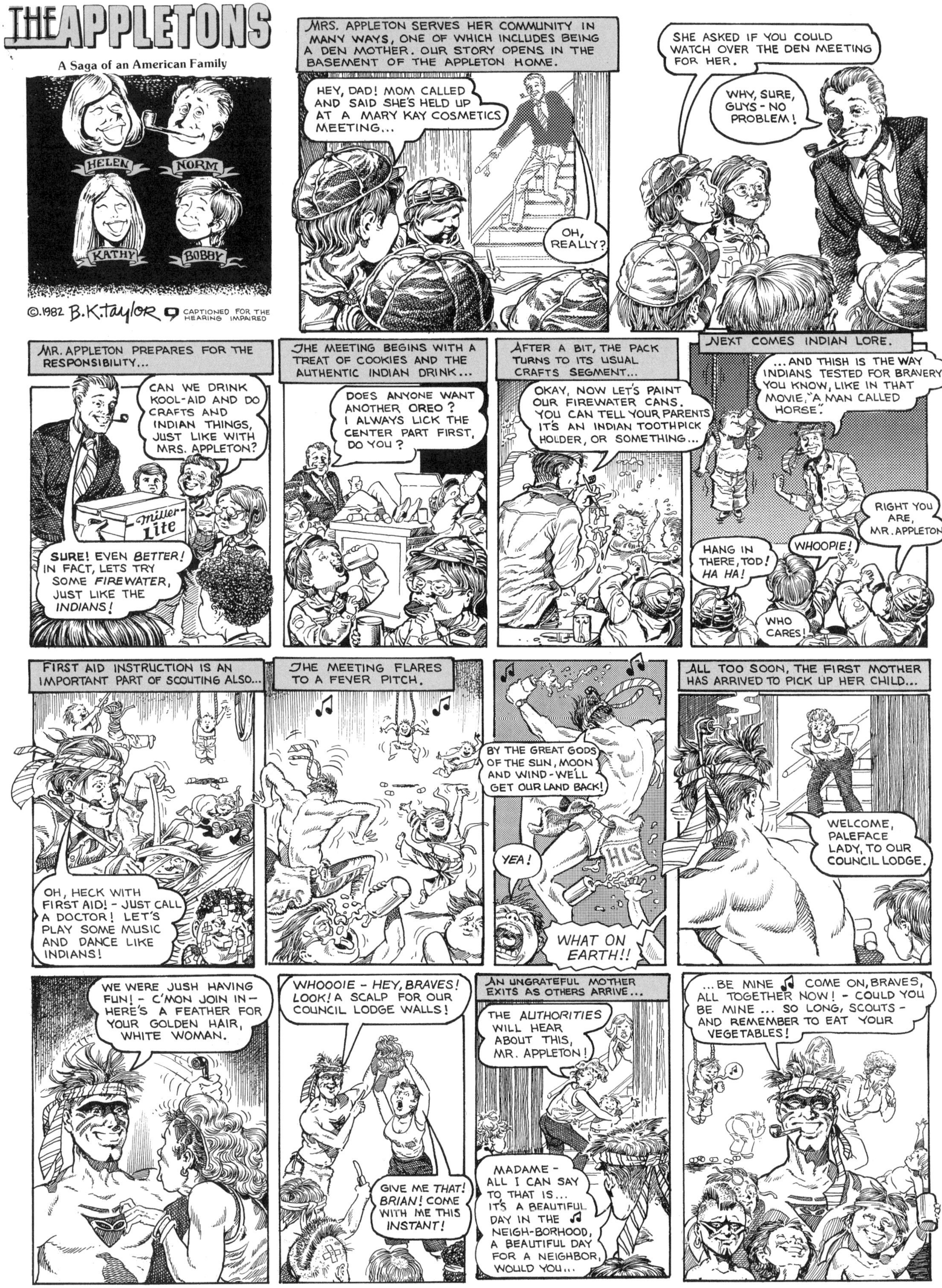

THE APPLETONS
A Saga of an American Family
HELEN
NORM
KATHY
BOBBY
©.1982 B.K.Taylor
CAPTIONED FOR THE HEARING IMPAIRED
MRS. APPLETON SERVES HER COMMUNITY IN MANY WAYS, ONE OF WHICH INCLUDES BEING A DEN MOTHER. OUR STORY OPENS IN THE BASEMENT OF THE APPLETON HOME.
HEY, DAD! MOM CALLED AND SAID SHE'S HELD UP AT A MARY KAY COSMETICS MEETING...
OH, REALLY?
SHE ASKED IF YOU COULD WATCH OVER THE DEN MEETING FOR HER.
WHY, SURE, GUYS - NO PROBLEM!
MR. APPLETON PREPARES FOR THE RESPONSIBILITY...
CAN WE DRINK KOOL-AID AND DO CRAFTS AND INDIAN THINGS, JUST LIKE WITH MRS. APPLETON?
Miller Lite
SURE! EVEN BETTER! IN FACT, LETS TRY SOME FIREWATER, JUST LIKE THE INDIANS!
THE MEETING BEGINS WITH A TREAT OF COOKIES AND THE AUTHENTIC INDIAN DRINK...
DOES ANYONE WANT ANOTHER OREO? I ALWAYS LICK THE CENTER PART FIRST, DO YOU?
AFTER A BIT, THE PACK TURNS TO ITS USUAL CRAFTS SEGMENT...
OKAY, NOW LET'S PAINT OUR FIREWATER CANS. YOU CAN TELL YOUR PARENTS IT'S AN INDIAN TOOTHPICK HOLDER, OR SOMETHING...
NEXT COMES INDIAN LORE.
...AND THISH IS THE WAY INDIANS TESTED FOR BRAVERY- YOU KNOW, LIKE IN THAT MOVIE, "A MAN CALLED HORSE."
RIGHT YOU ARE, MR. APPLETON
HANG IN THERE, TOD! HA HA!
WHOOPIE!
WHO CARES!
FIRST AID INSTRUCTION IS AN IMPORTANT PART OF SCOUTING ALSO...
OH, HECK WITH FIRST AID! - JUST CALL A DOCTOR! LET'S PLAY SOME MUSIC AND DANCE LIKE INDIANS!
THE MEETING FLARES TO A FEVER PITCH.
BY THE GREAT GODS OF THE SUN, MOON AND WIND - WE'LL GET OUR LAND BACK!
YEA!
WHAT ON EARTH!!
ALL TOO SOON, THE FIRST MOTHER HAS ARRIVED TO PICK UP HER CHILD...
WELCOME, PALEFACE LADY, TO OUR COUNCIL LODGE.
WE WERE JUSH HAVING FUN! - C'MON JOIN IN - HERE'S A FEATHER FOR YOUR GOLDEN HAIR, WHITE WOMAN.
WHOOOIE - HEY, BRAVES! LOOK! A SCALP FOR OUR COUNCIL LODGE WALLS!
GIVE ME THAT! BRIAN! COME WITH ME THIS INSTANT!
AN UNGRATEFUL MOTHER EXITS AS OTHERS ARRIVE...
THE AUTHORITIES WILL HEAR ABOUT THIS, MR. APPLETON!
MADAME - ALL I CAN SAY TO THAT IS... IT'S A BEAUTIFUL DAY IN THE NEIGH-BORHOOD, A BEAUTIFUL DAY FOR A NEIGHBOR, WOULD YOU...
...BE MINE COME ON, BRAVES, ALL TOGETHER NOW! - COULD YOU BE MINE ... SO LONG, SCOUTS - AND REMEMBER TO EAT YOUR VEGETABLES!

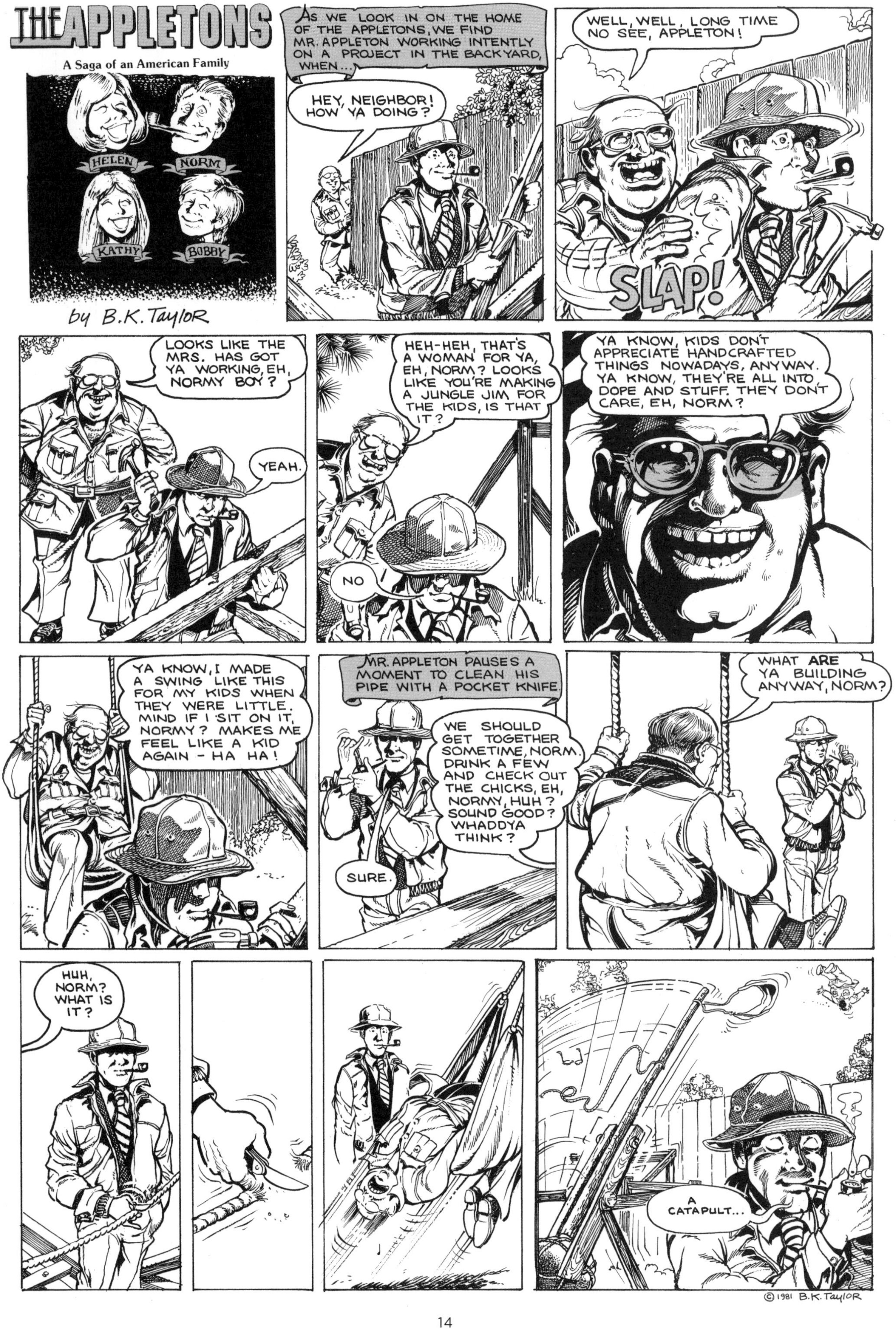
THE APPLETONS
A Saga of an American Family
HELEN
NORM
KATHY
BOBBY
by B.K. Taylor
AS WE LOOK IN ON THE HOME OF THE APPLETONS, WE FIND MR. APPLETON WORKING INTENTLY ON A PROJECT IN THE BACKYARD, WHEN...
HEY, NEIGHBOR! HOW YA DOING?
WELL, WELL, LONG TIME NO SEE, APPLETON!
SLAP!
LOOKS LIKE THE MRS. HAS GOT YA WORKING, EH, NORMY BOY?
YEAH.
HEH-HEH, THAT'S A WOMAN FOR YA, EH, NORM? LOOKS LIKE YOU'RE MAKING A JUNGLE JIM FOR THE KIDS, IS THAT IT?
NO
YA KNOW, KIDS DON'T APPRECIATE HANDCRAFTED THINGS NOWADAYS, ANYWAY. YA KNOW, THEY'RE ALL INTO DOPE AND STUFF. THEY DON'T CARE, EH, NORM?
YA KNOW, I MADE A SWING LIKE THIS FOR MY KIDS WHEN THEY WERE LITTLE. MIND IF I SIT ON IT, NORMY? MAKES ME FEEL LIKE A KID AGAIN - HA HA!
MR. APPLETON PAUSES A MOMENT TO CLEAN HIS PIPE WITH A POCKET KNIFE.
WE SHOULD GET TOGETHER SOMETIME, NORM. DRINK A FEW AND CHECK OUT THE CHICKS, EH, NORMY, HUH? SOUND GOOD? WHADDYA THINK?
SURE.
WHAT ARE YA BUILDING ANYWAY, NORM?
HUH, NORM? WHAT IS IT?
A CATAPULT...
©1981 B.K. Taylor

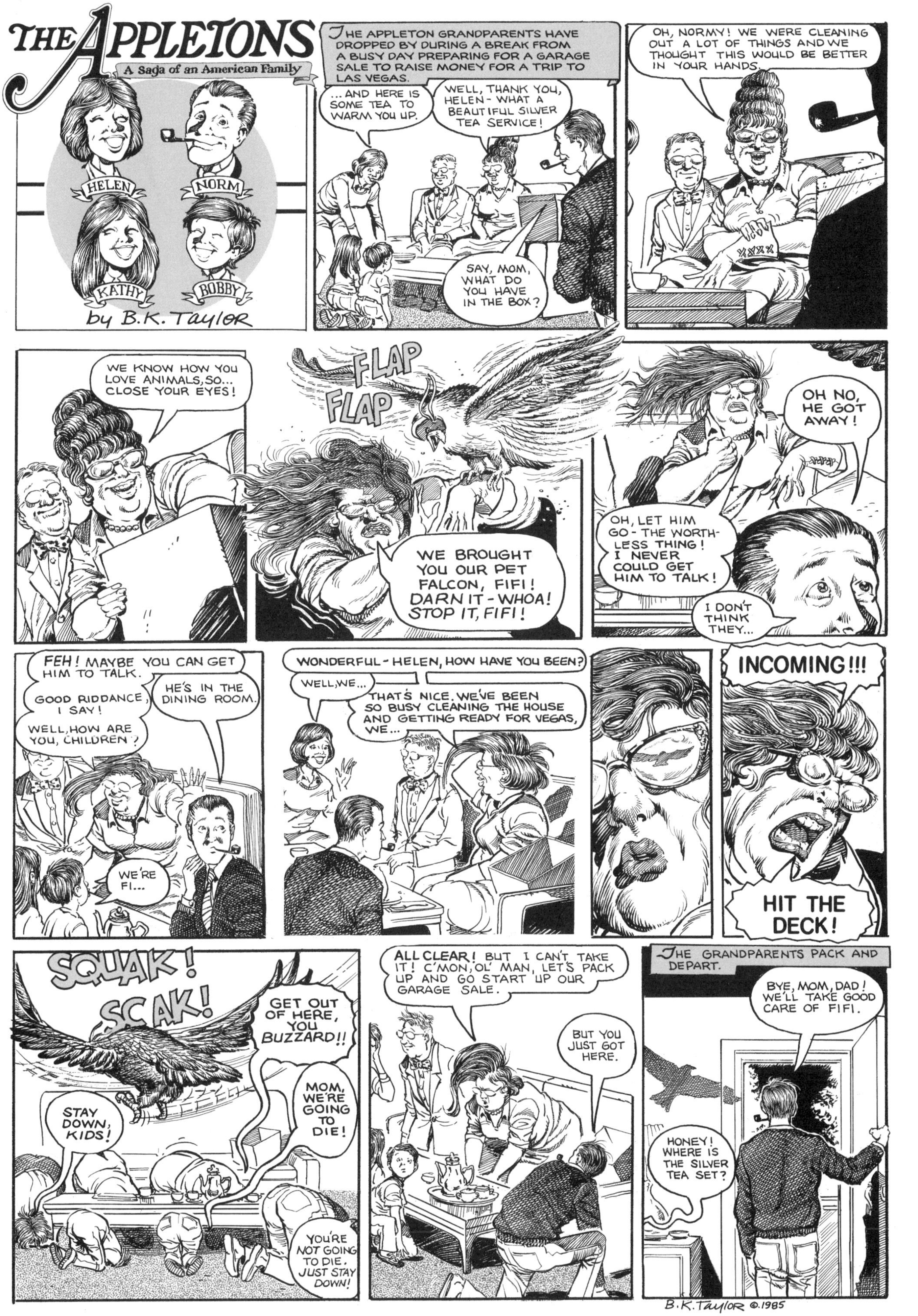
THE APPLETONS
A Saga of an American Family
HELEN
NORM
KATHY
BOBBY
by B.K. Taylor
THE APPLETON GRANDPARENTS HAVE DROPPED BY DURING A BREAK FROM A BUSY DAY PREPARING FOR A GARAGE SALE TO RAISE MONEY FOR A TRIP TO LAS VEGAS.
...AND HERE IS SOME TEA TO WARM YOU UP.
WELL, THANK YOU, HELEN - WHAT A BEAUTIFUL SILVER TEA SERVICE!
SAY, MOM, WHAT DO YOU HAVE IN THE BOX?
OH, NORMY! WE WERE CLEANING OUT A LOT OF THINGS AND WE THOUGHT THIS WOULD BE BETTER IN YOUR HANDS.
WE KNOW HOW YOU LOVE ANIMALS, SO... CLOSE YOUR EYES!
FLAP
FLAP
WE BROUGHT YOU OUR PET FALCON, FIFI! DARN IT - WHOA! STOP IT, FIFI!
OH NO, HE GOT AWAY!
OH, LET HIM GO - THE WORTHLESS THING! I NEVER COULD GET HIM TO TALK!
I DON'T THINK THEY...
FEH! MAYBE YOU CAN GET HIM TO TALK.
GOOD RIDDANCE, I SAY!
HE'S IN THE DINING ROOM.
WELL, HOW ARE YOU, CHILDREN?
WE'RE FI...
WONDERFUL - HELEN, HOW HAVE YOU BEEN?
WELL, WE...
THAT'S NICE. WE'VE BEEN SO BUSY CLEANING THE HOUSE AND GETTING READY FOR VEGAS, WE...
INCOMING!!!
HIT THE DECK!
SQUAK!
SCAK!
GET OUT OF HERE, YOU BUZZARD!!
STAY DOWN, KIDS!
MOM, WE'RE GOING TO DIE!
YOU'RE NOT GOING TO DIE. JUST STAY DOWN!
ALL CLEAR! BUT I CAN'T TAKE IT! C'MON, OL' MAN, LET'S PACK UP AND GO START UP OUR GARAGE SALE.
BUT YOU JUST GOT HERE.
THE GRANDPARENTS PACK AND DEPART.
BYE, MOM, DAD! WE'LL TAKE GOOD CARE OF FIFI.
HONEY! WHERE IS THE SILVER TEA SET?
B.K. Taylor ©1985

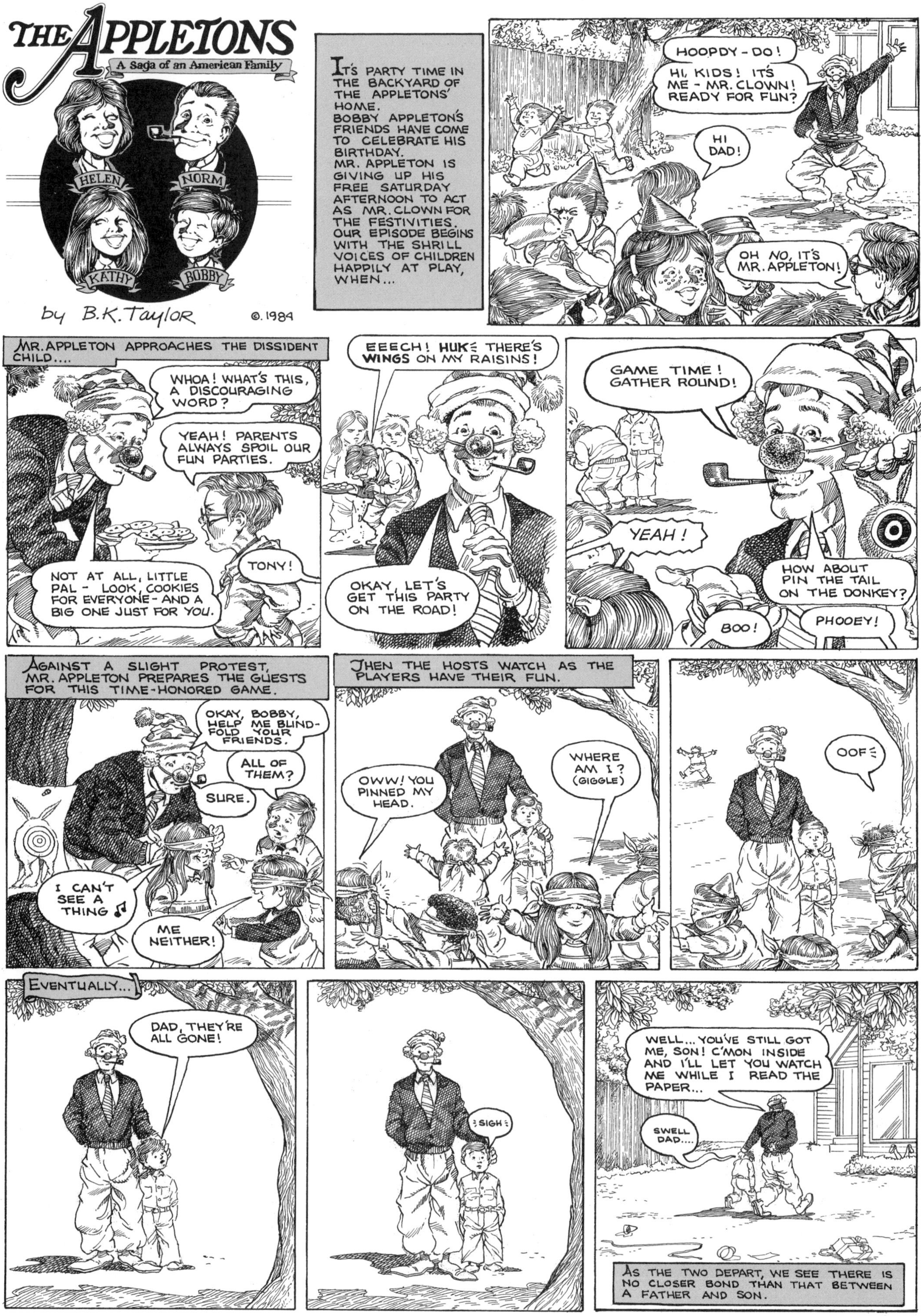
THE APPLETONS
A Saga of an American Family
HELEN
NORM
KATHY
BOBBY
by B.K. Taylor
©.1984
IT'S PARTY TIME IN THE BACKYARD OF THE APPLETONS' HOME. BOBBY APPLETON'S FRIENDS HAVE COME TO CELEBRATE HIS BIRTHDAY. MR. APPLETON IS GIVING UP HIS FREE SATURDAY AFTERNOON TO ACT AS MR. CLOWN FOR THE FESTIVITIES. OUR EPISODE BEGINS WITH THE SHRILL VOICES OF CHILDREN HAPPILY AT PLAY, WHEN...
HOOPDY-DO!
HI, KIDS! IT'S ME - MR. CLOWN! READY FOR FUN?
HI DAD!
OH NO, IT'S MR. APPLETON!
MR. APPLETON APPROACHES THE DISSIDENT CHILD....
WHOA! WHAT'S THIS, A DISCOURAGING WORD?
YEAH! PARENTS ALWAYS SPOIL OUR FUN PARTIES.
NOT AT ALL, LITTLE PAL - LOOK, COOKIES FOR EVERYONE - AND A BIG ONE JUST FOR YOU.
TONY!
EEECH! HUK! THERE'S WINGS ON MY RAISINS!
OKAY, LET'S GET THIS PARTY ON THE ROAD!
GAME TIME! GATHER ROUND!
YEAH!
HOW ABOUT PIN THE TAIL ON THE DONKEY?
BOO!
PHOOEY!
AGAINST A SLIGHT PROTEST, MR. APPLETON PREPARES THE GUESTS FOR THIS TIME-HONORED GAME.
OKAY, BOBBY, HELP ME BLIND-FOLD YOUR FRIENDS.
ALL OF THEM?
SURE.
I CAN'T SEE A THING ♪
ME NEITHER!
THEN THE HOSTS WATCH AS THE PLAYERS HAVE THEIR FUN.
OWW! YOU PINNED MY HEAD.
WHERE AM I? (GIGGLE)
OOF!
EVENTUALLY...
DAD, THEY'RE ALL GONE!
SIGH
WELL... YOU'VE STILL GOT ME, SON! C'MON INSIDE AND I'LL LET YOU WATCH ME WHILE I READ THE PAPER...
SWELL DAD....
AS THE TWO DEPART, WE SEE THERE IS NO CLOSER BOND THAN THAT BETWEEN A FATHER AND SON.

THE OFFICIAL CARTOON STRIP FOR THE 1984 OLYMPICS

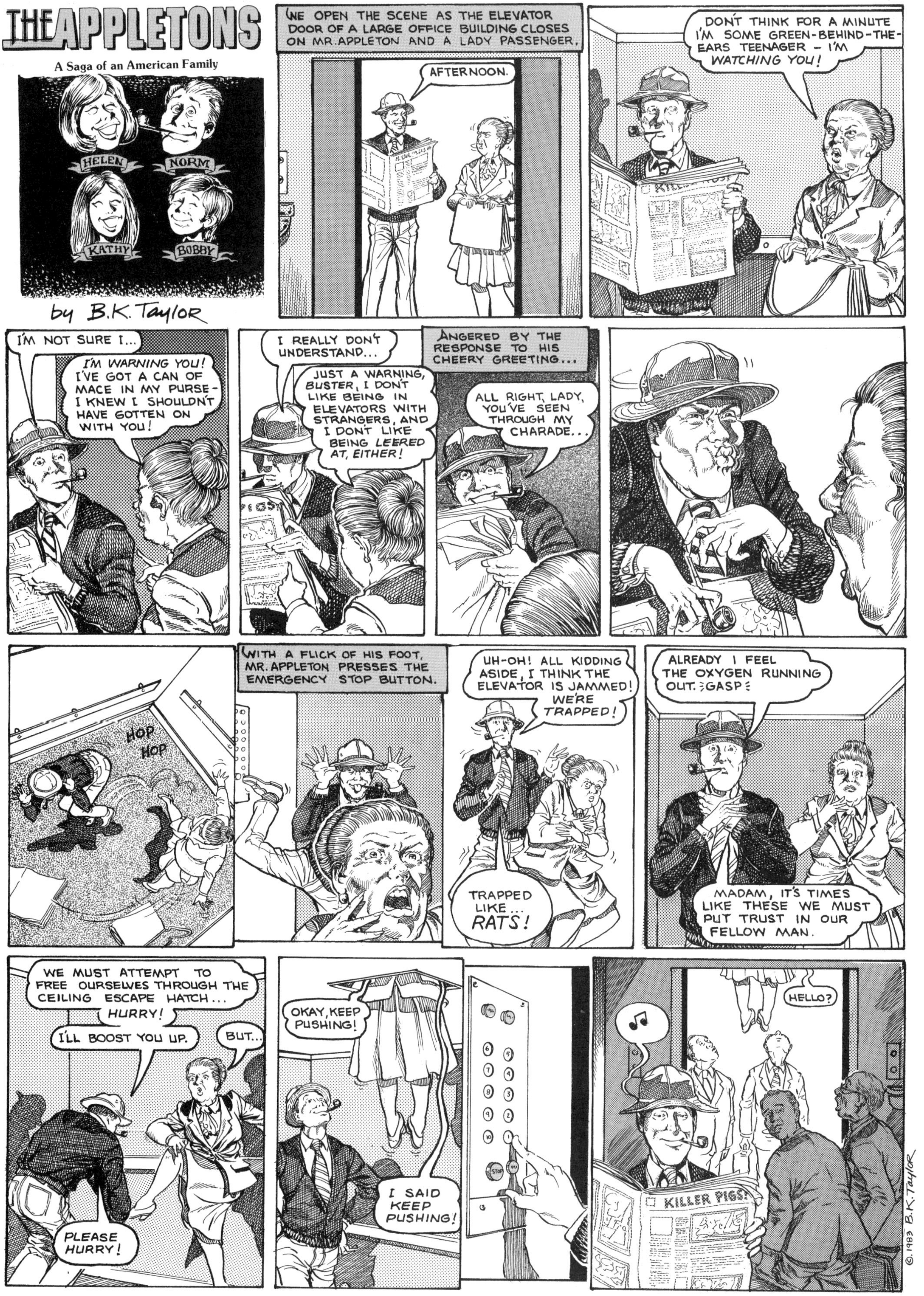
THE APPLETONS
A Saga of an American Family
HELEN
NORM
KATHY
BOBBY
by B.K. Taylor
WE OPEN THE SCENE AS THE ELEVATOR DOOR OF A LARGE OFFICE BUILDING CLOSES ON MR. APPLETON AND A LADY PASSENGER.
AFTERNOON.
DON'T THINK FOR A MINUTE I'M SOME GREEN-BEHIND-THE-EARS TEENAGER - I'M WATCHING YOU!
I'M NOT SURE I...
I'M WARNING YOU! I'VE GOT A CAN OF MACE IN MY PURSE - I KNEW I SHOULDN'T HAVE GOTTEN ON WITH YOU!
I REALLY DON'T UNDERSTAND...
JUST A WARNING, BUSTER, I DON'T LIKE BEING IN ELEVATORS WITH STRANGERS, AND I DON'T LIKE BEING LEERED AT, EITHER!
ANGERED BY THE RESPONSE TO HIS CHEERY GREETING...
ALL RIGHT, LADY, YOU'VE SEEN THROUGH MY CHARADE...
HOP HOP
WITH A FLICK OF HIS FOOT, MR. APPLETON PRESSES THE EMERGENCY STOP BUTTON.
UH-OH! ALL KIDDING ASIDE, I THINK THE ELEVATOR IS JAMMED! WE'RE TRAPPED!
TRAPPED LIKE... RATS!
ALREADY I FEEL THE OXYGEN RUNNING OUT. ⋮GASP⋮
MADAM, IT'S TIMES LIKE THESE WE MUST PUT TRUST IN OUR FELLOW MAN.
WE MUST ATTEMPT TO FREE OURSELVES THROUGH THE CEILING ESCAPE HATCH... HURRY!
I'LL BOOST YOU UP.
BUT...
PLEASE HURRY!
OKAY, KEEP PUSHING!
I SAID KEEP PUSHING!
HELLO?
KILLER PIGS!
©1983 B.K. Taylor

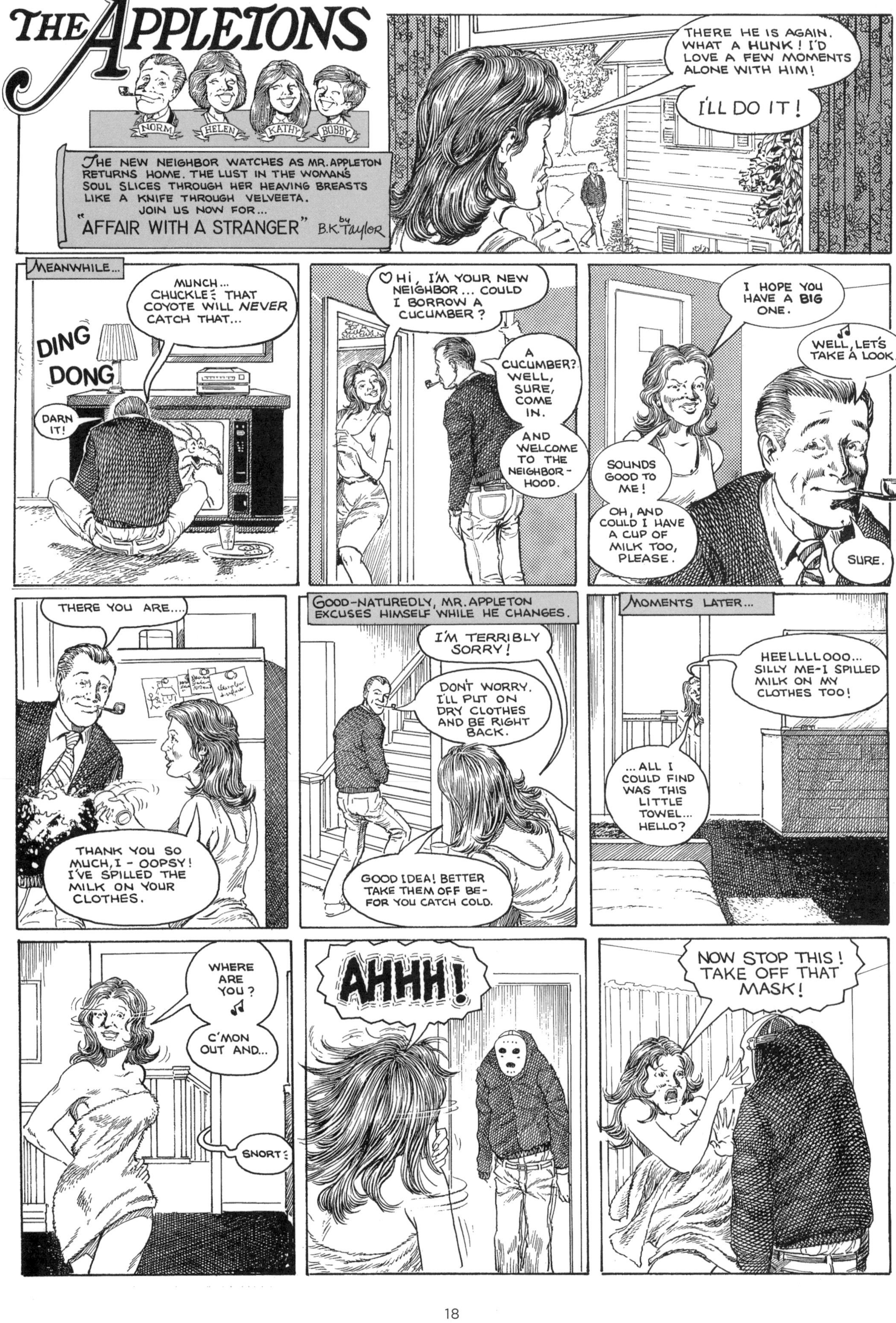

THE APPLETONS
NORM
HELEN
KATHY
BOBBY
THE NEW NEIGHBOR WATCHES AS MR. APPLETON RETURNS HOME. THE LUST IN THE WOMAN'S SOUL SLICES THROUGH HER HEAVING BREASTS LIKE A KNIFE THROUGH VELVEETA. JOIN US NOW FOR...
"AFFAIR WITH A STRANGER" by B.K. Taylor
THERE HE IS AGAIN. WHAT A HUNK! I'D LOVE A FEW MOMENTS ALONE WITH HIM!
I'LL DO IT!
MEANWHILE...
MUNCH... CHUCKLE: THAT COYOTE WILL NEVER CATCH THAT...
DING DONG
DARN IT!
HI, I'M YOUR NEW NEIGHBOR... COULD I BORROW A CUCUMBER?
A CUCUMBER? WELL, SURE, COME IN.
AND WELCOME TO THE NEIGHBOR-HOOD.
I HOPE YOU HAVE A BIG ONE.
WELL, LET'S TAKE A LOOK.
SOUNDS GOOD TO ME!
OH, AND COULD I HAVE A CUP OF MILK TOO, PLEASE.
SURE.
THERE YOU ARE....
THANK YOU SO MUCH, I - OOPSY! I'VE SPILLED THE MILK ON YOUR CLOTHES.
GOOD-NATUREDLY, MR. APPLETON EXCUSES HIMSELF WHILE HE CHANGES.
I'M TERRIBLY SORRY!
DON'T WORRY. I'LL PUT ON DRY CLOTHES AND BE RIGHT BACK.
GOOD IDEA! BETTER TAKE THEM OFF BE-FOR YOU CATCH COLD.
MOMENTS LATER...
HEELLLLOOO... SILLY ME-I SPILLED MILK ON MY CLOTHES TOO!
...ALL I COULD FIND WAS THIS LITTLE TOWEL... HELLO?
WHERE ARE YOU?
C'MON OUT AND...
SNORT
AHHH!
NOW STOP THIS! TAKE OFF THAT MASK!

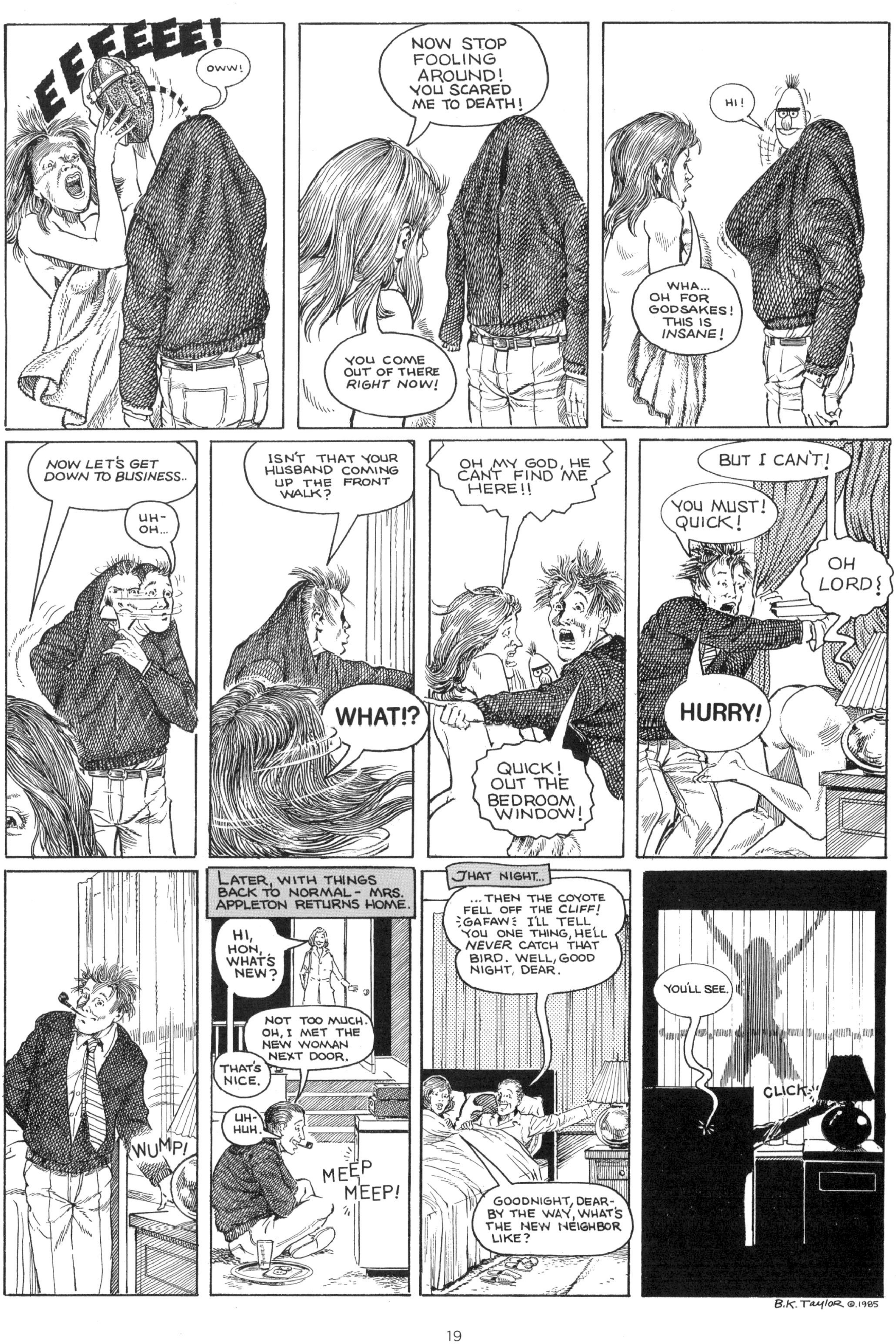
EEEEEE!
OWW!
NOW STOP FOOLING AROUND! YOU SCARED ME TO DEATH!
YOU COME OUT OF THERE RIGHT NOW!
HI!
WHA... OH FOR GODSAKES! THIS IS INSANE!
NOW LET'S GET DOWN TO BUSINESS..
UH-OH...
ISN'T THAT YOUR HUSBAND COMING UP THE FRONT WALK?
WHAT!?
OH MY GOD, HE CAN'T FIND ME HERE!!
QUICK! OUT THE BEDROOM WINDOW!
BUT I CAN'T!
YOU MUST! QUICK!
OH LORD!
HURRY!
WUMP!
LATER, WITH THINGS BACK TO NORMAL - MRS. APPLETON RETURNS HOME.
HI, HON, WHAT'S NEW?
NOT TOO MUCH. OH, I MET THE NEW WOMAN NEXT DOOR.
THAT'S NICE.
UH-HUH.
MEEP MEEP!
THAT NIGHT...
...THEN THE COYOTE FELL OFF THE CLIFF! GAFAW! I'LL TELL YOU ONE THING, HE'LL NEVER CATCH THAT BIRD. WELL, GOOD NIGHT, DEAR.
GOODNIGHT, DEAR- BY THE WAY, WHAT'S THE NEW NEIGHBOR LIKE?
YOU'LL SEE.
CLICK
B.K. TAYLOR ©.1985

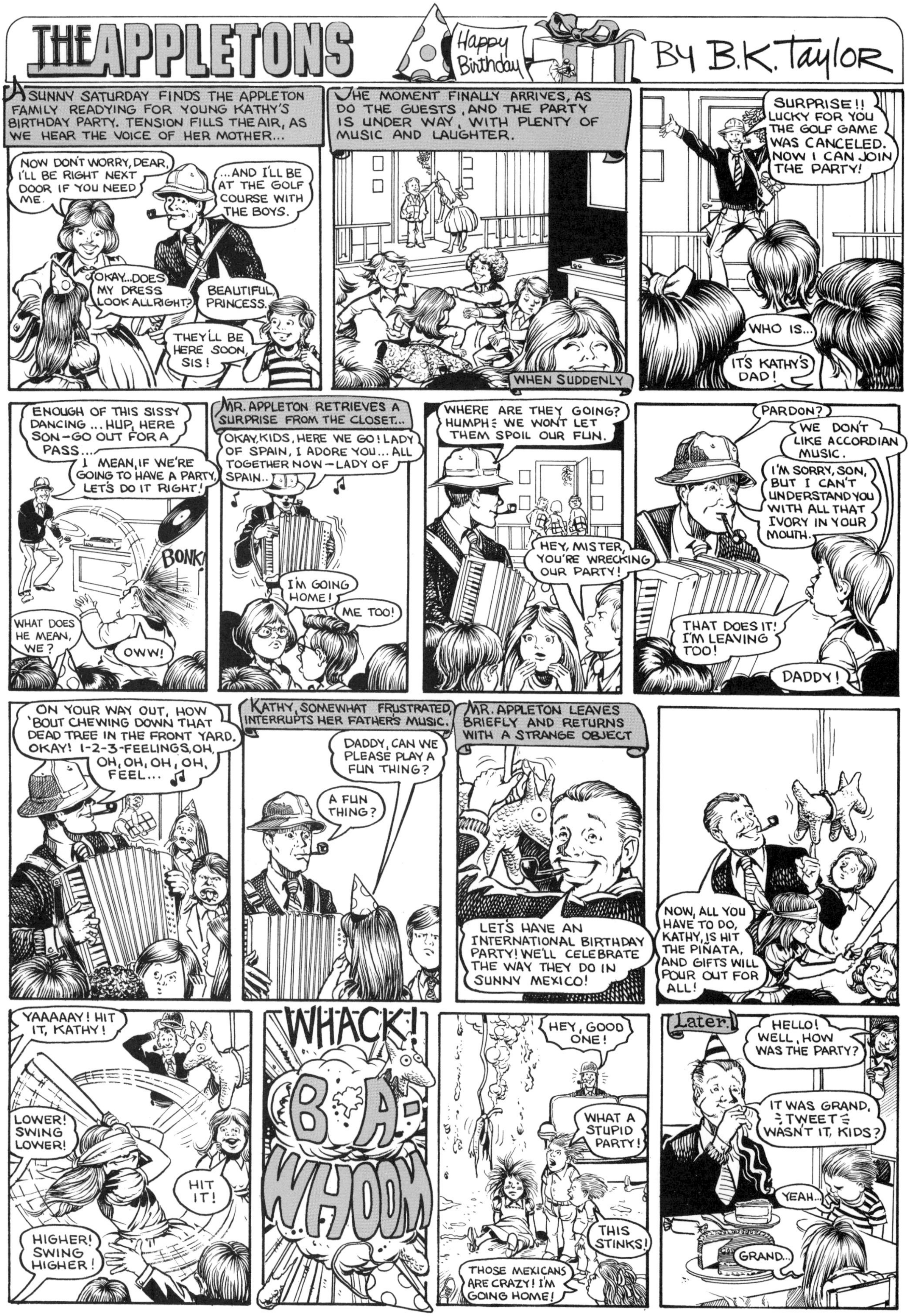
THE APPLETONS
Happy Birthday
BY B.K. Taylor
A SUNNY SATURDAY FINDS THE APPLETON FAMILY READYING FOR YOUNG KATHY'S BIRTHDAY PARTY. TENSION FILLS THE AIR, AS WE HEAR THE VOICE OF HER MOTHER...
NOW DON'T WORRY, DEAR, I'LL BE RIGHT NEXT DOOR IF YOU NEED ME.
...AND I'LL BE AT THE GOLF COURSE WITH THE BOYS.
OKAY...DOES MY DRESS LOOK ALLRIGHT?
BEAUTIFUL, PRINCESS.
THEY'LL BE HERE SOON, SIS!
THE MOMENT FINALLY ARRIVES, AS DO THE GUESTS, AND THE PARTY IS UNDER WAY, WITH PLENTY OF MUSIC AND LAUGHTER.
WHEN SUDDENLY
SURPRISE!! LUCKY FOR YOU THE GOLF GAME WAS CANCELED. NOW I CAN JOIN THE PARTY!
WHO IS...
IT'S KATHY'S DAD!
ENOUGH OF THIS SISSY DANCING... HUP, HERE SON—GO OUT FOR A PASS...
I MEAN, IF WE'RE GOING TO HAVE A PARTY, LET'S DO IT RIGHT!
BONK!
WHAT DOES HE MEAN, WE?
OWW!
MR. APPLETON RETRIEVES A SURPRISE FROM THE CLOSET...
OKAY, KIDS, HERE WE GO! LADY OF SPAIN, I ADORE YOU... ALL TOGETHER NOW—LADY OF SPAIN..
I'M GOING HOME!
ME TOO!
WHERE ARE THEY GOING? HUMPH! WE WON'T LET THEM SPOIL OUR FUN.
HEY, MISTER, YOU'RE WRECKING OUR PARTY!
PARDON?
WE DON'T LIKE ACCORDIAN MUSIC.
I'M SORRY, SON, BUT I CAN'T UNDERSTAND YOU WITH ALL THAT IVORY IN YOUR MOUTH.
THAT DOES IT! I'M LEAVING TOO!
DADDY!
ON YOUR WAY OUT, HOW 'BOUT CHEWING DOWN THAT DEAD TREE IN THE FRONT YARD. OKAY! 1-2-3-FEELINGS, OH, OH, OH, OH, OH, FEEL...
KATHY, SOMEWHAT FRUSTRATED, INTERRUPTS HER FATHER'S MUSIC.
DADDY, CAN WE PLEASE PLAY A FUN THING?
A FUN THING?
MR. APPLETON LEAVES BRIEFLY AND RETURNS WITH A STRANGE OBJECT
LET'S HAVE AN INTERNATIONAL BIRTHDAY PARTY! WE'LL CELEBRATE THE WAY THEY DO IN SUNNY MEXICO!
NOW, ALL YOU HAVE TO DO, KATHY, IS HIT THE PIÑATA, AND GIFTS WILL POUR OUT FOR ALL!
YAAAAAY! HIT IT, KATHY!
LOWER! SWING LOWER!
HIT IT!
HIGHER! SWING HIGHER!
WHACK!
B-A-WHOOM
HEY, GOOD ONE!
WHAT A STUPID PARTY!
THIS STINKS!
THOSE MEXICANS ARE CRAZY! I'M GOING HOME!
Later.
HELLO! WELL, HOW WAS THE PARTY?
IT WAS GRAND, TWEET WASN'T IT, KIDS?
YEAH...
GRAND...

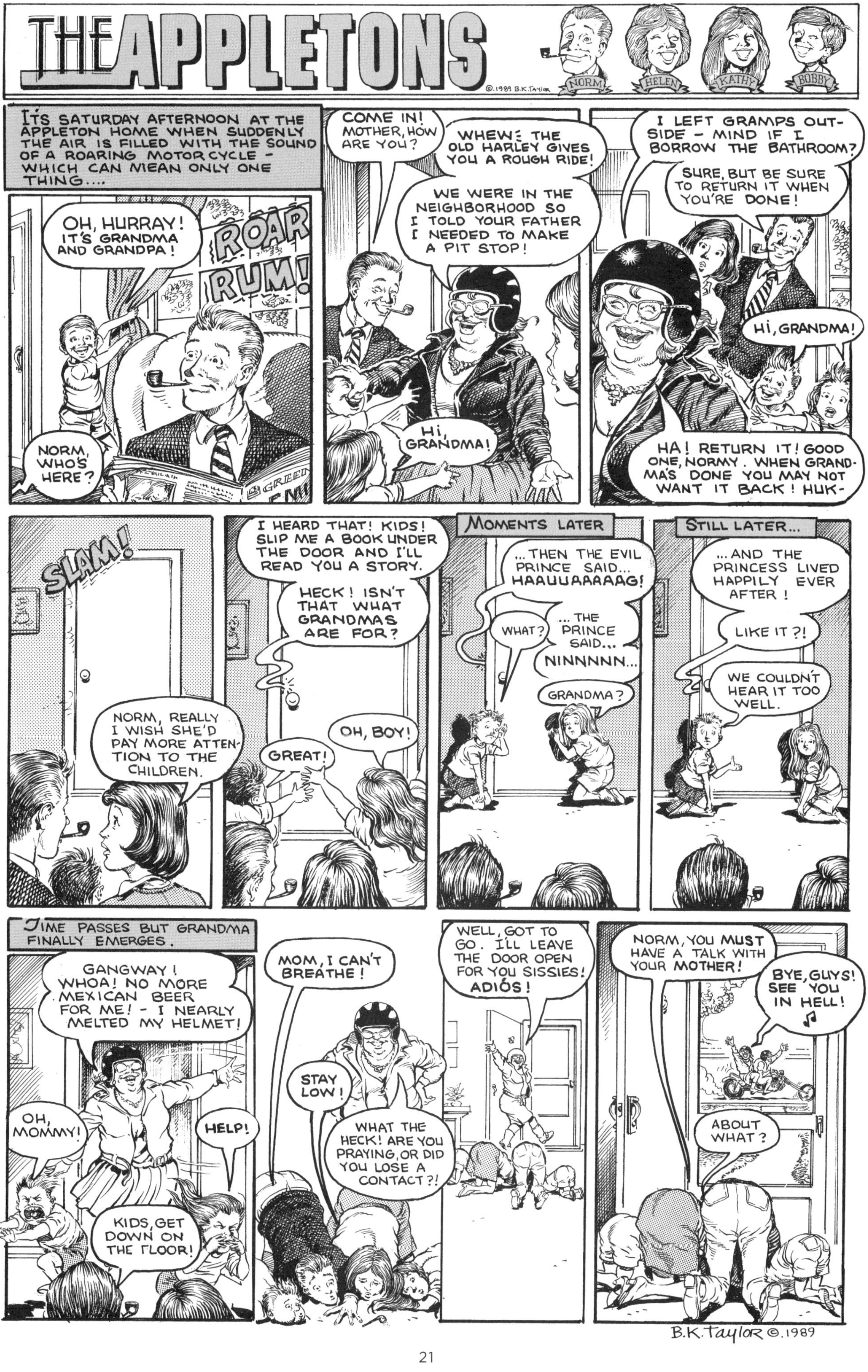
THE APPLETONS
©.1989 B.K.TAYLOR
NORM
HELEN
KATHY
BOBBY
IT'S SATURDAY AFTERNOON AT THE APPLETON HOME WHEN SUDDENLY THE AIR IS FILLED WITH THE SOUND OF A ROARING MOTORCYCLE - WHICH CAN MEAN ONLY ONE THING....
OH, HURRAY! IT'S GRANDMA AND GRANDPA!
ROAR
RUM!
NORM, WHO'S HERE?
COME IN! MOTHER, HOW ARE YOU?
WHEW! THE OLD HARLEY GIVES YOU A ROUGH RIDE!
WE WERE IN THE NEIGHBORHOOD SO I TOLD YOUR FATHER I NEEDED TO MAKE A PIT STOP!
HI, GRANDMA!
I LEFT GRAMPS OUTSIDE - MIND IF I BORROW THE BATHROOM?
SURE, BUT BE SURE TO RETURN IT WHEN YOU'RE DONE!
HI, GRANDMA!
HA! RETURN IT! GOOD ONE, NORMY. WHEN GRANDMA'S DONE YOU MAY NOT WANT IT BACK! HUK-
SLAM!
NORM, REALLY I WISH SHE'D PAY MORE ATTENTION TO THE CHILDREN.
I HEARD THAT! KIDS! SLIP ME A BOOK UNDER THE DOOR AND I'LL READ YOU A STORY.
HECK! ISN'T THAT WHAT GRANDMAS ARE FOR?
OH, BOY!
GREAT!
MOMENTS LATER
...THEN THE EVIL PRINCE SAID... HAAUUAAAAAG!
WHAT?
...THE PRINCE SAID... NINNNNN...
GRANDMA?
STILL LATER...
...AND THE PRINCESS LIVED HAPPILY EVER AFTER!
LIKE IT?!
WE COULDN'T HEAR IT TOO WELL.
TIME PASSES BUT GRANDMA FINALLY EMERGES.
GANGWAY! WHOA! NO MORE MEXICAN BEER FOR ME! - I NEARLY MELTED MY HELMET!
OH, MOMMY!
HELP!
KIDS, GET DOWN ON THE FLOOR!
MOM, I CAN'T BREATHE!
STAY LOW!
WHAT THE HECK! ARE YOU PRAYING, OR DID YOU LOSE A CONTACT?!
WELL, GOT TO GO. I'LL LEAVE THE DOOR OPEN FOR YOU SISSIES! ADIÓS!
NORM, YOU MUST HAVE A TALK WITH YOUR MOTHER!
BYE, GUYS! SEE YOU IN HELL!
ABOUT WHAT?
B.K.Taylor ©.1989

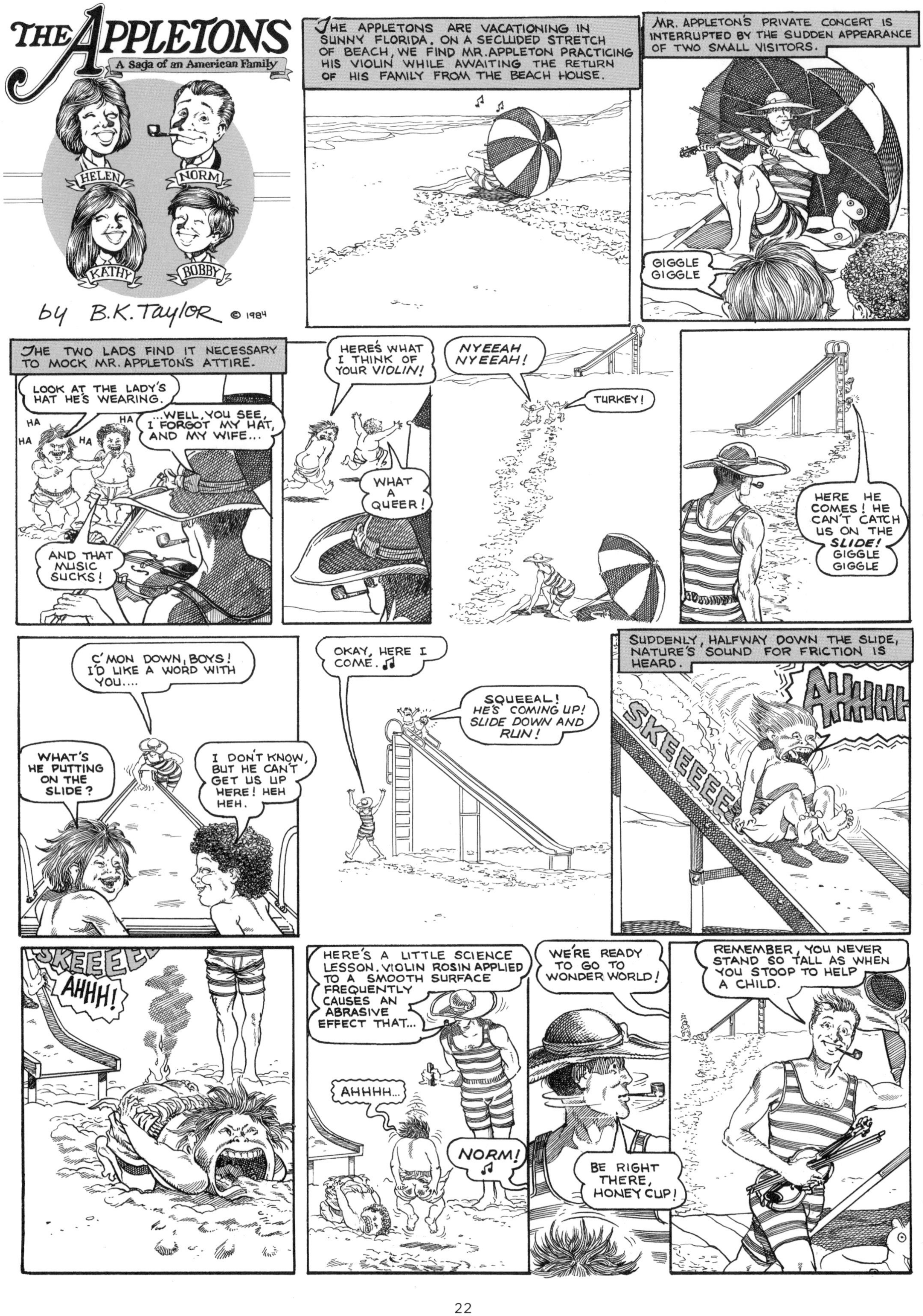
THE APPLETONS
A Saga of an American Family
HELEN
NORM
KATHY
BOBBY
by B.K. Taylor © 1984
THE APPLETONS ARE VACATIONING IN SUNNY FLORIDA. ON A SECLUDED STRETCH OF BEACH, WE FIND MR. APPLETON PRACTICING HIS VIOLIN WHILE AWAITING THE RETURN OF HIS FAMILY FROM THE BEACH HOUSE.
MR. APPLETON'S PRIVATE CONCERT IS INTERRUPTED BY THE SUDDEN APPEARANCE OF TWO SMALL VISITORS.
GIGGLE GIGGLE
THE TWO LADS FIND IT NECESSARY TO MOCK MR. APPLETON'S ATTIRE.
LOOK AT THE LADY'S HAT HE'S WEARING.
HA HA HA HA
...WELL, YOU SEE, I FORGOT MY HAT, AND MY WIFE...
AND THAT MUSIC SUCKS!
HERE'S WHAT I THINK OF YOUR VIOLIN!
WHAT A QUEER!
NYEEAH NYEEAH!
TURKEY!
HERE HE COMES! HE CAN'T CATCH US ON THE SLIDE! GIGGLE GIGGLE
C'MON DOWN, BOYS! I'D LIKE A WORD WITH YOU....
WHAT'S HE PUTTING ON THE SLIDE?
I DON'T KNOW, BUT HE CAN'T GET US UP HERE! HEH HEH.
OKAY, HERE I COME.
SQUEEAL! HE'S COMING UP! SLIDE DOWN AND RUN!
SUDDENLY, HALFWAY DOWN THE SLIDE, NATURE'S SOUND FOR FRICTION IS HEARD.
SKEEEEEE
AHHHH
SKEEEEE
AHHH!
HERE'S A LITTLE SCIENCE LESSON. VIOLIN ROSIN APPLIED TO A SMOOTH SURFACE FREQUENTLY CAUSES AN ABRASIVE EFFECT THAT...
AHHHH...
NORM!
WE'RE READY TO GO TO WONDER WORLD!
BE RIGHT THERE, HONEY CUP!
REMEMBER, YOU NEVER STAND SO TALL AS WHEN YOU STOOP TO HELP A CHILD.

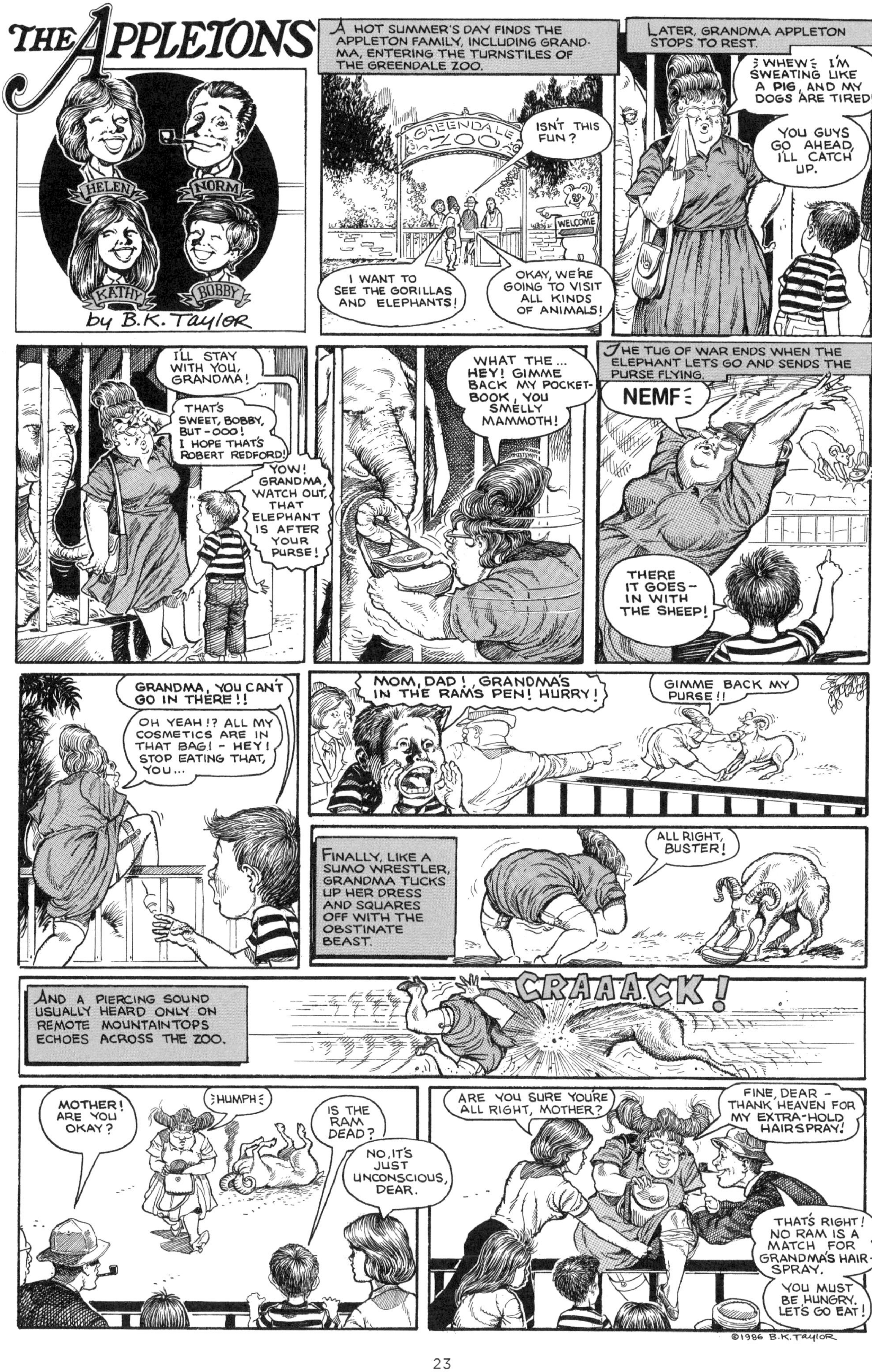
THE APPLETONS
HELEN
NORM
KATHY
BOBBY
by B.K. Taylor
A HOT SUMMER'S DAY FINDS THE APPLETON FAMILY, INCLUDING GRANDMA, ENTERING THE TURNSTILES OF THE GREENDALE ZOO.
GREENDALE ZOO
ISN'T THIS FUN?
WELCOME
I WANT TO SEE THE GORILLAS AND ELEPHANTS!
OKAY, WE'RE GOING TO VISIT ALL KINDS OF ANIMALS!
LATER, GRANDMA APPLETON STOPS TO REST.
WHEW! I'M SWEATING LIKE A PIG, AND MY DOGS ARE TIRED!
YOU GUYS GO AHEAD, I'LL CATCH UP.
I'LL STAY WITH YOU, GRANDMA!
THAT'S SWEET, BOBBY, BUT-OOO! I HOPE THAT'S ROBERT REDFORD!
YOW! GRANDMA, WATCH OUT, THAT ELEPHANT IS AFTER YOUR PURSE!
WHAT THE... HEY! GIMME BACK MY POCKETBOOK, YOU SMELLY MAMMOTH!
THE TUG OF WAR ENDS WHEN THE ELEPHANT LETS GO AND SENDS THE PURSE FLYING.
NEMF
THERE IT GOES - IN WITH THE SHEEP!
GRANDMA, YOU CAN'T GO IN THERE!!
OH YEAH!? ALL MY COSMETICS ARE IN THAT BAG! - HEY! STOP EATING THAT, YOU...
MOM, DAD! GRANDMA'S IN THE RAM'S PEN! HURRY!
GIMME BACK MY PURSE!!
FINALLY, LIKE A SUMO WRESTLER, GRANDMA TUCKS UP HER DRESS AND SQUARES OFF WITH THE OBSTINATE BEAST.
ALL RIGHT, BUSTER!
AND A PIERCING SOUND USUALLY HEARD ONLY ON REMOTE MOUNTAINTOPS ECHOES ACROSS THE ZOO.
CRAAACK!
MOTHER! ARE YOU OKAY?
HUMPH
IS THE RAM DEAD?
NO, IT'S JUST UNCONSCIOUS, DEAR.
ARE YOU SURE YOU'RE ALL RIGHT, MOTHER?
FINE, DEAR - THANK HEAVEN FOR MY EXTRA-HOLD HAIRSPRAY!
THAT'S RIGHT! NO RAM IS A MATCH FOR GRANDMA'S HAIRSPRAY.
YOU MUST BE HUNGRY. LET'S GO EAT!
©1986 B.K. TAYLOR

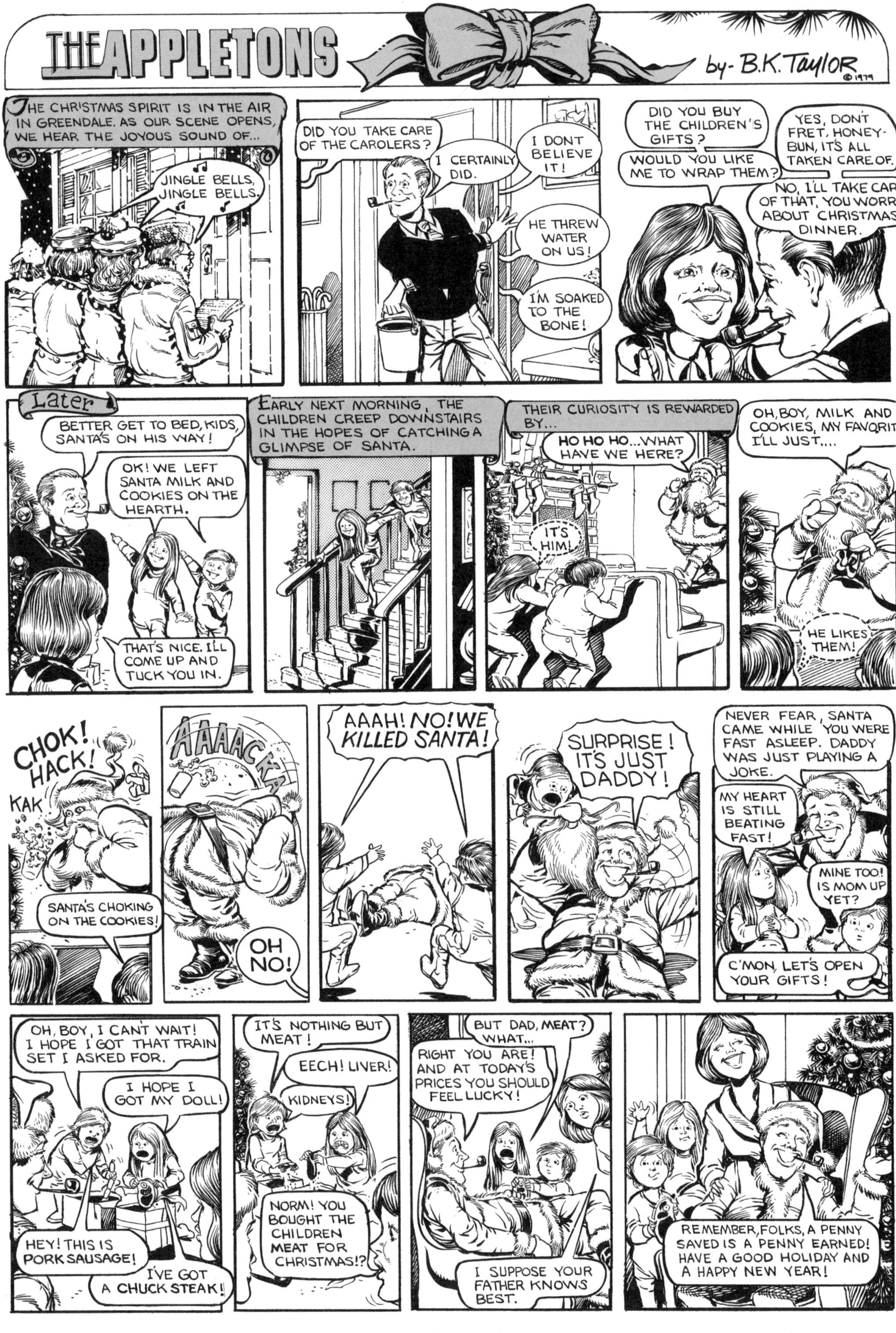
THE APPLETONS
by- B.K. Taylor ©1979
THE CHRISTMAS SPIRIT IS IN THE AIR IN GREENDALE. AS OUR SCENE OPENS, WE HEAR THE JOYOUS SOUND OF...
JINGLE BELLS, JINGLE BELLS.
DID YOU TAKE CARE OF THE CAROLERS?
I CERTAINLY DID.
I DONT BELIEVE IT!
HE THREW WATER ON US!
I'M SOAKED TO THE BONE!
DID YOU BUY THE CHILDREN'S GIFTS?
YES, DON'T FRET, HONEY-BUN, IT'S ALL TAKEN CARE OF.
WOULD YOU LIKE ME TO WRAP THEM?
NO, I'LL TAKE CARE OF THAT, YOU WORRY ABOUT CHRISTMAS DINNER.
Later
BETTER GET TO BED, KIDS, SANTA'S ON HIS WAY!
OK! WE LEFT SANTA MILK AND COOKIES ON THE HEARTH.
THAT'S NICE. I'LL COME UP AND TUCK YOU IN.
EARLY NEXT MORNING, THE CHILDREN CREEP DOWNSTAIRS IN THE HOPES OF CATCHING A GLIMPSE OF SANTA.
THEIR CURIOSITY IS REWARDED BY...
HO HO HO...WHAT HAVE WE HERE?
IT'S HIM!
OH, BOY, MILK AND COOKIES, MY FAVORITE. I'LL JUST....
HE LIKES THEM!
CHOK! HACK!
KAK
SANTA'S CHOKING ON THE COOKIES!
AAAACKA
OH NO!
AAAH! NO! WE KILLED SANTA!
SURPRISE! IT'S JUST DADDY!
NEVER FEAR, SANTA CAME WHILE YOU WERE FAST ASLEEP. DADDY WAS JUST PLAYING A JOKE.
MY HEART IS STILL BEATING FAST!
MINE TOO! IS MOM UP YET?
C'MON, LET'S OPEN YOUR GIFTS!
OH, BOY, I CAN'T WAIT! I HOPE I GOT THAT TRAIN SET I ASKED FOR.
I HOPE I GOT MY DOLL!
HEY! THIS IS PORK SAUSAGE!
I'VE GOT A CHUCK STEAK!
IT'S NOTHING BUT MEAT!
EECH! LIVER!
KIDNEYS!
NORM! YOU BOUGHT THE CHILDREN MEAT FOR CHRISTMAS!?
BUT DAD, MEAT? WHAT...
RIGHT YOU ARE! AND AT TODAY'S PRICES YOU SHOULD FEEL LUCKY!
I SUPPOSE YOUR FATHER KNOWS BEST.
REMEMBER, FOLKS, A PENNY SAVED IS A PENNY EARNED! HAVE A GOOD HOLIDAY AND A HAPPY NEW YEAR!

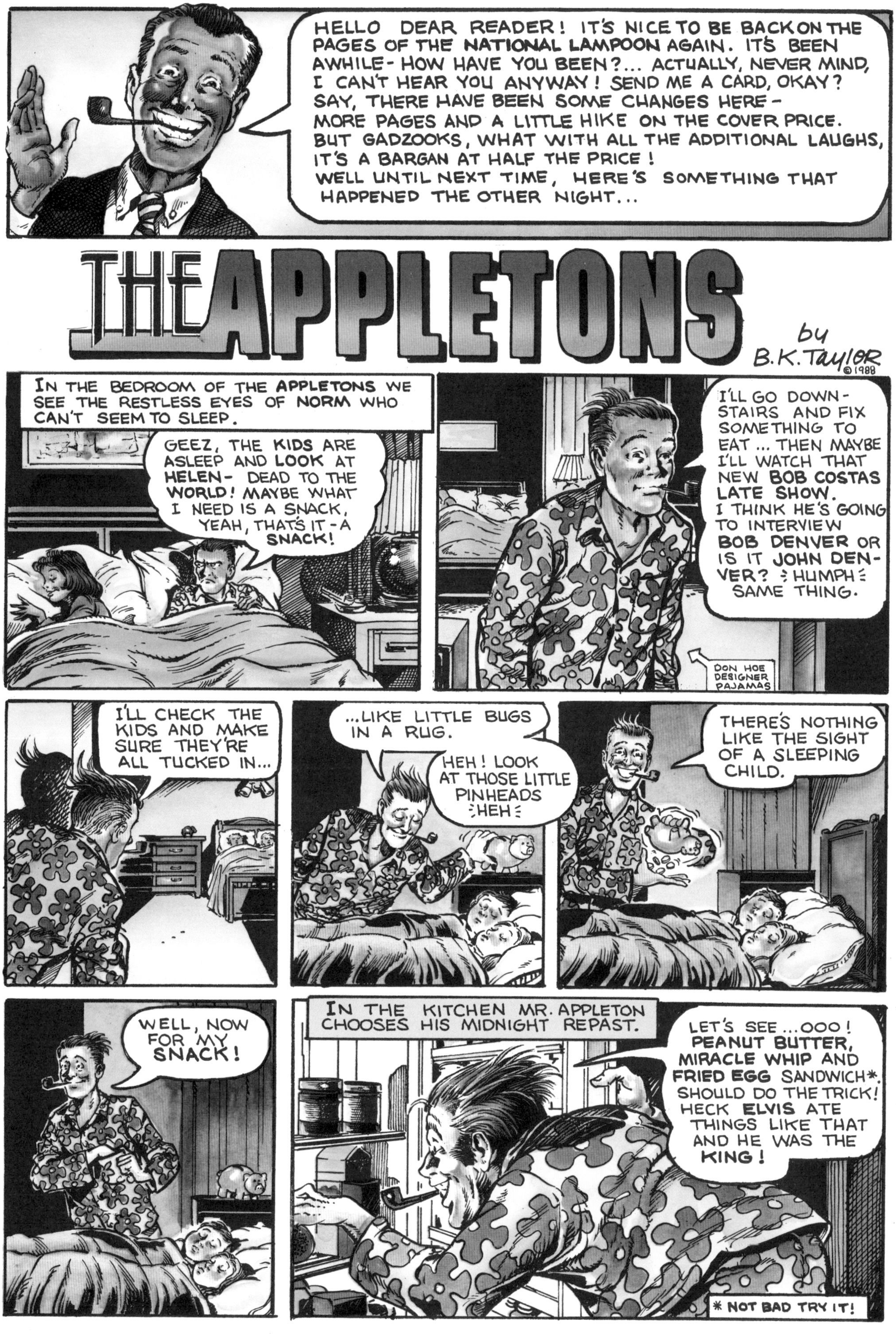
HELLO DEAR READER! IT'S NICE TO BE BACK ON THE PAGES OF THE NATIONAL LAMPOON AGAIN. IT'S BEEN AWHILE- HOW HAVE YOU BEEN?... ACTUALLY, NEVER MIND, I CAN'T HEAR YOU ANYWAY! SEND ME A CARD, OKAY? SAY, THERE HAVE BEEN SOME CHANGES HERE- MORE PAGES AND A LITTLE HIKE ON THE COVER PRICE. BUT GADZOOKS, WHAT WITH ALL THE ADDITIONAL LAUGHS, IT'S A BARGAN AT HALF THE PRICE! WELL UNTIL NEXT TIME, HERE'S SOMETHING THAT HAPPENED THE OTHER NIGHT...
THE APPLETONS
by B.K. TAYLOR ©1988
IN THE BEDROOM OF THE APPLETONS WE SEE THE RESTLESS EYES OF NORM WHO CAN'T SEEM TO SLEEP.
GEEZ, THE KIDS ARE ASLEEP AND LOOK AT HELEN- DEAD TO THE WORLD! MAYBE WHAT I NEED IS A SNACK, YEAH, THAT'S IT-A SNACK!
I'LL GO DOWN-STAIRS AND FIX SOMETHING TO EAT... THEN MAYBE I'LL WATCH THAT NEW BOB COSTAS LATE SHOW. I THINK HE'S GOING TO INTERVIEW BOB DENVER OR IS IT JOHN DENVER? HUMPH SAME THING.
DON HOE DESIGNER PAJAMAS
I'LL CHECK THE KIDS AND MAKE SURE THEY'RE ALL TUCKED IN...
...LIKE LITTLE BUGS IN A RUG.
HEH! LOOK AT THOSE LITTLE PINHEADS HEH
THERE'S NOTHING LIKE THE SIGHT OF A SLEEPING CHILD.
WELL, NOW FOR MY SNACK!
IN THE KITCHEN MR. APPLETON CHOOSES HIS MIDNIGHT REPAST.
LET'S SEE...OOO! PEANUT BUTTER, MIRACLE WHIP AND FRIED EGG SANDWICH*. SHOULD DO THE TRICK! HECK ELVIS ATE THINGS LIKE THAT AND HE WAS THE KING!
* NOT BAD TRY IT!

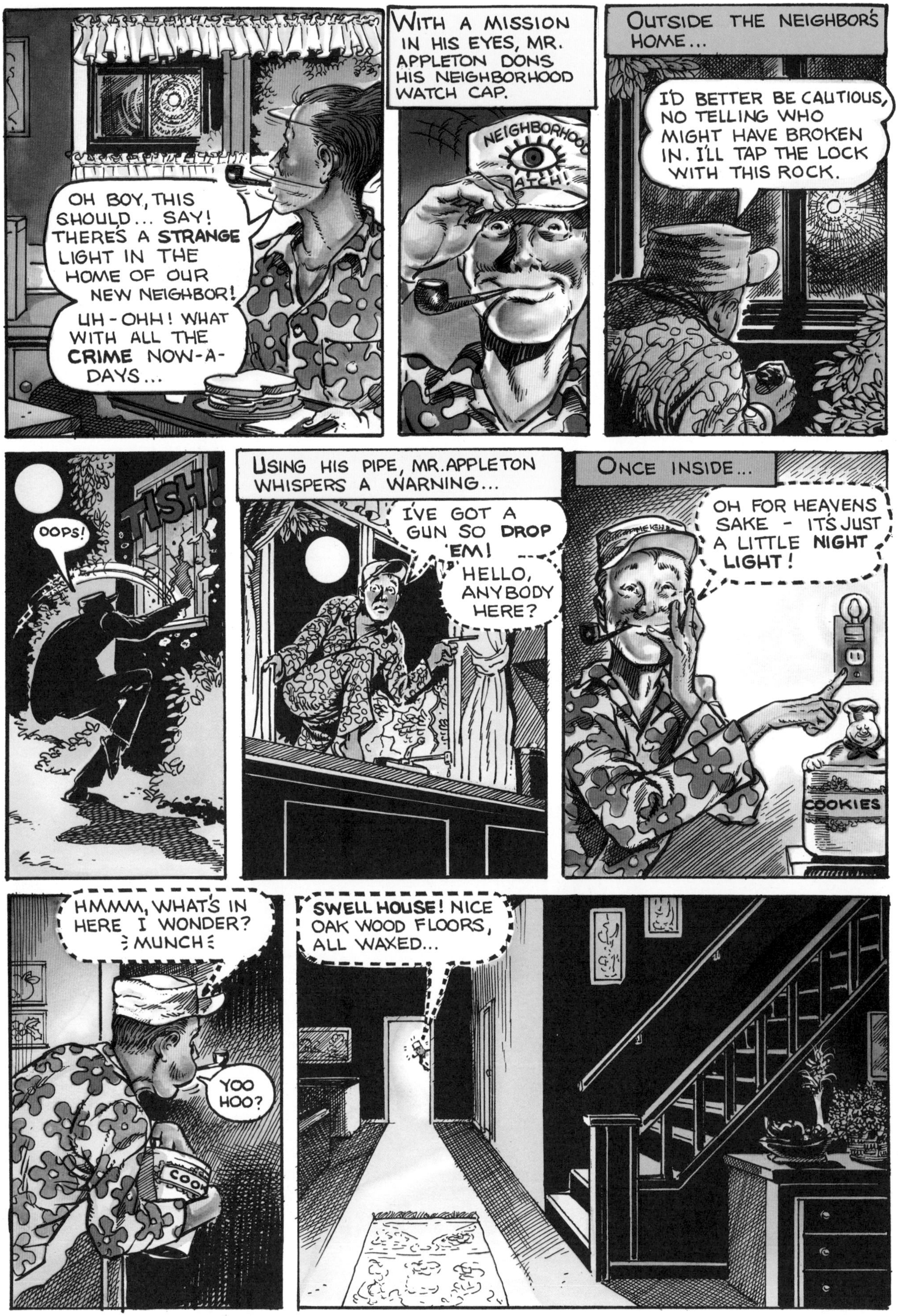
OH BOY, THIS SHOULD... SAY! THERE'S A STRANGE LIGHT IN THE HOME OF OUR NEW NEIGHBOR!
UH-OHH! WHAT WITH ALL THE CRIME NOW-A-DAYS...
WITH A MISSION IN HIS EYES, MR. APPLETON DONS HIS NEIGHBORHOOD WATCH CAP.
NEIGHBORHOOD WATCH!
OUTSIDE THE NEIGHBOR'S HOME...
I'D BETTER BE CAUTIOUS, NO TELLING WHO MIGHT HAVE BROKEN IN. I'LL TAP THE LOCK WITH THIS ROCK.
TISH!
OOPS!
USING HIS PIPE, MR. APPLETON WHISPERS A WARNING...
I'VE GOT A GUN SO DROP 'EM!
HELLO, ANYBODY HERE?
ONCE INSIDE...
OH FOR HEAVENS SAKE - IT'S JUST A LITTLE NIGHT LIGHT!
COOKIES
HMMM, WHAT'S IN HERE I WONDER? MUNCH
YOO HOO?
COO
SWELL HOUSE! NICE OAK WOOD FLOORS, ALL WAXED...

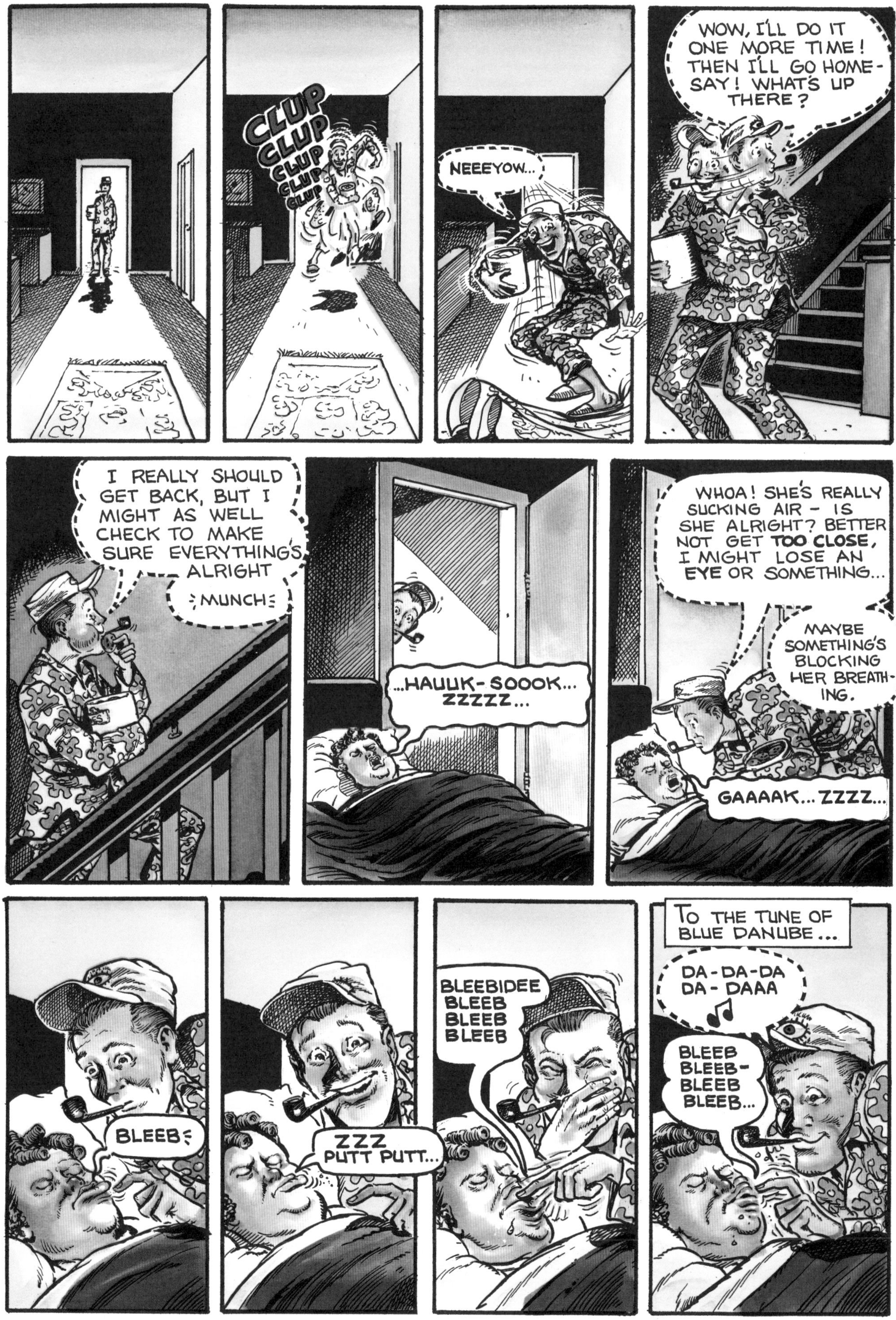
CLUP CLUP CLUP CLUP CLUP
NEEEYOW...
WOW, I'LL DO IT ONE MORE TIME! THEN I'LL GO HOME- SAY! WHAT'S UP THERE?
I REALLY SHOULD GET BACK, BUT I MIGHT AS WELL CHECK TO MAKE SURE EVERYTHING'S ALRIGHT
MUNCH
...HAUUK-SOOOK... ZZZZZ...
WHOA! SHE'S REALLY SUCKING AIR - IS SHE ALRIGHT? BETTER NOT GET TOO CLOSE, I MIGHT LOSE AN EYE OR SOMETHING...
MAYBE SOMETHING'S BLOCKING HER BREATH-ING.
GAAAAK... ZZZZ...
BLEEB
ZZZ PUTT PUTT...
BLEEBIDEE BLEEB BLEEB BLEEB
TO THE TUNE OF BLUE DANUBE...
DA-DA-DA DA-DAAA
BLEEB BLEEB-BLEEB BLEEB...

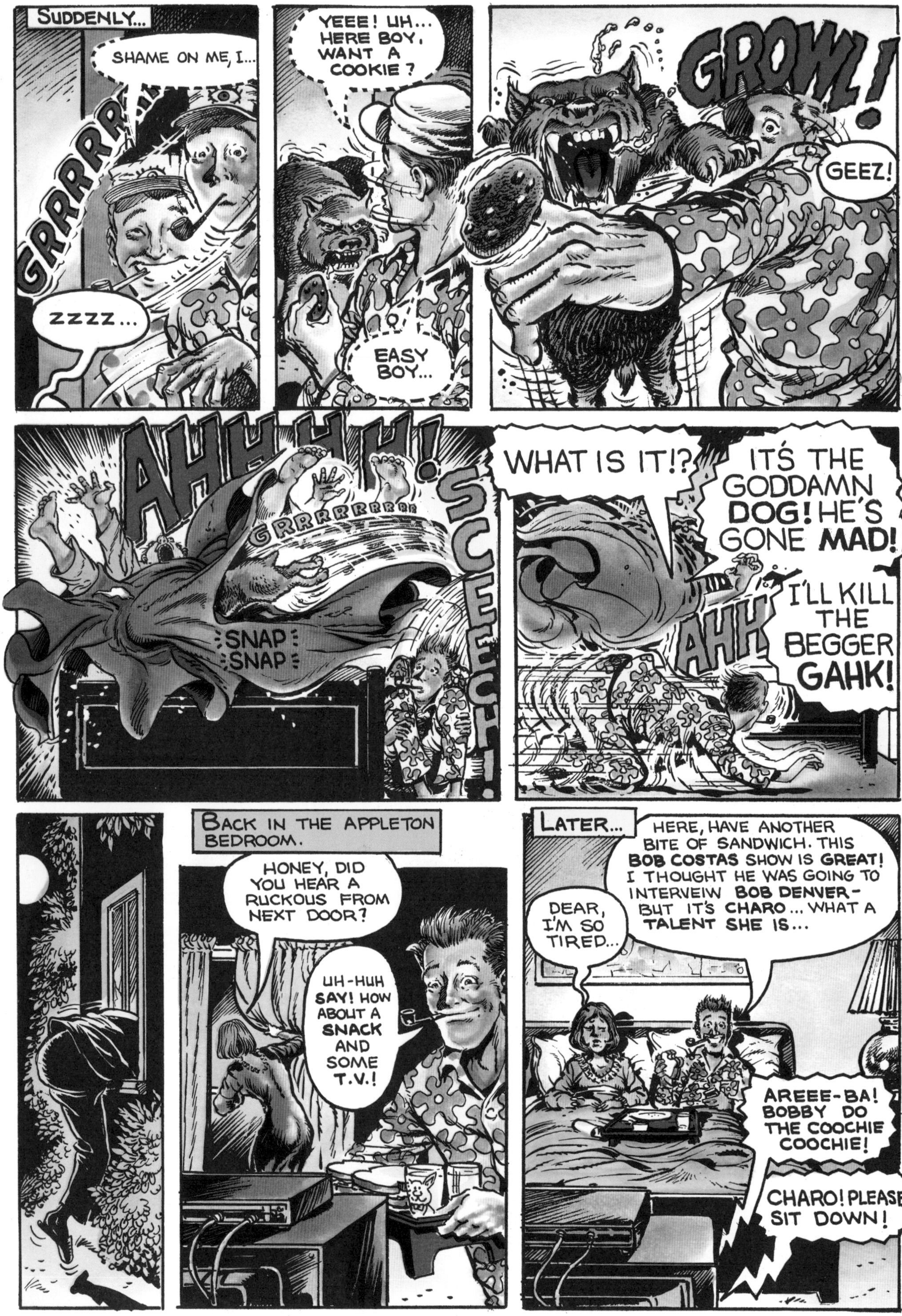

SUDDENLY...
SHAME ON ME, I...
GRRRRR...
ZZZZ...
YEEE! UH... HERE BOY, WANT A COOKIE?
EASY BOY...
GROWL!
GEEZ!
AHHHHH!
GRRRRRRRRR
SNAP SNAP
SCEECH!
WHAT IS IT!?
IT'S THE GODDAMN DOG! HE'S GONE MAD!
AHH
I'LL KILL THE BEGGER GAHK!
BACK IN THE APPLETON BEDROOM.
HONEY, DID YOU HEAR A RUCKOUS FROM NEXT DOOR?
UH-HUH SAY! HOW ABOUT A SNACK AND SOME T.V.!
LATER...
DEAR, I'M SO TIRED...
HERE, HAVE ANOTHER BITE OF SANDWICH. THIS BOB COSTAS SHOW IS GREAT! I THOUGHT HE WAS GOING TO INTERVEIW BOB DENVER- BUT IT'S CHARO... WHAT A TALENT SHE IS...
AREEE-BA! BOBBY DO THE COOCHIE COOCHIE!
CHARO! PLEASE SIT DOWN!

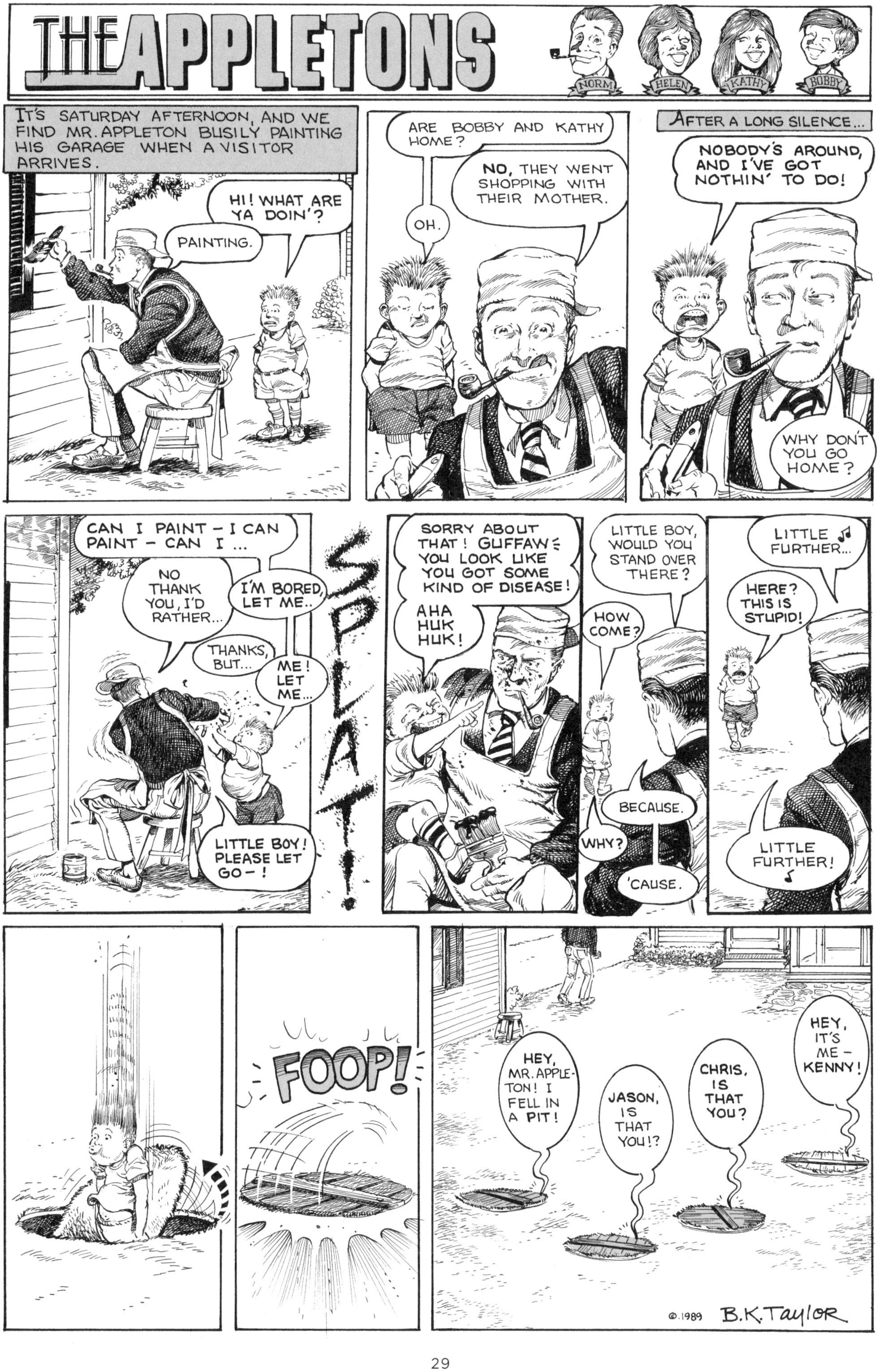
THE APPLETONS
NORM
HELEN
KATHY
BOBBY
IT'S SATURDAY AFTERNOON, AND WE FIND MR. APPLETON BUSILY PAINTING HIS GARAGE WHEN A VISITOR ARRIVES.
HI! WHAT ARE YA DOIN'?
PAINTING.
ARE BOBBY AND KATHY HOME?
NO, THEY WENT SHOPPING WITH THEIR MOTHER.
OH.
AFTER A LONG SILENCE...
NOBODY'S AROUND, AND I'VE GOT NOTHIN' TO DO!
WHY DON'T YOU GO HOME?
CAN I PAINT - I CAN PAINT - CAN I ...
NO THANK YOU, I'D RATHER...
I'M BORED, LET ME..
THANKS, BUT...
ME! LET ME...
LITTLE BOY! PLEASE LET GO - !
SPLAT!
SORRY ABOUT THAT! GUFFAW
YOU LOOK LIKE YOU GOT SOME KIND OF DISEASE!
AHA HUK HUK!
LITTLE BOY, WOULD YOU STAND OVER THERE?
HOW COME?
BECAUSE.
WHY?
'CAUSE.
LITTLE FURTHER...
HERE? THIS IS STUPID!
LITTLE FURTHER!
FOOP!
HEY, MR. APPLETON! I FELL IN A PIT!
JASON, IS THAT YOU!?
CHRIS, IS THAT YOU?
HEY, IT'S ME - KENNY!
©.1989 B.K. Taylor

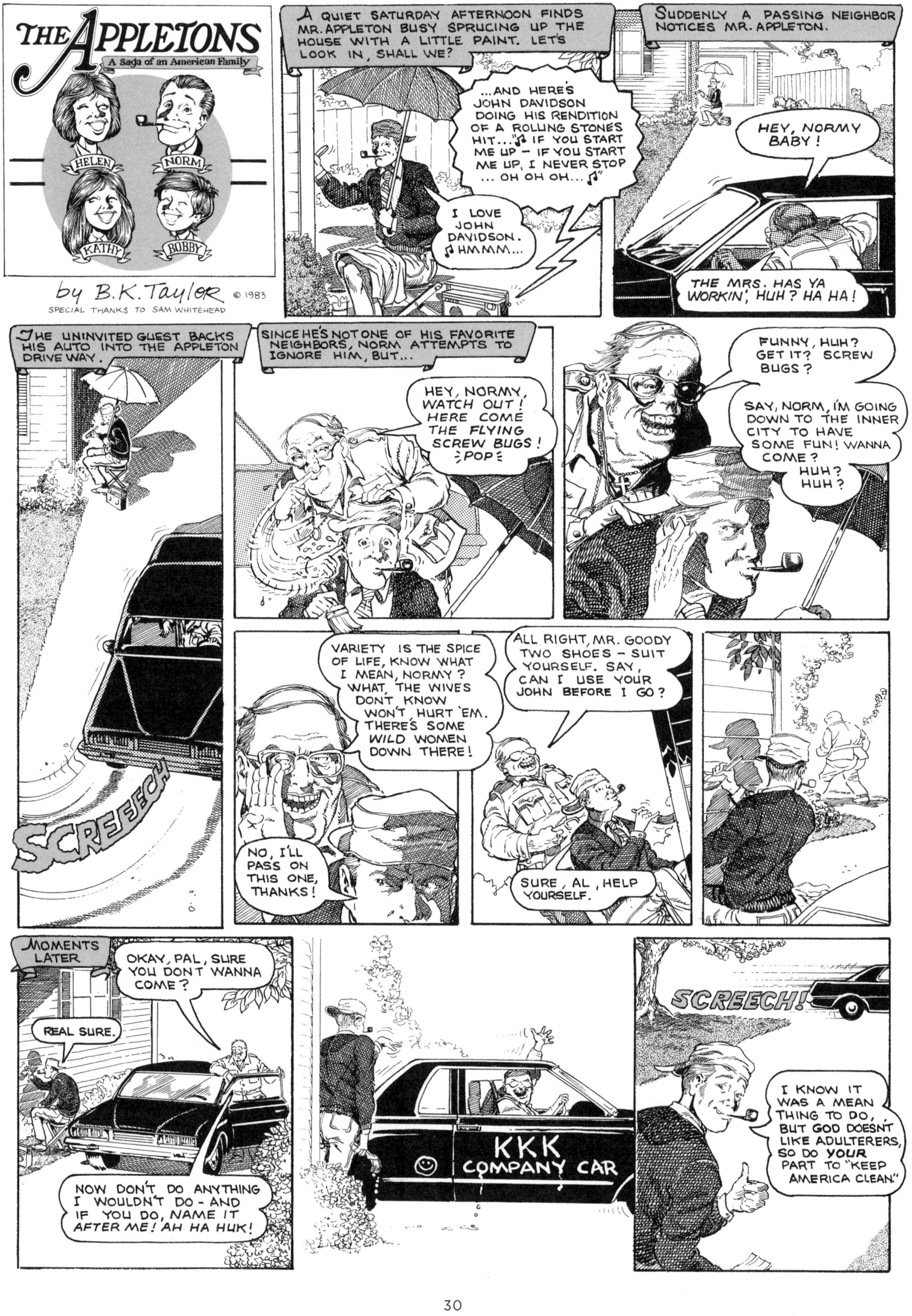
THE APPLETONS
A Saga of an American Family
HELEN
NORM
KATHY
BOBBY
by B.K. Taylor © 1983
SPECIAL THANKS TO SAM WHITEHEAD
A QUIET SATURDAY AFTERNOON FINDS MR. APPLETON BUSY SPRUCING UP THE HOUSE WITH A LITTLE PAINT. LET'S LOOK IN, SHALL WE?
...AND HERE'S JOHN DAVIDSON DOING HIS RENDITION OF A ROLLING STONES HIT... ♫ IF YOU START ME UP - IF YOU START ME UP, I NEVER STOP ... OH OH OH... ♫"
I LOVE JOHN DAVIDSON. ♫ HMMM...
SUDDENLY A PASSING NEIGHBOR NOTICES MR. APPLETON.
HEY, NORMY BABY!
THE MRS. HAS YA WORKIN', HUH? HA HA!
THE UNINVITED GUEST BACKS HIS AUTO INTO THE APPLETON DRIVE WAY.
SCREEECH
SINCE HE'S NOT ONE OF HIS FAVORITE NEIGHBORS, NORM ATTEMPTS TO IGNORE HIM, BUT...
HEY, NORMY, WATCH OUT! HERE COME THE FLYING SCREW BUGS! POP
FUNNY, HUH? GET IT? SCREW BUGS?
SAY, NORM, I'M GOING DOWN TO THE INNER CITY TO HAVE SOME FUN! WANNA COME? HUH? HUH?
VARIETY IS THE SPICE OF LIFE, KNOW WHAT I MEAN, NORMY? WHAT THE WIVES DON'T KNOW WON'T HURT 'EM. THERE'S SOME WILD WOMEN DOWN THERE!
NO, I'LL PASS ON THIS ONE, THANKS!
ALL RIGHT, MR. GOODY TWO SHOES - SUIT YOURSELF. SAY, CAN I USE YOUR JOHN BEFORE I GO?
SURE, AL, HELP YOURSELF.
MOMENTS LATER
OKAY, PAL, SURE YOU DONT WANNA COME?
REAL SURE.
NOW DON'T DO ANYTHING I WOULDN'T DO - AND IF YOU DO, NAME IT AFTER ME! AH HA HUK!
KKK COMPANY CAR
SCREECH!
I KNOW IT WAS A MEAN THING TO DO, BUT GOD DOESN'T LIKE ADULTERERS, SO DO YOUR PART TO "KEEP AMERICA CLEAN."

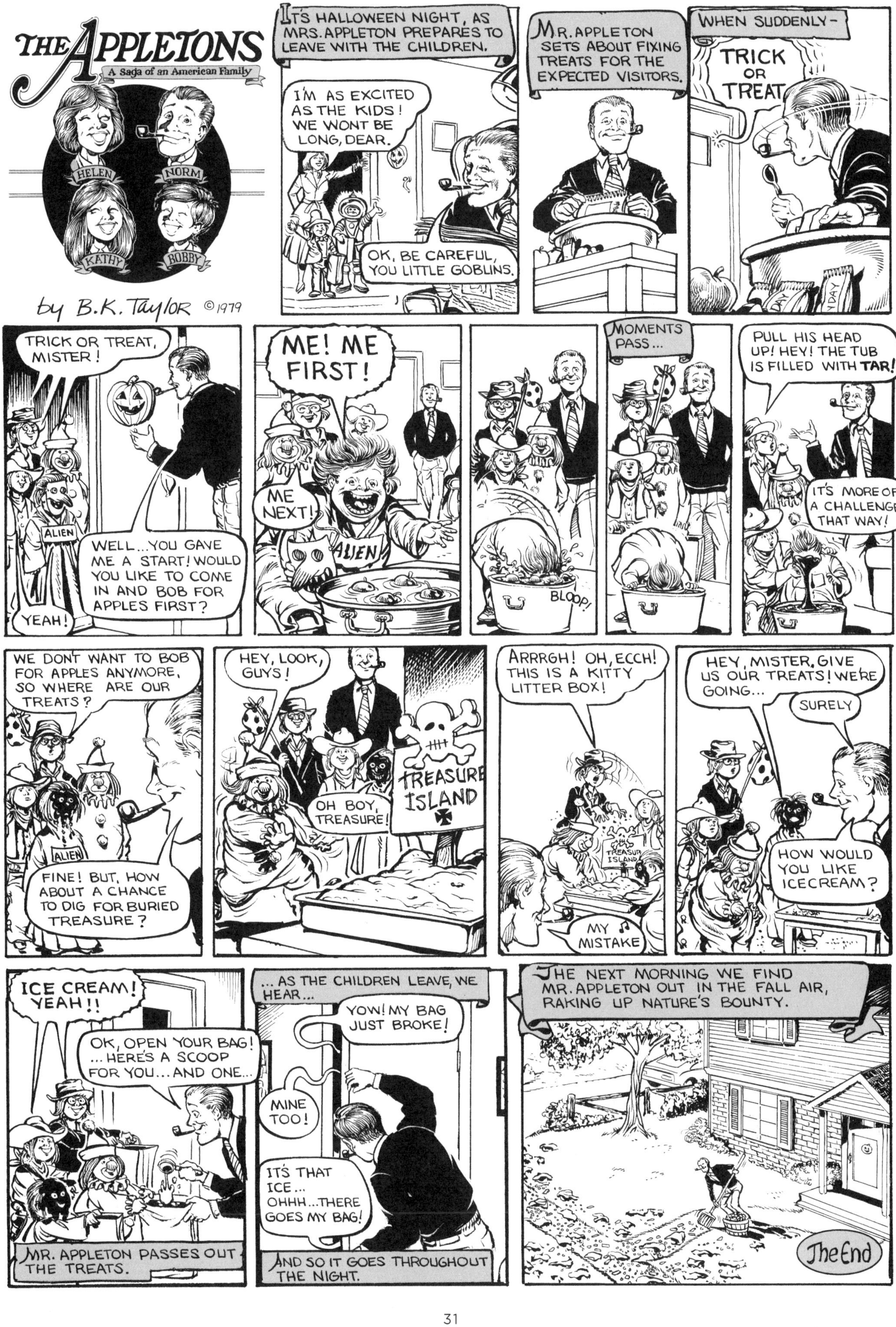
THE APPLETONS
A Saga of an American Family
HELEN
NORM
KATHY
BOBBY
by B.K. Taylor ©1979
IT'S HALLOWEEN NIGHT, AS MRS. APPLETON PREPARES TO LEAVE WITH THE CHILDREN.
I'M AS EXCITED AS THE KIDS! WE WONT BE LONG, DEAR.
OK, BE CAREFUL, YOU LITTLE GOBLINS.
MR. APPLETON SETS ABOUT FIXING TREATS FOR THE EXPECTED VISITORS.
WHEN SUDDENLY-
TRICK OR TREAT
TRICK OR TREAT, MISTER!
WELL...YOU GAVE ME A START! WOULD YOU LIKE TO COME IN AND BOB FOR APPLES FIRST?
YEAH!
ALIEN
ME! ME FIRST!
ME NEXT!
ALIEN
BLOOP!
MOMENTS PASS...
PULL HIS HEAD UP! HEY! THE TUB IS FILLED WITH TAR!
IT'S MORE OF A CHALLENGE THAT WAY!
WE DONT WANT TO BOB FOR APPLES ANYMORE, SO WHERE ARE OUR TREATS?
ALIEN
FINE! BUT, HOW ABOUT A CHANCE TO DIG FOR BURIED TREASURE?
HEY, LOOK, GUYS!
TREASURE ISLAND
OH BOY, TREASURE!
ARRRGH! OH, ECCH! THIS IS A KITTY LITTER BOX!
MY MISTAKE
HEY, MISTER, GIVE US OUR TREATS! WE'RE GOING...
SURELY
HOW WOULD YOU LIKE ICECREAM?
ICE CREAM! YEAH!!
OK, OPEN YOUR BAG! ...HERE'S A SCOOP FOR YOU...AND ONE...
MR. APPLETON PASSES OUT THE TREATS.
...AS THE CHILDREN LEAVE, WE HEAR...
YOW! MY BAG JUST BROKE!
MINE TOO!
IT'S THAT ICE... OHHH...THERE GOES MY BAG!
AND SO IT GOES THROUGHOUT THE NIGHT.
THE NEXT MORNING WE FIND MR. APPLETON OUT IN THE FALL AIR, RAKING UP NATURE'S BOUNTY.
The End

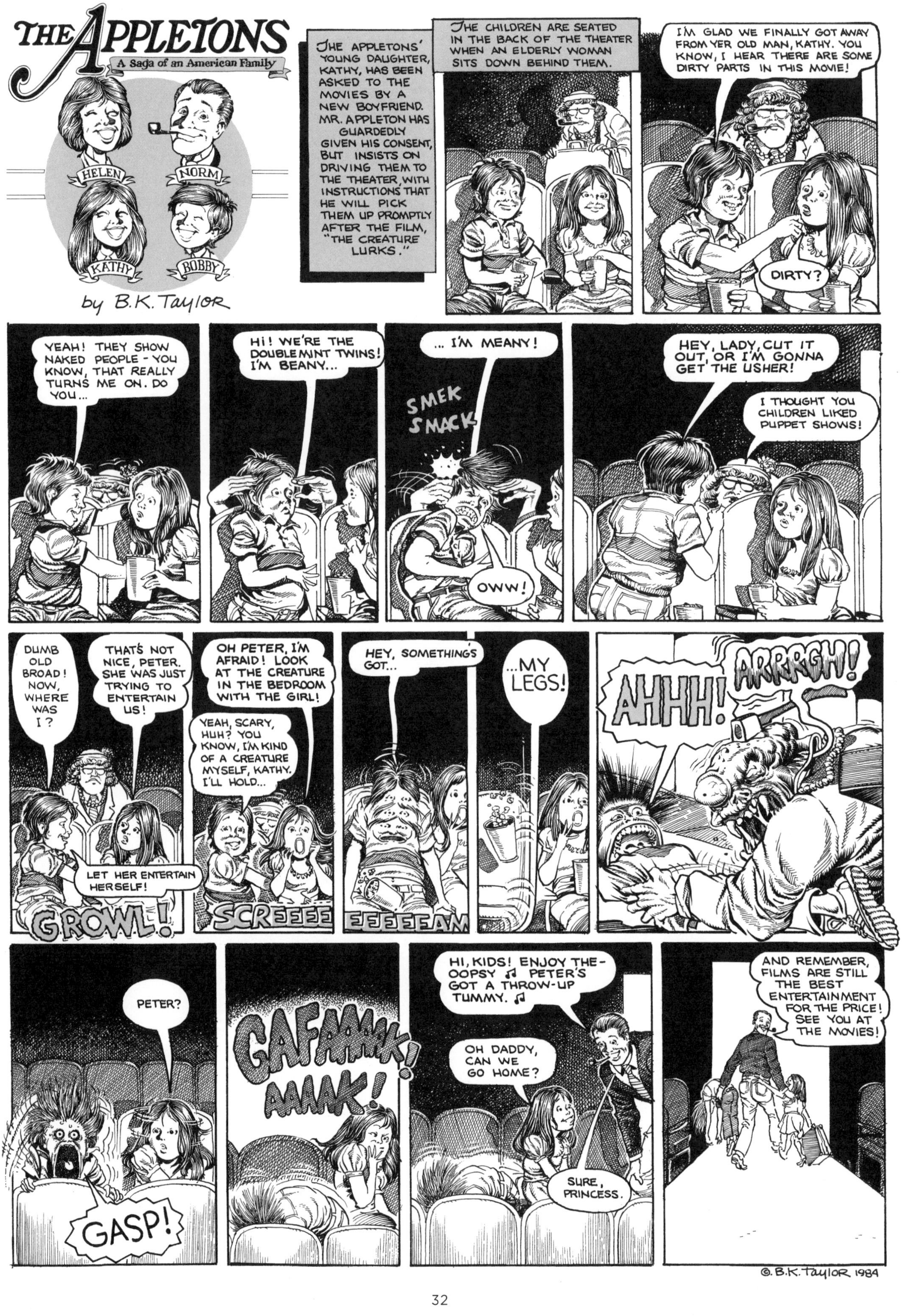
THE APPLETONS
A Saga of an American Family
HELEN
NORM
KATHY
BOBBY
by B.K. Taylor
THE APPLETONS' YOUNG DAUGHTER, KATHY, HAS BEEN ASKED TO THE MOVIES BY A NEW BOYFRIEND. MR. APPLETON HAS GUARDEDLY GIVEN HIS CONSENT, BUT INSISTS ON DRIVING THEM TO THE THEATER, WITH INSTRUCTIONS THAT HE WILL PICK THEM UP PROMPTLY AFTER THE FILM, "THE CREATURE LURKS."
THE CHILDREN ARE SEATED IN THE BACK OF THE THEATER WHEN AN ELDERLY WOMAN SITS DOWN BEHIND THEM.
I'M GLAD WE FINALLY GOT AWAY FROM YER OLD MAN, KATHY. YOU KNOW, I HEAR THERE ARE SOME DIRTY PARTS IN THIS MOVIE!
DIRTY?
YEAH! THEY SHOW NAKED PEOPLE - YOU KNOW, THAT REALLY TURNS ME ON. DO YOU...
HI! WE'RE THE DOUBLEMINT TWINS! I'M BEANY...
... I'M MEANY!
SMEK
SMACK
OWW!
HEY, LADY, CUT IT OUT, OR I'M GONNA GET THE USHER!
I THOUGHT YOU CHILDREN LIKED PUPPET SHOWS!
DUMB OLD BROAD! NOW, WHERE WAS I?
THAT'S NOT NICE, PETER. SHE WAS JUST TRYING TO ENTERTAIN US!
LET HER ENTERTAIN HERSELF!
GROWL!
OH PETER, I'M AFRAID! LOOK AT THE CREATURE IN THE BEDROOM WITH THE GIRL!
YEAH, SCARY, HUH? YOU KNOW, I'M KIND OF A CREATURE MYSELF, KATHY. I'LL HOLD...
SCREEEEE
HEY, SOMETHING'S GOT...
...MY LEGS!
EEEEEEAM
AHHH!
ARRRGH!
PETER?
GASP!
GAFAAAK! AAAAK!
HI, KIDS! ENJOY THE- OOPSY ♫ PETER'S GOT A THROW-UP TUMMY. ♫
OH DADDY, CAN WE GO HOME?
SURE, PRINCESS.
AND REMEMBER, FILMS ARE STILL THE BEST ENTERTAINMENT FOR THE PRICE! SEE YOU AT THE MOVIES!
©. B.K. Taylor 1984

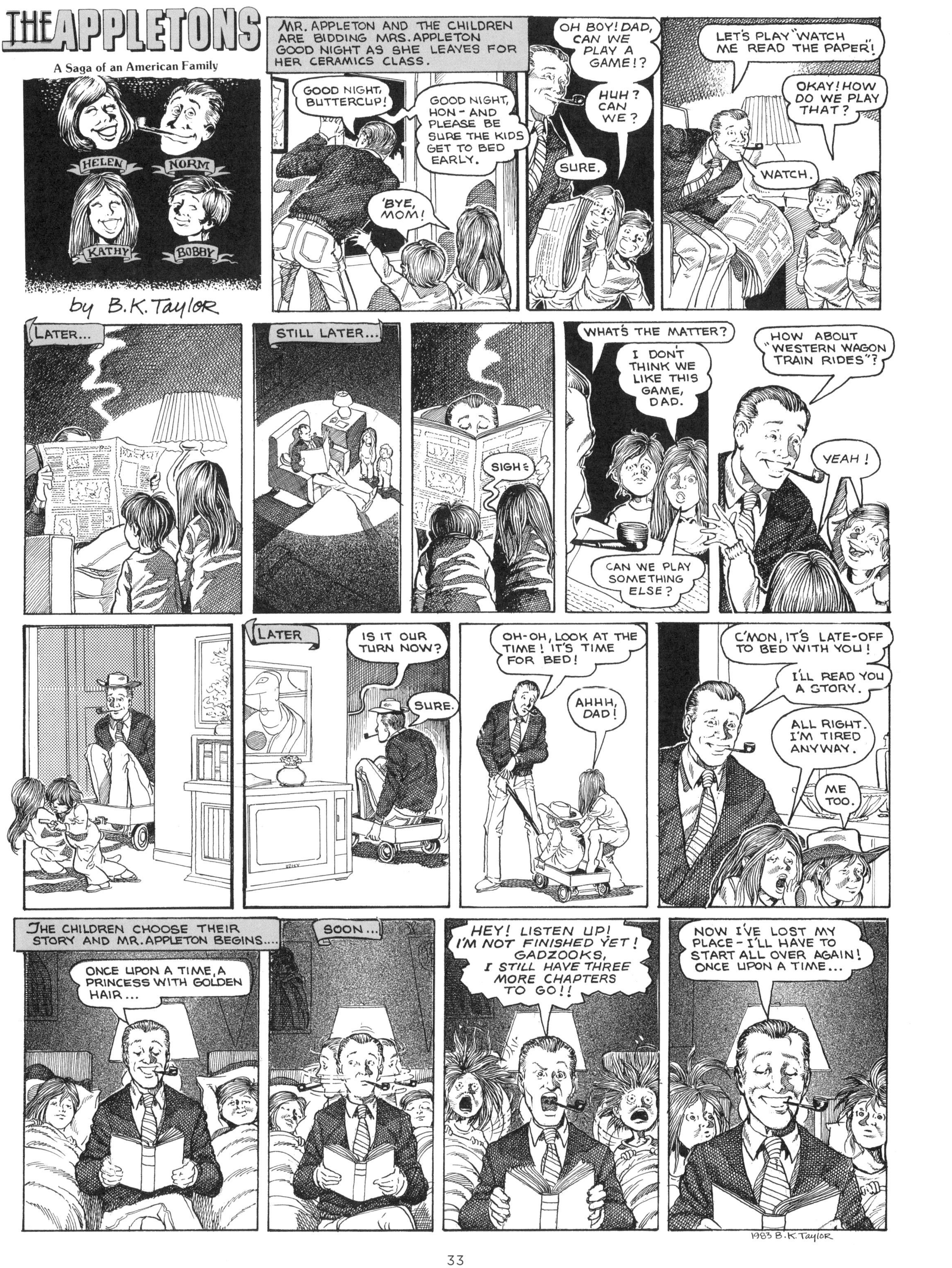
THE APPLETONS
A Saga of an American Family
HELEN
NORM
KATHY
BOBBY
by B.K. Taylor
MR. APPLETON AND THE CHILDREN ARE BIDDING MRS. APPLETON GOOD NIGHT AS SHE LEAVES FOR HER CERAMICS CLASS.
GOOD NIGHT, BUTTERCUP!
GOOD NIGHT, HON - AND PLEASE BE SURE THE KIDS GET TO BED EARLY.
'BYE, MOM!
OH BOY! DAD, CAN WE PLAY A GAME!?
HUH? CAN WE?
SURE.
LET'S PLAY "WATCH ME READ THE PAPER"!
OKAY! HOW DO WE PLAY THAT?
WATCH.
LATER...
STILL LATER...
SIGH
WHAT'S THE MATTER?
I DON'T THINK WE LIKE THIS GAME, DAD.
CAN WE PLAY SOMETHING ELSE?
HOW ABOUT "WESTERN WAGON TRAIN RIDES"?
YEAH!
LATER
IS IT OUR TURN NOW?
SURE.
OH-OH, LOOK AT THE TIME! IT'S TIME FOR BED!
AHHH, DAD!
C'MON, IT'S LATE-OFF TO BED WITH YOU!
I'LL READ YOU A STORY.
ALL RIGHT. I'M TIRED ANYWAY.
ME TOO.
THE CHILDREN CHOOSE THEIR STORY AND MR. APPLETON BEGINS....
ONCE UPON A TIME, A PRINCESS WITH GOLDEN HAIR...
SOON...
HEY! LISTEN UP! I'M NOT FINISHED YET! GADZOOKS, I STILL HAVE THREE MORE CHAPTERS TO GO!!
NOW I'VE LOST MY PLACE - I'LL HAVE TO START ALL OVER AGAIN! ONCE UPON A TIME...
1983 B.K. Taylor

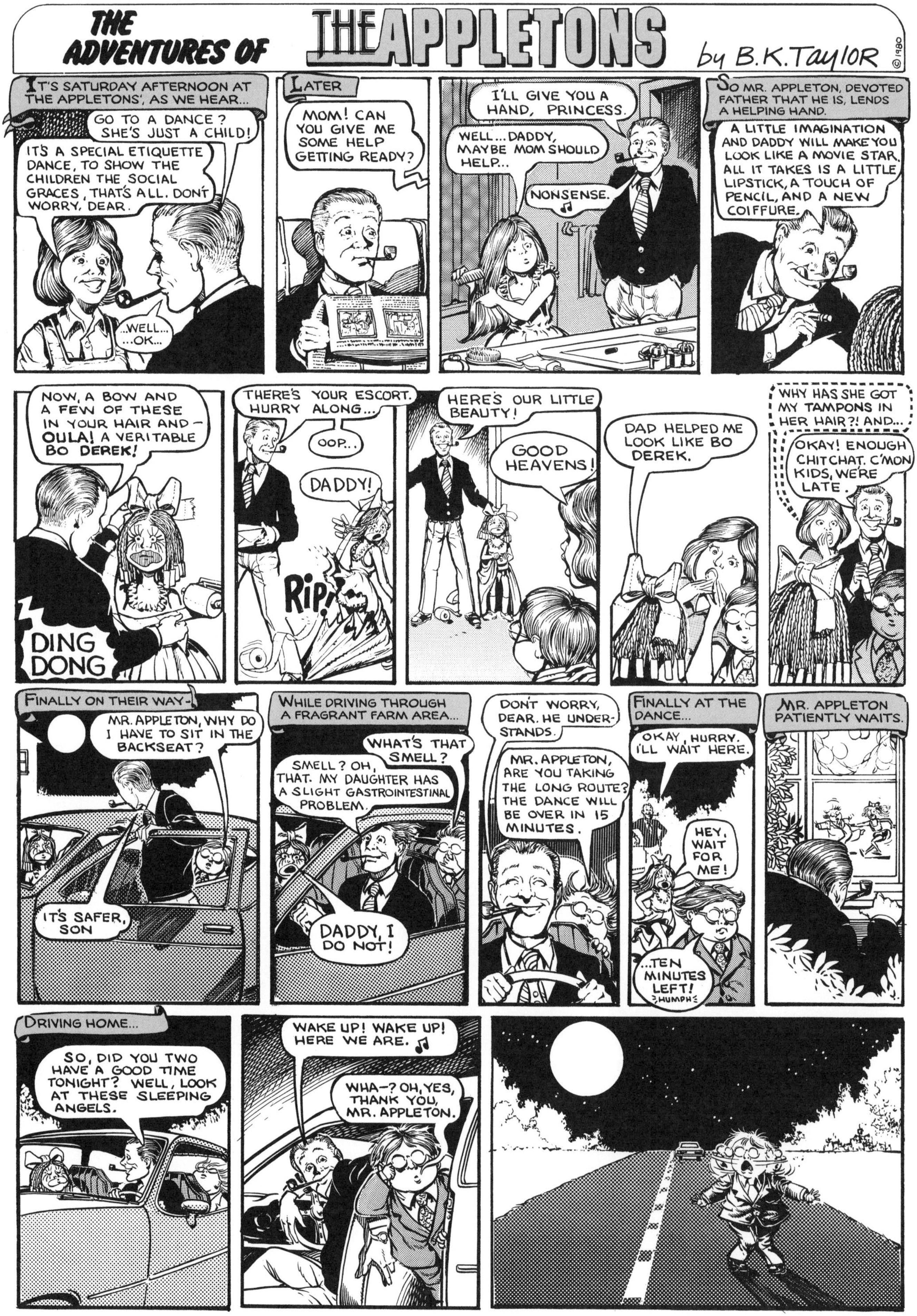
THE ADVENTURES OF THE APPLETONS
by B.K.Taylor
©1980
IT'S SATURDAY AFTERNOON AT THE APPLETONS', AS WE HEAR...
GO TO A DANCE? SHE'S JUST A CHILD!
IT'S A SPECIAL ETIQUETTE DANCE, TO SHOW THE CHILDREN THE SOCIAL GRACES, THAT'S ALL. DON'T WORRY, DEAR.
...WELL... ...OK...
LATER
MOM! CAN YOU GIVE ME SOME HELP GETTING READY?
I'LL GIVE YOU A HAND, PRINCESS.
WELL... DADDY, MAYBE MOM SHOULD HELP...
NONSENSE.
SO MR. APPLETON, DEVOTED FATHER THAT HE IS, LENDS A HELPING HAND.
A LITTLE IMAGINATION AND DADDY WILL MAKE YOU LOOK LIKE A MOVIE STAR, ALL IT TAKES IS A LITTLE LIPSTICK, A TOUCH OF PENCIL, AND A NEW COIFFURE.
NOW, A BOW AND A FEW OF THESE IN YOUR HAIR AND- OULA! A VERITABLE BO DEREK!
DING DONG
THERE'S YOUR ESCORT. HURRY ALONG...
OOP...
DADDY!
RIP!
HERE'S OUR LITTLE BEAUTY!
GOOD HEAVENS!
DAD HELPED ME LOOK LIKE BO DEREK.
WHY HAS SHE GOT MY TAMPONS IN HER HAIR?! AND...
OKAY! ENOUGH CHITCHAT. C'MON KIDS, WE'RE LATE.
FINALLY ON THEIR WAY-
MR. APPLETON, WHY DO I HAVE TO SIT IN THE BACKSEAT?
IT'S SAFER, SON
WHILE DRIVING THROUGH A FRAGRANT FARM AREA...
WHAT'S THAT SMELL?
SMELL? OH, THAT. MY DAUGHTER HAS A SLIGHT GASTROINTESTINAL PROBLEM.
DADDY, I DO NOT!
DON'T WORRY, DEAR. HE UNDERSTANDS.
MR. APPLETON, ARE YOU TAKING THE LONG ROUTE? THE DANCE WILL BE OVER IN 15 MINUTES.
FINALLY AT THE DANCE...
OKAY, HURRY. I'LL WAIT HERE.
HEY, WAIT FOR ME!
...TEN MINUTES LEFT!
HUMPH
MR. APPLETON PATIENTLY WAITS.
DRIVING HOME...
SO, DID YOU TWO HAVE A GOOD TIME TONIGHT? WELL, LOOK AT THESE SLEEPING ANGELS.
WAKE UP! WAKE UP! HERE WE ARE.
WHA-? OH, YES, THANK YOU, MR. APPLETON.

THE APPLETONS

A Saga of an American Family

HELEN • NORM
KATHY • BOBBY

by – B.K. Taylor © 1983

OUR SENIOR CITIZENS OFTEN FACE LONELINESS AND BOREDOM IN THEIR GOLDEN YEARS. THE APPLETONS ARE DOING THEIR PART TO MAKE SURE THIS WON'T HAPPEN TO THEIR OLDER LOVED ONES. HELEN APPLETON HAS JUST BAKED A PIE FOR DESSERT, AS WE JOIN THEM IN "A VISIT TO GRANDMOTHER'S HOUSE."

YOO HOO! ANYONE HOME?

WELL, WHAT A SURPRISE! EXCUSE THE ATTIRE, BUT WE WERE PLAYING STARWARS, AND I WAS PRINCESS LEIA!

GOODNESS SAKE! HOMEMADE PIE. THANK YOU! ¦MUNCH¦ I'LL CALL GRANDFATHER.... LAMAR!!... WHERE IS HE? LAMAR!!... DARTH!!

WATCH OUT! THERE'S A DOBERMAN PINSCHER LOOSE! PINCH!!

THERE YOU ARE, YOU RASCAL!

HERE – HAVE SOME PIE THE KIDS BROUGHT OVER!

SAY, LOOKS GOOD, THANKS!

C'MON IN, KIDS! TAKE A LOAD OFF YOUR FEET.

¦MUNCH¦ ¦GRUMF¦

WHEW! HE WAS HUNGRY!

YOU'LL HAVE TO EXCUSE THE MESS, BUT WHEN WE PLAY STAR WARS, WE REALLY GO AT IT!

OH BOY! CAN WE PLAY!?

GRANDMOTHERS BEING WHAT THEY ARE, WILL ALWAYS MAKE TIME FOR A CHILD'S REQUEST.

OKAY, HOW ABOUT A QUICK COSMIC PILLOW FIGHT... READY?

YEAH!!

WUMP!

NORMY, THESE KIDS ARE SOFT! ARE YOU FEEDING THEM RIGHT?

ROAR!

OH-OH, IT'S TIME FOR OUR GRAY PANTHERS MEETING!

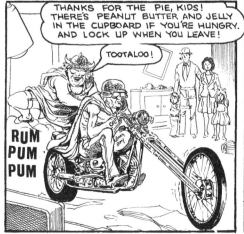

THANKS FOR THE PIE, KIDS! THERE'S PEANUT BUTTER AND JELLY IN THE CUPBOARD IF YOU'RE HUNGRY. AND LOCK UP WHEN YOU LEAVE!

TOOTALOO!

RUM PUM PUM

WE CAN ONLY HOPE THAT WE GROW OLD AS GRACEFULLY AS THEY HAVE.

AND SO ENDS ANOTHER VISIT TO "GRANDMOTHER'S HOUSE".

THE OFFICIAL CARTOON STRIP FOR THE 1984 OLYMPICS

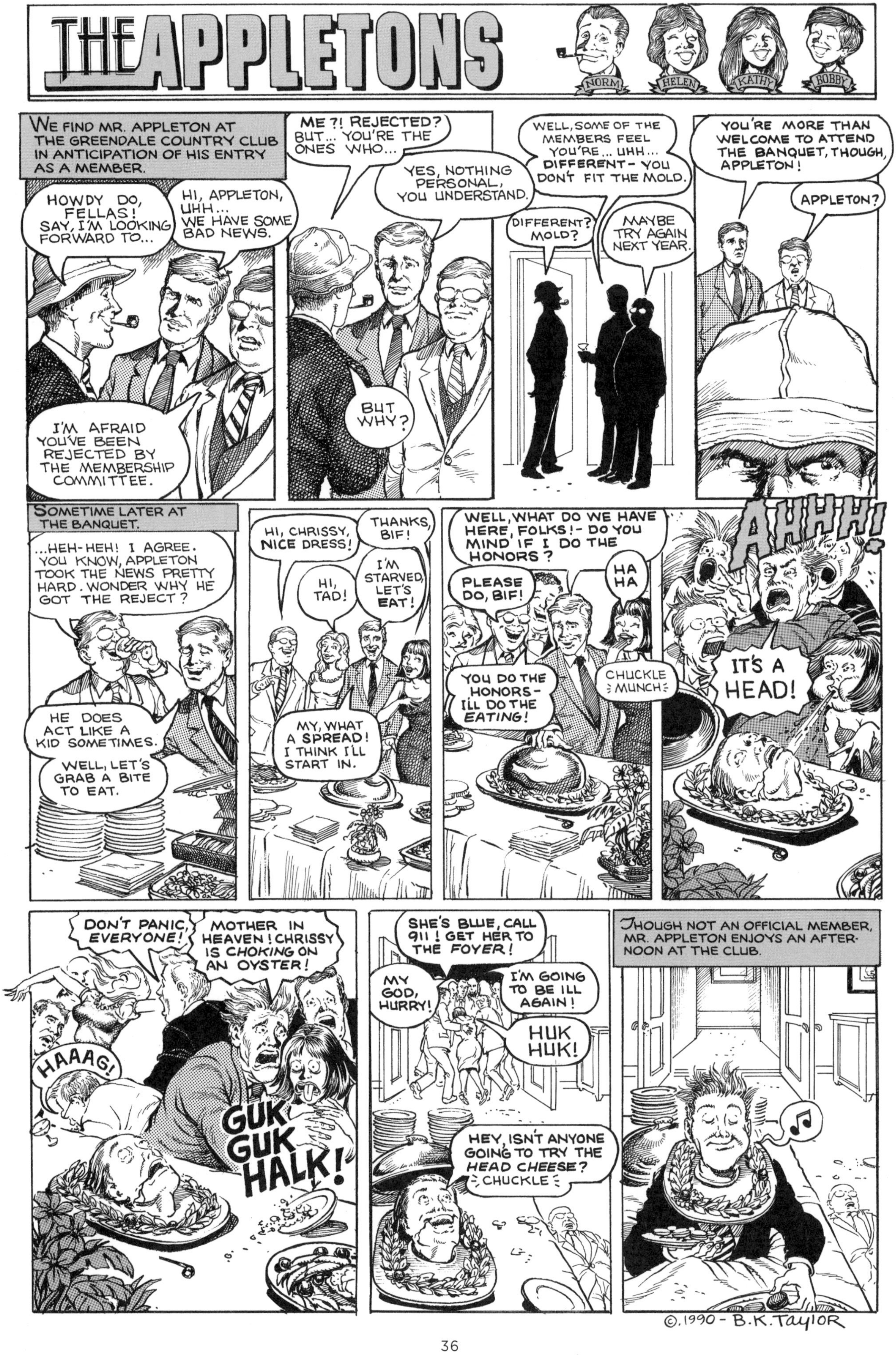
THE APPLETONS
NORM
HELEN
KATHY
BOBBY
WE FIND MR. APPLETON AT THE GREENDALE COUNTRY CLUB IN ANTICIPATION OF HIS ENTRY AS A MEMBER.
HOWDY DO, FELLAS! SAY, I'M LOOKING FORWARD TO...
HI, APPLETON, UHH... WE HAVE SOME BAD NEWS.
I'M AFRAID YOU'VE BEEN REJECTED BY THE MEMBERSHIP COMMITTEE.
ME ?! REJECTED? BUT... YOU'RE THE ONES WHO...
YES, NOTHING PERSONAL, YOU UNDERSTAND.
BUT WHY?
WELL, SOME OF THE MEMBERS FEEL YOU'RE... UHH... DIFFERENT - YOU DON'T FIT THE MOLD.
DIFFERENT? MOLD?
MAYBE TRY AGAIN NEXT YEAR.
YOU'RE MORE THAN WELCOME TO ATTEND THE BANQUET, THOUGH, APPLETON!
APPLETON?
SOMETIME LATER AT THE BANQUET.
...HEH-HEH! I AGREE. YOU KNOW, APPLETON TOOK THE NEWS PRETTY HARD. WONDER WHY HE GOT THE REJECT?
HE DOES ACT LIKE A KID SOMETIMES.
WELL, LET'S GRAB A BITE TO EAT.
HI, CHRISSY, NICE DRESS!
THANKS, BIF!
HI, TAD!
I'M STARVED, LET'S EAT!
MY, WHAT A SPREAD! I THINK I'LL START IN.
WELL, WHAT DO WE HAVE HERE, FOLKS! - DO YOU MIND IF I DO THE HONORS?
PLEASE DO, BIF!
HA HA
YOU DO THE HONORS - I'LL DO THE EATING!
CHUCKLE MUNCH
AHHH!
IT'S A HEAD!
DON'T PANIC, EVERYONE!
MOTHER IN HEAVEN! CHRISSY IS CHOKING ON AN OYSTER!
HAAAG!
GUK GUK HALK!
SHE'S BLUE, CALL 911! GET HER TO THE FOYER!
MY GOD, HURRY!
I'M GOING TO BE ILL AGAIN!
HUK HUK!
HEY, ISN'T ANYONE GOING TO TRY THE HEAD CHEESE? CHUCKLE
THOUGH NOT AN OFFICIAL MEMBER, MR. APPLETON ENJOYS AN AFTERNOON AT THE CLUB.
©. 1990 - B.K. TAYLOR

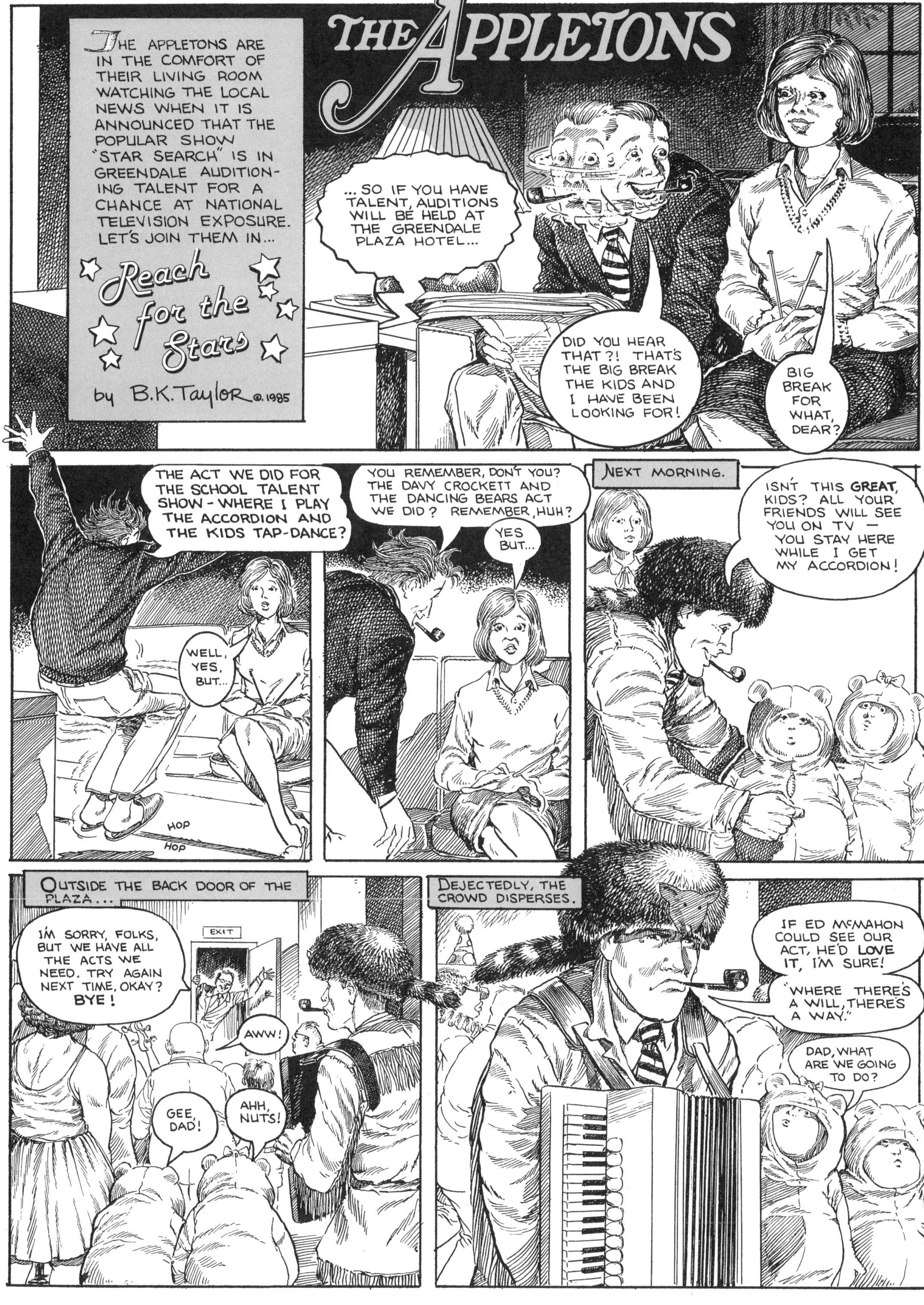
THE APPLETONS
THE APPLETONS ARE IN THE COMFORT OF THEIR LIVING ROOM WATCHING THE LOCAL NEWS WHEN IT IS ANNOUNCED THAT THE POPULAR SHOW "STAR SEARCH" IS IN GREENDALE AUDITIONING TALENT FOR A CHANCE AT NATIONAL TELEVISION EXPOSURE. LET'S JOIN THEM IN...
Reach for the Stars
by B.K.Taylor ©.1985
... SO IF YOU HAVE TALENT, AUDITIONS WILL BE HELD AT THE GREENDALE PLAZA HOTEL...
DID YOU HEAR THAT?! THAT'S THE BIG BREAK THE KIDS AND I HAVE BEEN LOOKING FOR!
BIG BREAK FOR WHAT, DEAR?
THE ACT WE DID FOR THE SCHOOL TALENT SHOW - WHERE I PLAY THE ACCORDION AND THE KIDS TAP-DANCE?
WELL, YES, BUT...
HOP
HOP
YOU REMEMBER, DON'T YOU? THE DAVY CROCKETT AND THE DANCING BEARS ACT WE DID? REMEMBER, HUH?
YES BUT...
NEXT MORNING.
ISN'T THIS GREAT, KIDS? ALL YOUR FRIENDS WILL SEE YOU ON TV — YOU STAY HERE WHILE I GET MY ACCORDION!
OUTSIDE THE BACK DOOR OF THE PLAZA...
EXIT
I'M SORRY, FOLKS, BUT WE HAVE ALL THE ACTS WE NEED. TRY AGAIN NEXT TIME, OKAY? BYE!
AWW!
GEE, DAD!
AHH, NUTS!
DEJECTEDLY, THE CROWD DISPERSES.
IF ED McMAHON COULD SEE OUR ACT, HE'D LOVE IT, I'M SURE!
"WHERE THERE'S A WILL, THERE'S A WAY."
DAD, WHAT ARE WE GOING TO DO?

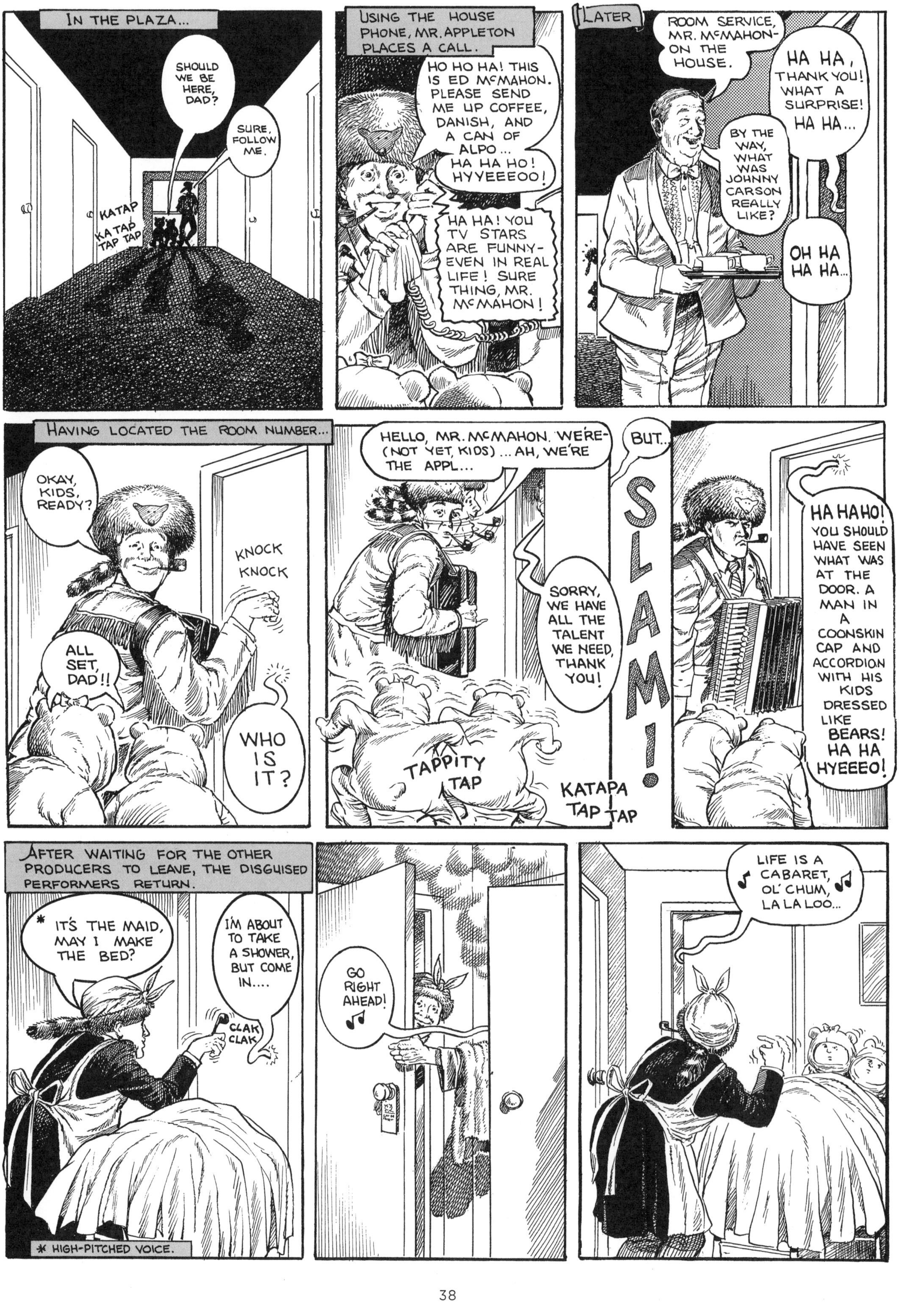
IN THE PLAZA...
SHOULD WE BE HERE, DAD?
SURE, FOLLOW ME.
KATAP KATAP TAP TAP
USING THE HOUSE PHONE, MR. APPLETON PLACES A CALL.
HO HO HA! THIS IS ED McMAHON. PLEASE SEND ME UP COFFEE, DANISH, AND A CAN OF ALPO ... HA HA HO! HYYEEEOO!
HA HA! YOU TV STARS ARE FUNNY- EVEN IN REAL LIFE! SURE THING, MR. McMAHON!
LATER
ROOM SERVICE, MR. McMAHON- ON THE HOUSE.
HA HA, THANK YOU! WHAT A SURPRISE! HA HA...
BY THE WAY, WHAT WAS JOHNNY CARSON REALLY LIKE?
OH HA HA HA...
HAVING LOCATED THE ROOM NUMBER...
OKAY, KIDS, READY?
KNOCK KNOCK
ALL SET, DAD!!
WHO IS IT?
HELLO, MR. McMAHON. WE'RE- (NOT YET, KIDS) ... AH, WE'RE THE APPL...
BUT...
SORRY, WE HAVE ALL THE TALENT WE NEED, THANK YOU!
SLAM!
TAPPITY TAP
KATAPA TAP TAP
HA HA HO! YOU SHOULD HAVE SEEN WHAT WAS AT THE DOOR. A MAN IN A COONSKIN CAP AND ACCORDION WITH HIS KIDS DRESSED LIKE BEARS! HA HA HYEEEO!
AFTER WAITING FOR THE OTHER PRODUCERS TO LEAVE, THE DISGUISED PERFORMERS RETURN.
* IT'S THE MAID, MAY I MAKE THE BED?
I'M ABOUT TO TAKE A SHOWER, BUT COME IN....
CLAK CLAK
* HIGH-PITCHED VOICE.
GO RIGHT AHEAD! ♪
LIFE IS A CABARET, OL' CHUM, LA LA LOO...

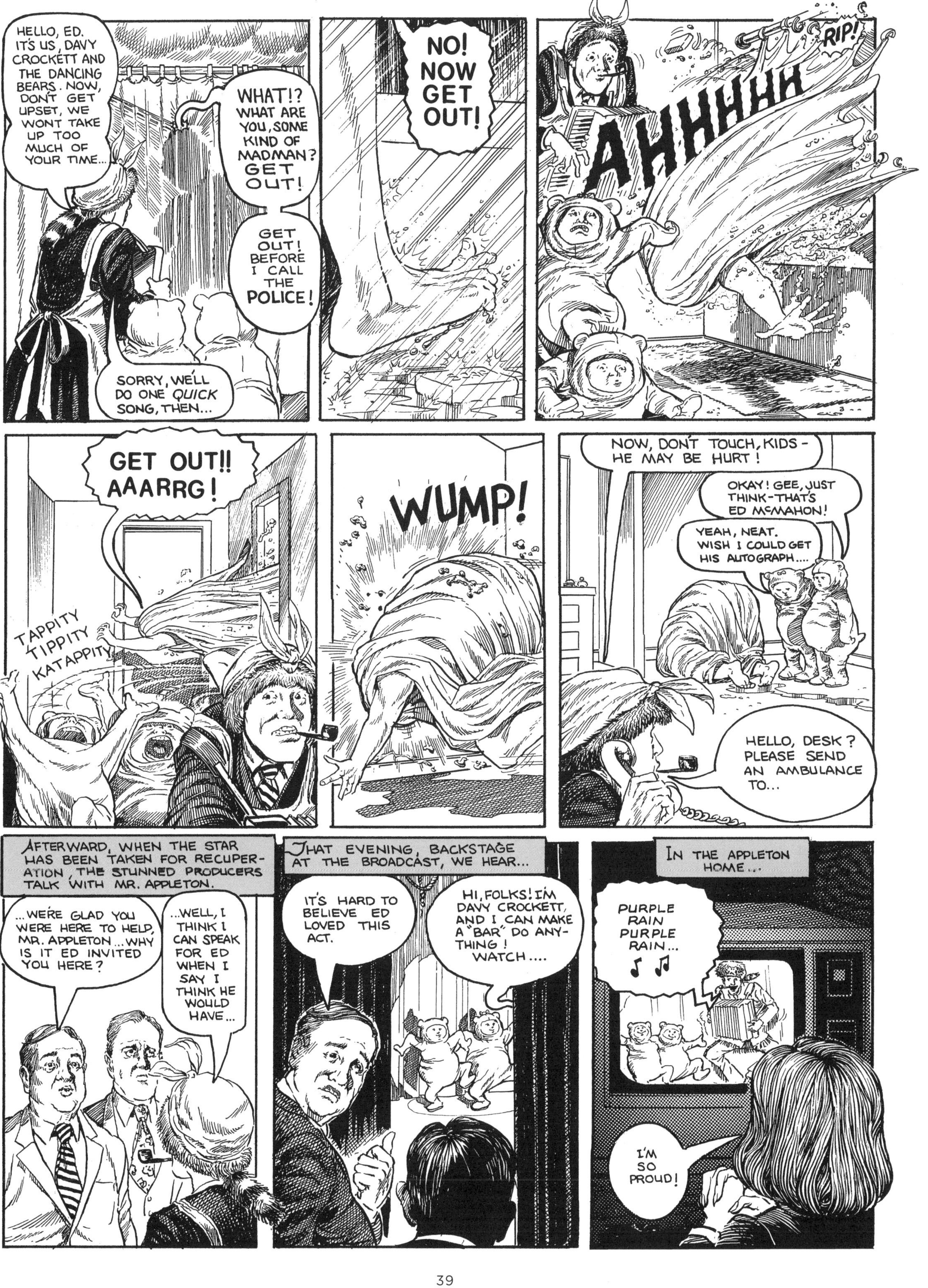
HELLO, ED. IT'S US, DAVY CROCKETT AND THE DANCING BEARS. NOW, DON'T GET UPSET, WE WONT TAKE UP TOO MUCH OF YOUR TIME...
WHAT!? WHAT ARE YOU, SOME KIND OF MADMAN? GET OUT!
GET OUT! BEFORE I CALL THE POLICE!
SORRY, WE'LL DO ONE QUICK SONG, THEN...
NO! NOW GET OUT!
RIP!
AHHHHH
GET OUT!! AAARRG!
TAPPITY TIPPITY KATAPPITY
WUMP!
NOW, DON'T TOUCH, KIDS - HE MAY BE HURT!
OKAY! GEE, JUST THINK-THAT'S ED McMAHON!
YEAH, NEAT. WISH I COULD GET HIS AUTOGRAPH....
HELLO, DESK? PLEASE SEND AN AMBULANCE TO...
AFTERWARD, WHEN THE STAR HAS BEEN TAKEN FOR RECUPERATION, THE STUNNED PRODUCERS TALK WITH MR. APPLETON.
...WE'RE GLAD YOU WERE HERE TO HELP, MR. APPLETON... WHY IS IT ED INVITED YOU HERE?
...WELL, I THINK I CAN SPEAK FOR ED WHEN I SAY I THINK HE WOULD HAVE...
THAT EVENING, BACKSTAGE AT THE BROADCAST, WE HEAR...
IT'S HARD TO BELIEVE ED LOVED THIS ACT.
HI, FOLKS! I'M DAVY CROCKETT, AND I CAN MAKE A "BAR" DO ANYTHING! WATCH....
IN THE APPLETON HOME...
PURPLE RAIN PURPLE RAIN...
I'M SO PROUD!

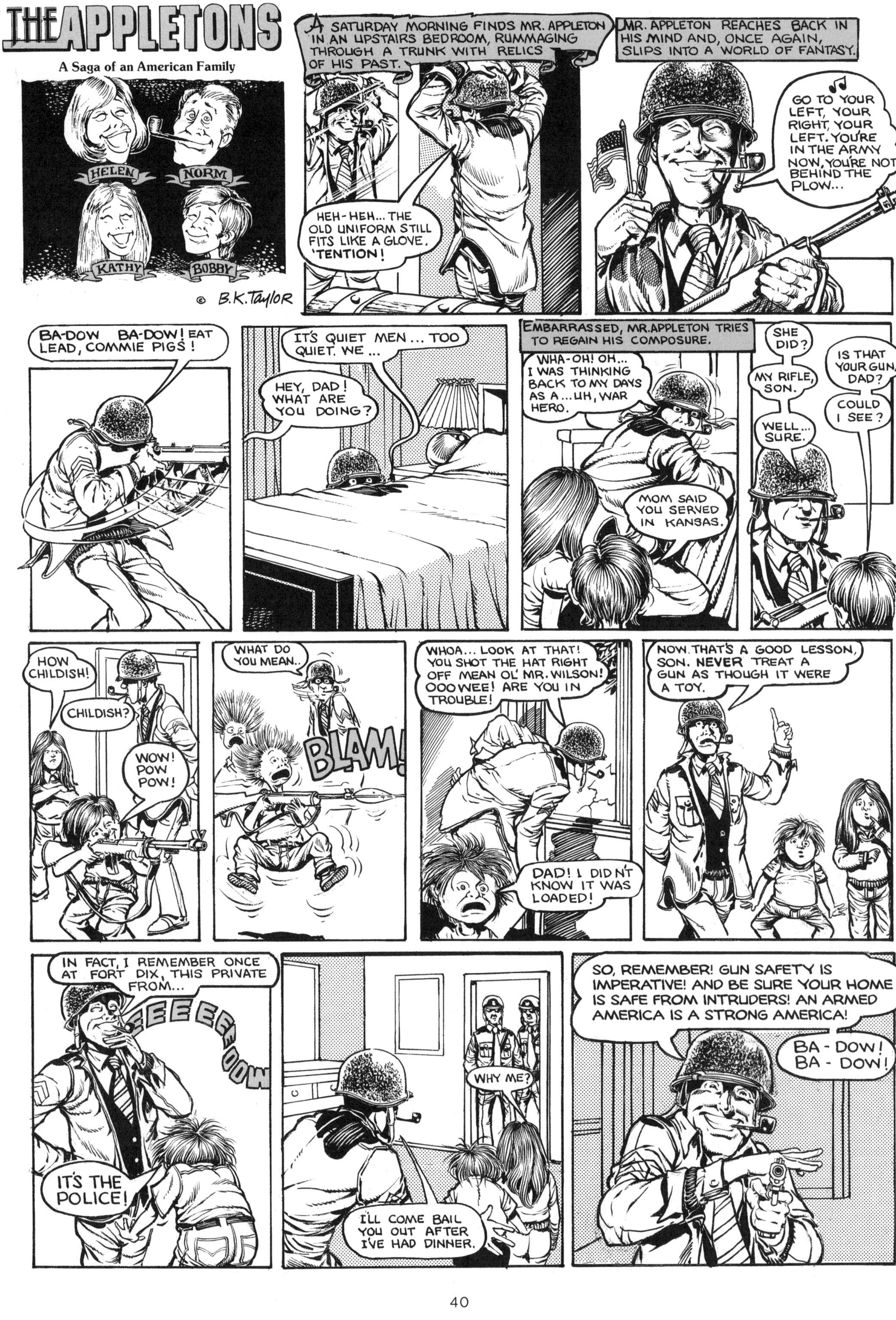
THE APPLETONS
A Saga of an American Family
HELEN
NORM
KATHY
BOBBY
© B.K.Taylor
A SATURDAY MORNING FINDS MR. APPLETON IN AN UPSTAIRS BEDROOM, RUMMAGING THROUGH A TRUNK WITH RELICS OF HIS PAST.
HEH-HEH... THE OLD UNIFORM STILL FITS LIKE A GLOVE. 'TENTION!
MR. APPLETON REACHES BACK IN HIS MIND AND, ONCE AGAIN, SLIPS INTO A WORLD OF FANTASY.
GO TO YOUR LEFT, YOUR RIGHT, YOUR LEFT. YOU'RE IN THE ARMY NOW, YOU'RE NOT BEHIND THE PLOW...
BA-DOW BA-DOW! EAT LEAD, COMMIE PIGS!
IT'S QUIET MEN... TOO QUIET. WE...
HEY, DAD! WHAT ARE YOU DOING?
EMBARRASSED, MR. APPLETON TRIES TO REGAIN HIS COMPOSURE.
WHA-OH! OH... I WAS THINKING BACK TO MY DAYS AS A... UH, WAR HERO.
MOM SAID YOU SERVED IN KANSAS.
SHE DID?
MY RIFLE, SON.
IS THAT YOUR GUN, DAD?
COULD I SEE?
WELL... SURE.
HOW CHILDISH!
CHILDISH?
WOW! POW POW!
WHAT DO YOU MEAN..
BLAM!
WHOA... LOOK AT THAT! YOU SHOT THE HAT RIGHT OFF MEAN OL' MR. WILSON! OOOWEE! ARE YOU IN TROUBLE!
DAD! I DIDN'T KNOW IT WAS LOADED!
NOW. THAT'S A GOOD LESSON, SON. NEVER TREAT A GUN AS THOUGH IT WERE A TOY.
IN FACT, I REMEMBER ONCE AT FORT DIX, THIS PRIVATE FROM...
EEEEEEOOOW
IT'S THE POLICE!
WHY ME?
I'LL COME BAIL YOU OUT AFTER I'VE HAD DINNER.
SO, REMEMBER! GUN SAFETY IS IMPERATIVE! AND BE SURE YOUR HOME IS SAFE FROM INTRUDERS! AN ARMED AMERICA IS A STRONG AMERICA!
BA-DOW! BA-DOW!

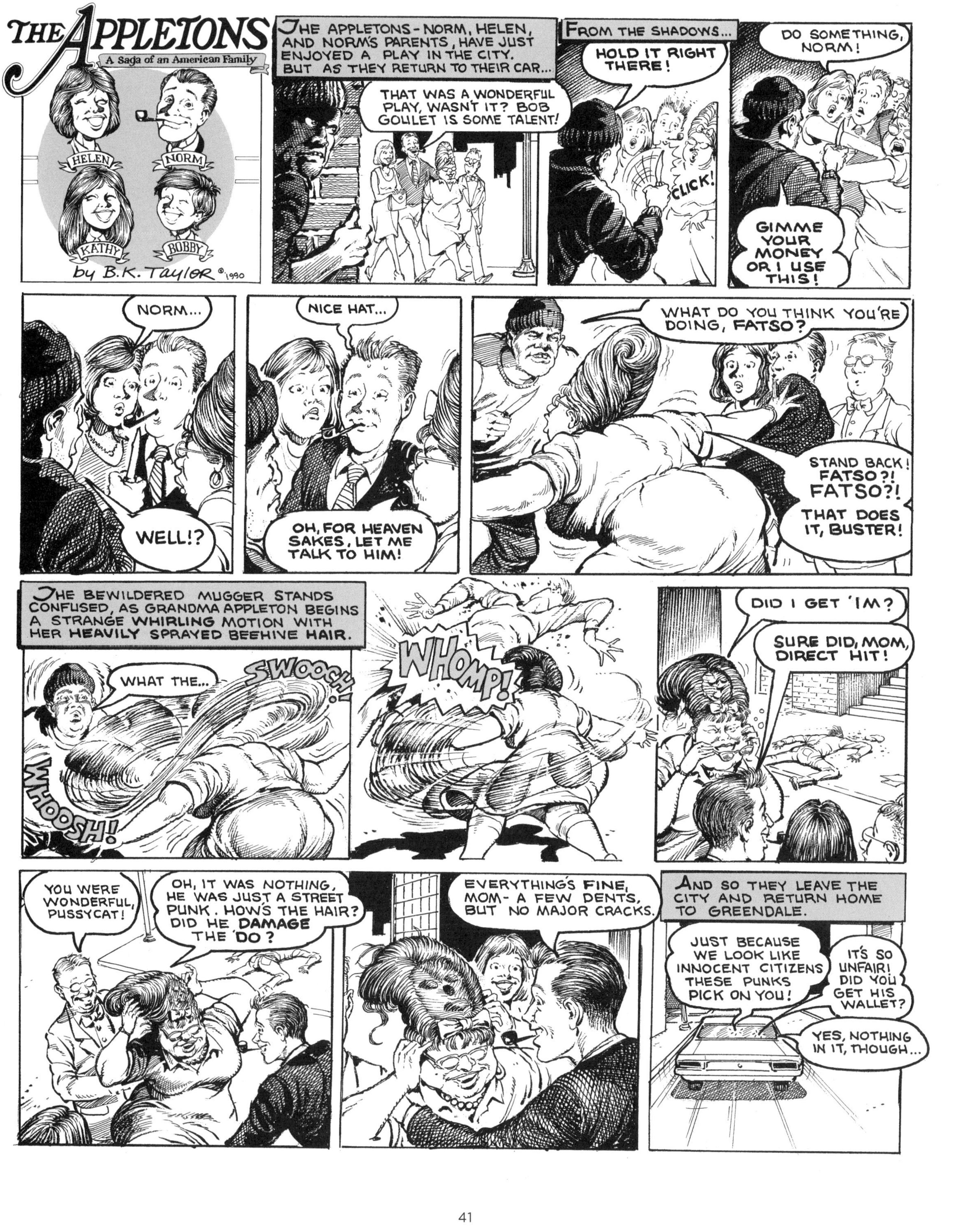
THE APPLETONS
A Saga of an American Family
HELEN
NORM
KATHY
BOBBY
by B.K. Taylor ©1990
THE APPLETONS - NORM, HELEN, AND NORM'S PARENTS, HAVE JUST ENJOYED A PLAY IN THE CITY. BUT AS THEY RETURN TO THEIR CAR...
THAT WAS A WONDERFUL PLAY, WASN'T IT? BOB GOULET IS SOME TALENT!
FROM THE SHADOWS...
HOLD IT RIGHT THERE!
CLICK!
DO SOMETHING, NORM!
GIMME YOUR MONEY OR I USE THIS!
NORM...
WELL!?
NICE HAT...
OH, FOR HEAVEN SAKES, LET ME TALK TO HIM!
WHAT DO YOU THINK YOU'RE DOING, FATSO?
STAND BACK! FATSO?! FATSO?! THAT DOES IT, BUSTER!
THE BEWILDERED MUGGER STANDS CONFUSED, AS GRANDMA APPLETON BEGINS A STRANGE WHIRLING MOTION WITH HER HEAVILY SPRAYED BEEHIVE HAIR.
WHAT THE...
SWOOSH!
WHOOSH!
WHOMP!
DID I GET 'IM?
SURE DID, MOM, DIRECT HIT!
YOU WERE WONDERFUL, PUSSYCAT!
OH, IT WAS NOTHING, HE WAS JUST A STREET PUNK. HOW'S THE HAIR? DID HE DAMAGE THE 'DO?
EVERYTHING'S FINE, MOM- A FEW DENTS, BUT NO MAJOR CRACKS.
AND SO THEY LEAVE THE CITY AND RETURN HOME TO GREENDALE.
JUST BECAUSE WE LOOK LIKE INNOCENT CITIZENS THESE PUNKS PICK ON YOU!
IT'S SO UNFAIR! DID YOU GET HIS WALLET?
YES, NOTHING IN IT, THOUGH...

THE APPLETONS
A Saga of an American Family
HELEN
NORM
KATHY
BOBBY
by B.K. Taylor
MR. APPLETON IS ENJOYING A MIDDAY REPAST AT A LOCAL DINER. IN THE NEXT BOOTH A MAN AND HIS DOG ARE DOING THE SAME....
SUDDENLY...
MOTHER OF MERCY!
EXCUSE ME, SIR! YOUR DOG JUST SNATCHED FOOD FROM MY PLATE!
S'MATTER, YOU DON'T LIKE DOGS?
WELL, YES, BUT...
THEN MIND YOUR OWN BUSINESS, HE'S ON A LEASH!
THE WAITRESS BRINGS A FRESH PLATE OF FOOD.
MOMENTS PASS AS MR. APPLETON THINKS THE SITUATION OVER.
THEN...
PSSST... HERE, BOY!
GUK!
HUP!
NEXT...
JESUS CHRIST!!
HUP!
MR. APPLETON PASSES THE ENTANGLED PATRON AS HE LEAVES TO PAY HIS CHECK.
FETCH BOY!
AAAHRG...
HUKAAAARG
AT THE COUNTER...
HOW WAS EVERYTHING?
FINE, JUST FINE!
©.1983 B.K.Taylor
THE OFFICIAL CARTOON STRIP FOR THE 1984 OLYMPICS

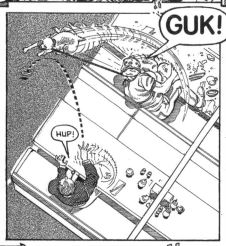

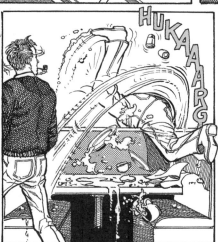

THE APPLETONS

NORM   HELEN   KATHY   BOBBY

WE FIND THE APPLETON FAMILY ATTENDING THE GREENDALE ART FESTIVAL, ENJOYING AN AFTERNOON OF CULTURE.

THIS IS INTERESTING.

LOOKS LIKE OUR CAR WINDSHIELD **AFTER** A VACATION.

GIGGLE.

THE FAMILY ENJOYS THE WRY COMMENT BY MR. APPLETON.

OH NORM, YOU'RE A CUTUP!

HUK HUK — I JUST THOUGHT OF THAT! SORRY ⧸ GUFFAW ⧸

DAD, YOU'RE SO FUNNY YOU SHOULD WRITE FOR **PAT SAJAK** OR SOMEBODY.

SUDDENLY, FROM BEHIND, ONE OF NORM APPLETON'S LEAST FAVORITE PERSONS APPEARS.

YOU KNOW, I'VE OFTEN THOUGHT.... OH NO!

HEY, DAD, LOOK! A CLOWN!

THAT'S A MIME, DEAR.

WOW! HE'S PULLING A ROPE THAT'S **NOT THERE!**

THANK YOU — VERY NICE — IF YOU'LL EXCUSE US...

MR. APPLETON ATTEMPTS TO PASS BY BUT...

EXCUSE ME BUT I'D... OOF ⧸

OH DEAR

DAD!

AFTER THE ACCIDENT THE MIME EXPRESSES HIS SADNESS....

NO NEED TO HELP, I'M ALL RIGHT.

THE MIME ATTEMPTS TO LESSEN THE PAIN OF THE SITUATION WITH HUMOR.

ZOW! HE PULLED FLOWERS FROM BEHIND DAD'S EAR!

YOU ALL GO AHEAD, I'M GOING TO VISIT THE MEN'S ROOM.

THE PERSISTENT MIME FOLLOWS.

MUMPH WUMP!

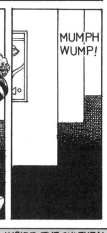

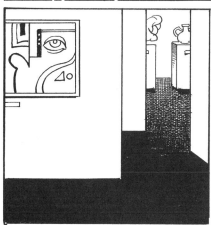

LATER   MR. APPLETON RETURNS.

THERE YOU ARE!

SAY, I THINK WE'VE SEEN ENOUGH — HOW ABOUT A TREAT AT THE MALT SHOP!

OH BOY!

LET'S GO!

MEANWHILE, BACK INSIDE THE CULTURAL CENTER, TWO PEOPLE VIEW THE DISPLAYS.

I THINK IT REPRESENTS THE CYCLE OF LIFE.

I THINK IT'S DISGUSTING!

B.K. Taylor
© 1989

43

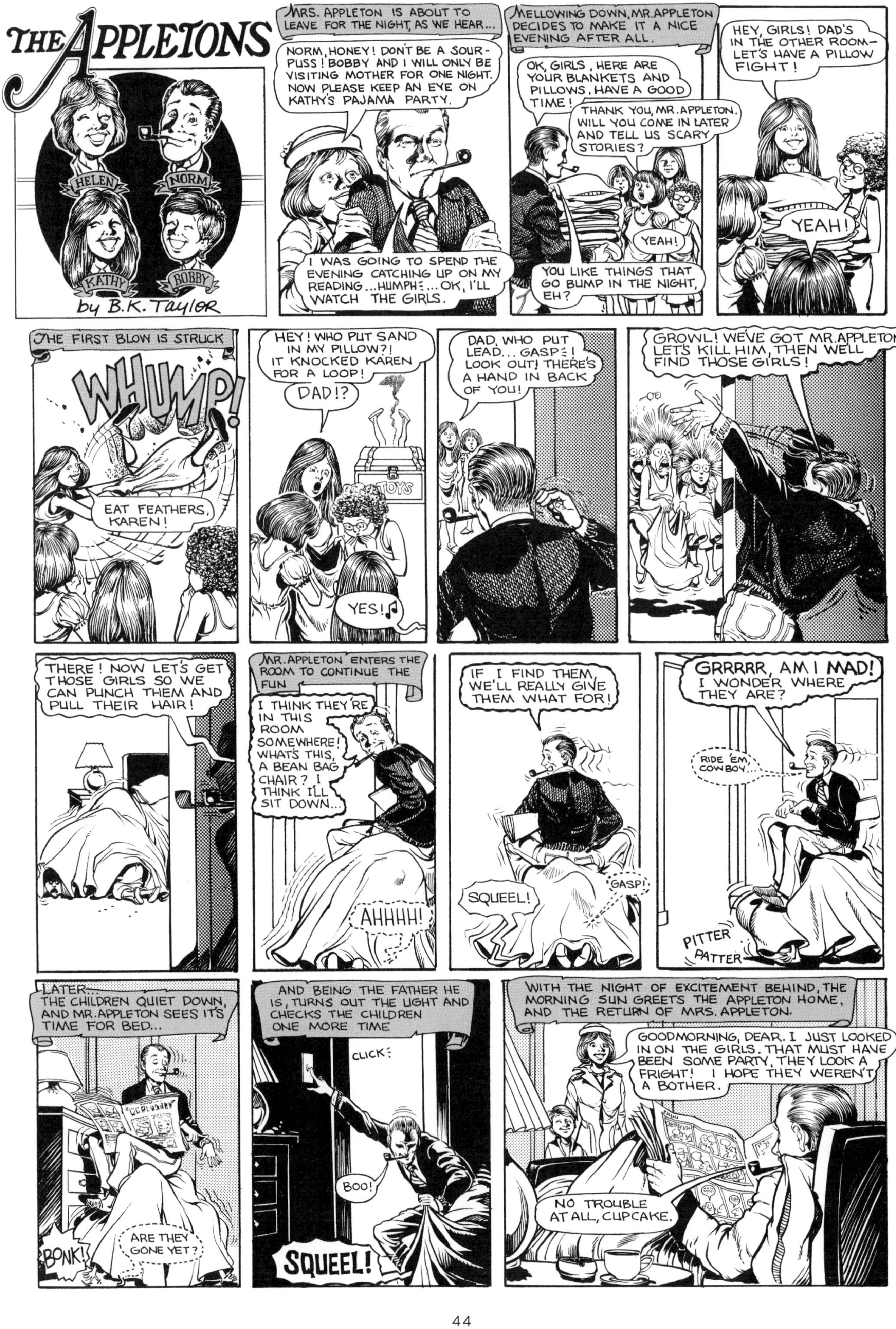
THE APPLETONS
HELEN
NORM
KATHY
BOBBY
by B.K. Taylor
MRS. APPLETON IS ABOUT TO LEAVE FOR THE NIGHT, AS WE HEAR...
NORM, HONEY! DON'T BE A SOUR-PUSS! BOBBY AND I WILL ONLY BE VISITING MOTHER FOR ONE NIGHT. NOW PLEASE KEEP AN EYE ON KATHY'S PAJAMA PARTY.
I WAS GOING TO SPEND THE EVENING CATCHING UP ON MY READING...HUMPH!...OK, I'LL WATCH THE GIRLS.
MELLOWING DOWN, MR. APPLETON DECIDES TO MAKE IT A NICE EVENING AFTER ALL.
OK, GIRLS, HERE ARE YOUR BLANKETS AND PILLOWS, HAVE A GOOD TIME!
THANK YOU, MR. APPLETON. WILL YOU COME IN LATER AND TELL US SCARY STORIES?
YEAH!
YOU LIKE THINGS THAT GO BUMP IN THE NIGHT, EH?
HEY, GIRLS! DAD'S IN THE OTHER ROOM-LET'S HAVE A PILLOW FIGHT!
YEAH!
THE FIRST BLOW IS STRUCK
WHUMP!
EAT FEATHERS, KAREN!
HEY! WHO PUT SAND IN MY PILLOW?! IT KNOCKED KAREN FOR A LOOP!
DAD!?
TOYS
YES!
DAD, WHO PUT LEAD... GASP!! LOOK OUT! THERE'S A HAND IN BACK OF YOU!
GROWL! WE'VE GOT MR. APPLETON! LET'S KILL HIM, THEN WE'LL FIND THOSE GIRLS!
THERE! NOW LET'S GET THOSE GIRLS SO WE CAN PUNCH THEM AND PULL THEIR HAIR!
MR. APPLETON ENTERS THE ROOM TO CONTINUE THE FUN
I THINK THEY'RE IN THIS ROOM SOMEWHERE! WHAT'S THIS, A BEAN BAG CHAIR? I THINK I'LL SIT DOWN...
AHHHH!
IF I FIND THEM, WE'LL REALLY GIVE THEM WHAT FOR!
SQUEEL!
GASP!
GRRRRR, AM I MAD! I WONDER WHERE THEY ARE?
RIDE 'EM COWBOY...
PITTER PATTER
LATER... THE CHILDREN QUIET DOWN, AND MR. APPLETON SEES IT'S TIME FOR BED...
BONK!
ARE THEY GONE YET?
AND BEING THE FATHER HE IS, TURNS OUT THE LIGHT AND CHECKS THE CHILDREN ONE MORE TIME
CLICK!
BOO!
SQUEEL!
WITH THE NIGHT OF EXCITEMENT BEHIND, THE MORNING SUN GREETS THE APPLETON HOME, AND THE RETURN OF MRS. APPLETON.
GOODMORNING, DEAR. I JUST LOOKED IN ON THE GIRLS. THAT MUST HAVE BEEN SOME PARTY, THEY LOOK A FRIGHT! I HOPE THEY WEREN'T A BOTHER.
NO TROUBLE AT ALL, CUPCAKE.

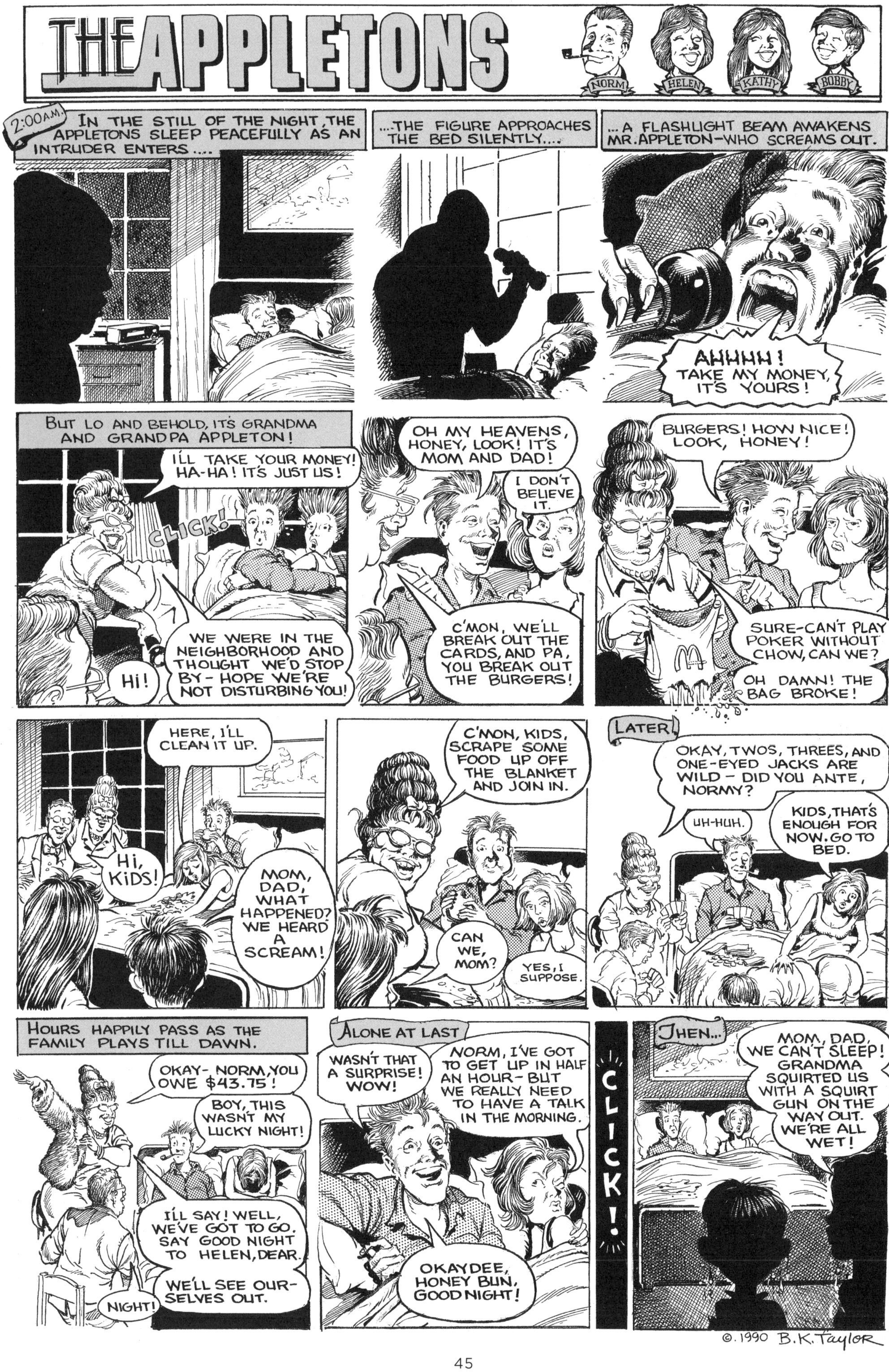
THE APPLETONS
NORM
HELEN
KATHY
BOBBY
2:00 A.M.
IN THE STILL OF THE NIGHT, THE APPLETONS SLEEP PEACEFULLY AS AN INTRUDER ENTERS....
...THE FIGURE APPROACHES THE BED SILENTLY....
...A FLASHLIGHT BEAM AWAKENS MR. APPLETON—WHO SCREAMS OUT.
AHHHH! TAKE MY MONEY, IT'S YOURS!
BUT LO AND BEHOLD, IT'S GRANDMA AND GRANDPA APPLETON!
I'LL TAKE YOUR MONEY! HA-HA! IT'S JUST US!
CLICK!
WE WERE IN THE NEIGHBORHOOD AND THOUGHT WE'D STOP BY- HOPE WE'RE NOT DISTURBING YOU!
HI!
OH MY HEAVENS, HONEY, LOOK! IT'S MOM AND DAD!
I DON'T BELIEVE IT.
C'MON, WE'LL BREAK OUT THE CARDS, AND PA, YOU BREAK OUT THE BURGERS!
BURGERS! HOW NICE! LOOK, HONEY!
SURE-CAN'T PLAY POKER WITHOUT CHOW, CAN WE?
OH DAMN! THE BAG BROKE!
HERE, I'LL CLEAN IT UP.
HI, KIDS!
MOM, DAD, WHAT HAPPENED? WE HEARD A SCREAM!
C'MON, KIDS, SCRAPE SOME FOOD UP OFF THE BLANKET AND JOIN IN.
CAN WE, MOM?
YES, I SUPPOSE.
LATER!
OKAY, TWOS, THREES, AND ONE-EYED JACKS ARE WILD - DID YOU ANTE, NORMY?
UH-HUH.
KIDS, THAT'S ENOUGH FOR NOW. GO TO BED.
HOURS HAPPILY PASS AS THE FAMILY PLAYS TILL DAWN.
OKAY- NORM, YOU OWE $43.75!
BOY, THIS WASN'T MY LUCKY NIGHT!
I'LL SAY! WELL, WE'VE GOT TO GO. SAY GOOD NIGHT TO HELEN, DEAR.
WE'LL SEE OURSELVES OUT.
NIGHT!
ALONE AT LAST
WASN'T THAT A SURPRISE! WOW!
NORM, I'VE GOT TO GET UP IN HALF AN HOUR- BUT WE REALLY NEED TO HAVE A TALK IN THE MORNING.
OKAYDEE, HONEY BUN, GOOD NIGHT!
CLICK!
THEN...
MOM, DAD, WE CAN'T SLEEP! GRANDMA SQUIRTED US WITH A SQUIRT GUN ON THE WAY OUT. WE'RE ALL WET!
©. 1990 B.K. Taylor

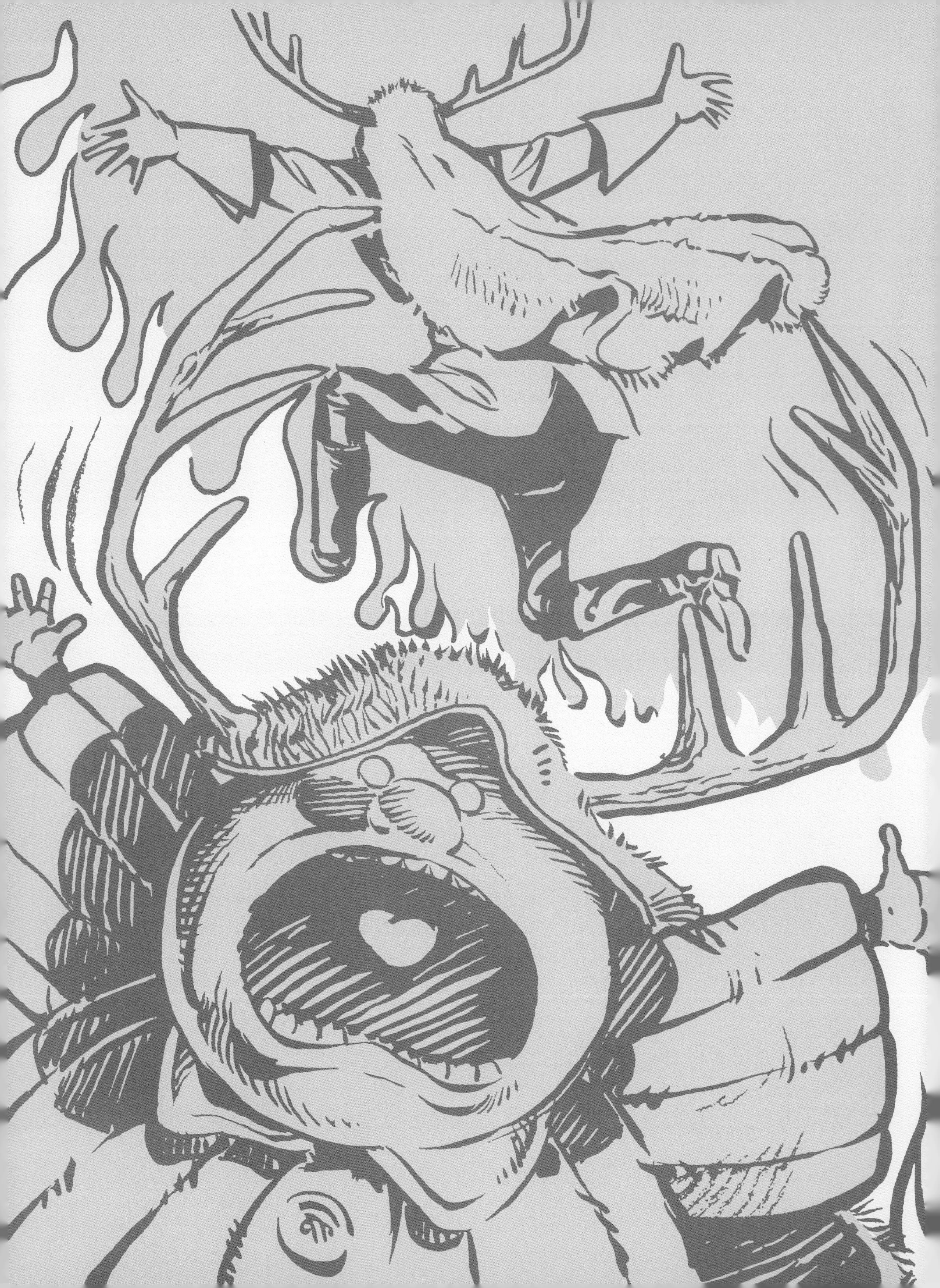

Whereas *The Appletons* is the saga of an American family, *Timberland Tales* is purely Canadian. Set in the Canadian North in a virginal settlement, this isolated and somewhat naïve group of characters encounters the outside world and its trials of everyday life.

Our cast:

Maurice

Maurice, the pre-adolescent, innocent, and very curious French/First Nations boy, is our lead character. Maurice's origin is sketchy, but it was believed he was left in a basket on the doorstep of Dr. Rogers's cabin (the settlement's veterinarian). Pinned to Maurice's baby blanket was a note that read, "Here is your bonus gift — signed, Mary Kay Cosmetics." Consequently, Dr. Rogers was saddled with the responsibility of raising this bonus gift. As time passes, we find Maurice is now discovering the beginnings of manhood, and his curiosity and naïveté are rampant. His best friend is ...

Doctor Rogers

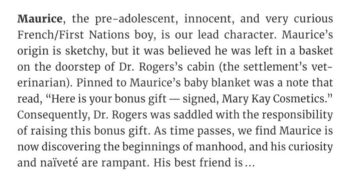

Constable Tom

Constable Tom, who, legend has it, suffered a bit of brain damage as a boy, yet now stands tall as a proud symbol of a Canadian Mountie ... (well, stands tall, anyway). Constable Tom never speaks, except in the very first strip. He is young Maurice's constant companion.

Foamy, Maurice's almost faithful dog, sports a bit of foam around his mouth, and thus is thought by many to be slightly mad. He's not exactly a Lassie or Rin Tin Tin, but as most dog owners know, it's the luck of the draw when finding a good dog.

Kathleen

Dr. Rogers, a straitlaced and ambitious veterinarian and surrogate father figure to Maurice. Ever since finding Maurice on his doorstep, Dr. Rogers has shared the duties of raising him with ...

Foamy

Kathleen, a missionary and romantic interest to Dr. Rogers. She, like the doctor, has committed herself as a mentor (and parental figure) to young Maurice and his adolescent curiosity and penchant for creating chaos.

The cast lives an intimate and simple life in their remote corner of the Canadian North, but there are times when interaction with the outside world brings unexpected surprises and discovery, as you will see ...

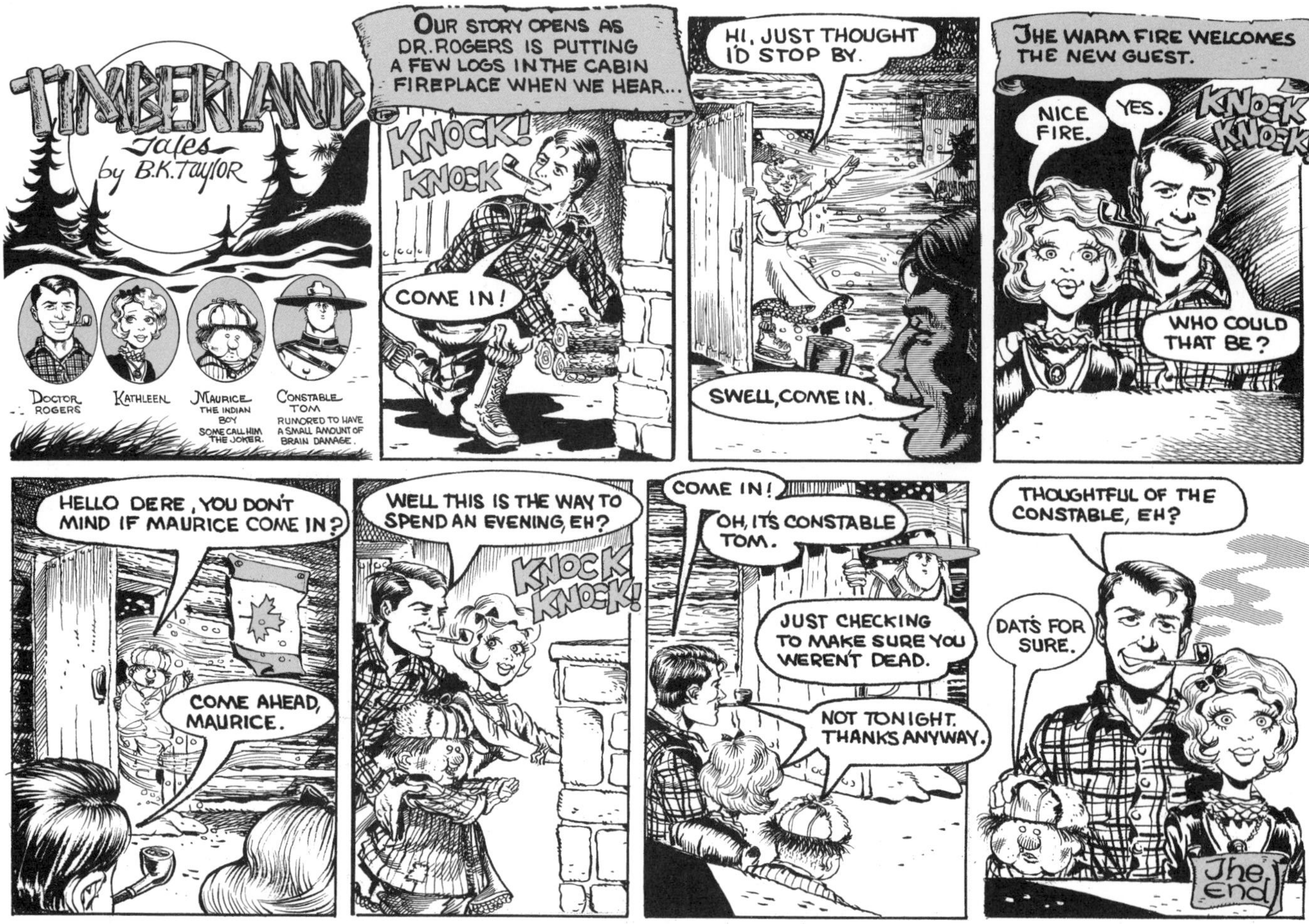
TIMBERLAND
Tales
by B.K.Taylor
DOCTOR ROGERS
KATHLEEN
MAURICE THE INDIAN BOY SOME CALL HIM THE JOKER.
CONSTABLE TOM RUMORED TO HAVE A SMALL AMOUNT OF BRAIN DAMAGE.
OUR STORY OPENS AS DR. ROGERS IS PUTTING A FEW LOGS IN THE CABIN FIREPLACE WHEN WE HEAR...
KNOCK! KNOCK
COME IN!
HI, JUST THOUGHT I'D STOP BY.
SWELL, COME IN.
THE WARM FIRE WELCOMES THE NEW GUEST.
NICE FIRE.
YES.
KNOCK KNOCK!
WHO COULD THAT BE?
HELLO DERE, YOU DON'T MIND IF MAURICE COME IN?
COME AHEAD, MAURICE.
WELL THIS IS THE WAY TO SPEND AN EVENING, EH?
KNOCK KNOCK!
COME IN!
OH, IT'S CONSTABLE TOM.
JUST CHECKING TO MAKE SURE YOU WEREN'T DEAD.
NOT TONIGHT. THANKS ANYWAY.
THOUGHTFUL OF THE CONSTABLE, EH?
DAT'S FOR SURE.
The End

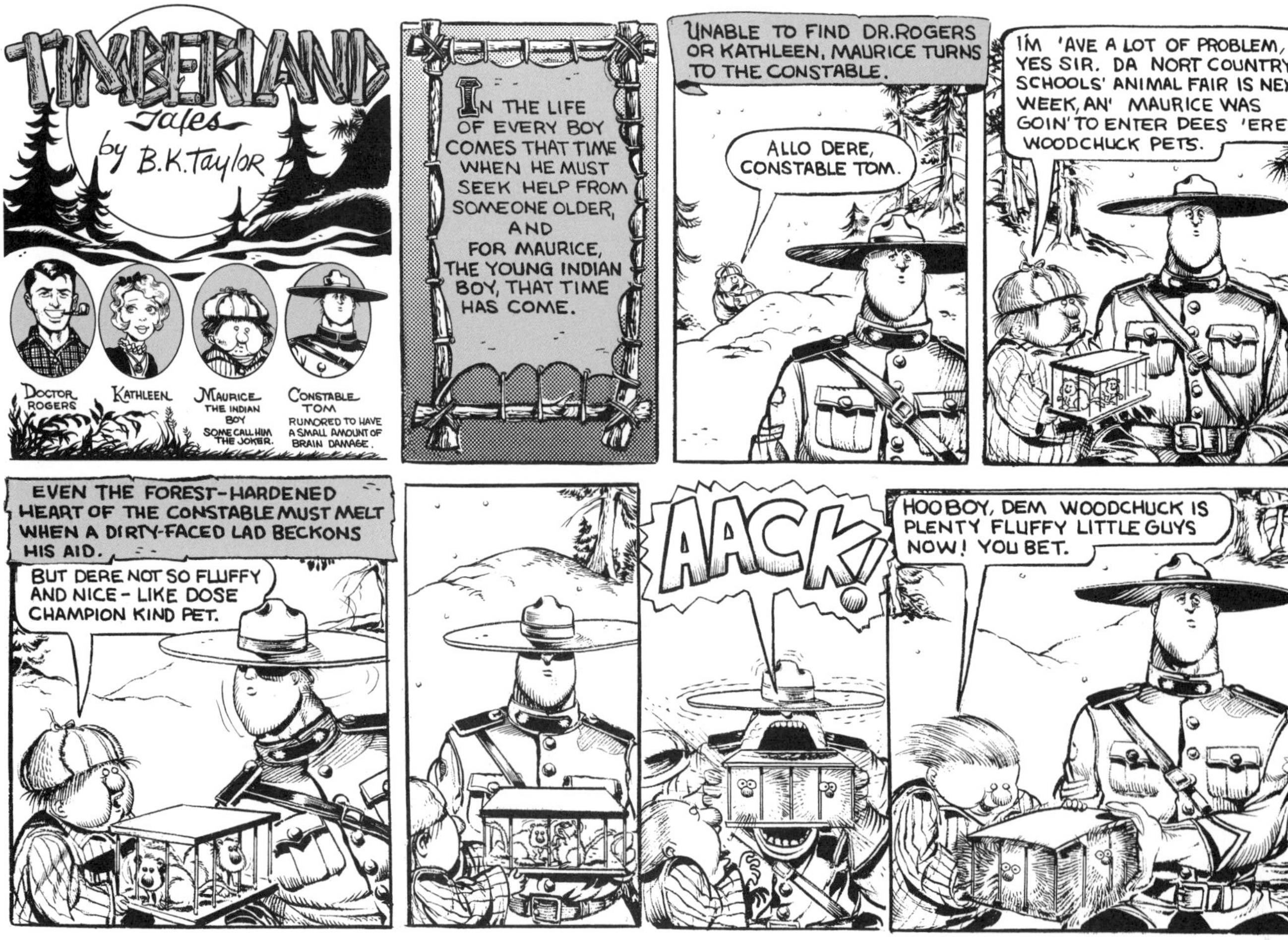
TIMBERLAND
Tales
by B.K.Taylor
DOCTOR ROGERS
KATHLEEN
MAURICE THE INDIAN BOY SOME CALL HIM THE JOKER.
CONSTABLE TOM RUMORED TO HAVE A SMALL AMOUNT OF BRAIN DAMAGE.
IN THE LIFE OF EVERY BOY COMES THAT TIME WHEN HE MUST SEEK HELP FROM SOMEONE OLDER, AND FOR MAURICE, THE YOUNG INDIAN BOY, THAT TIME HAS COME.
UNABLE TO FIND DR. ROGERS OR KATHLEEN, MAURICE TURNS TO THE CONSTABLE.
ALLO DERE, CONSTABLE TOM.
I'M 'AVE A LOT OF PROBLEM, YES SIR. DA NORT COUNTRY SCHOOLS' ANIMAL FAIR IS NEXT WEEK, AN' MAURICE WAS GOIN' TO ENTER DEES 'ERE WOODCHUCK PETS.
EVEN THE FOREST-HARDENED HEART OF THE CONSTABLE MUST MELT WHEN A DIRTY-FACED LAD BECKONS HIS AID.
BUT DERE NOT SO FLUFFY AND NICE - LIKE DOSE CHAMPION KIND PET.
AACK!
HOO BOY, DEM WOODCHUCK IS PLENTY FLUFFY LITTLE GUYS NOW! YOU BET.

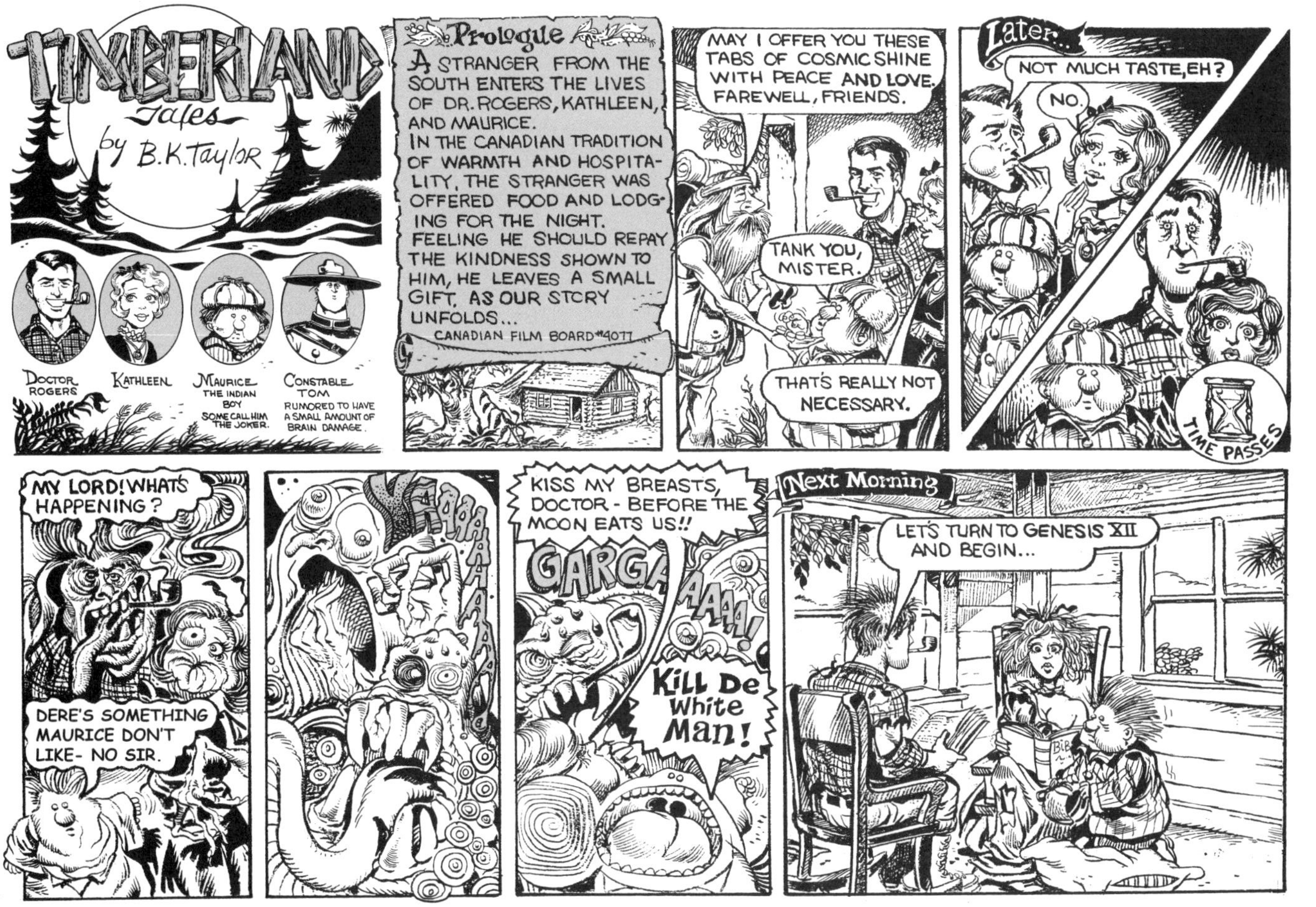
TIMBERLAND
Tales
by B.K.Taylor
DOCTOR ROGERS
KATHLEEN
MAURICE THE INDIAN BOY SOME CALL HIM THE JOKER.
CONSTABLE TOM RUMORED TO HAVE A SMALL AMOUNT OF BRAIN DAMAGE.
Prologue
A STRANGER FROM THE SOUTH ENTERS THE LIVES OF DR. ROGERS, KATHLEEN, AND MAURICE.
IN THE CANADIAN TRADITION OF WARMTH AND HOSPITALITY, THE STRANGER WAS OFFERED FOOD AND LODGING FOR THE NIGHT.
FEELING HE SHOULD REPAY THE KINDNESS SHOWN TO HIM, HE LEAVES A SMALL GIFT, AS OUR STORY UNFOLDS...
CANADIAN FILM BOARD #4077
MAY I OFFER YOU THESE TABS OF COSMIC SHINE WITH PEACE AND LOVE. FAREWELL, FRIENDS.
TANK YOU, MISTER.
THAT'S REALLY NOT NECESSARY.
Later...
NOT MUCH TASTE, EH?
NO.
TIME PASSES
MY LORD! WHAT'S HAPPENING?
DERE'S SOMETHING MAURICE DON'T LIKE- NO SIR.
YAAAAAAAAAA
KISS MY BREASTS, DOCTOR - BEFORE THE MOON EATS US!!
GARGAAAAA!
Kill De White Man!
Next Morning
LET'S TURN TO GENESIS XII AND BEGIN...

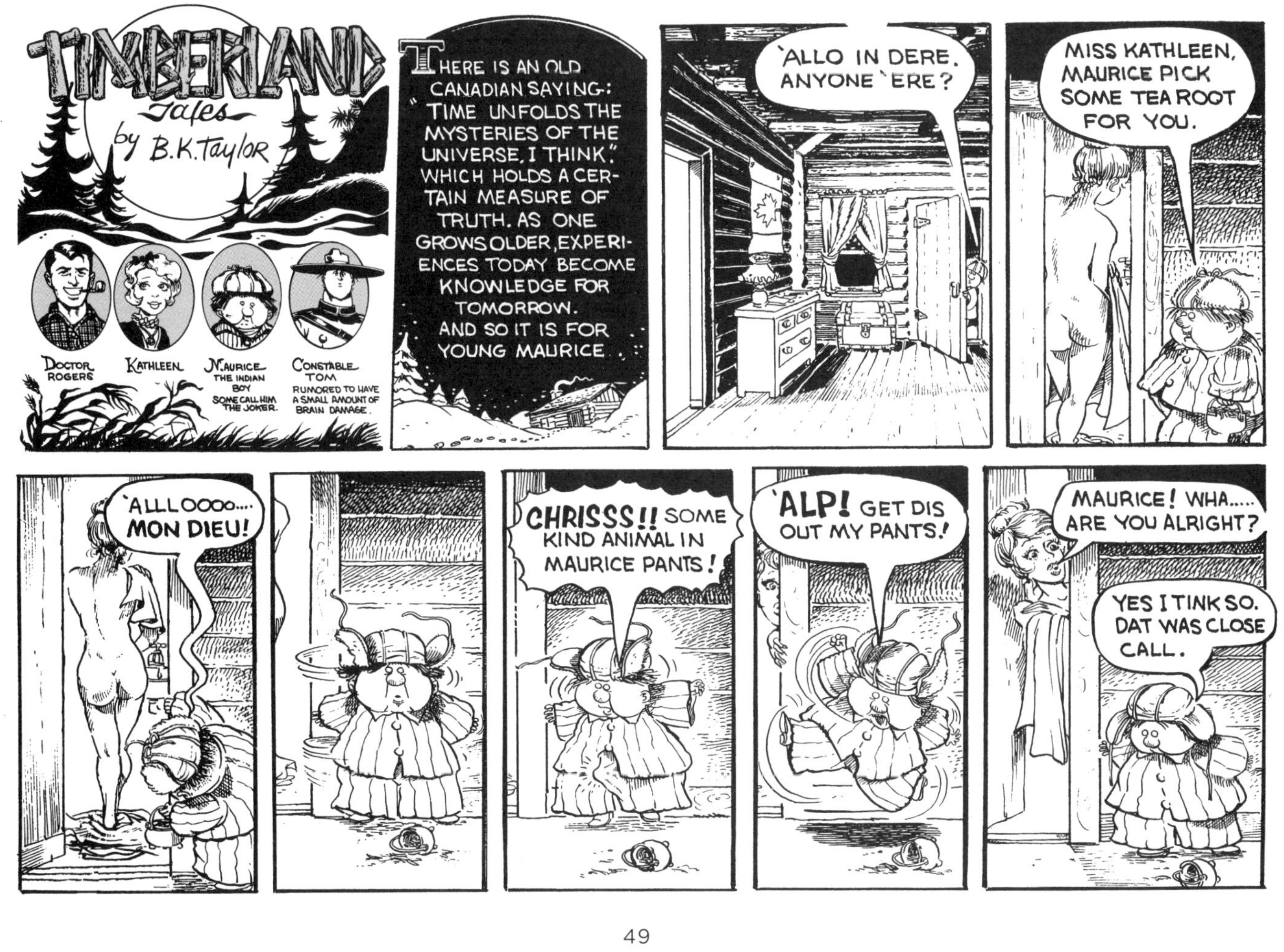
TIMBERLAND
Tales
by B.K.Taylor
DOCTOR ROGERS
KATHLEEN
MAURICE THE INDIAN BOY SOME CALL HIM THE JOKER.
CONSTABLE TOM RUMORED TO HAVE A SMALL AMOUNT OF BRAIN DAMAGE.
THERE IS AN OLD CANADIAN SAYING: "TIME UNFOLDS THE MYSTERIES OF THE UNIVERSE, I THINK." WHICH HOLDS A CERTAIN MEASURE OF TRUTH. AS ONE GROWS OLDER, EXPERIENCES TODAY BECOME KNOWLEDGE FOR TOMORROW. AND SO IT IS FOR YOUNG MAURICE...
'ALLO IN DERE. ANYONE 'ERE?
MISS KATHLEEN, MAURICE PICK SOME TEA ROOT FOR YOU.
'ALLLOOOO.... MON DIEU!
CHRISSS!! SOME KIND ANIMAL IN MAURICE PANTS!
'ALP! GET DIS OUT MY PANTS!
MAURICE! WHA..... ARE YOU ALRIGHT?
YES I TINK SO. DAT WAS CLOSE CALL.

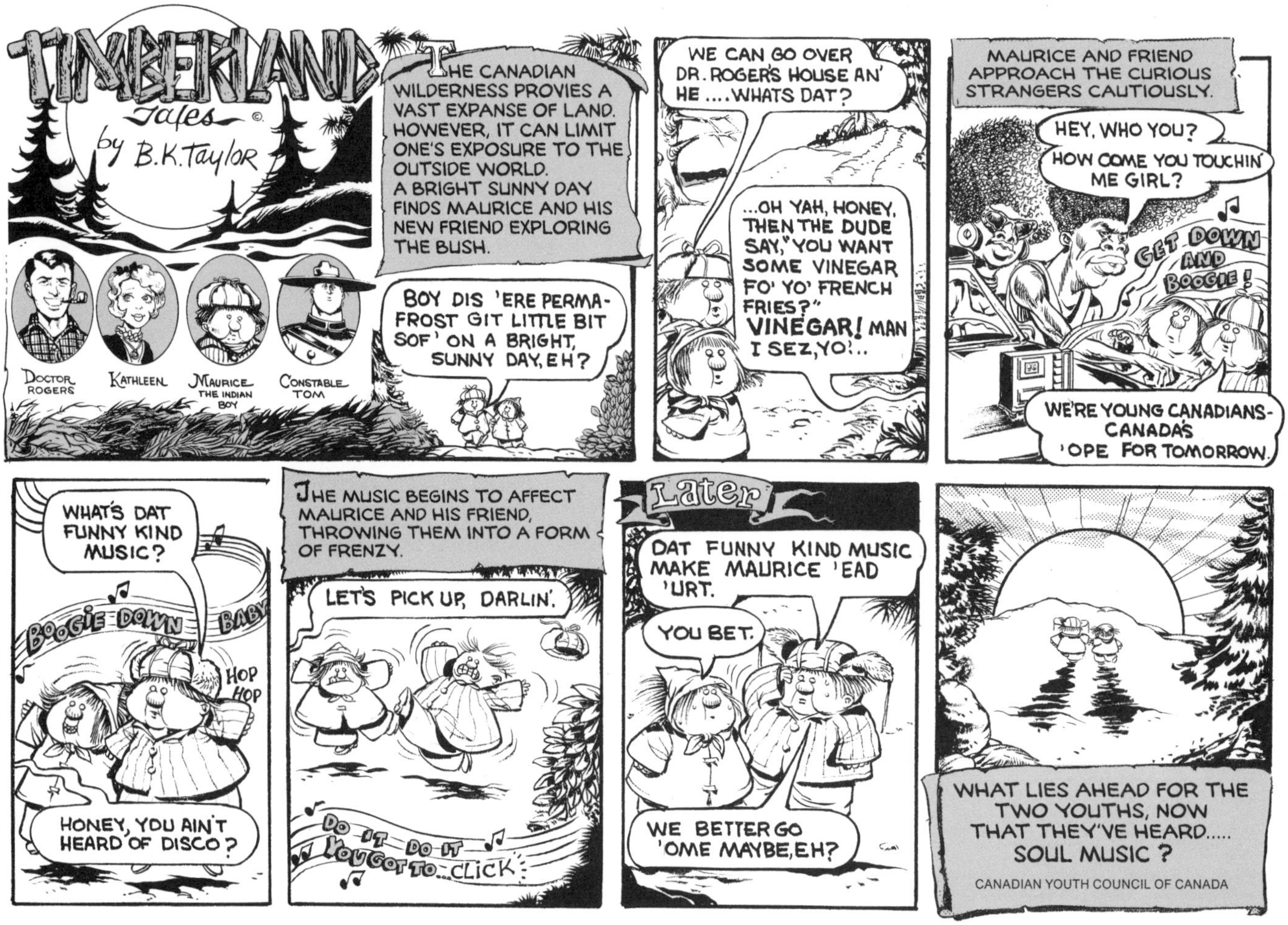

TIMBERLAND Tales ©
by B.K.Taylor
Doctor Rogers
Kathleen
Maurice the Indian boy
Constable Tom
The Canadian wilderness provies a vast expanse of land. However, it can limit one's exposure to the outside world. A bright sunny day finds Maurice and his new friend exploring the bush.
BOY DIS 'ERE PERMA-FROST GIT LITTLE BIT SOF' ON A BRIGHT, SUNNY DAY, EH?
WE CAN GO OVER DR. ROGER'S HOUSE AN' HE .... WHATS DAT?
...OH YAH, HONEY, THEN THE DUDE SAY, "YOU WANT SOME VINEGAR FO' YO' FRENCH FRIES?" VINEGAR! MAN I SEZ, YO'...
MAURICE AND FRIEND APPROACH THE CURIOUS STRANGERS CAUTIOUSLY.
HEY, WHO YOU?
HOW COME YOU TOUCHIN' ME GIRL?
GET DOWN AND BOOGIE!
WE'RE YOUNG CANADIANS- CANADA'S 'OPE FOR TOMORROW.
WHAT'S DAT FUNNY KIND MUSIC?
BOOGIE DOWN BABY
HOP HOP
HONEY, YOU AIN'T HEARD OF DISCO?
THE MUSIC BEGINS TO AFFECT MAURICE AND HIS FRIEND, THROWING THEM INTO A FORM OF FRENZY.
LET'S PICK UP, DARLIN'.
DO IT DO IT YOU GOT TO...CLICK
Later
DAT FUNNY KIND MUSIC MAKE MAURICE 'EAD 'URT.
YOU BET.
WE BETTER GO 'OME MAYBE, EH?
WHAT LIES AHEAD FOR THE TWO YOUTHS, NOW THAT THEY'VE HEARD..... SOUL MUSIC?
CANADIAN YOUTH COUNCIL OF CANADA

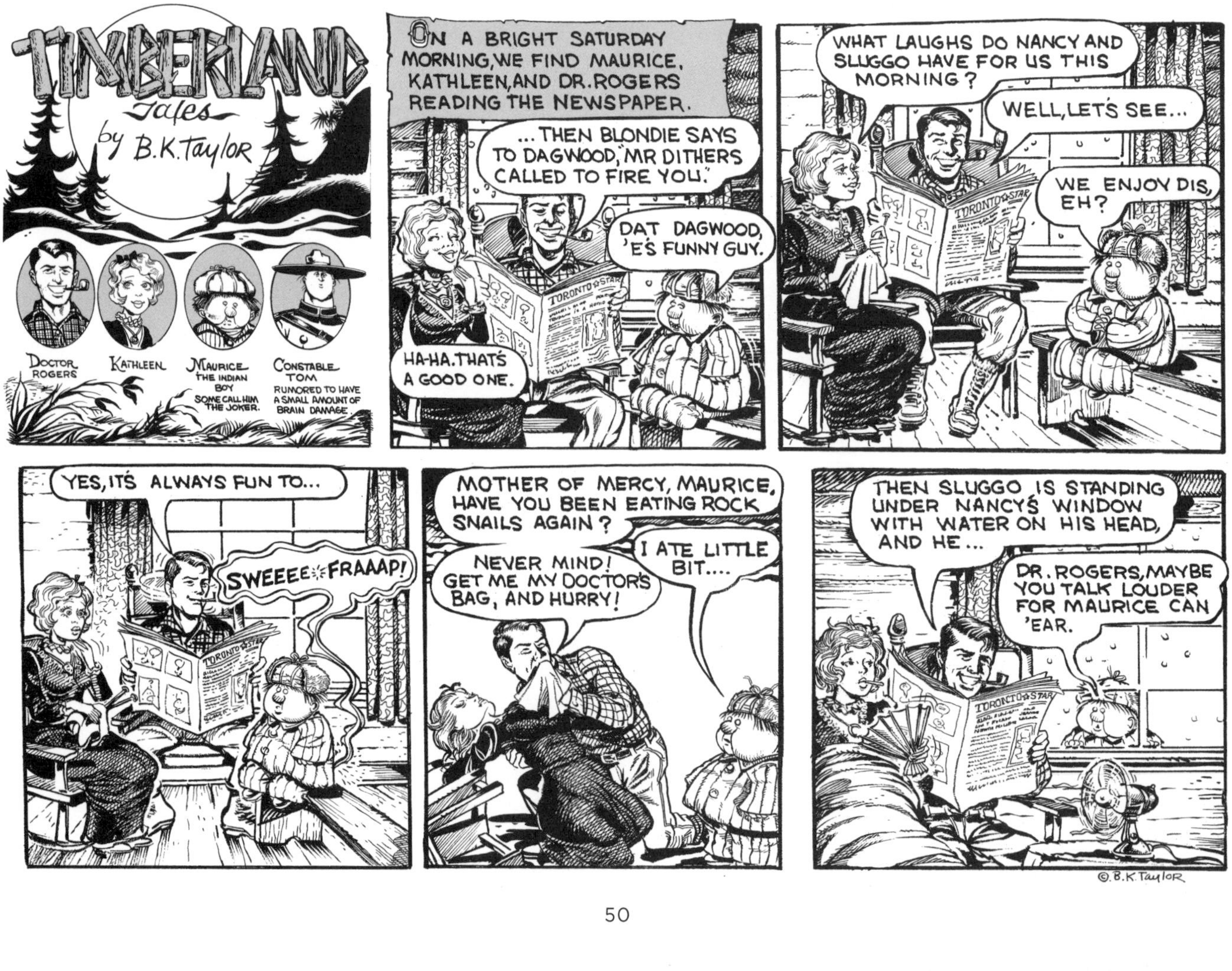

TIMBERLAND Tales
by B.K.Taylor
Doctor Rogers
Kathleen
Maurice the Indian boy some call him the joker.
Constable Tom rumored to have a small amount of brain damage.
ON A BRIGHT SATURDAY MORNING, WE FIND MAURICE, KATHLEEN, AND DR. ROGERS READING THE NEWSPAPER.
... THEN BLONDIE SAYS TO DAGWOOD, "MR DITHERS CALLED TO FIRE YOU."
DAT DAGWOOD, 'E'S FUNNY GUY.
HA-HA. THAT'S A GOOD ONE.
WHAT LAUGHS DO NANCY AND SLUGGO HAVE FOR US THIS MORNING?
WELL, LET'S SEE...
WE ENJOY DIS, EH?
YES, IT'S ALWAYS FUN TO...
SWEEEE FRAAAP!
MOTHER OF MERCY, MAURICE, HAVE YOU BEEN EATING ROCK SNAILS AGAIN?
NEVER MIND! GET ME MY DOCTOR'S BAG, AND HURRY!
I ATE LITTLE BIT....
THEN SLUGGO IS STANDING UNDER NANCY'S WINDOW WITH WATER ON HIS HEAD, AND HE ...
DR. ROGERS, MAYBE YOU TALK LOUDER FOR MAURICE CAN 'EAR.
©B.K.Taylor

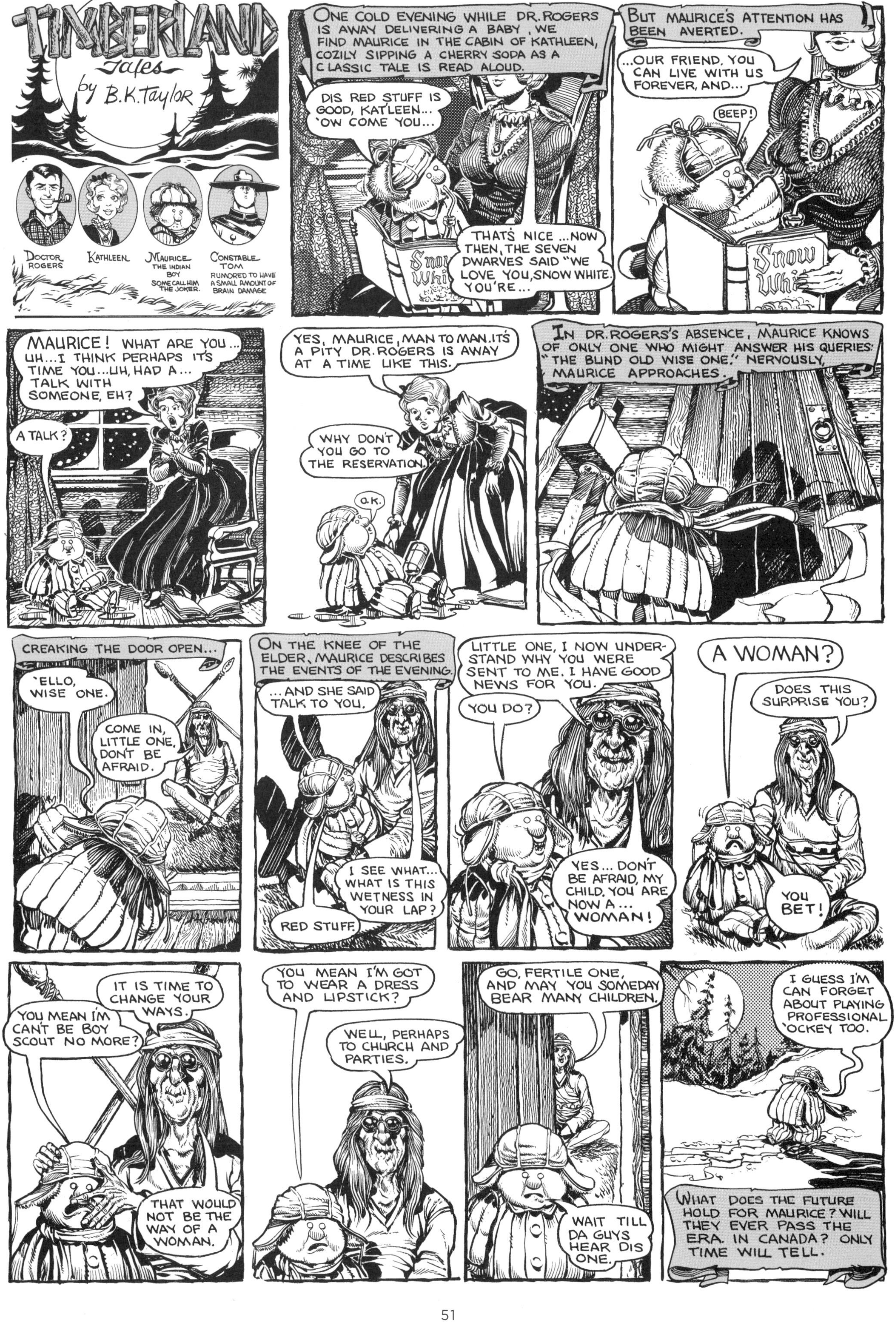
TIMBERLAND Tales
by B.K. Taylor
DOCTOR ROGERS
KATHLEEN
MAURICE THE INDIAN BOY SOME CALL HIM THE JOKER.
CONSTABLE TOM RUMORED TO HAVE A SMALL AMOUNT OF BRAIN DAMAGE
ONE COLD EVENING WHILE DR. ROGERS IS AWAY DELIVERING A BABY, WE FIND MAURICE IN THE CABIN OF KATHLEEN, COZILY SIPPING A CHERRY SODA AS A CLASSIC TALE IS READ ALOUD.
DIS RED STUFF IS GOOD, KAT'LEEN... 'OW COME YOU...
THAT'S NICE ...NOW THEN, THE SEVEN DWARVES SAID "WE LOVE YOU, SNOW WHITE. YOU'RE...
BUT MAURICE'S ATTENTION HAS BEEN AVERTED.
...OUR FRIEND, YOU CAN LIVE WITH US FOREVER, AND...
BEEP!
Snow White
MAURICE! WHAT ARE YOU... UH...I THINK PERHAPS IT'S TIME YOU...UH, HAD A... TALK WITH SOMEONE, EH?
A TALK?
YES, MAURICE, MAN TO MAN. IT'S A PITY DR. ROGERS IS AWAY AT A TIME LIKE THIS.
WHY DON'T YOU GO TO THE RESERVATION.
O.K.
IN DR. ROGERS'S ABSENCE, MAURICE KNOWS OF ONLY ONE WHO MIGHT ANSWER HIS QUERIES: "THE BLIND OLD WISE ONE." NERVOUSLY, MAURICE APPROACHES.
CREAKING THE DOOR OPEN...
`ELLO, WISE ONE.
COME IN, LITTLE ONE. DON'T BE AFRAID.
ON THE KNEE OF THE ELDER, MAURICE DESCRIBES THE EVENTS OF THE EVENING.
...AND SHE SAID TALK TO YOU.
I SEE WHAT... WHAT IS THIS WETNESS IN YOUR LAP?
RED STUFF.
LITTLE ONE, I NOW UNDERSTAND WHY YOU WERE SENT TO ME. I HAVE GOOD NEWS FOR YOU.
YOU DO?
YES... DON'T BE AFRAID, MY CHILD, YOU ARE NOW A ... WOMAN!
A WOMAN?
DOES THIS SURPRISE YOU?
YOU BET!
IT IS TIME TO CHANGE YOUR WAYS.
YOU MEAN I'M CAN'T BE BOY SCOUT NO MORE?
THAT WOULD NOT BE THE WAY OF A WOMAN.
YOU MEAN I'M GOT TO WEAR A DRESS AND LIPSTICK?
WELL, PERHAPS TO CHURCH AND PARTIES.
GO, FERTILE ONE, AND MAY YOU SOMEDAY BEAR MANY CHILDREN.
WAIT TILL DA GUYS HEAR DIS ONE.
I GUESS I'M CAN FORGET ABOUT PLAYING PROFESSIONAL 'OCKEY TOO.
WHAT DOES THE FUTURE HOLD FOR MAURICE? WILL THEY EVER PASS THE ERA. IN CANADA? ONLY TIME WILL TELL.

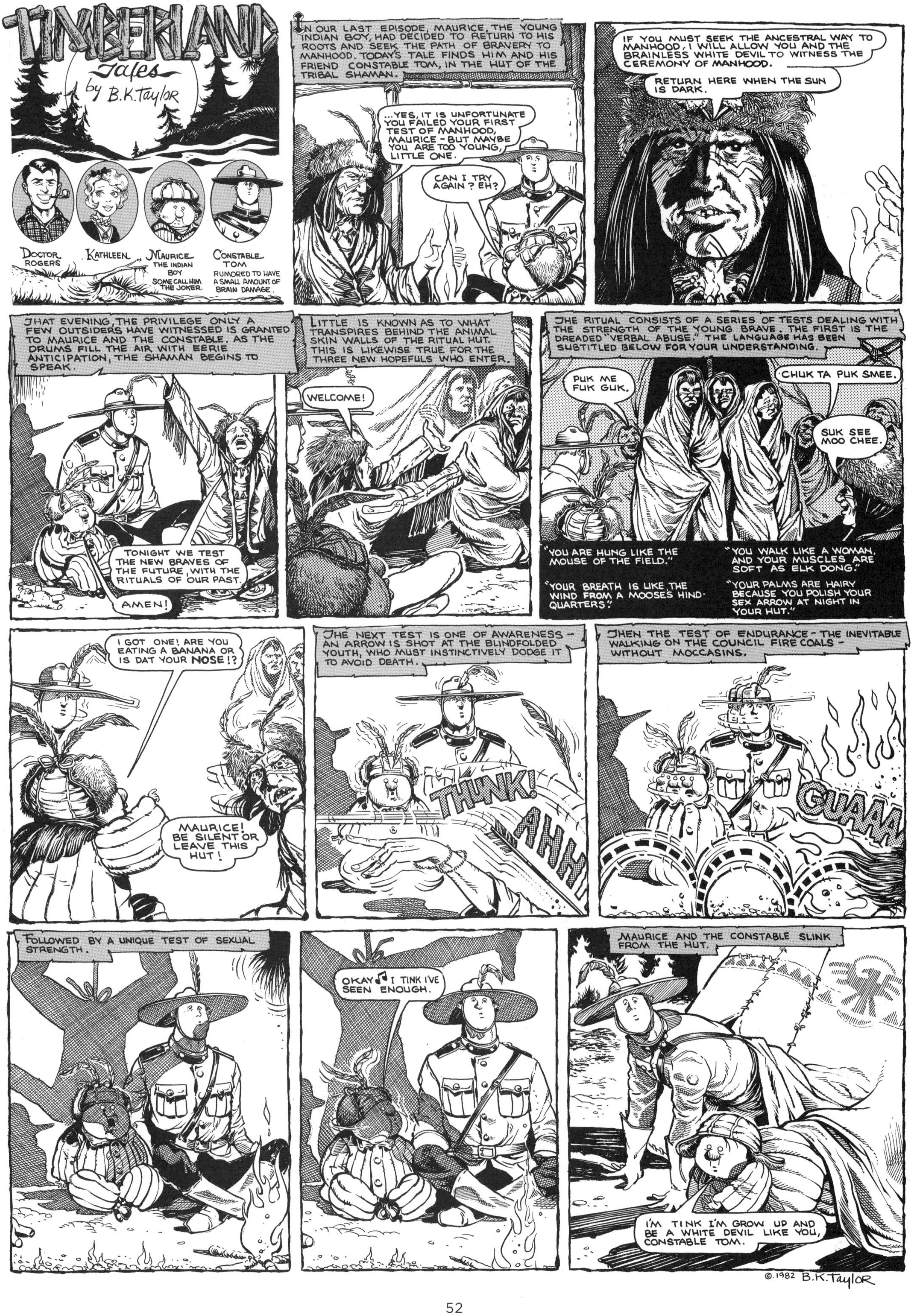
TIMBERLAND Tales by B.K.Taylor
DOCTOR ROGERS
KATHLEEN
MAURICE THE INDIAN BOY SOME CALL HIM THE JOKER.
CONSTABLE TOM RUMORED TO HAVE A SMALL AMOUNT OF BRAIN DAMAGE.
IN OUR LAST EPISODE, MAURICE, THE YOUNG INDIAN BOY, HAD DECIDED TO RETURN TO HIS ROOTS AND SEEK THE PATH OF BRAVERY TO MANHOOD. TODAY'S TALE FINDS HIM AND HIS FRIEND CONSTABLE TOM, IN THE HUT OF THE TRIBAL SHAMAN.
...YES, IT IS UNFORTUNATE YOU FAILED YOUR FIRST TEST OF MANHOOD, MAURICE - BUT MAYBE YOU ARE TOO YOUNG, LITTLE ONE.
CAN I TRY AGAIN? EH?
IF YOU MUST SEEK THE ANCESTRAL WAY TO MANHOOD, I WILL ALLOW YOU AND THE BRAINLESS WHITE DEVIL TO WITNESS THE CEREMONY OF MANHOOD.
RETURN HERE WHEN THE SUN IS DARK.
THAT EVENING, THE PRIVILEGE ONLY A FEW OUTSIDERS HAVE WITNESSED IS GRANTED TO MAURICE AND THE CONSTABLE. AS THE DRUMS FILL THE AIR WITH EERIE ANTICIPATION, THE SHAMAN BEGINS TO SPEAK.
TONIGHT WE TEST THE NEW BRAVES OF THE FUTURE, WITH THE RITUALS OF OUR PAST.
AMEN!
LITTLE IS KNOWN AS TO WHAT TRANSPIRES BEHIND THE ANIMAL SKIN WALLS OF THE RITUAL HUT. THIS IS LIKEWISE TRUE FOR THE THREE NEW HOPEFULS WHO ENTER.
WELCOME!
THE RITUAL CONSISTS OF A SERIES OF TESTS DEALING WITH THE STRENGTH OF THE YOUNG BRAVE. THE FIRST IS THE DREADED "VERBAL ABUSE." THE LANGUAGE HAS BEEN SUBTITLED BELOW FOR YOUR UNDERSTANDING.
PUK ME FUK GUK.
CHUK TA PUK SMEE.
SUK SEE MOO CHEE.
"YOU ARE HUNG LIKE THE MOUSE OF THE FIELD."
"YOUR BREATH IS LIKE THE WIND FROM A MOOSES HIND-QUARTERS."
"YOU WALK LIKE A WOMAN, AND YOUR MUSCLES ARE SOFT AS ELK DONG."
"YOUR PALMS ARE HAIRY BECAUSE YOU POLISH YOUR SEX ARROW AT NIGHT IN YOUR HUT."
I GOT ONE! ARE YOU EATING A BANANA OR IS DAT YOUR NOSE!?
MAURICE! BE SILENT OR LEAVE THIS HUT!
THE NEXT TEST IS ONE OF AWARENESS - AN ARROW IS SHOT AT THE BLINDFOLDED YOUTH, WHO MUST INSTINCTIVELY DODGE IT TO AVOID DEATH.
THUNK!
AHH
THEN THE TEST OF ENDURANCE - THE INEVITABLE WALKING ON THE COUNCIL FIRE COALS - WITHOUT MOCCASINS.
GUAAA
FOLLOWED BY A UNIQUE TEST OF SEXUAL STRENGTH.
OKAY♪ I TINK I'VE SEEN ENOUGH.
MAURICE AND THE CONSTABLE SLINK FROM THE HUT.
I'M TINK I'M GROW UP AND BE A WHITE DEVIL LIKE YOU, CONSTABLE TOM.
©.1982 B.K.Taylor

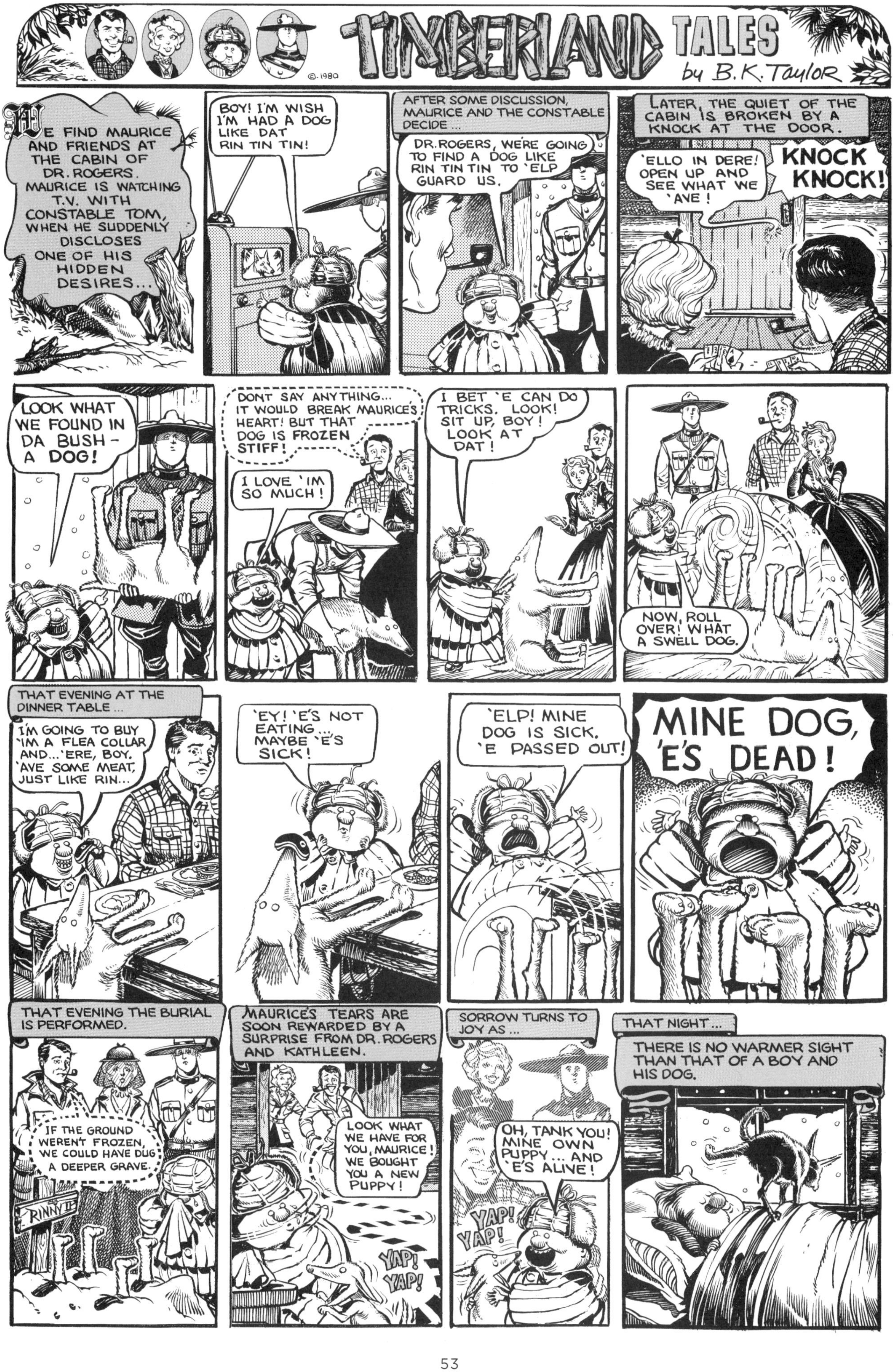
TIMBERLAND TALES
by B.K. Taylor
©. 1980
WE FIND MAURICE AND FRIENDS AT THE CABIN OF DR. ROGERS. MAURICE IS WATCHING T.V. WITH CONSTABLE TOM, WHEN HE SUDDENLY DISCLOSES ONE OF HIS HIDDEN DESIRES...
BOY! I'M WISH I'M HAD A DOG LIKE DAT RIN TIN TIN!
AFTER SOME DISCUSSION, MAURICE AND THE CONSTABLE DECIDE ...
DR. ROGERS, WE'RE GOING TO FIND A DOG LIKE RIN TIN TIN TO 'ELP GUARD US.
LATER, THE QUIET OF THE CABIN IS BROKEN BY A KNOCK AT THE DOOR.
'ELLO IN DERE! OPEN UP AND SEE WHAT WE 'AVE!
KNOCK KNOCK!
LOOK WHAT WE FOUND IN DA BUSH - A DOG!
DONT SAY ANYTHING... IT WOULD BREAK MAURICES HEART! BUT THAT DOG IS FROZEN STIFF!
I LOVE 'IM SO MUCH!
I BET 'E CAN DO TRICKS. LOOK! SIT UP, BOY! LOOK AT DAT!
NOW, ROLL OVER! WHAT A SWELL DOG.
THAT EVENING AT THE DINNER TABLE ...
I'M GOING TO BUY 'IM A FLEA COLLAR AND... 'ERE, BOY. 'AVE SOME MEAT, JUST LIKE RIN...
'EY! 'E'S NOT EATING... MAYBE 'E'S SICK!
'ELP! MINE DOG IS SICK. 'E PASSED OUT!
MINE DOG, 'E'S DEAD!
THAT EVENING THE BURIAL IS PERFORMED.
IF THE GROUND WEREN'T FROZEN, WE COULD HAVE DUG A DEEPER GRAVE.
RINNY II
MAURICE'S TEARS ARE SOON REWARDED BY A SURPRISE FROM DR. ROGERS AND KATHLEEN.
LOOK WHAT WE HAVE FOR YOU, MAURICE! WE BOUGHT YOU A NEW PUPPY!
YAP! YAP!
SORROW TURNS TO JOY AS ...
OH, TANK YOU! MINE OWN PUPPY... AND 'E'S ALIVE!
YAP! YAP!
THAT NIGHT...
THERE IS NO WARMER SIGHT THAN THAT OF A BOY AND HIS DOG.

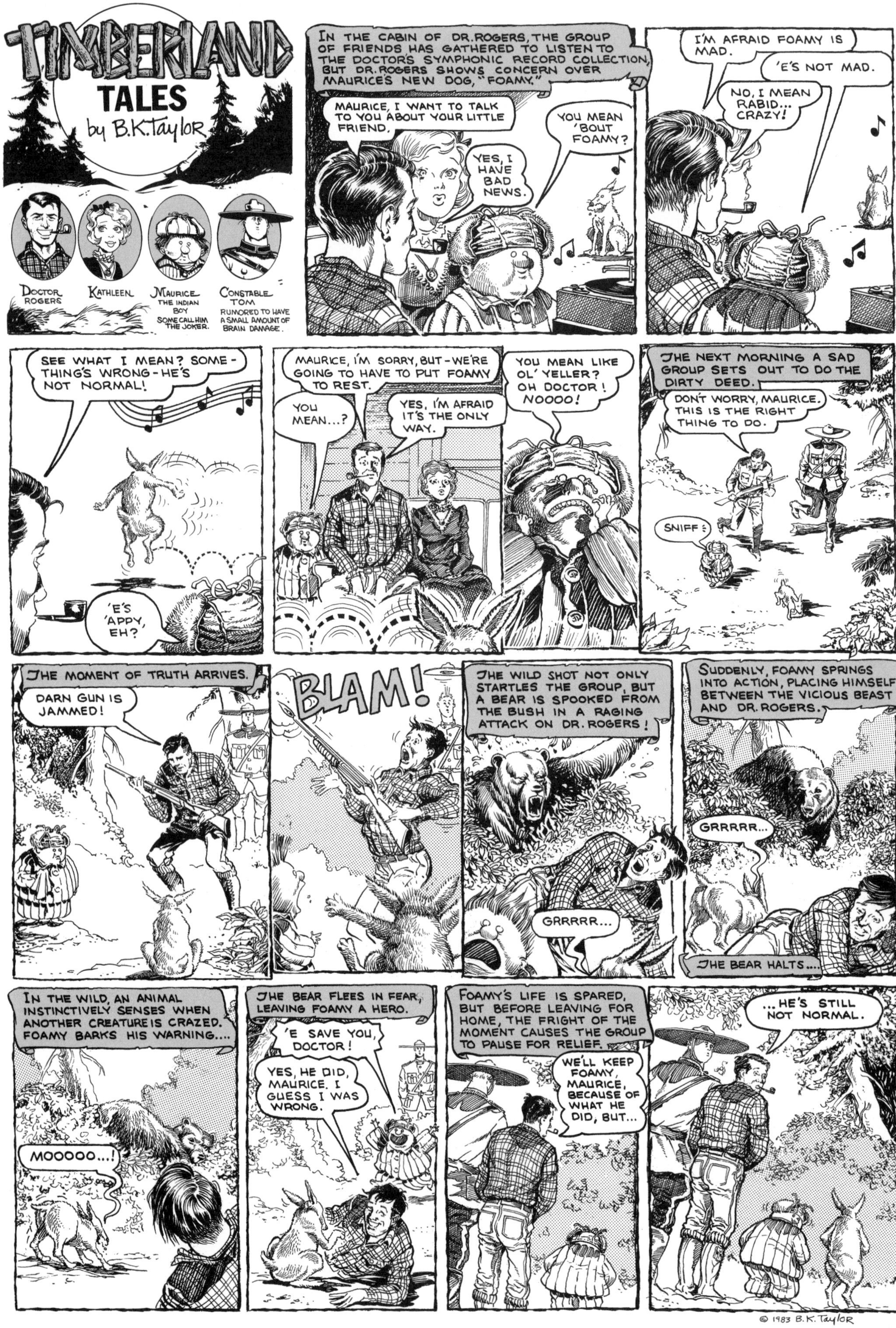
TIMBERLAND TALES
by B.K. Taylor
DOCTOR ROGERS
KATHLEEN
MAURICE THE INDIAN BOY SOME CALL HIM THE JOKER.
CONSTABLE TOM RUMORED TO HAVE A SMALL AMOUNT OF BRAIN DAMAGE.
IN THE CABIN OF DR. ROGERS, THE GROUP OF FRIENDS HAS GATHERED TO LISTEN TO THE DOCTOR'S SYMPHONIC RECORD COLLECTION, BUT DR. ROGERS SHOWS CONCERN OVER MAURICE'S NEW DOG, "FOAMY."
MAURICE, I WANT TO TALK TO YOU ABOUT YOUR LITTLE FRIEND.
YOU MEAN 'BOUT FOAMY?
YES, I HAVE BAD NEWS.
I'M AFRAID FOAMY IS MAD.
'E'S NOT MAD.
NO, I MEAN RABID... CRAZY!
SEE WHAT I MEAN? SOMETHING'S WRONG - HE'S NOT NORMAL!
'E'S 'APPY, EH?
MAURICE, I'M SORRY, BUT - WE'RE GOING TO HAVE TO PUT FOAMY TO REST.
YOU MEAN...?
YES, I'M AFRAID IT'S THE ONLY WAY.
YOU MEAN LIKE OL' YELLER? OH DOCTOR! NOOOO!
THE NEXT MORNING A SAD GROUP SETS OUT TO DO THE DIRTY DEED.
DON'T WORRY, MAURICE. THIS IS THE RIGHT THING TO DO.
SNIFF
THE MOMENT OF TRUTH ARRIVES.
DARN GUN IS JAMMED!
BLAM!
THE WILD SHOT NOT ONLY STARTLES THE GROUP, BUT A BEAR IS SPOOKED FROM THE BUSH IN A RAGING ATTACK ON DR. ROGERS!
GRRRRR...
SUDDENLY, FOAMY SPRINGS INTO ACTION, PLACING HIMSELF BETWEEN THE VICIOUS BEAST AND DR. ROGERS.
GRRRRR...
THE BEAR HALTS....
IN THE WILD, AN ANIMAL INSTINCTIVELY SENSES WHEN ANOTHER CREATURE IS CRAZED. FOAMY BARKS HIS WARNING....
MOOOOO...!
THE BEAR FLEES IN FEAR, LEAVING FOAMY A HERO.
'E SAVE YOU, DOCTOR!
YES, HE DID, MAURICE. I GUESS I WAS WRONG.
FOAMY'S LIFE IS SPARED, BUT BEFORE LEAVING FOR HOME, THE FRIGHT OF THE MOMENT CAUSES THE GROUP TO PAUSE FOR RELIEF.
WE'LL KEEP FOAMY, MAURICE, BECAUSE OF WHAT HE DID, BUT...
...HE'S STILL NOT NORMAL.

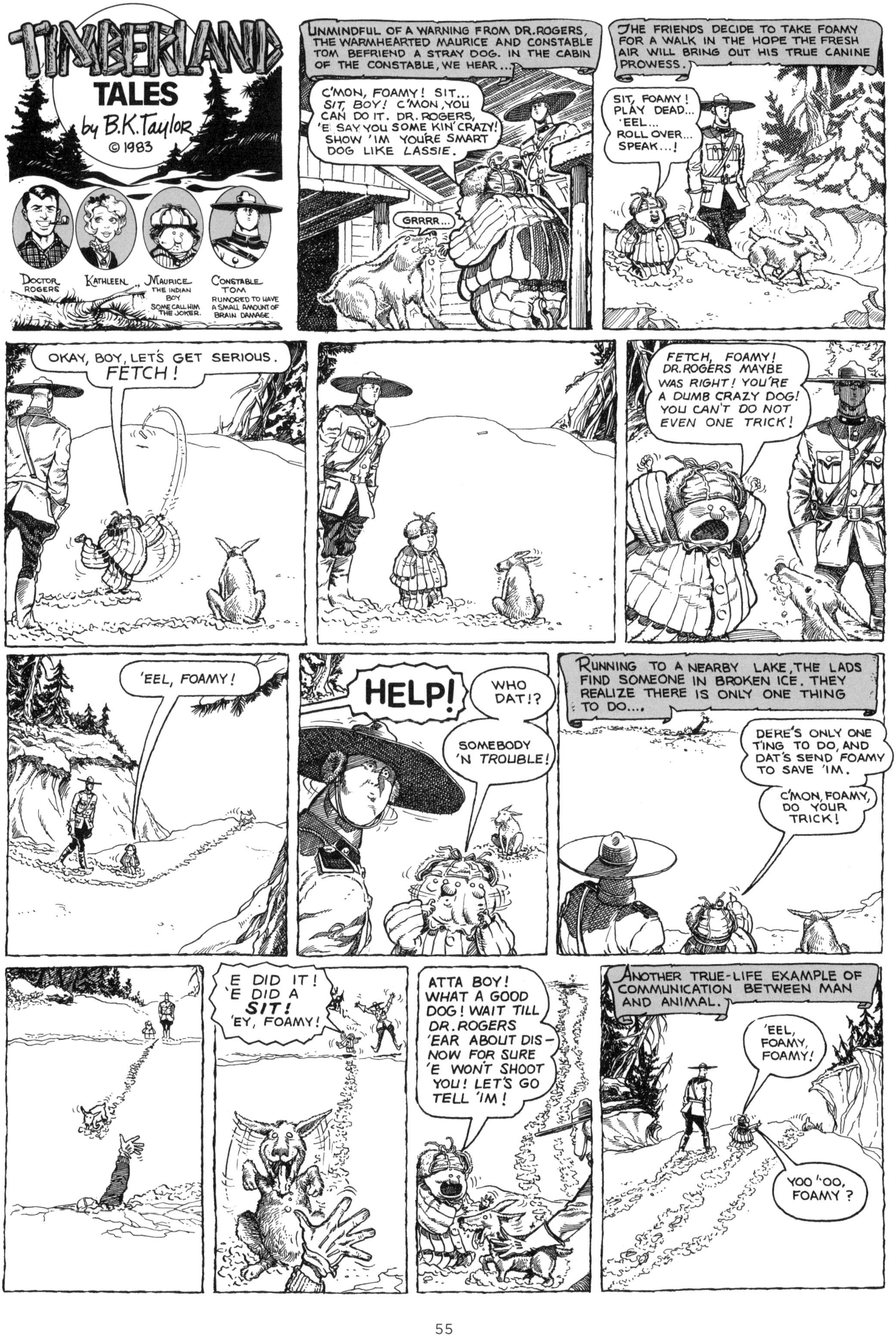
TIMBERLAND TALES
by B.K. Taylor
© 1983
DOCTOR ROGERS
KATHLEEN
MAURICE THE INDIAN BOY SOME CALL HIM THE JOKER.
CONSTABLE TOM RUMORED TO HAVE A SMALL AMOUNT OF BRAIN DAMAGE.
UNMINDFUL OF A WARNING FROM DR. ROGERS, THE WARMHEARTED MAURICE AND CONSTABLE TOM BEFRIEND A STRAY DOG. IN THE CABIN OF THE CONSTABLE, WE HEAR...
C'MON, FOAMY! SIT... SIT, BOY! C'MON, YOU CAN DO IT. DR. ROGERS, 'E SAY YOU SOME KIN' CRAZY! SHOW 'IM YOU'RE SMART DOG LIKE LASSIE.
GRRRR...
THE FRIENDS DECIDE TO TAKE FOAMY FOR A WALK IN THE HOPE THE FRESH AIR WILL BRING OUT HIS TRUE CANINE PROWESS.
SIT, FOAMY! PLAY DEAD... 'EEL... ROLL OVER... SPEAK...!
OKAY, BOY, LET'S GET SERIOUS. FETCH!
FETCH, FOAMY! DR. ROGERS MAYBE WAS RIGHT! YOU'RE A DUMB CRAZY DOG! YOU CAN'T DO NOT EVEN ONE TRICK!
'EEL, FOAMY!
HELP!
WHO DAT!?
SOMEBODY 'N TROUBLE!
RUNNING TO A NEARBY LAKE, THE LADS FIND SOMEONE IN BROKEN ICE. THEY REALIZE THERE IS ONLY ONE THING TO DO....
DERE'S ONLY ONE TING TO DO, AND DAT'S SEND FOAMY TO SAVE 'IM.
C'MON, FOAMY, DO YOUR TRICK!
'E DID IT! 'E DID A SIT! 'EY, FOAMY!
ATTA BOY! WHAT A GOOD DOG! WAIT TILL DR. ROGERS 'EAR ABOUT DIS — NOW FOR SURE 'E WON'T SHOOT YOU! LET'S GO TELL 'IM!
ANOTHER TRUE-LIFE EXAMPLE OF COMMUNICATION BETWEEN MAN AND ANIMAL.
'EEL, FOAMY, FOAMY!
YOO 'OO, FOAMY?

TIMBERLAND TALES
by B.K. Taylor

DOCTOR ROGERS — KATHLEEN — MAURICE THE INDIAN BOY SOME CALL HIM THE JOKER. — CONSTABLE TOM RUMORED TO HAVE A SMALL AMOUNT OF BRAIN DAMAGE.

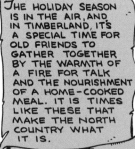

THE HOLIDAY SEASON IS IN THE AIR, AND IN TIMBERLAND, IT'S A SPECIAL TIME FOR OLD FRIENDS TO GATHER TOGETHER BY THE WARMTH OF A FIRE FOR TALK AND THE NOURISHMENT OF A HOME-COOKED MEAL. IT IS TIMES LIKE THESE THAT MAKE THE NORTH COUNTRY WHAT IT IS.

LET'S LOOK IN AND EXPERIENCE A TASTE OF THIS GLORIOUS OCCASION. IN THE CABIN OF KATHLEEN, WE HEAR...

WELL, LOOK WHAT THE CAT DRAGGED IN, EH? HEH-HEH!

MERRY CHRISTMAS!

THE FEAST WILL BE READY SOON — I HOPE YOU CAME WITH AN EMPTY STOMACH!

YOU BET! AND I'M BE READY FOR CHRISTMAS SHENANIGANS, TOO!

THE FIRST EVENT OF THE EVENING WAS A SING-ALONG, WITH ARMS ENTWINED, SWAYING BACK AND FORTH BY A CRACKLING FIRE.

♪ KATHY PATHY PO-PATHY ♪ BONANA-PANA PO-PATHY...

NEXT, OF COURSE, WAS THE DECORATING OF THE TREE...

THEN A HEATED GAME OF CHARADES.

MOON RIVER?

THE OLD GRAY MARE?

DAT'S RIGHT!

AT LAST, WHAT EVERYONE HAS BEEN WAITING FOR... THE CHRISTMAS MEAL.

IT'S SO NICE HAVING YOU ALL HERE TOGETHER — ESPECIALLY YOU, CONSTABLE TOM. IT'S BEEN SUCH A LONG TIME SINCE YOU'VE JOINED US FOR DINNER.

I CAN'T WAIT!

ME TOO!

IT MAY BE COLD AND SNOWY OUTSIDE, BUT WE'RE WARM AND COZY IN HERE, AREN'T WE?

INDEED WE ARE, AND WITH A FINE MEAL BEFORE US, KATHLEEN!

LET'S EAT, EH?

KATHLEEN TURNS TO CONSTABLE TOM WITH A SPECIAL REQUEST...

WOULD YOU CARE TO SAY THE BLESSING THIS EVENING, CONSTABLE TOM?

NOW I LAY ME DOWN TO SLEEP, I PRAY THEE FOR MY SOUL TO KEEP ... AMEN.

... WOULD ANYONE CARE FOR DESSERT?

GRUMBLE

Happy Holidays

1981 © B.K. Taylor

56

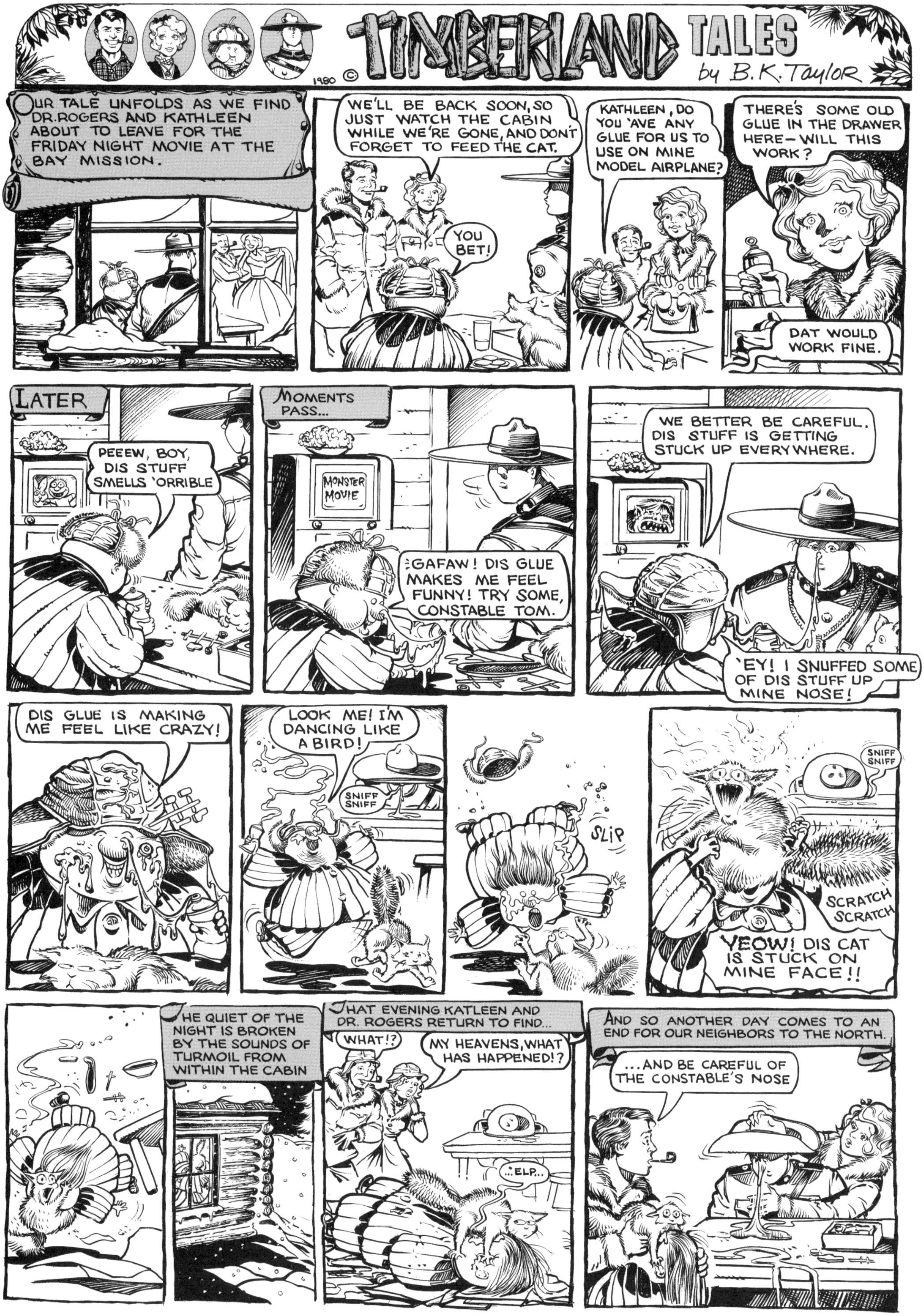
TIMBERLAND TALES
1980 ©
by B.K. Taylor
OUR TALE UNFOLDS AS WE FIND DR. ROGERS AND KATHLEEN ABOUT TO LEAVE FOR THE FRIDAY NIGHT MOVIE AT THE BAY MISSION.
WE'LL BE BACK SOON, SO JUST WATCH THE CABIN WHILE WE'RE GONE, AND DON'T FORGET TO FEED THE CAT.
YOU BET!
KATHLEEN, DO YOU 'AVE ANY GLUE FOR US TO USE ON MINE MODEL AIRPLANE?
THERE'S SOME OLD GLUE IN THE DRAWER HERE— WILL THIS WORK?
DAT WOULD WORK FINE.
LATER
PEEEW, BOY, DIS STUFF SMELLS 'ORRIBLE
MOMENTS PASS...
MONSTER MOVIE
GAFAW! DIS GLUE MAKES ME FEEL FUNNY! TRY SOME, CONSTABLE TOM.
WE BETTER BE CAREFUL. DIS STUFF IS GETTING STUCK UP EVERYWHERE.
'EY! I SNUFFED SOME OF DIS STUFF UP MINE NOSE!
DIS GLUE IS MAKING ME FEEL LIKE CRAZY!
LOOK ME! I'M DANCING LIKE A BIRD!
SNIFF SNIFF
SLIP
SNIFF SNIFF
SCRATCH SCRATCH
YEOW! DIS CAT IS STUCK ON MINE FACE!!
THE QUIET OF THE NIGHT IS BROKEN BY THE SOUNDS OF TURMOIL FROM WITHIN THE CABIN
THAT EVENING KATLEEN AND DR. ROGERS RETURN TO FIND...
WHAT!?
MY HEAVENS, WHAT HAS HAPPENED!?
...ELP...
AND SO ANOTHER DAY COMES TO AN END FOR OUR NEIGHBORS TO THE NORTH.
...AND BE CAREFUL OF THE CONSTABLE'S NOSE

TIMBERLAND Tales
by B.K. Taylor
DOCTOR ROGERS
KATHLEEN
MAURICE THE INDIAN BOY SOME CALL HIM THE JOKER.
CONSTABLE TOM RUMORED TO HAVE A SMALL AMOUNT OF BRAIN DAMAGE.
THROUGH THE PAGES OF HISTORY, NEVER HAS THERE BEEN A CLOSER RELATIONSHIP BETWEEN TWO NATIONS THAN THAT OF CANADA AND THE U.S.A. OTHER NATIONS MARVEL AT THIS KINSHIP, WHICH, QUITE SIMPLY, IS BASED ON THE PEOPLE – THE SMALL ACTS OF FRIENDSHIP AND CONCERN FOR ONE ANOTHER.
HERE IS ONE SMALL EXAMPLE:
NIK NAK PADDY W'AK, GIVE DAT DOG A BONE.
HELP!
OVER HERE. HELP!
W'AT YOU DOING DOWN DERE, MISTER?
THANK GOD YOU FOUND ME!
YOU BET! YOU LOOK MAYBE YOU'RE IN SOME KIND TROUBLE, EH? 'EY, ARE YOU ONE DEM YANKEE GUYS?
YES, YES, NOW WILL YOU PLEASE GRAB THIS GUIDE-LINE AND HELP PULL ME UP?
OKEY DOKEY, MAURICE GOT IT NOW!
GOOD, NOW HOLD IT TIGHT.
O.K., 'ANG ON! 'EY, YOU GUYS STILL GOT DAT PRESIDENT DAT DOES DAT FUNNY TING?
WHAT? HEY, LISTEN, JUST HOLD THE LINE, OK?
O.K., BUT YOU STILL GOT HIM?
JESUS CHRIST! WHAT PRESIDENT ARE YOU TALKING ABOUT- CARTER?
NO, DAT GUY DAT GOES LIKE DIS....
NO DON'T YOU DUMB SHIT
NIK NAK PADDY W'AK, GIVE DAT DOG A BONE.

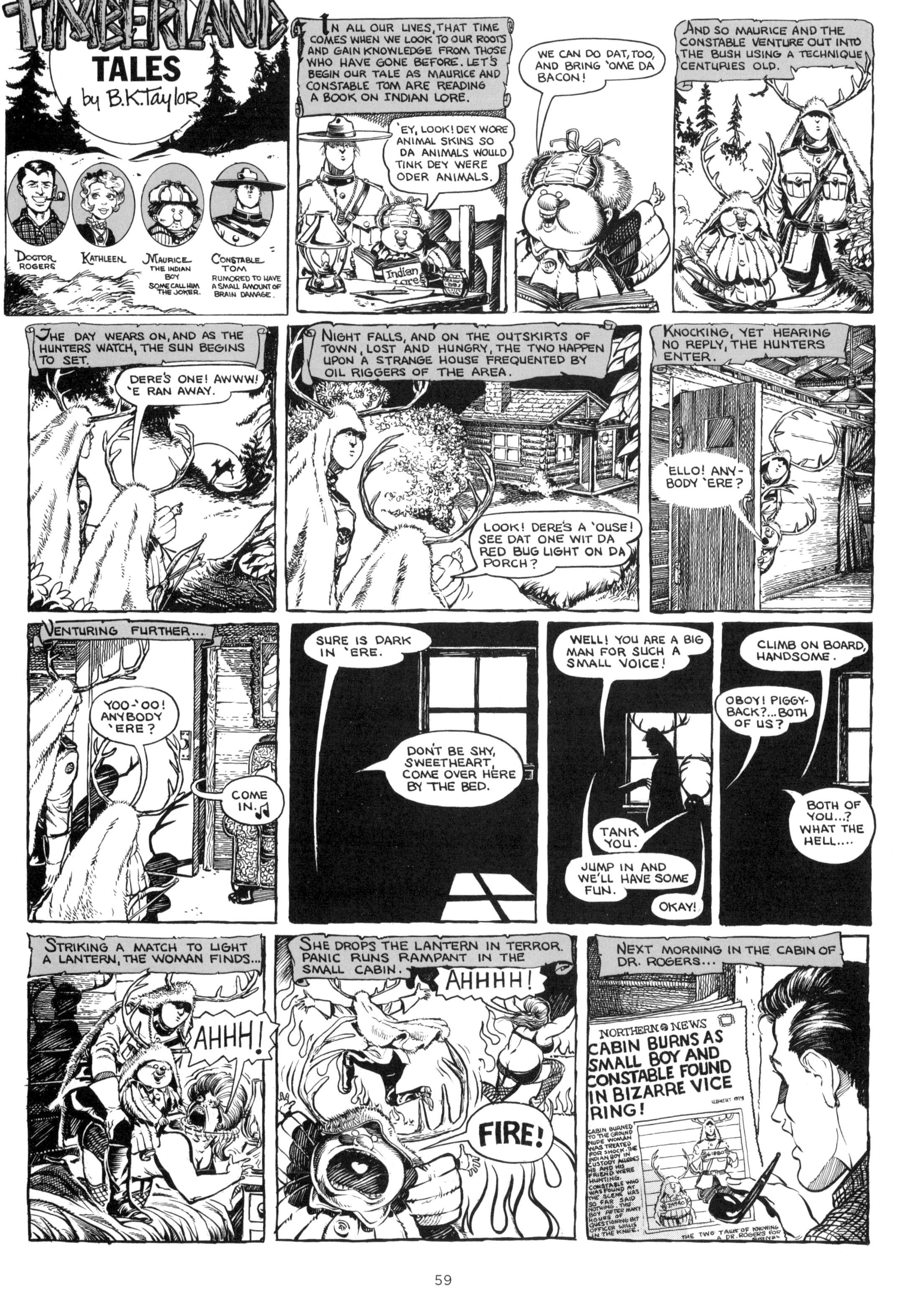
TIMBERLAND TALES
by B.K. Taylor
DOCTOR ROGERS
KATHLEEN
MAURICE THE INDIAN BOY SOME CALL HIM THE JOKER.
CONSTABLE TOM RUMORED TO HAVE A SMALL AMOUNT OF BRAIN DAMAGE.
IN ALL OUR LIVES, THAT TIME COMES WHEN WE LOOK TO OUR ROOTS AND GAIN KNOWLEDGE FROM THOSE WHO HAVE GONE BEFORE. LET'S BEGIN OUR TALE AS MAURICE AND CONSTABLE TOM ARE READING A BOOK ON INDIAN LORE.
'EY, LOOK! DEY WORE ANIMAL SKINS SO DA ANIMALS WOULD TINK DEY WERE ODER ANIMALS.
Indian Lore
WE CAN DO DAT, TOO, AND BRING 'OME DA BACON!
AND SO MAURICE AND THE CONSTABLE VENTURE OUT INTO THE BUSH USING A TECHNIQUE CENTURIES OLD.
THE DAY WEARS ON, AND AS THE HUNTERS WATCH, THE SUN BEGINS TO SET.
DERE'S ONE! AWWW! 'E RAN AWAY.
NIGHT FALLS, AND ON THE OUTSKIRTS OF TOWN, LOST AND HUNGRY, THE TWO HAPPEN UPON A STRANGE HOUSE FREQUENTED BY OIL RIGGERS OF THE AREA.
LOOK! DERE'S A 'OUSE! SEE DAT ONE WIT DA RED BUG LIGHT ON DA PORCH?
KNOCKING, YET HEARING NO REPLY, THE HUNTERS ENTER.
'ELLO! ANY-BODY 'ERE?
VENTURING FURTHER...
YOO-'OO! ANYBODY 'ERE?
COME IN.♪
SURE IS DARK IN 'ERE.
DON'T BE SHY, SWEETHEART, COME OVER HERE BY THE BED.
WELL! YOU ARE A BIG MAN FOR SUCH A SMALL VOICE!
TANK YOU.
JUMP IN AND WE'LL HAVE SOME FUN.
OKAY!
CLIMB ON BOARD, HANDSOME.
OBOY! PIGGY-BACK?...BOTH OF US?
BOTH OF YOU...? WHAT THE HELL....
STRIKING A MATCH TO LIGHT A LANTERN, THE WOMAN FINDS...
AHHH!
SHE DROPS THE LANTERN IN TERROR. PANIC RUNS RAMPANT IN THE SMALL CABIN.
AHHHH!
FIRE!
NEXT MORNING IN THE CABIN OF DR. ROGERS...
NORTHERN NEWS
CABIN BURNS AS SMALL BOY AND CONSTABLE FOUND IN BIZARRE VICE RING!
CABIN BURNED TO THE GROUND NUDE WOMAN WAS TREATED FOR SHOCK. THE INDIAN BOY IN CUSTODY ALLEGES HE AND HIS FRIEND WERE HUNTING. CONSTABLE WHO WAS FOUND AT THE SCENE HAS SO FAR SAID NOTHING. THE BOY AFTER MANY HOURS OF QUESTIONING BIT OFFICER WILLIS IN THE KNEE.
61880
24940
THE TWO TALK OF KNOWING A DR. ROGERS FOR

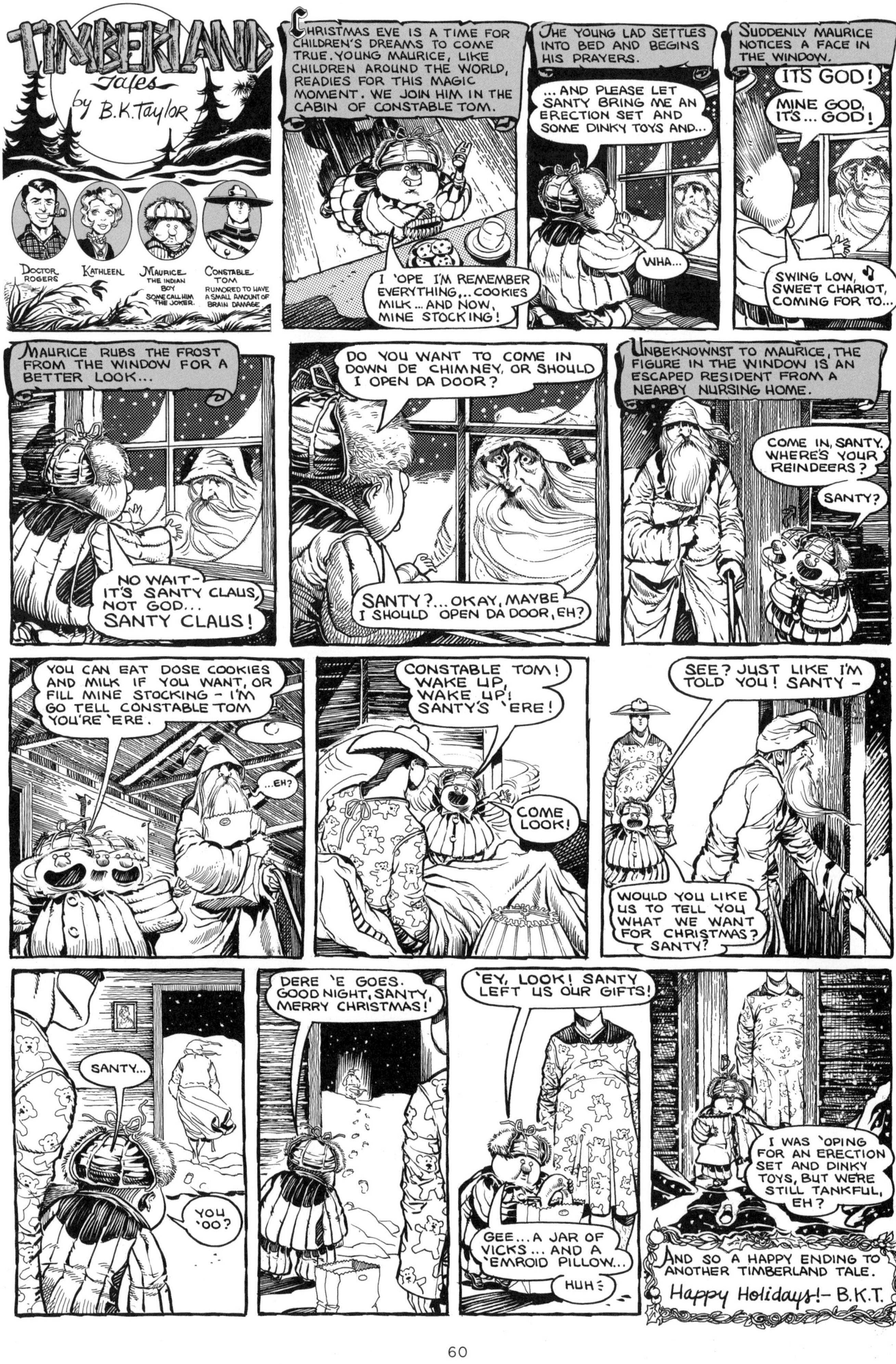
TIMBERLAND Tales
by B.K.Taylor
DOCTOR ROGERS
KATHLEEN
MAURICE THE INDIAN BOY SOME CALL HIM THE JOKER.
CONSTABLE TOM RUMORED TO HAVE A SMALL AMOUNT OF BRAIN DAMAGE
CHRISTMAS EVE IS A TIME FOR CHILDREN'S DREAMS TO COME TRUE. YOUNG MAURICE, LIKE CHILDREN AROUND THE WORLD, READIES FOR THIS MAGIC MOMENT. WE JOIN HIM IN THE CABIN OF CONSTABLE TOM.
I 'OPE I'M REMEMBER EVERYTHING,.. COOKIES MILK ... AND NOW, MINE STOCKING!
THE YOUNG LAD SETTLES INTO BED AND BEGINS HIS PRAYERS.
...AND PLEASE LET SANTY BRING ME AN ERECTION SET AND SOME DINKY TOYS AND...
WHA...
SUDDENLY MAURICE NOTICES A FACE IN THE WINDOW.
ITS GOD!
MINE GOD, ITS... GOD!
SWING LOW, SWEET CHARIOT, COMING FOR TO...
MAURICE RUBS THE FROST FROM THE WINDOW FOR A BETTER LOOK...
NO WAIT- IT'S SANTY CLAUS, NOT GOD... SANTY CLAUS!
DO YOU WANT TO COME IN DOWN DE CHIMNEY, OR SHOULD I OPEN DA DOOR?
SANTY?... OKAY, MAYBE I SHOULD OPEN DA DOOR, EH?
UNBEKNOWNST TO MAURICE, THE FIGURE IN THE WINDOW IS AN ESCAPED RESIDENT FROM A NEARBY NURSING HOME.
COME IN, SANTY. WHERE'S YOUR REINDEERS?
SANTY?
YOU CAN EAT DOSE COOKIES AND MILK IF YOU WANT, OR FILL MINE STOCKING - I'M GO TELL CONSTABLE TOM YOU'RE 'ERE.
...EH?
CONSTABLE TOM! WAKE UP, WAKE UP! SANTY'S 'ERE!
COME LOOK!
SEE? JUST LIKE I'M TOLD YOU! SANTY -
WOULD YOU LIKE US TO TELL YOU WHAT WE WANT FOR CHRISTMAS? SANTY?
SANTY...
YOU 'OO?
DERE 'E GOES. GOOD NIGHT, SANTY, MERRY CHRISTMAS!
'EY, LOOK! SANTY LEFT US OUR GIFTS!
GEE... A JAR OF VICKS... AND A 'EMROID PILLOW...
HUH?
I WAS 'OPING FOR AN ERECTION SET AND DINKY TOYS, BUT WE'RE STILL TANKFUL, EH?
AND SO A HAPPY ENDING TO ANOTHER TIMBERLAND TALE.
Happy Holidays!- B.K.T.

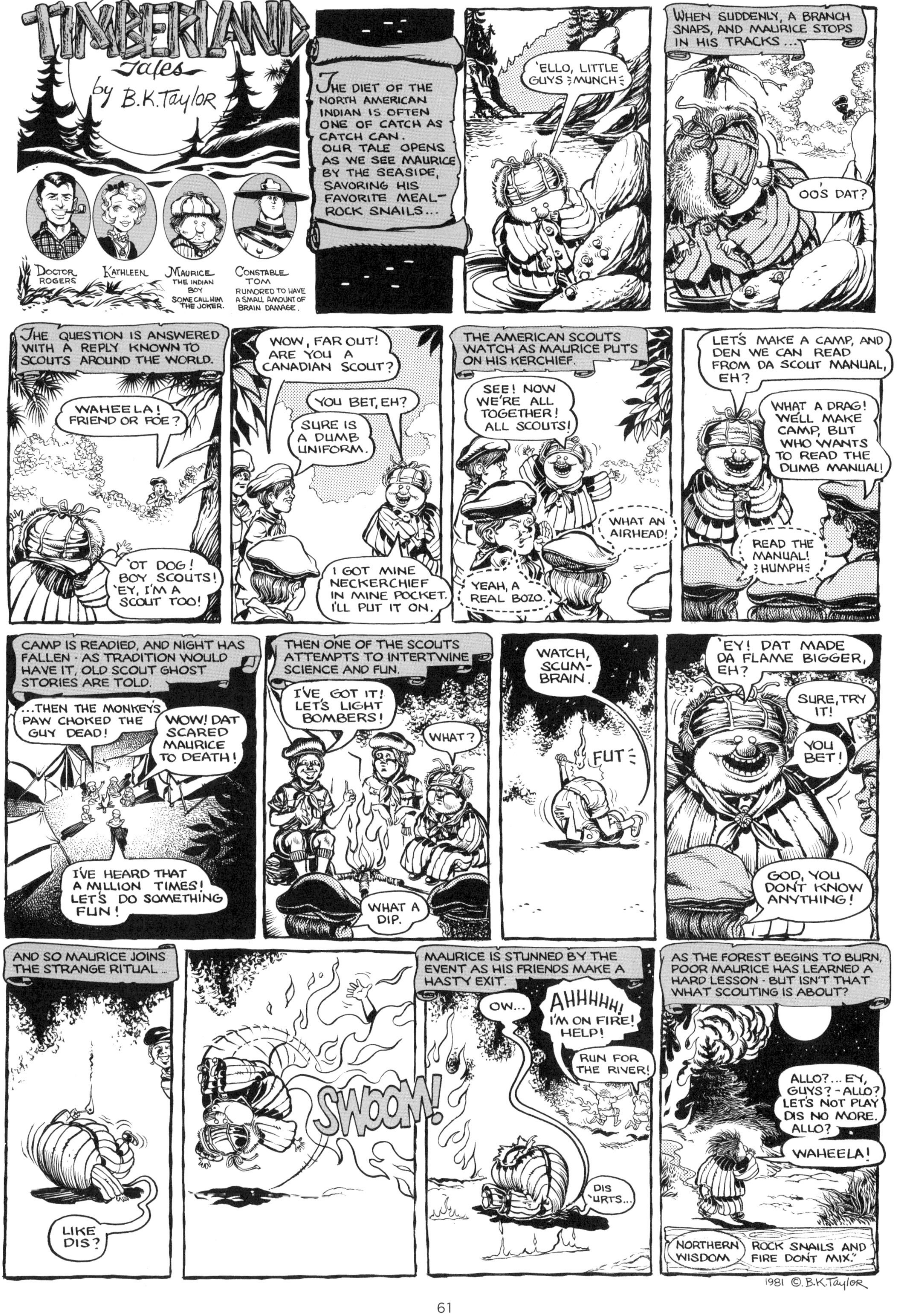
TIMBERLAND Tales
by B.K.Taylor
DOCTOR ROGERS
KATHLEEN
MAURICE THE INDIAN BOY SOME CALL HIM THE JOKER.
CONSTABLE TOM RUMORED TO HAVE A SMALL AMOUNT OF BRAIN DAMAGE.
THE DIET OF THE NORTH AMERICAN INDIAN IS OFTEN ONE OF CATCH AS CATCH CAN. OUR TALE OPENS AS WE SEE MAURICE BY THE SEASIDE, SAVORING HIS FAVORITE MEAL-ROCK SNAILS...
'ELLO, LITTLE GUYS MUNCH
WHEN SUDDENLY, A BRANCH SNAPS, AND MAURICE STOPS IN HIS TRACKS...
OO'S DAT?
THE QUESTION IS ANSWERED WITH A REPLY KNOWN TO SCOUTS AROUND THE WORLD.
WAHEELA! FRIEND OR FOE?
'OT DOG! BOY SCOUTS! 'EY, I'M A SCOUT TOO!
WOW, FAR OUT! ARE YOU A CANADIAN SCOUT?
YOU BET, EH?
SURE IS A DUMB UNIFORM.
I GOT MINE NECKERCHIEF IN MINE POCKET. I'LL PUT IT ON.
THE AMERICAN SCOUTS WATCH AS MAURICE PUTS ON HIS KERCHIEF.
SEE! NOW WE'RE ALL TOGETHER! ALL SCOUTS!
WHAT AN AIRHEAD!
YEAH, A REAL BOZO.
LET'S MAKE A CAMP, AND DEN WE CAN READ FROM DA SCOUT MANUAL, EH?
WHAT A DRAG! WE'LL MAKE CAMP, BUT WHO WANTS TO READ THE DUMB MANUAL!
READ THE MANUAL! HUMPH
CAMP IS READIED, AND NIGHT HAS FALLEN - AS TRADITION WOULD HAVE IT, OLD SCOUT GHOST STORIES ARE TOLD.
...THEN THE MONKEY'S PAW CHOKED THE GUY DEAD!
WOW! DAT SCARED MAURICE TO DEATH!
I'VE HEARD THAT A MILLION TIMES! LET'S DO SOMETHING FUN!
THEN ONE OF THE SCOUTS ATTEMPTS TO INTERTWINE SCIENCE AND FUN.
I'VE GOT IT! LET'S LIGHT BOMBERS!
WHAT?
WHAT A DIP.
WATCH, SCUM-BRAIN.
FUT
'EY! DAT MADE DA FLAME BIGGER, EH?
SURE, TRY IT!
YOU BET!
GOD, YOU DON'T KNOW ANYTHING!
AND SO MAURICE JOINS THE STRANGE RITUAL...
LIKE DIS?
SWOOM!
MAURICE IS STUNNED BY THE EVENT AS HIS FRIENDS MAKE A HASTY EXIT.
OW...
AHHHHH! I'M ON FIRE! HELP!
RUN FOR THE RIVER!
DIS 'URTS...
AS THE FOREST BEGINS TO BURN, POOR MAURICE HAS LEARNED A HARD LESSON - BUT ISN'T THAT WHAT SCOUTING IS ABOUT?
ALLO?... EY, GUYS? - ALLO? LET'S NOT PLAY DIS NO MORE. ALLO?
WAHEELA!
NORTHERN WISDOM
"ROCK SNAILS AND FIRE DON'T MIX."
1981 ©. B.K.Taylor

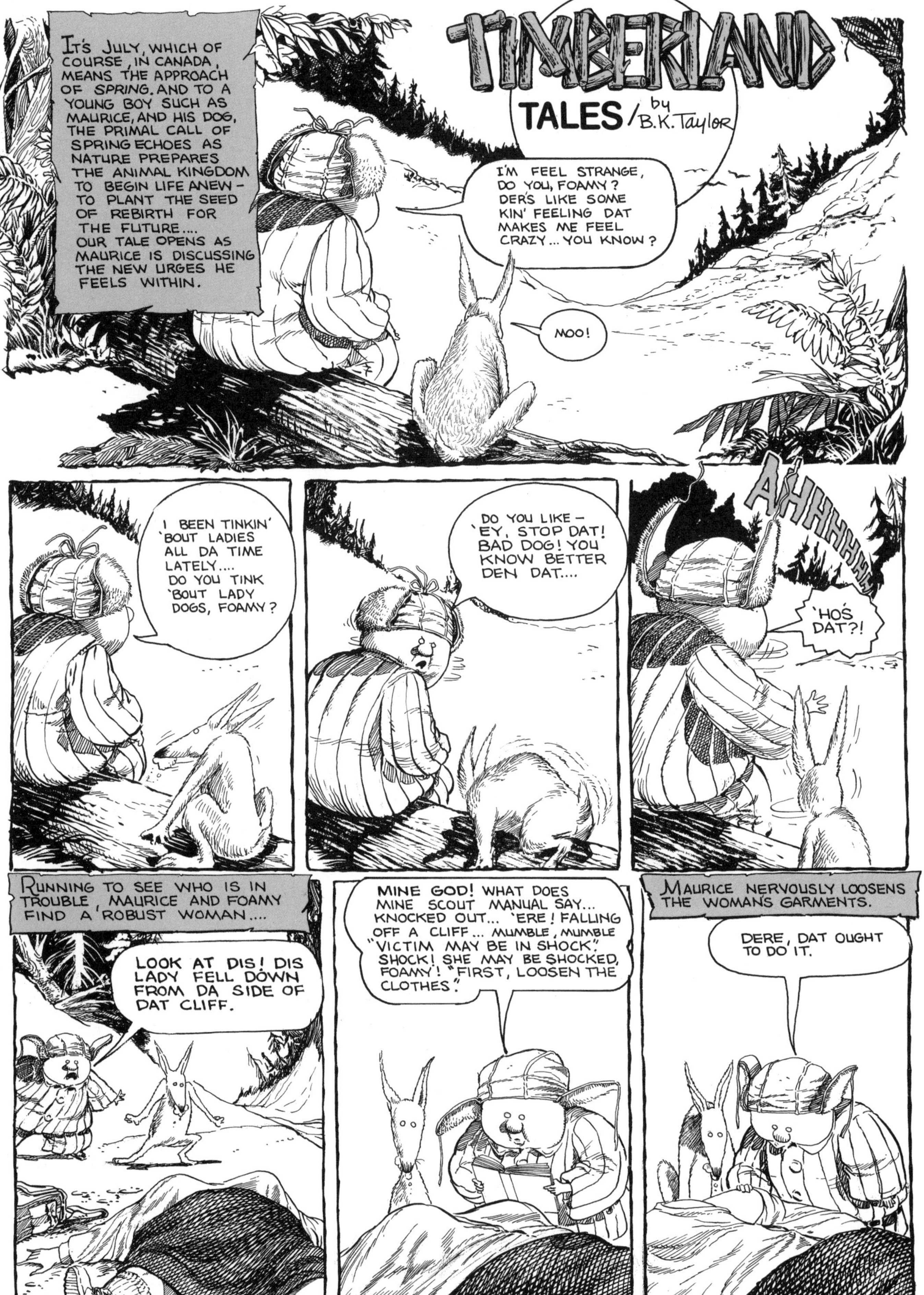
TIMBERLAND TALES / by B.K. Taylor
IT'S JULY, WHICH OF COURSE, IN CANADA, MEANS THE APPROACH OF SPRING. AND TO A YOUNG BOY SUCH AS MAURICE, AND HIS DOG, THE PRIMAL CALL OF SPRING ECHOES AS NATURE PREPARES THE ANIMAL KINGDOM TO BEGIN LIFE ANEW - TO PLANT THE SEED OF REBIRTH FOR THE FUTURE.... OUR TALE OPENS AS MAURICE IS DISCUSSING THE NEW URGES HE FEELS WITHIN.
I'M FEEL STRANGE, DO YOU, FOAMY? DER'S LIKE SOME KIN' FEELING DAT MAKES ME FEEL CRAZY... YOU KNOW?
MOO!
I BEEN TINKIN' 'BOUT LADIES ALL DA TIME LATELY.... DO YOU TINK 'BOUT LADY DOGS, FOAMY?
DO YOU LIKE - 'EY, STOP DAT! BAD DOG! YOU KNOW BETTER DEN DAT....
AHHHHHH
'HO'S DAT?!
RUNNING TO SEE WHO IS IN TROUBLE, MAURICE AND FOAMY FIND A ROBUST WOMAN....
LOOK AT DIS! DIS LADY FELL DOWN FROM DA SIDE OF DAT CLIFF.
MINE GOD! WHAT DOES MINE SCOUT MANUAL SAY... KNOCKED OUT... 'ERE! FALLING OFF A CLIFF... MUMBLE, MUMBLE "VICTIM MAY BE IN SHOCK." SHOCK! SHE MAY BE SHOCKED, FOAMY! "FIRST, LOOSEN THE CLOTHES."
MAURICE NERVOUSLY LOOSENS THE WOMAN'S GARMENTS.
DERE, DAT OUGHT TO DO IT.

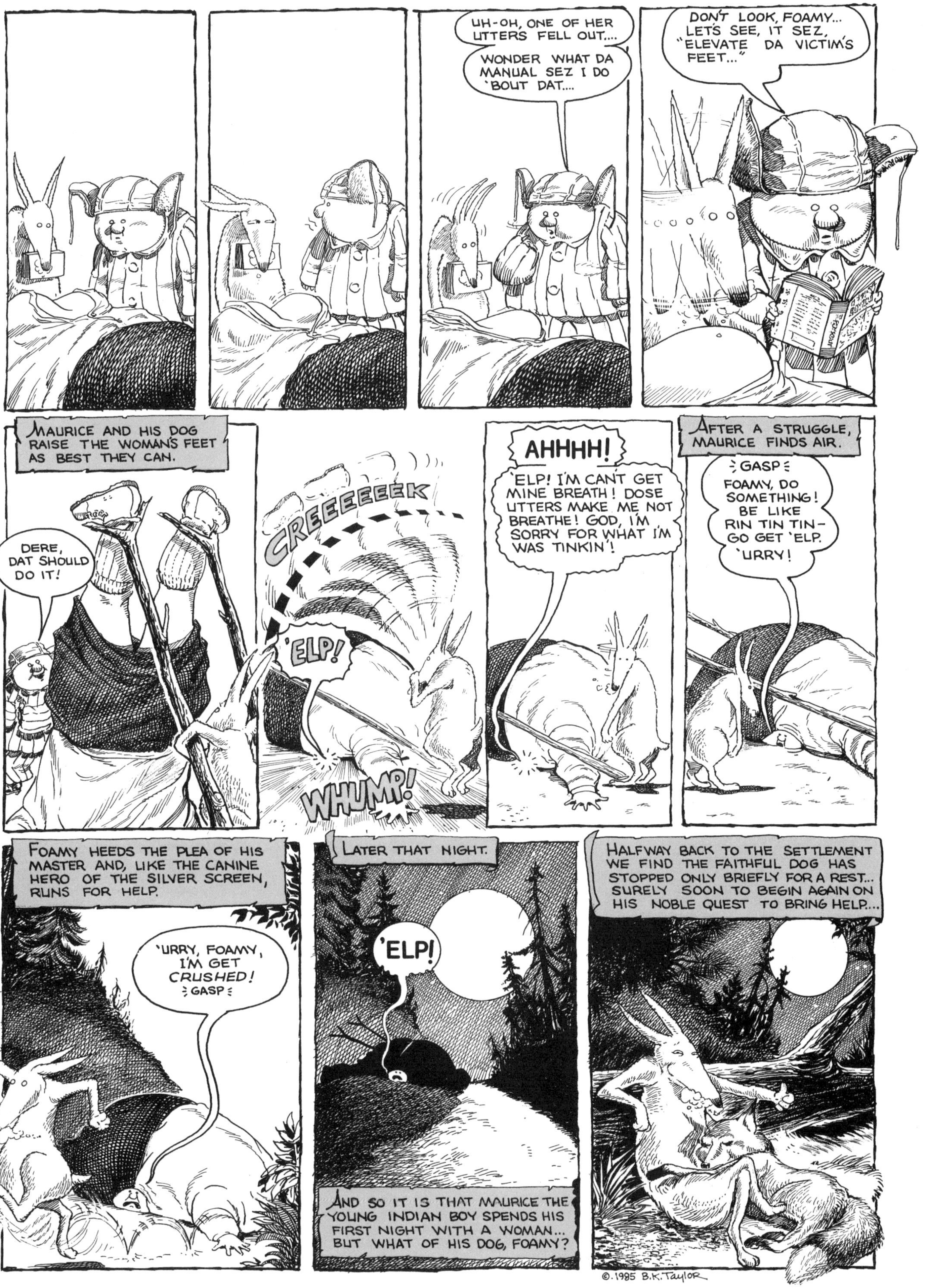
UH-OH, ONE OF HER UTTERS FELL OUT....
WONDER WHAT DA MANUAL SEZ I DO 'BOUT DAT....
DON'T LOOK, FOAMY... LET'S SEE, IT SEZ, "ELEVATE DA VICTIM'S FEET..."
MAURICE AND HIS DOG RAISE THE WOMAN'S FEET AS BEST THEY CAN.
DERE, DAT SHOULD DO IT!
CREEEEEEK
'ELP!
WHUMP!
AHHHH!
'ELP! I'M CAN'T GET MINE BREATH! DOSE UTTERS MAKE ME NOT BREATHE! GOD, I'M SORRY FOR WHAT I'M WAS TINKIN'!
AFTER A STRUGGLE, MAURICE FINDS AIR.
GASP
FOAMY, DO SOMETHING! BE LIKE RIN TIN TIN- GO GET 'ELP. 'URRY!
FOAMY HEEDS THE PLEA OF HIS MASTER AND, LIKE THE CANINE HERO OF THE SILVER SCREEN, RUNS FOR HELP.
'URRY, FOAMY, I'M GET CRUSHED! GASP
LATER THAT NIGHT.
'ELP!
AND SO IT IS THAT MAURICE THE YOUNG INDIAN BOY SPENDS HIS FIRST NIGHT WITH A WOMAN... BUT WHAT OF HIS DOG, FOAMY?
HALFWAY BACK TO THE SETTLEMENT WE FIND THE FAITHFUL DOG HAS STOPPED ONLY BRIEFLY FOR A REST... SURELY SOON TO BEGIN AGAIN ON HIS NOBLE QUEST TO BRING HELP....
©.1985 B.K. TAYLOR

TIMBERLAND Tales
by B.K. Taylor
DOCTOR ROGERS
KATHLEEN
MAURICE THE INDIAN BOY SOME CALL HIM THE JOKER.
CONSTABLE TOM RUMORED TO HAVE A SMALL AMOUNT OF BRAIN DAMAGE.
IN THE CABIN OF DR. ROGERS, MAURICE AND CONSTABLE TOM ARE WATCHING THE DOCTOR'S TELEVISION WHILE HE DOES A BIT OF SHOPPING.
I LOVE DIS GENERAL 'OSPITAL, DON'T YOU?
...I'LL BET YOU DO.
INSPIRED AFTER VIEWING THE PROGRAM, MAURICE LOOKS FOR SOMETHING TO DO.
FINDING DR. ROGERS'S MEDICAL BAG, MAURICE BEAMS WITH EXCITEMENT.
EH! WHAT'S DIS?!
STUD CITY ANIMAL STIMULANT
THE LAD RETURNS TO HIS FRIEND WITH HIS NEWFOUND TREASURES.
OKAY, I'M DA DOCTOR - TIME FOR SOME MEDICINE!
MAURICE CONTINUES HIS MEDICAL EXAM, UNTIL...
NOW LET'S LISTEN TO DAT 'EART.
DOCTOR ROGERS!!
MOMENTS LATER, AS MAURICE RETURNS TO THE CABIN WITH DR. ROGERS AND KATHLEEN...
CONSTABLE TOM?!
'E WAS 'ERE...
THEIR SEARCH FOR THE CONSTABLE IS INTERRUPTED BY A FRANTIC COMMOTION OUTSIDE THE DOOR.
LOOK!
THE GROUP GIVES CHASE, BUT THEIR FRIEND EVADES CAPTURE.
IT ISN'T UNTIL LATE THAT EVENING, WHEN CONSTABLE TOM IS CAUGHT WITH A WELL-PLACED SNARE, THAT THE TURMOIL ENDS.
BUT ALL IS WELL IN THE END. THE CONSTABLE IS SECURED TO BED FOR A FEW DAYS AND, OUTSIDE OF THE LOSS OF SOME WILDLIFE, THINGS RETURN TO NORMAL IN TIMBERLAND.
1982 ©. B.K. Taylor

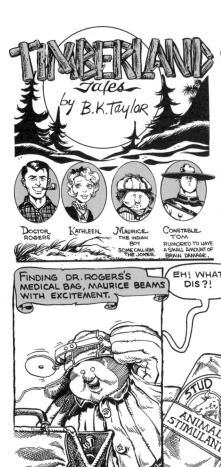

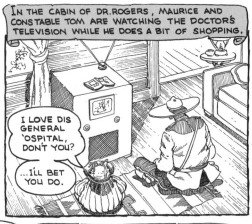

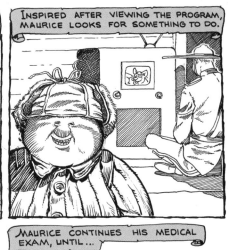

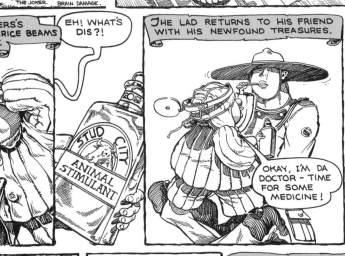

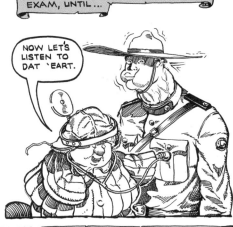

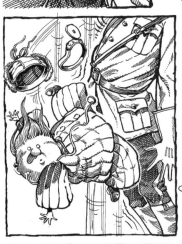

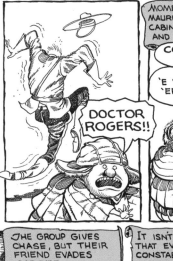

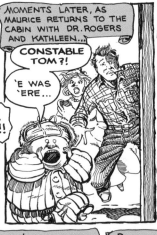

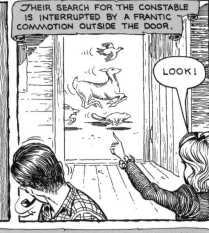

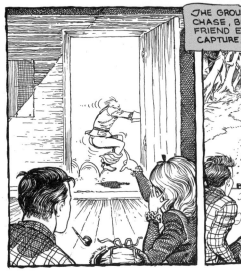

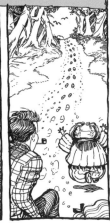

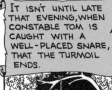

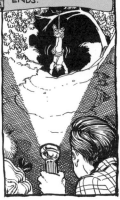

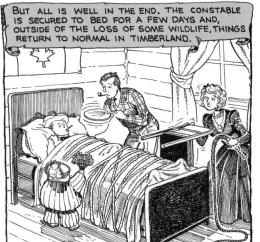

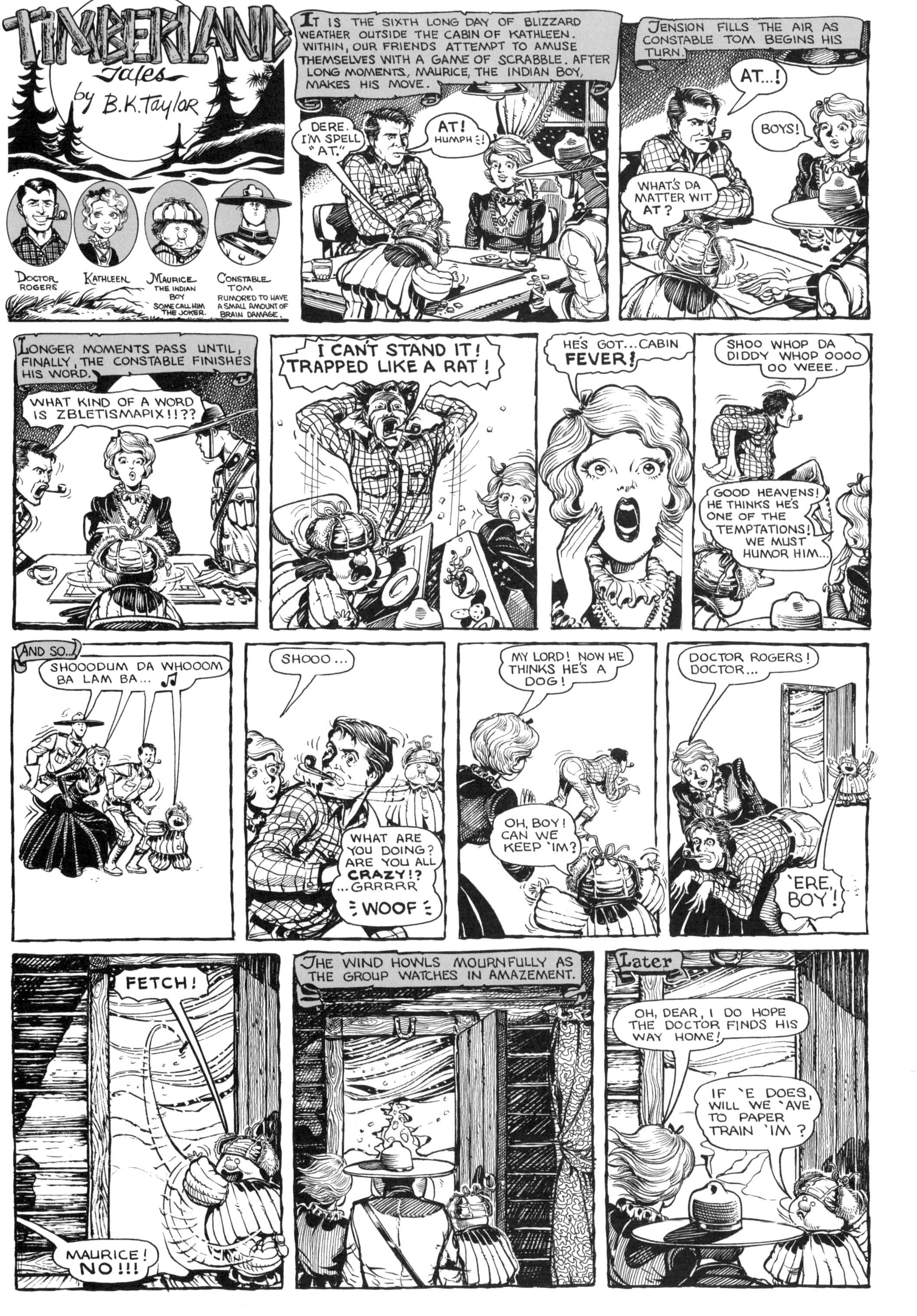
TIMBERLAND
Tales
by B.K.Taylor
DOCTOR ROGERS
KATHLEEN
MAURICE THE INDIAN BOY SOME CALL HIM THE JOKER.
CONSTABLE TOM RUMORED TO HAVE A SMALL AMOUNT OF BRAIN DAMAGE.
IT IS THE SIXTH LONG DAY OF BLIZZARD WEATHER OUTSIDE THE CABIN OF KATHLEEN. WITHIN, OUR FRIENDS ATTEMPT TO AMUSE THEMSELVES WITH A GAME OF SCRABBLE. AFTER LONG MOMENTS, MAURICE, THE INDIAN BOY, MAKES HIS MOVE.
DERE. I'M SPELL "AT."
AT! HUMPH!
TENSION FILLS THE AIR AS CONSTABLE TOM BEGINS HIS TURN.
AT...!
BOYS!
WHAT'S DA MATTER WIT AT?
LONGER MOMENTS PASS UNTIL, FINALLY, THE CONSTABLE FINISHES HIS WORD.
WHAT KIND OF A WORD IS ZBLETISMAPIX!!??
I CAN'T STAND IT! TRAPPED LIKE A RAT!
HE'S GOT... CABIN FEVER!
SHOO WHOP DA DIDDY WHOP OOOO OO WEEE.
GOOD HEAVENS! HE THINKS HE'S ONE OF THE TEMPTATIONS! WE MUST HUMOR HIM...
AND SO...
SHOOODUM DA WHOOOM BA LAM BA... ♪
SHOOO...
WHAT ARE YOU DOING? ARE YOU ALL CRAZY!? ...GRRRRR
WOOF
MY LORD! NOW HE THINKS HE'S A DOG!
OH, BOY! CAN WE KEEP 'IM?
DOCTOR ROGERS! DOCTOR...
'ERE, BOY!
FETCH!
MAURICE! NO!!!
THE WIND HOWLS MOURNFULLY AS THE GROUP WATCHES IN AMAZEMENT.
Later
OH, DEAR, I DO HOPE THE DOCTOR FINDS HIS WAY HOME!
IF 'E DOES, WILL WE 'AVE TO PAPER TRAIN 'IM?

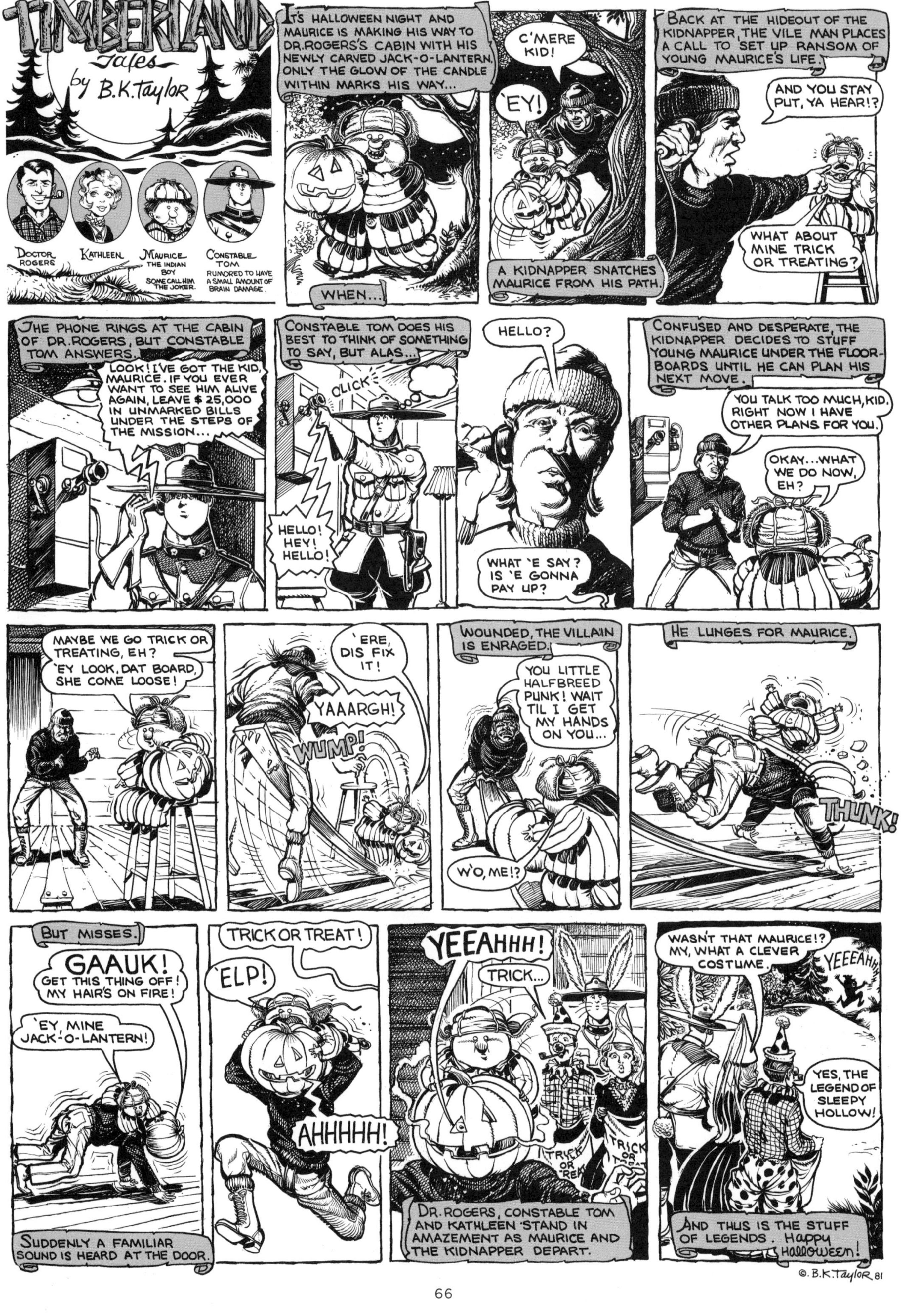
TIMBERLAND Tales
by B.K.Taylor
DOCTOR ROGERS
KATHLEEN
MAURICE THE INDIAN BOY SOME CALL HIM THE JOKER.
CONSTABLE TOM RUMORED TO HAVE A SMALL AMOUNT OF BRAIN DAMAGE.
IT'S HALLOWEEN NIGHT AND MAURICE IS MAKING HIS WAY TO DR.ROGERS'S CABIN WITH HIS NEWLY CARVED JACK-O-LANTERN. ONLY THE GLOW OF THE CANDLE WITHIN MARKS HIS WAY...
WHEN...
C'MERE KID!
'EY!
A KIDNAPPER SNATCHES MAURICE FROM HIS PATH.
BACK AT THE HIDEOUT OF THE KIDNAPPER, THE VILE MAN PLACES A CALL TO SET UP RANSOM OF YOUNG MAURICE'S LIFE.
AND YOU STAY PUT, YA HEAR!?
WHAT ABOUT MINE TRICK OR TREATING?
THE PHONE RINGS AT THE CABIN OF DR.ROGERS, BUT CONSTABLE TOM ANSWERS.
LOOK! I'VE GOT THE KID, MAURICE. IF YOU EVER WANT TO SEE HIM ALIVE AGAIN, LEAVE $ 25,000 IN UNMARKED BILLS UNDER THE STEPS OF THE MISSION...
CONSTABLE TOM DOES HIS BEST TO THINK OF SOMETHING TO SAY, BUT ALAS...
CLICK
HELLO! HEY! HELLO!
HELLO?
WHAT 'E SAY? IS 'E GONNA PAY UP?
CONFUSED AND DESPERATE, THE KIDNAPPER DECIDES TO STUFF YOUNG MAURICE UNDER THE FLOOR-BOARDS UNTIL HE CAN PLAN HIS NEXT MOVE.
YOU TALK TOO MUCH, KID. RIGHT NOW I HAVE OTHER PLANS FOR YOU.
OKAY...WHAT WE DO NOW, EH?
MAYBE WE GO TRICK OR TREATING, EH?
'EY LOOK, DAT BOARD, SHE COME LOOSE!
'ERE, DIS FIX IT!
YAAARGH!
WUMP!
WOUNDED, THE VILLAIN IS ENRAGED.
YOU LITTLE HALFBREED PUNK! WAIT TIL I GET MY HANDS ON YOU...
W'O, ME!?
HE LUNGES FOR MAURICE.
THUNK!
BUT MISSES.
GAAUK! GET THIS THING OFF! MY HAIR'S ON FIRE!
'EY, MINE JACK-O-LANTERN!
SUDDENLY A FAMILIAR SOUND IS HEARD AT THE DOOR.
TRICK OR TREAT!
'ELP!
AHHHHH!
YEEAHHH!
TRICK...
TRICK OR TREAT
TRICK OR
DR.ROGERS, CONSTABLE TOM AND KATHLEEN STAND IN AMAZEMENT AS MAURICE AND THE KIDNAPPER DEPART.
WASN'T THAT MAURICE!? MY, WHAT A CLEVER COSTUME.
YEEEAHH
YES, THE LEGEND OF SLEEPY HOLLOW!
AND THUS IS THE STUFF OF LEGENDS. Happy HALLOWEEN!
©. B.K.TAYLOR 81

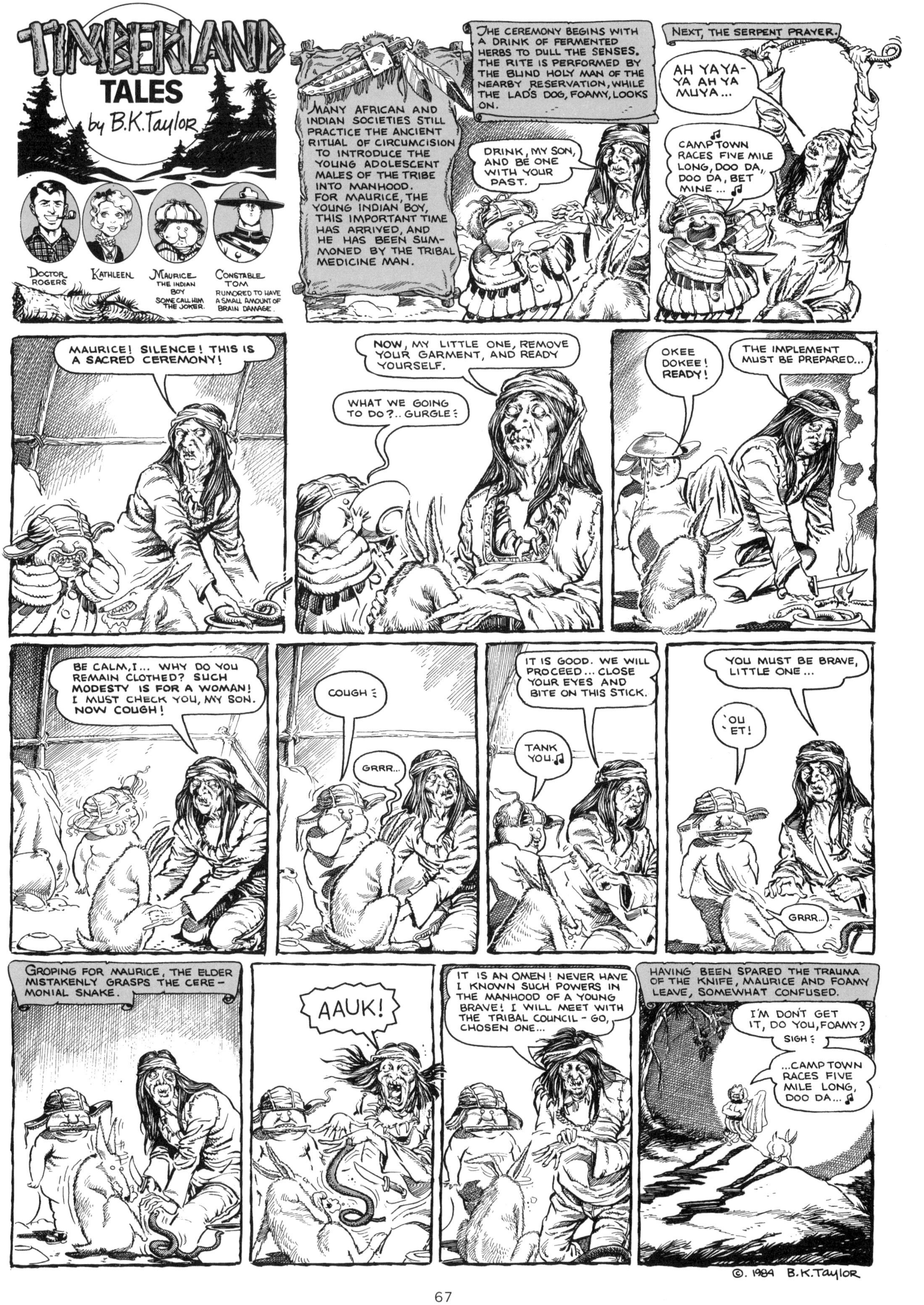

TIMBERLAND TALES
by B.K.Taylor
DOCTOR ROGERS
KATHLEEN
MAURICE THE INDIAN BOY SOME CALL HIM THE JOKER.
CONSTABLE TOM RUMORED TO HAVE A SMALL AMOUNT OF BRAIN DAMAGE.
MANY AFRICAN AND INDIAN SOCIETIES STILL PRACTICE THE ANCIENT RITUAL OF CIRCUMCISION TO INTRODUCE THE YOUNG ADOLESCENT MALES OF THE TRIBE INTO MANHOOD. FOR MAURICE, THE YOUNG INDIAN BOY, THIS IMPORTANT TIME HAS ARRIVED, AND HE HAS BEEN SUMMONED BY THE TRIBAL MEDICINE MAN.
THE CEREMONY BEGINS WITH A DRINK OF FERMENTED HERBS TO DULL THE SENSES. THE RITE IS PERFORMED BY THE BLIND HOLY MAN OF THE NEARBY RESERVATION, WHILE THE LAD'S DOG, FOAMY, LOOKS ON.
DRINK, MY SON, AND BE ONE WITH YOUR PAST.
NEXT, THE SERPENT PRAYER.
AH YAYA-YA AH YA MUYA...
CAMPTOWN RACES FIVE MILE LONG, DOO DA, DOO DA, BET MINE...
MAURICE! SILENCE! THIS IS A SACRED CEREMONY!
NOW, MY LITTLE ONE, REMOVE YOUR GARMENT, AND READY YOURSELF.
WHAT WE GOING TO DO?.. GURGLE
OKEE DOKEE! READY!
THE IMPLEMENT MUST BE PREPARED...
BE CALM, I... WHY DO YOU REMAIN CLOTHED? SUCH MODESTY IS FOR A WOMAN! I MUST CHECK YOU, MY SON. NOW COUGH!
COUGH
GRRR...
IT IS GOOD. WE WILL PROCEED... CLOSE YOUR EYES AND BITE ON THIS STICK.
TANK YOU.
YOU MUST BE BRAVE, LITTLE ONE...
`OU `ET!
GRRR...
GROPING FOR MAURICE, THE ELDER MISTAKENLY GRASPS THE CERE-MONIAL SNAKE.
AAUK!
IT IS AN OMEN! NEVER HAVE I KNOWN SUCH POWERS IN THE MANHOOD OF A YOUNG BRAVE! I WILL MEET WITH THE TRIBAL COUNCIL - GO, CHOSEN ONE...
HAVING BEEN SPARED THE TRAUMA OF THE KNIFE, MAURICE AND FOAMY LEAVE, SOMEWHAT CONFUSED.
I'M DON'T GET IT, DO YOU, FOAMY?
SIGH
...CAMPTOWN RACES FIVE MILE LONG, DOO DA...
©. 1984 B.K.TAYLOR

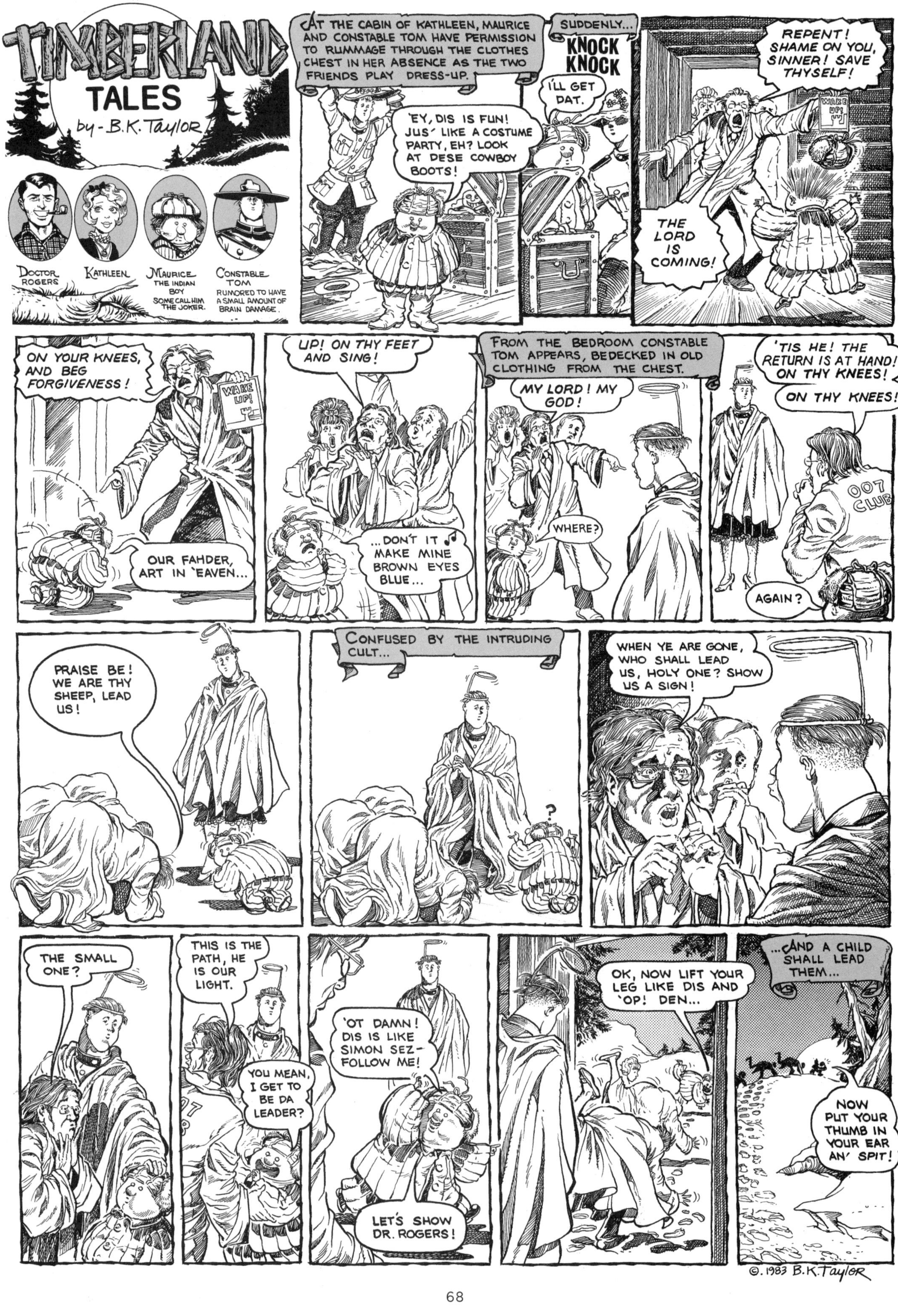
TIMBERLAND TALES
by - B.K. Taylor
DOCTOR ROGERS
KATHLEEN
MAURICE THE INDIAN BOY SOME CALL HIM THE JOKER.
CONSTABLE TOM RUMORED TO HAVE A SMALL AMOUNT OF BRAIN DAMAGE.
AT THE CABIN OF KATHLEEN, MAURICE AND CONSTABLE TOM HAVE PERMISSION TO RUMMAGE THROUGH THE CLOTHES CHEST IN HER ABSENCE AS THE TWO FRIENDS PLAY DRESS-UP.
'EY, DIS IS FUN! JUS' LIKE A COSTUME PARTY, EH? LOOK AT DESE COWBOY BOOTS!
SUDDENLY...
KNOCK KNOCK
I'LL GET DAT.
REPENT! SHAME ON YOU, SINNER! SAVE THYSELF!
WAKE UP!
THE LORD IS COMING!
ON YOUR KNEES, AND BEG FORGIVENESS!
WAKE UP!
OUR FAHDER, ART IN 'EAVEN...
UP! ON THY FEET AND SING!
...DON'T IT MAKE MINE BROWN EYES BLUE...
FROM THE BEDROOM CONSTABLE TOM APPEARS, BEDECKED IN OLD CLOTHING FROM THE CHEST.
MY LORD! MY GOD!
WHERE?
'TIS HE! THE RETURN IS AT HAND! ON THY KNEES!
ON THY KNEES!
007 CLUB
AGAIN?
PRAISE BE! WE ARE THY SHEEP, LEAD US!
CONFUSED BY THE INTRUDING CULT...
?
WHEN YE ARE GONE, WHO SHALL LEAD US, HOLY ONE? SHOW US A SIGN!
THE SMALL ONE?
THIS IS THE PATH, HE IS OUR LIGHT.
YOU MEAN, I GET TO BE DA LEADER?
'OT DAMN! DIS IS LIKE SIMON SEZ-FOLLOW ME!
LET'S SHOW DR. ROGERS!
OK, NOW LIFT YOUR LEG LIKE DIS AND 'OP! DEN...
...AND A CHILD SHALL LEAD THEM...
NOW PUT YOUR THUMB IN YOUR EAR AN' SPIT!
©. 1983 B.K. Taylor

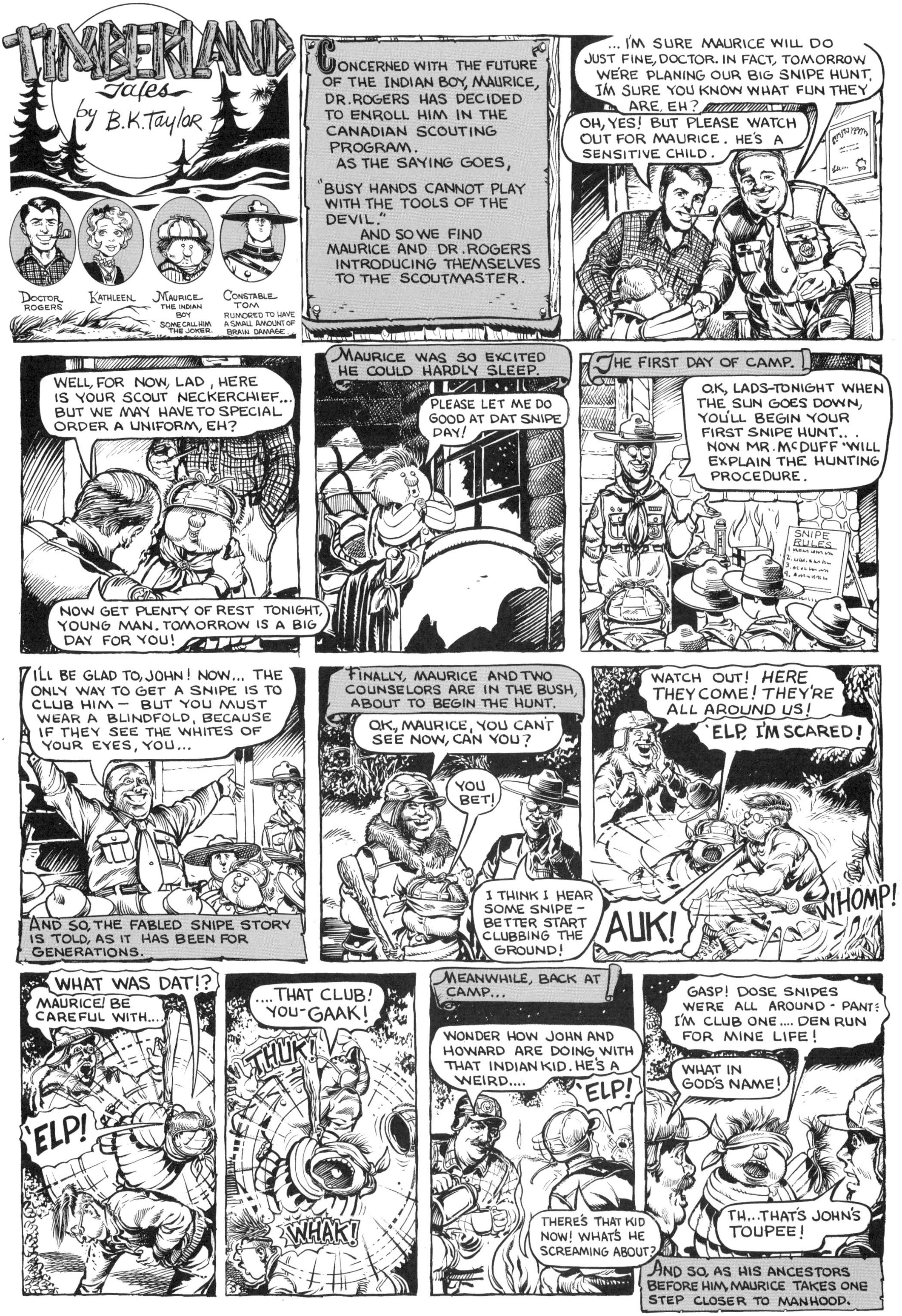
TIMBERLAND Tales
by B.K.Taylor
DOCTOR ROGERS
KATHLEEN
MAURICE THE INDIAN BOY SOME CALL HIM THE JOKER.
CONSTABLE TOM RUMORED TO HAVE A SMALL AMOUNT OF BRAIN DAMAGE
CONCERNED WITH THE FUTURE OF THE INDIAN BOY, MAURICE, DR. ROGERS HAS DECIDED TO ENROLL HIM IN THE CANADIAN SCOUTING PROGRAM. AS THE SAYING GOES, "BUSY HANDS CANNOT PLAY WITH THE TOOLS OF THE DEVIL." AND SO WE FIND MAURICE AND DR. ROGERS INTRODUCING THEMSELVES TO THE SCOUTMASTER.
... I'M SURE MAURICE WILL DO JUST FINE, DOCTOR. IN FACT, TOMORROW WE'RE PLANING OUR BIG SNIPE HUNT. I'M SURE YOU KNOW WHAT FUN THEY ARE, EH?
OH, YES! BUT PLEASE WATCH OUT FOR MAURICE. HE'S A SENSITIVE CHILD.
WELL, FOR NOW, LAD, HERE IS YOUR SCOUT NECKERCHIEF... BUT WE MAY HAVE TO SPECIAL ORDER A UNIFORM, EH?
NOW GET PLENTY OF REST TONIGHT, YOUNG MAN. TOMORROW IS A BIG DAY FOR YOU!
MAURICE WAS SO EXCITED HE COULD HARDLY SLEEP.
PLEASE LET ME DO GOOD AT DAT SNIPE DAY!
THE FIRST DAY OF CAMP.
O.K, LADS–TONIGHT WHEN THE SUN GOES DOWN, YOU'LL BEGIN YOUR FIRST SNIPE HUNT.. . NOW MR. McDUFF WILL EXPLAIN THE HUNTING PROCEDURE.
SNIPE RULES
I'LL BE GLAD TO, JOHN! NOW... THE ONLY WAY TO GET A SNIPE IS TO CLUB HIM — BUT YOU MUST WEAR A BLINDFOLD, BECAUSE IF THEY SEE THE WHITES OF YOUR EYES, YOU...
AND SO, THE FABLED SNIPE STORY IS TOLD, AS IT HAS BEEN FOR GENERATIONS.
FINALLY, MAURICE AND TWO COUNSELORS ARE IN THE BUSH, ABOUT TO BEGIN THE HUNT.
O.K., MAURICE, YOU CAN'T SEE NOW, CAN YOU?
YOU BET!
I THINK I HEAR SOME SNIPE – BETTER START CLUBBING THE GROUND!
WATCH OUT! HERE THEY COME! THEY'RE ALL AROUND US!
'ELP, I'M SCARED!
AUK!
WHOMP!
WHAT WAS DAT!?
MAURICE! BE CAREFUL WITH....
'ELP!
....THAT CLUB! YOU-GAAK!
THUK!
WHAK!
MEANWHILE, BACK AT CAMP...
WONDER HOW JOHN AND HOWARD ARE DOING WITH THAT INDIAN KID. HE'S A WEIRD....
'ELP!
THERE'S THAT KID NOW! WHAT'S HE SCREAMING ABOUT?
GASP! DOSE SNIPES WERE ALL AROUND - PANT! I'M CLUB ONE.... DEN RUN FOR MINE LIFE!
WHAT IN GOD'S NAME!
TH...THAT'S JOHN'S TOUPEE!
AND SO, AS HIS ANCESTORS BEFORE HIM, MAURICE TAKES ONE STEP CLOSER TO MANHOOD.

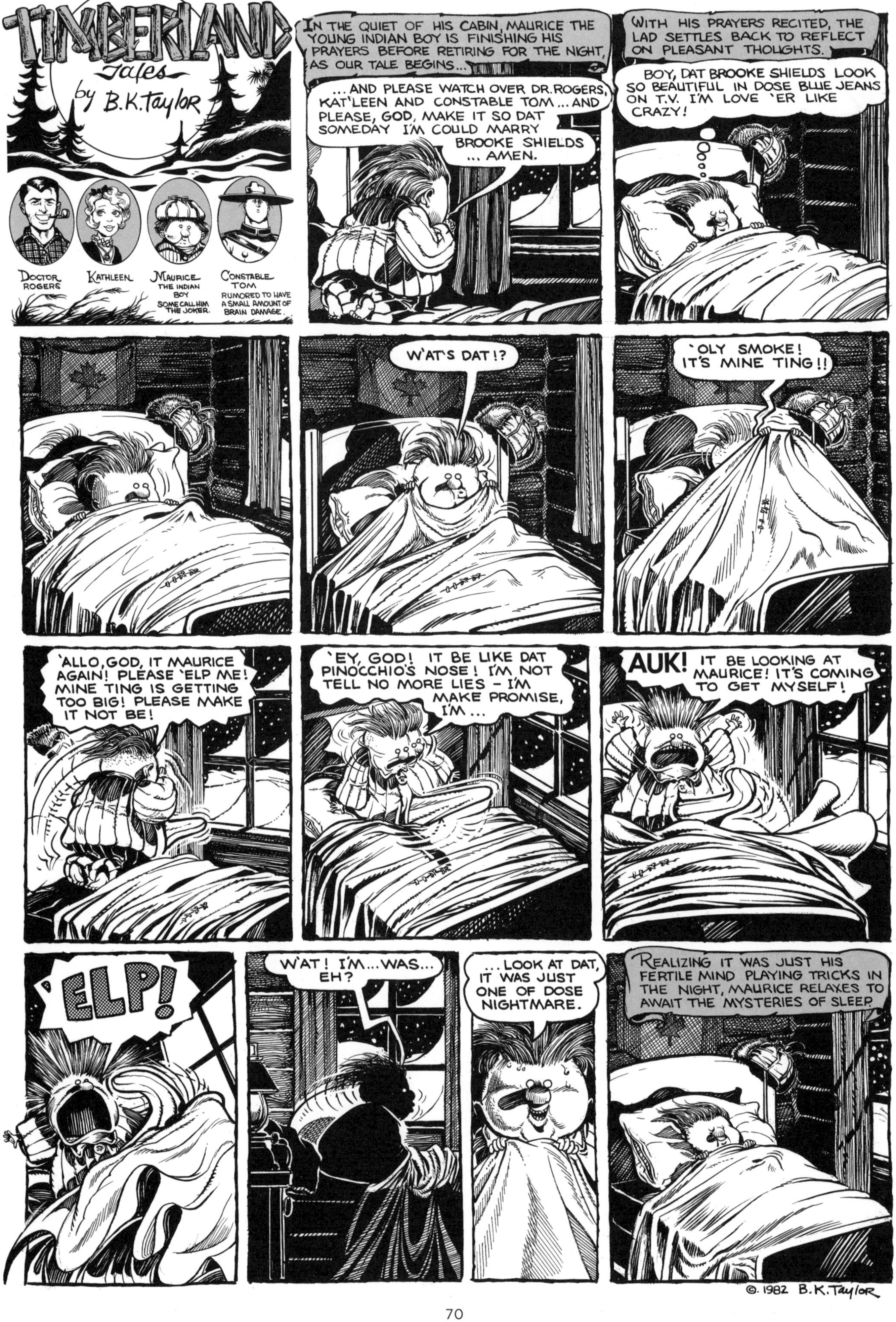
TIMBERLAND Tales
by B.K.Taylor
DOCTOR ROGERS
KATHLEEN
MAURICE THE INDIAN BOY SOME CALL HIM THE JOKER.
CONSTABLE TOM RUMORED TO HAVE A SMALL AMOUNT OF BRAIN DAMAGE.
IN THE QUIET OF HIS CABIN, MAURICE THE YOUNG INDIAN BOY IS FINISHING HIS PRAYERS BEFORE RETIRING FOR THE NIGHT, AS OUR TALE BEGINS...
...AND PLEASE WATCH OVER DR. ROGERS, KAT'LEEN AND CONSTABLE TOM... AND PLEASE, GOD, MAKE IT SO DAT SOMEDAY I'M COULD MARRY BROOKE SHIELDS ... AMEN.
WITH HIS PRAYERS RECITED, THE LAD SETTLES BACK TO REFLECT ON PLEASANT THOUGHTS.
BOY, DAT BROOKE SHIELDS LOOK SO BEAUTIFUL IN DOSE BLUE JEANS ON T.V. I'M LOVE 'ER LIKE CRAZY!
W'AT'S DAT!?
'OLY SMOKE! IT'S MINE TING!!
'ALLO, GOD, IT MAURICE AGAIN! PLEASE 'ELP ME! MINE TING IS GETTING TOO BIG! PLEASE MAKE IT NOT BE!
'EY, GOD! IT BE LIKE DAT PINOCCHIO'S NOSE! I'M NOT TELL NO MORE LIES - I'M MAKE PROMISE, I'M ...
AUK! IT BE LOOKING AT MAURICE! IT'S COMING TO GET MYSELF!
'ELP!
W'AT! I'M... WAS... EH?
... LOOK AT DAT, IT WAS JUST ONE OF DOSE NIGHTMARE.
REALIZING IT WAS JUST HIS FERTILE MIND PLAYING TRICKS IN THE NIGHT, MAURICE RELAXES TO AWAIT THE MYSTERIES OF SLEEP.
©. 1982 B.K.Taylor

TIMBERLAND TALES
by B.K. Taylor

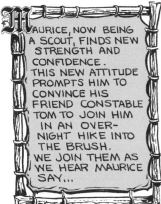

MAURICE, NOW BEING A SCOUT, FINDS NEW STRENGTH AND CONFIDENCE. THIS NEW ATTITUDE PROMPTS HIM TO CONVINCE HIS FRIEND CONSTABLE TOM TO JOIN HIM IN AN OVERNIGHT HIKE INTO THE BRUSH. WE JOIN THEM AS WE HEAR MAURICE SAY...

BOY, DIS IS DA LIFE, EH, CONSTABLE TOM? OUT 'ERE IN DA WOODS WIT BIRDS AND...

MOAN...

SUDDENLY ...

EH! LOOK DERE! ANODDER GUY IS OUD 'ERE.

WHAT'S DA MATTER DERE, MISTER?

I SEEM TO HAVE SPRAINED MY ANKLE.

UH-OH! DAT LOOKS SERIOUS! WE BETTER GIVE YOU FIRST AID.

NO, REALLY. IF YOU COULD JUST...

WE GOT A **RED ALERT**, CONSTABLE TOM! YOU LIE BACK, MISTER, AND DON'T WORRY, I'M A BOY SCOUT!

REALLY — I...

WITH THE HELP OF CONSTABLE TOM, MAURICE FASHIONS A STRETCHER FROM WOOD AND TWINE.

DAT SHOULD DO IT. WE BETTER 'URRY AND GET 'IM TO DR. ROGERS. DIS GUY'S IN TROUBLE!

WILL YOU PLEASE PUT ME DOWN! I'LL BE FINE

SENSING THE URGENCY OF THE SITUATION, MAURICE AND CONSTABLE TOM WASTE NO TIME.

I INSIST I'M ALL RIGHT, NOW LET...

WATCH DIS BRANCH!

BONK!

ACROSS RIVERS AND STREAMS THEY MARCH.

BOY! DIS WATER IS DEEP.

EVEN STEEP RAVINES DON'T STAND IN THEIR WAY.

OKAY...! BOMBS AWAY!

NO!

AAAAAAH!

THOOMP!

MOMENTS LATER.

ONE, TWO, TREE, PULL!

BUMP
KNOCK

ONWARD THEY MARCH.

WHEW! DIS SCOUT BUSINESS IS 'ARD, BUT WE'RE GETTING CLOSE TO 'OME, EH?

TURN ME OVER.

HOURS LATER.

DR. ROGERS, 'URRY! DERE'S A GUY READY TO **CROAK!**

DR. ROGERS HURRIES TO THE SCENE.

IT'S A GOOD THING YOU BROUGHT HIM IN WHEN YOU DID THIS MAN IS AT DEATH'S DOOR.

DAT'S WHAT I TOUGHT.

REMEMBER! BEING A SCOUT IS MORE THAN A JOB, IT'S AN ADVENTURE.

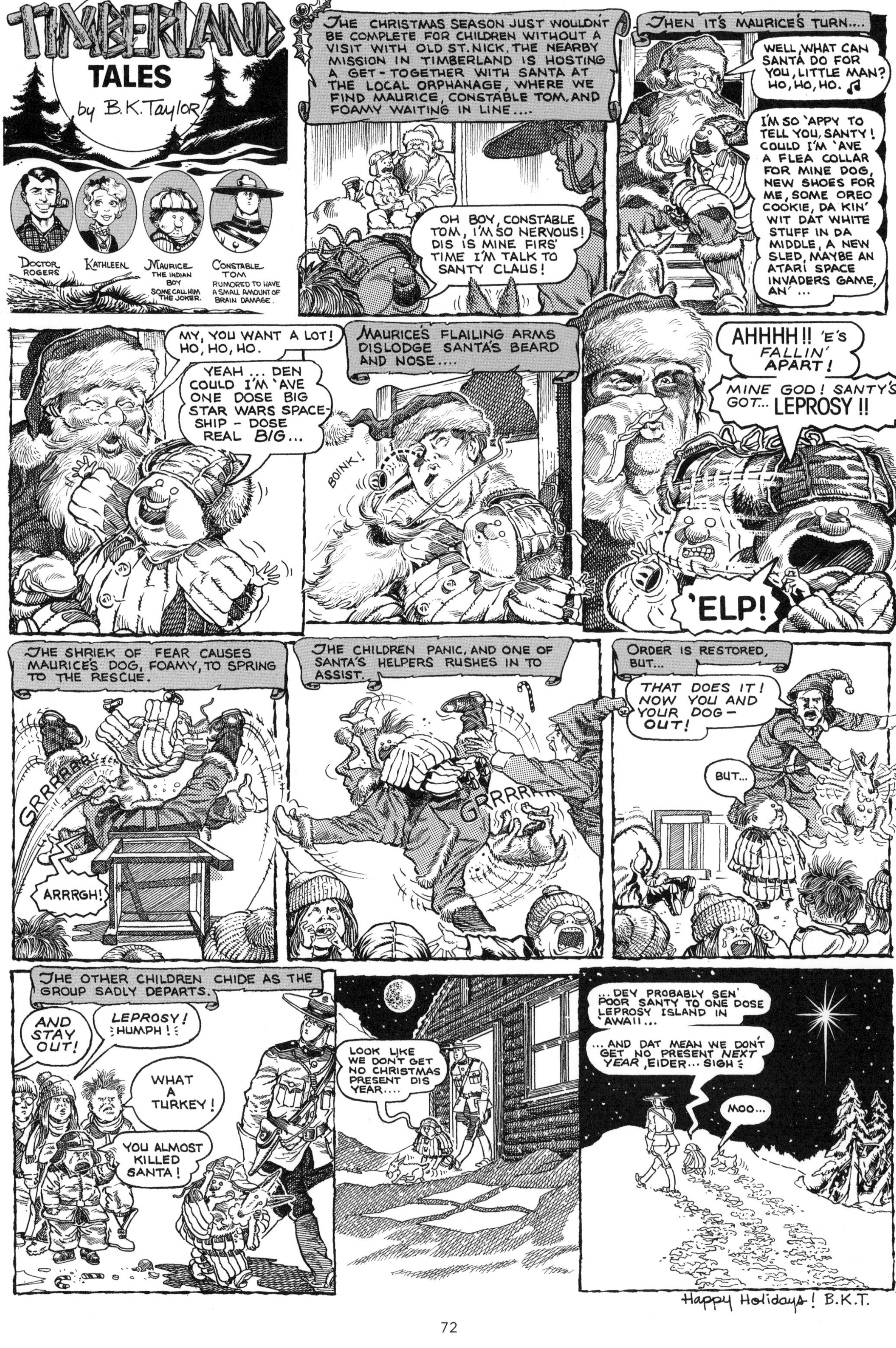
TIMBERLAND TALES
by B.K. Taylor
DOCTOR ROGERS
KATHLEEN
MAURICE THE INDIAN BOY SOME CALL HIM THE JOKER.
CONSTABLE TOM RUMORED TO HAVE A SMALL AMOUNT OF BRAIN DAMAGE.
THE CHRISTMAS SEASON JUST WOULDN'T BE COMPLETE FOR CHILDREN WITHOUT A VISIT WITH OLD ST. NICK. THE NEARBY MISSION IN TIMBERLAND IS HOSTING A GET-TOGETHER WITH SANTA AT THE LOCAL ORPHANAGE, WHERE WE FIND MAURICE, CONSTABLE TOM, AND FOAMY WAITING IN LINE....
OH BOY, CONSTABLE TOM, I'M SO NERVOUS! DIS IS MINE FIRS' TIME I'M TALK TO SANTY CLAUS!
THEN IT'S MAURICE'S TURN....
WELL, WHAT CAN SANTA DO FOR YOU, LITTLE MAN? HO, HO, HO. ♫
I'M SO 'APPY TO TELL YOU, SANTY! COULD I'M 'AVE A FLEA COLLAR FOR MINE DOG, NEW SHOES FOR ME, SOME OREO COOKIE, DA KIN' WIT DAT WHITE STUFF IN DA MIDDLE, A NEW SLED, MAYBE AN ATARI SPACE INVADERS GAME, AN' ...
MY, YOU WANT A LOT! HO, HO, HO.
YEAH ... DEN COULD I'M 'AVE ONE DOSE BIG STAR WARS SPACE-SHIP - DOSE REAL BIG...
MAURICE'S FLAILING ARMS DISLODGE SANTA'S BEARD AND NOSE....
BOINK!
AHHHH!! 'E'S FALLIN' APART!
MINE GOD! SANTY'S GOT... LEPROSY!!
'ELP!
THE SHRIEK OF FEAR CAUSES MAURICE'S DOG, FOAMY, TO SPRING TO THE RESCUE.
GRRRRR!
ARRRGH!
THE CHILDREN PANIC, AND ONE OF SANTA'S HELPERS RUSHES IN TO ASSIST.
GRRRRR!
ORDER IS RESTORED, BUT...
THAT DOES IT! NOW YOU AND YOUR DOG - OUT!
BUT...
THE OTHER CHILDREN CHIDE AS THE GROUP SADLY DEPARTS.
AND STAY OUT!
LEPROSY! HUMPH!
WHAT A TURKEY!
YOU ALMOST KILLED SANTA!
LOOK LIKE WE DON'T GET NO CHRISTMAS PRESENT DIS YEAR....
...DEY PROBABLY SEN' POOR SANTY TO ONE DOSE LEPROSY ISLAND IN 'AWAII...
...AND DAT MEAN WE DON'T GET NO PRESENT NEXT YEAR, EIDER... SIGH
MOO...
©. 1983 B.K. Taylor
Happy Holidays! B.K.T.

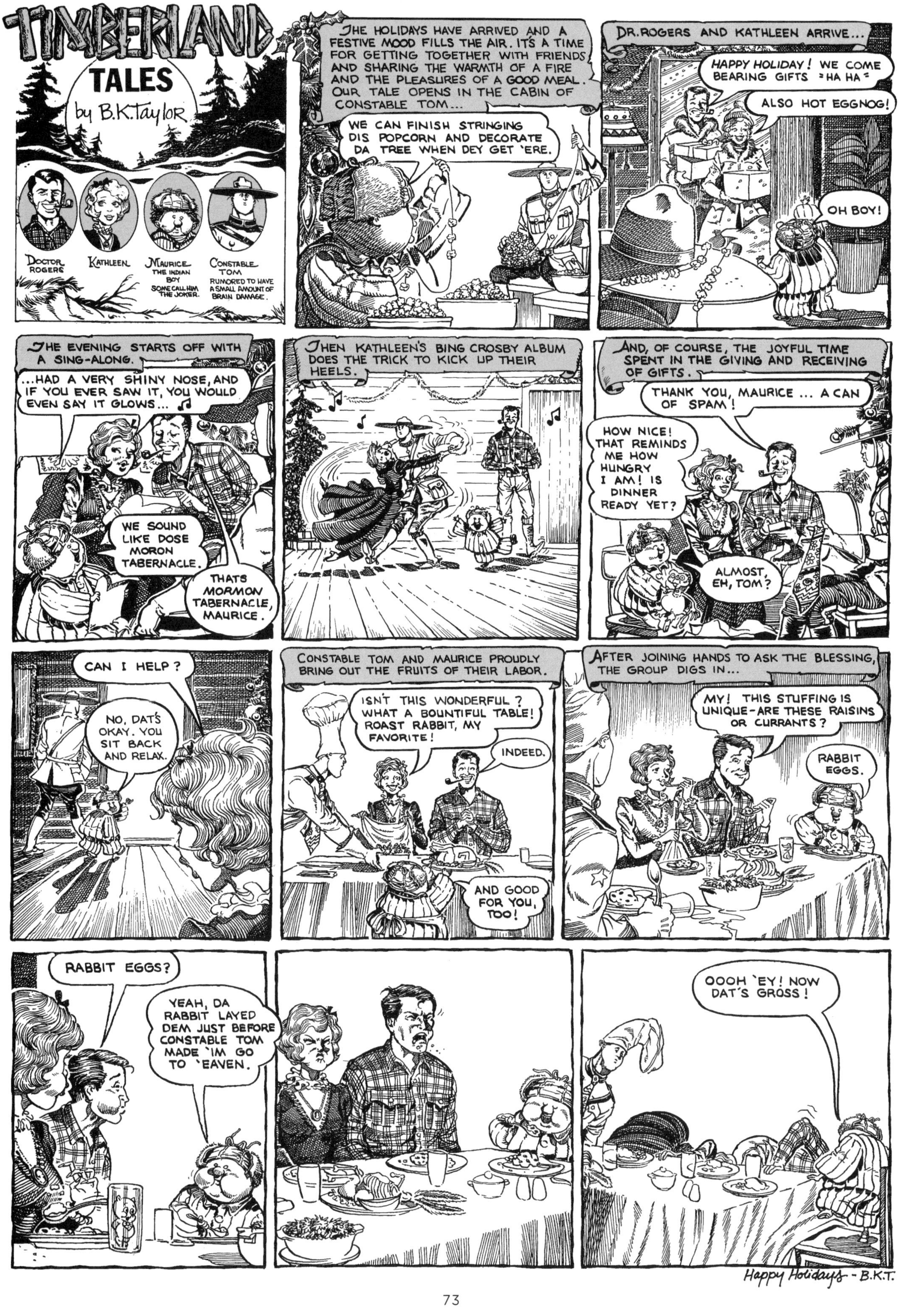
TIMBERLAND TALES
by B.K.Taylor
DOCTOR ROGERS
KATHLEEN
MAURICE THE INDIAN BOY SOME CALL HIM THE JOKER.
CONSTABLE TOM RUMORED TO HAVE A SMALL AMOUNT OF BRAIN DAMAGE.
THE HOLIDAYS HAVE ARRIVED AND A FESTIVE MOOD FILLS THE AIR. IT'S A TIME FOR GETTING TOGETHER WITH FRIENDS AND SHARING THE WARMTH OF A FIRE AND THE PLEASURES OF A GOOD MEAL. OUR TALE OPENS IN THE CABIN OF CONSTABLE TOM...
WE CAN FINISH STRINGING DIS POPCORN AND DECORATE DA TREE WHEN DEY GET 'ERE.
DR. ROGERS AND KATHLEEN ARRIVE...
HAPPY HOLIDAY! WE COME BEARING GIFTS =HA HA=
ALSO HOT EGGNOG!
OH BOY!
THE EVENING STARTS OFF WITH A SING-ALONG.
...HAD A VERY SHINY NOSE, AND IF YOU EVER SAW IT, YOU WOULD EVEN SAY IT GLOWS...
WE SOUND LIKE DOSE MORON TABERNACLE.
THATS MORMON TABERNACLE, MAURICE.
THEN KATHLEEN'S BING CROSBY ALBUM DOES THE TRICK TO KICK UP THEIR HEELS.
AND, OF COURSE, THE JOYFUL TIME SPENT IN THE GIVING AND RECEIVING OF GIFTS.
THANK YOU, MAURICE ... A CAN OF SPAM!
HOW NICE! THAT REMINDS ME HOW HUNGRY I AM! IS DINNER READY YET?
ALMOST, EH, TOM?
CAN I HELP?
NO, DAT'S OKAY. YOU SIT BACK AND RELAX.
CONSTABLE TOM AND MAURICE PROUDLY BRING OUT THE FRUITS OF THEIR LABOR.
ISN'T THIS WONDERFUL? WHAT A BOUNTIFUL TABLE! ROAST RABBIT, MY FAVORITE!
INDEED.
AND GOOD FOR YOU, TOO!
AFTER JOINING HANDS TO ASK THE BLESSING, THE GROUP DIGS IN...
MY! THIS STUFFING IS UNIQUE-ARE THESE RAISINS OR CURRANTS?
RABBIT EGGS.
RABBIT EGGS?
YEAH, DA RABBIT LAYED DEM JUST BEFORE CONSTABLE TOM MADE 'IM GO TO 'EAVEN.
OOOH 'EY! NOW DAT'S GROSS!
Happy Holidays - B.K.T.

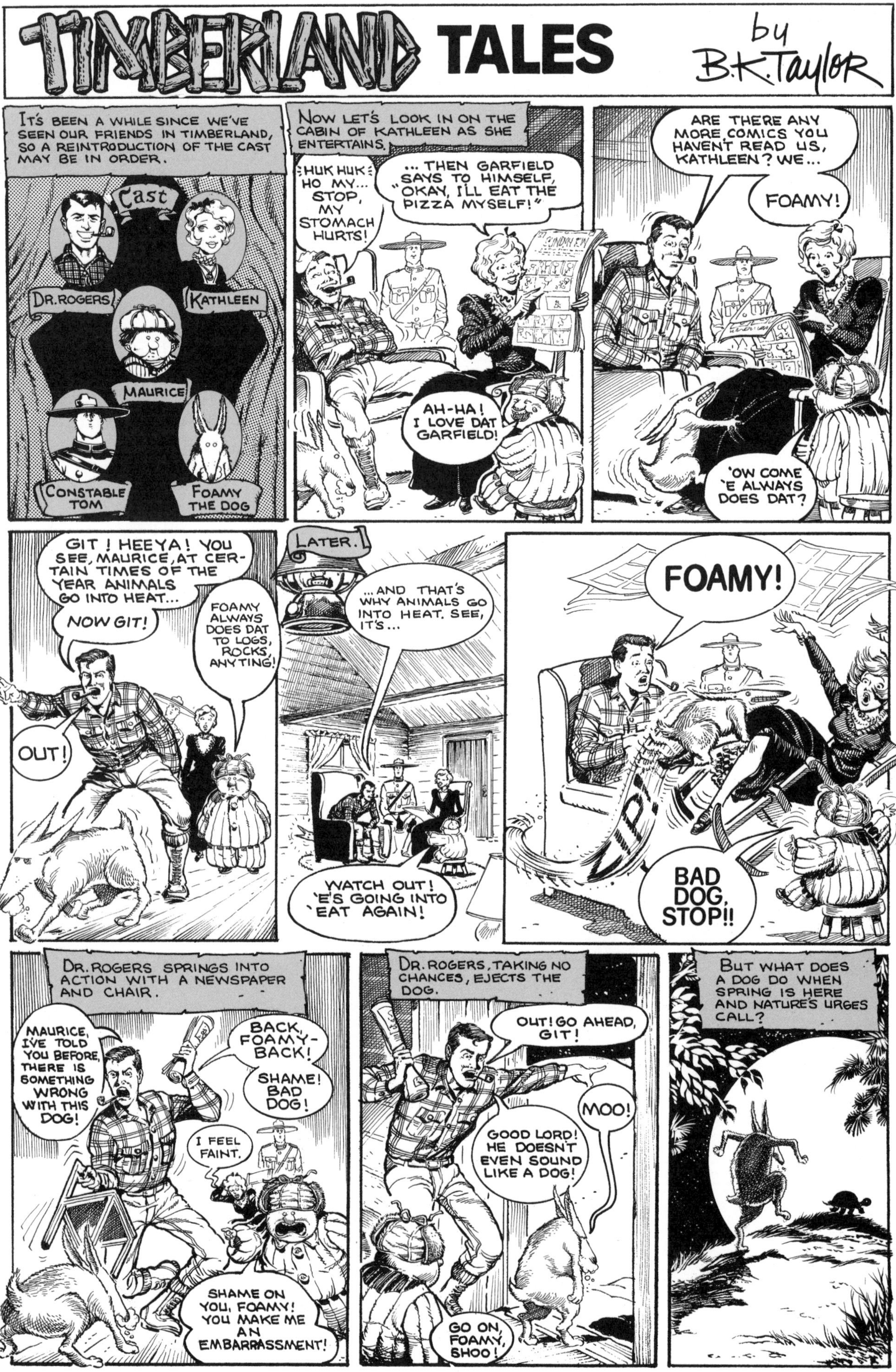
TIMBERLAND TALES
by B.K.Taylor
IT'S BEEN A WHILE SINCE WE'VE SEEN OUR FRIENDS IN TIMBERLAND, SO A REINTRODUCTION OF THE CAST MAY BE IN ORDER.
Cast
DR.ROGERS
KATHLEEN
MAURICE
CONSTABLE TOM
FOAMY THE DOG
NOW LET'S LOOK IN ON THE CABIN OF KATHLEEN AS SHE ENTERTAINS.
HUK HUK HO MY... STOP, MY STOMACH HURTS!
...THEN GARFIELD SAYS TO HIMSELF, "OKAY, I'LL EAT THE PIZZA MYSELF!"
AH-HA! I LOVE DAT GARFIELD!
ARE THERE ANY MORE COMICS YOU HAVEN'T READ US, KATHLEEN? WE...
FOAMY!
'OW COME 'E ALWAYS DOES DAT?
GIT! HEEYA! YOU SEE, MAURICE, AT CERTAIN TIMES OF THE YEAR ANIMALS GO INTO HEAT...
NOW GIT!
FOAMY ALWAYS DOES DAT TO LOGS, ROCKS, ANYTING!
OUT!
LATER.
...AND THAT'S WHY ANIMALS GO INTO HEAT. SEE, IT'S...
WATCH OUT! 'E'S GOING INTO 'EAT AGAIN!
FOAMY!
BAD DOG, STOP!!
DR.ROGERS SPRINGS INTO ACTION WITH A NEWSPAPER AND CHAIR.
MAURICE, I'VE TOLD YOU BEFORE, THERE IS SOMETHING WRONG WITH THIS DOG!
BACK, FOAMY- BACK!
SHAME! BAD DOG!
I FEEL FAINT.
SHAME ON YOU, FOAMY! YOU MAKE ME AN EMBARRASSMENT!
DR.ROGERS, TAKING NO CHANCES, EJECTS THE DOG.
OUT! GO AHEAD, GIT!
MOO!
GOOD LORD! HE DOESN'T EVEN SOUND LIKE A DOG!
GO ON, FOAMY, SHOO!
BUT WHAT DOES A DOG DO WHEN SPRING IS HERE AND NATURE'S URGES CALL?

TIMBERLAND TALES
by B.K. Taylor

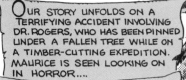

OUR STORY UNFOLDS ON A TERRIFYING ACCIDENT INVOLVING DR. ROGERS, WHO HAS BEEN PINNED UNDER A FALLEN TREE WHILE ON A TIMBER-CUTTING EXPEDITION. MAURICE IS SEEN LOOKING ON IN HORROR....

GEE.

MAURICE! DO SOMETHING— I'M TRAPPED!

A-HUK! I'M CAN'T REACH YOU!

HAND ME AN END OF THE ROPE — I'LL TIE IT AROUND MY CHEST AND THEN YOU CAN PULL ME OUT!

MAURICE FOLLOWS THE INSTRUCTIONS AND ATTEMPTS TO FREE THE DOCTOR, BUT ALAS...

NEVER MIND, YOU'RE NOT STRONG ENOUGH. TRY SOMETHING ELSE!

HA-YEEEE...

MAURICE, GO AND GET CONSTABLE TOM- HE'S STRONG....

MAURICE?!

MAURICE, ARE YOU THERE?

MOO.

FOAMY, WHERE'S MAURICE? OWW! WHAT'S HAPPENING?

OKEY DOKEY, YOU CAN BE OUT IN A JIFFY!

IS THE CONSTABLE HERE?

NOPE, I'M TIED DA ROPE TO A LOGGING TRUCK!

YOU WHAT!? A LOGGING TRUCK!! WHY DIDN'T YOU JUST TELL THEM I'M...

RRRRR

RRRRR!

WHOOWHEEE! 'E REALLY CLEARED A TRAIL! I 'OPE DEY KNOW WHERE 'E LIVES.

WELL, WE BETTER GET BACK.... OKAY, 'EEL, FOAMY... FOAMY! C'MON, 'EEL, FOAMY....

TIMBERLAND Tales
by B.K.Taylor
©79
DOCTOR ROGERS
KATHLEEN
MAURICE THE INDIAN BOY SOME CALL HIM THE JOKER.
CONSTABLE TOM RUMORED TO HAVE A SMALL AMOUNT OF BRAIN DAMAGE.
FOR A YOUTH, THERE IS NO GREATER JOY THAN THAT SPECIAL SURPRISE THAT ARRIVES IN THE MAIL. TODAY IS JUST SUCH A DAY FOR MAURICE, THE YOUNG INDIAN BOY... IN A TALE CALLED "THE THRILL OF IT ALL."
I'M WON! DR. ROGERS! I'M WON DAT CONTEST TO VISIT MR. PRETEND'S T.V. LAND!
MAURICE, HOW WONDERFUL! THIS WILL BE YOUR FIRST VISIT TO TORONTO.
MAURICE ARRIVES IN TORONTO TO THE SMILING FACE OF MR. PRETEND.
WELCOME, MAURICE! I'M MR. PRETEND, COME WITH ME AND I'LL SHOW YOU HOW TELEVISION WORKS.
T'ANKS!
EXCITEMENT FILLS THE AIR AS MAURICE TOURS THE STUDIO.
THE TIME DRAWS CLOSER TO AIRTIME, UNTIL...
THE RED LIGHT ON THE CAMERA MEANS IT'S TIME FOR MR. PRETEND!
HI, CHILDREN! WE HAVE MANY FUN THINGS ON THE SHOW TODAY. FIRST WE'LL VISIT PUPPET CORNER, SO DON'T GO AWAY... PLUS OUR SPECIAL GUEST IS THE WINNER OF THE BE-ON-T.V. CONTEST, OUR NEW FRIEND, MAURICE!
HI, MAURICE! I'M SO GLAD YOU COULD VISIT TODAY. MY NAME IS ROSCO.
WOW!
SAY, YOU REALLY LIKE ROSCO, EH?
YOU BET!... 'EY, EVERYBODY, LOOK AT DIS LITTLE GUY!
HI, MAURICE!
♪ IT'S TEATIME - TIME FOR TEA, TIME TO SHARE WITH YOU AND ME. ♪
MAURICE, WE ALWAYS STOP WHAT WE'RE DOING AT THIS POINT AND HAVE TEA AND A BLESSING. HERE'S YOURS...
KOOTCHY KOO...
CAN YOU COME UP TO PLAY?
OH MINE GOD! I'M PULLED OUT ROSCO'S GUTS!
AHHHHH! THAT'S IT, I QUIT!
BUMP
WHAT THE...
WITH ROSCO LIFELESS AND DANGLING FROM ONE ARM, MAURICE GLARES ACCUSINGLY AT "MR. PRETEND"... SUDDENLY A DARK THOUGHT ENTERS HIS MIND...
'EY... ARE YOU... ADOLF HITLER!?
WHAT? ME? WHY... NO! NO!
PEELING THE LATEX FROM HIS FACE, THE IMPOSTER READIES HIS ESCAPE!
BUT NOT FAST ENOUGH! FOR MAURICE JUMPS HIM AND HOLDS HIM DOWN UNTIL HELP ARRIVES.
THANKS, MAURICE. YOU'RE A HERO! WE'VE BEEN LOOKING FOR THIS MUG FOR A LONG TIME!
IT'S DA LEAST I COULD DO FOR DA FREE WORLD.
ACH, DU LIEBER!
WHAT THE HELL! SOME TIMES YOU CAN'T COME UP WITH AN ENDING SO YOU DO THE BEST YOU CAN! —B.K.T.

TIMBERLAND TALES
by B.K. Taylor

Doctor Rogers

Kathleen

Maurice THE INDIAN BOY SOME CALL HIM THE JOKER.

Constable Tom RUMORED TO HAVE A SMALL AMOUNT OF BRAIN DAMAGE.

EXCITEMENT IS IN THE AIR IN TIMBERLAND AS ONE OF THE LARGER TOWNS BEGINS ITS CENTENNIAL CELEBRATION. PEOPLE ARE DRAWN FROM MILES AROUND, AND DR. ROGERS, KATHLEEN, CONSTABLE TOM, AND MAURICE ARE NO EXCEPTION. THE RIDE TO THE FESTIVITIES HAS BEEN ONE FILLED WITH ANTICIPATION.

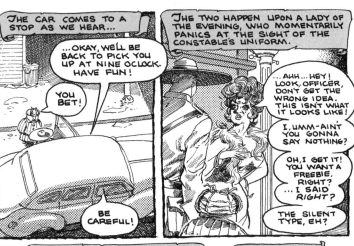

THE CAR COMES TO A STOP AS WE HEAR...

...OKAY, WE'LL BE BACK TO PICK YOU UP AT NINE O'CLOCK. HAVE FUN!

YOU BET!

BE CAREFUL!

THE TWO HAPPEN UPON A LADY OF THE EVENING, WHO MOMENTARILY PANICS AT THE SIGHT OF THE CONSTABLE'S UNIFORM.

...AHH... HEY! LOOK, OFFICER, DON'T GET THE WRONG IDEA. THIS ISN'T WHAT IT LOOKS LIKE!

I, UMM-AIN'T YOU GONNA SAY NOTHING?

OH, I GET IT! YOU WANT A FREEBIE, RIGHT? ...I SAID RIGHT?

THE SILENT TYPE, EH?

GETTING NO RESPONSE FROM THE CONSTABLE, SHE DRAWS HER OWN CONCLUSIONS AND ESCORTS THE BOYS UPSTAIRS.

C'MON, YOU GUYS. YOU KNOW, I STILL THINK IT'S SICK TO BRING A KID ALONG. BUT I'LL PLAY YOUR GAME.

WHAT GAME?

ONCE IN THE ROOM

LOOK, I HAVE TO FRESHEN UP, SO TAKE YOUR CLOTHES OFF, SHERLOCK - AND I'LL BE RIGHT BACK.

TAKE OUR CLOTHES OFF?

?

THE TWO ADVENTURERS DO AS THEY'RE TOLD, UNAWARE THAT THEIR NEW FRIEND HAS MADE A PERMANENT EXIT.

DIS IS SOME KIN' STRANGE CENTENNIAL, EH, CONSTABLE?

TIME PASSES.

§ SIGH § DIS IS BORING.

'EY! LOOK AT DIS!

A TREASURE CHEST!

WOW! LOOK AT DIS STUFF! WE CAN PLAY STAR WARRIORS! 'ERE, TRY SOME DIS STUFF ON!

SO THE FRIENDS TRY OUT THEIR NEWFOUND TOYS....

...AND LOOK 'ERE, A RUBBER LADY! WE CAN MAKE 'ER DA PRINCESS OF DA EMPIRE!

YOU'RE STRONG, YOU BLOW 'ER UP, OKAY?

LATER

I TINK MAYBE DAT'S ENOUGH....

DAT'S ENOUGH!

BWOOM!

IT'S NINE O'CLOCK, AND DR. ROGERS AND KATHLEEN ARE WAITING IN THE CAR, CHATTING, AS MAURICE AND THE CONSTABLE ENTER....

WASN'T THE PARADE JUST WONDERFUL?

...YES! AND THOSE CLOWNS WERE SO - OH LOOK! HERE THEY ARE! WELL, LADS, DID YOU HAVE...

...A GOOD TIME?

YEAH! LOOK WHAT WE FOUND! BUT I CAN'T GET DIS RUBBER LADY OFF MINE 'EAD!

© B.K. Taylor 1989

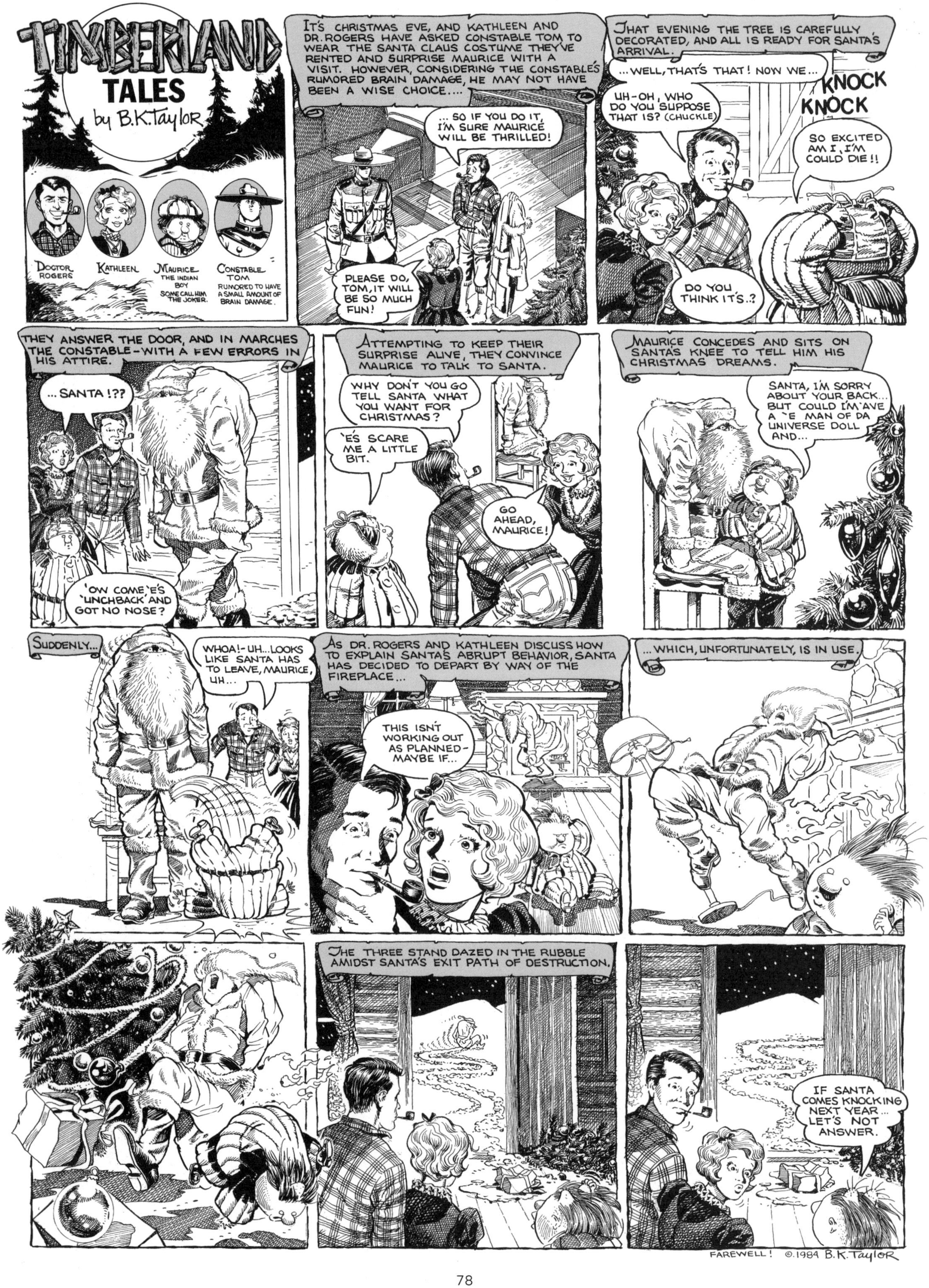
TIMBERLAND TALES
by B.K.Taylor
DOCTOR ROGERS
KATHLEEN
MAURICE THE INDIAN BOY SOME CALL HIM THE JOKER.
CONSTABLE TOM RUMORED TO HAVE A SMALL AMOUNT OF BRAIN DAMAGE.
IT'S CHRISTMAS EVE, AND KATHLEEN AND DR. ROGERS HAVE ASKED CONSTABLE TOM TO WEAR THE SANTA CLAUS COSTUME THEY'VE RENTED AND SURPRISE MAURICE WITH A VISIT. HOWEVER, CONSIDERING THE CONSTABLE'S RUMORED BRAIN DAMAGE, HE MAY NOT HAVE BEEN A WISE CHOICE....
... SO IF YOU DO IT, I'M SURE MAURICE WILL BE THRILLED!
PLEASE DO, TOM, IT WILL BE SO MUCH FUN!
THAT EVENING THE TREE IS CAREFULLY DECORATED, AND ALL IS READY FOR SANTA'S ARRIVAL.
... WELL, THAT'S THAT! NOW WE...
KNOCK KNOCK
UH-OH, WHO DO YOU SUPPOSE THAT IS? (CHUCKLE)
SO EXCITED AM I, I'M COULD DIE!!
DO YOU THINK IT'S..?
THEY ANSWER THE DOOR, AND IN MARCHES THE CONSTABLE-WITH A FEW ERRORS IN HIS ATTIRE.
... SANTA!??
'OW COME 'E'S 'UNCHBACK AND GOT NO NOSE?
ATTEMPTING TO KEEP THEIR SURPRISE ALIVE, THEY CONVINCE MAURICE TO TALK TO SANTA.
WHY DON'T YOU GO TELL SANTA WHAT YOU WANT FOR CHRISTMAS?
'E'S SCARE ME A LITTLE BIT.
GO AHEAD, MAURICE!
MAURICE CONCEDES AND SITS ON SANTA'S KNEE TO TELL HIM HIS CHRISTMAS DREAMS.
SANTA, I'M SORRY ABOUT YOUR BACK... BUT COULD I'M 'AVE A 'E MAN OF DA UNIVERSE DOLL AND...
SUDDENLY...
WHOA!-UH... LOOKS LIKE SANTA HAS TO LEAVE, MAURICE, UH...
AS DR. ROGERS AND KATHLEEN DISCUSS HOW TO EXPLAIN SANTA'S ABRUPT BEHAVIOR, SANTA HAS DECIDED TO DEPART BY WAY OF THE FIREPLACE...
THIS ISN'T WORKING OUT AS PLANNED-MAYBE IF...
... WHICH, UNFORTUNATELY, IS IN USE.
THE THREE STAND DAZED IN THE RUBBLE AMIDST SANTA'S EXIT PATH OF DESTRUCTION.
IF SANTA COMES KNOCKING NEXT YEAR... LET'S NOT ANSWER.
FAREWELL! ©1984 B.K.Taylor

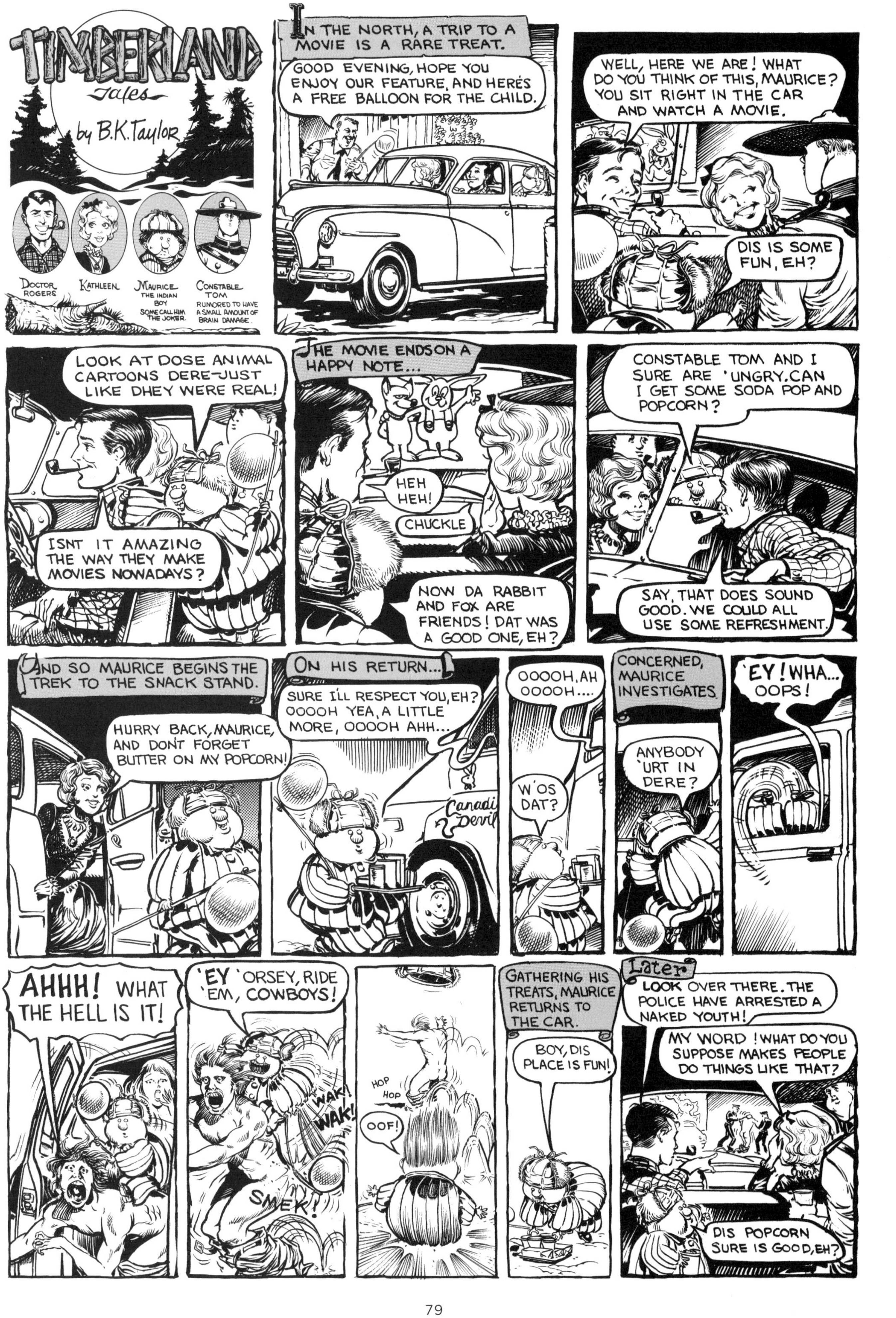
TIMBERLAND
Tales
by B.K.Taylor
DOCTOR ROGERS
KATHLEEN
MAURICE THE INDIAN BOY SOME CALL HIM THE JOKER.
CONSTABLE TOM RUMORED TO HAVE A SMALL AMOUNT OF BRAIN DAMAGE.
IN THE NORTH, A TRIP TO A MOVIE IS A RARE TREAT.
GOOD EVENING, HOPE YOU ENJOY OUR FEATURE, AND HERE'S A FREE BALLOON FOR THE CHILD.
WELL, HERE WE ARE! WHAT DO YOU THINK OF THIS, MAURICE? YOU SIT RIGHT IN THE CAR AND WATCH A MOVIE.
DIS IS SOME FUN, EH?
LOOK AT DOSE ANIMAL CARTOONS DERE-JUST LIKE DHEY WERE REAL!
ISNT IT AMAZING THE WAY THEY MAKE MOVIES NOWADAYS?
THE MOVIE ENDS ON A HAPPY NOTE...
HEH HEH!
CHUCKLE
NOW DA RABBIT AND FOX ARE FRIENDS! DAT WAS A GOOD ONE, EH?
CONSTABLE TOM AND I SURE ARE 'UNGRY. CAN I GET SOME SODA POP AND POPCORN?
SAY, THAT DOES SOUND GOOD. WE COULD ALL USE SOME REFRESHMENT.
AND SO MAURICE BEGINS THE TREK TO THE SNACK STAND.
HURRY BACK, MAURICE, AND DON'T FORGET BUTTER ON MY POPCORN!
ON HIS RETURN...
SURE I'LL RESPECT YOU, EH? OOOOH YEA, A LITTLE MORE, OOOOH AHH...
Canadi Devil
OOOOH, AH OOOOH....
W'OS DAT?
CONCERNED, MAURICE INVESTIGATES.
ANYBODY 'URT IN DERE?
'EY! WHA... OOPS!
AHHH! WHAT THE HELL IS IT!
'EY 'ORSEY, RIDE 'EM, COWBOYS!
WAK! WAK!
SMEK!
HOP HOP
OOF!
GATHERING HIS TREATS, MAURICE RETURNS TO THE CAR.
BOY, DIS PLACE IS FUN!
Later
LOOK OVER THERE. THE POLICE HAVE ARRESTED A NAKED YOUTH!
MY WORD! WHAT DO YOU SUPPOSE MAKES PEOPLE DO THINGS LIKE THAT?
DIS POPCORN SURE IS GOOD, EH?

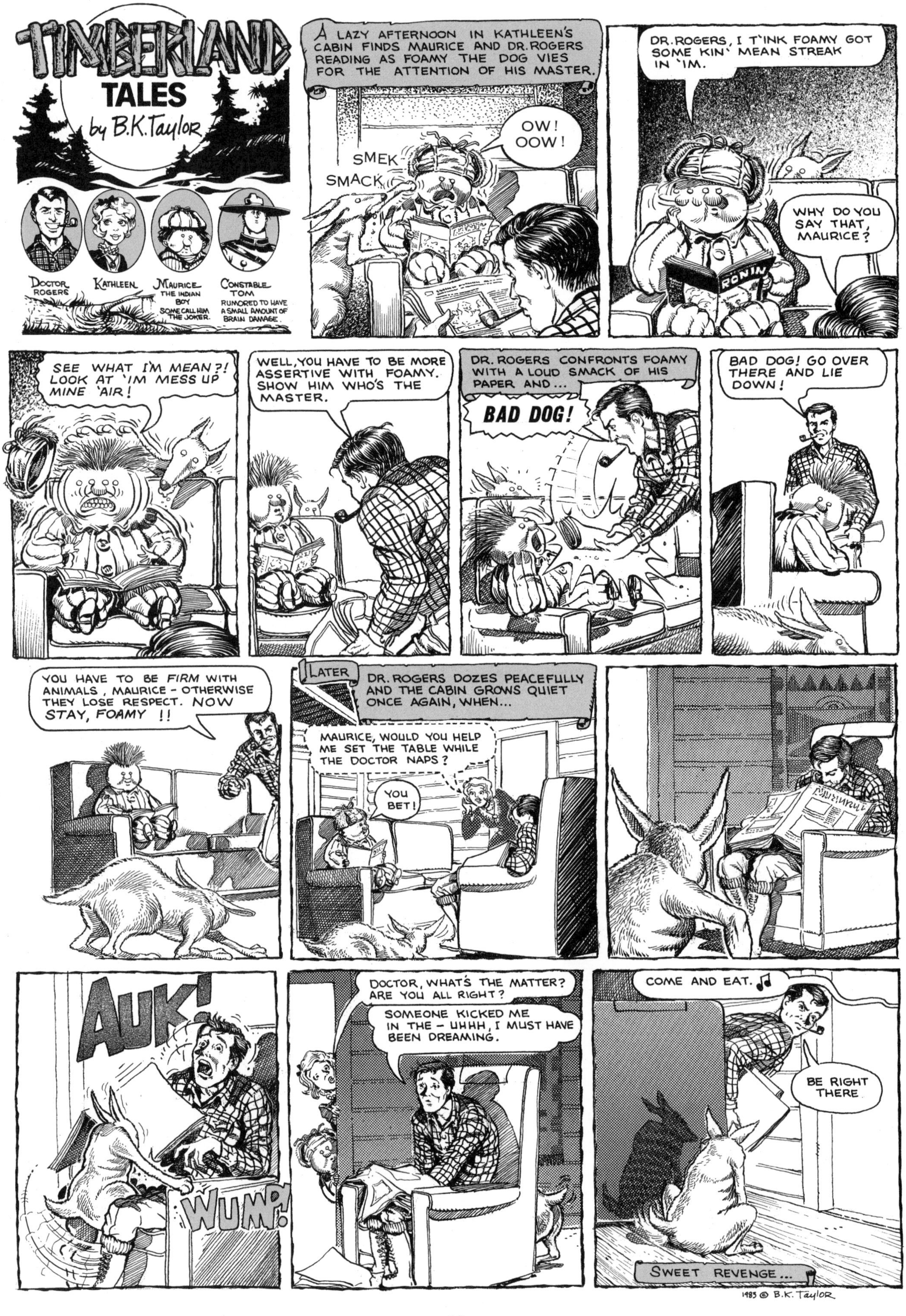
TIMBERLAND TALES
by B.K. Taylor
DOCTOR ROGERS
KATHLEEN
MAURICE THE INDIAN BOY SOME CALL HIM THE JOKER.
CONSTABLE TOM RUMORED TO HAVE A SMALL AMOUNT OF BRAIN DAMAGE.
A LAZY AFTERNOON IN KATHLEEN'S CABIN FINDS MAURICE AND DR. ROGERS READING AS FOAMY THE DOG VIES FOR THE ATTENTION OF HIS MASTER.
SMEK
SMACK
OW! OOW!
DR. ROGERS, I T'INK FOAMY GOT SOME KIN' MEAN STREAK IN 'IM.
RONIN
WHY DO YOU SAY THAT, MAURICE?
SEE WHAT I'M MEAN?! LOOK AT 'IM MESS UP MINE 'AIR!
WELL, YOU HAVE TO BE MORE ASSERTIVE WITH FOAMY. SHOW HIM WHO'S THE MASTER.
DR. ROGERS CONFRONTS FOAMY WITH A LOUD SMACK OF HIS PAPER AND...
BAD DOG!
BAD DOG! GO OVER THERE AND LIE DOWN!
YOU HAVE TO BE FIRM WITH ANIMALS, MAURICE - OTHERWISE THEY LOSE RESPECT. NOW STAY, FOAMY !!
LATER
DR. ROGERS DOZES PEACEFULLY AND THE CABIN GROWS QUIET ONCE AGAIN, WHEN...
MAURICE, WOULD YOU HELP ME SET THE TABLE WHILE THE DOCTOR NAPS?
YOU BET!
AUK!
WUMP!
DOCTOR, WHAT'S THE MATTER? ARE YOU ALL RIGHT?
SOMEONE KICKED ME IN THE - UHHH, I MUST HAVE BEEN DREAMING.
COME AND EAT.
BE RIGHT THERE
SWEET REVENGE...
1983 © B.K. Taylor

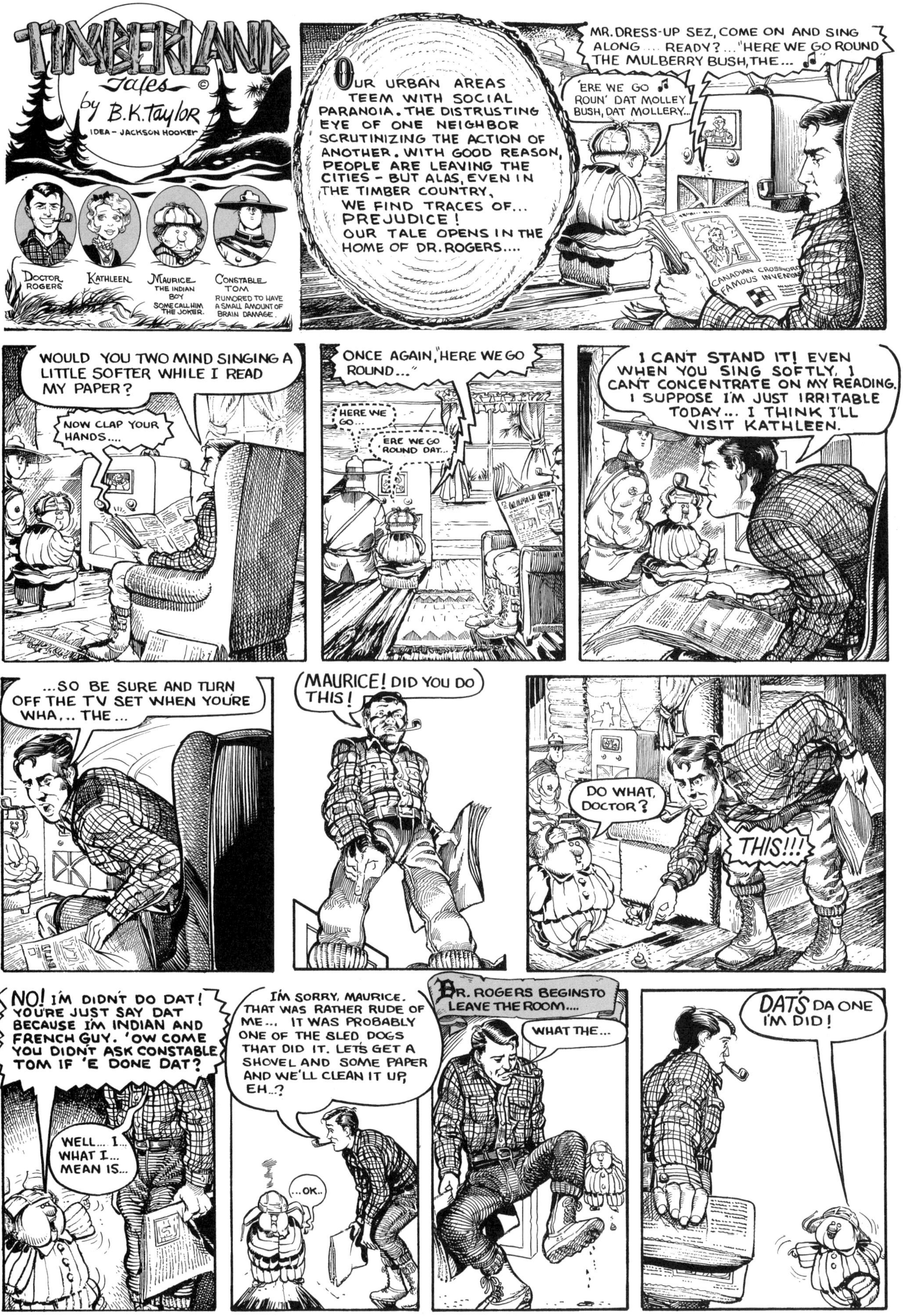
TIMBERLAND Tales ©
by B.K. Taylor
IDEA - JACKSON HOOKER
DOCTOR ROGERS
KATHLEEN
MAURICE THE INDIAN BOY SOME CALL HIM THE JOKER.
CONSTABLE TOM RUMORED TO HAVE A SMALL AMOUNT OF BRAIN DAMAGE.
OUR URBAN AREAS TEEM WITH SOCIAL PARANOIA. THE DISTRUSTING EYE OF ONE NEIGHBOR SCRUTINIZING THE ACTION OF ANOTHER. WITH GOOD REASON, PEOPLE ARE LEAVING THE CITIES - BUT ALAS, EVEN IN THE TIMBER COUNTRY, WE FIND TRACES OF... PREJUDICE! OUR TALE OPENS IN THE HOME OF DR. ROGERS....
MR. DRESS-UP SEZ, COME ON AND SING ALONG.... READY?... "HERE WE GO ROUND THE MULBERRY BUSH, THE...
'ERE WE GO ROUN' DAT MOLLEY BUSH, DAT MOLLERY...
CANADIAN CROSSWORD
FAMOUS INVENTORS
WOULD YOU TWO MIND SINGING A LITTLE SOFTER WHILE I READ MY PAPER?
NOW CLAP YOUR HANDS....
ONCE AGAIN, "HERE WE GO ROUND..."
HERE WE GO...
ERE WE GO ROUND DAT...
I CAN'T STAND IT! EVEN WHEN YOU SING SOFTLY, I CAN'T CONCENTRATE ON MY READING. I SUPPOSE I'M JUST IRRITABLE TODAY... I THINK I'LL VISIT KATHLEEN.
...SO BE SURE AND TURN OFF THE TV SET WHEN YOU'RE WHA,.. THE...
MAURICE! DID YOU DO THIS!
DO WHAT, DOCTOR?
THIS!!!
NO! I'M DIDN'T DO DAT! YOU'RE JUST SAY DAT BECAUSE I'M INDIAN AND FRENCH GUY. 'OW COME YOU DIDN'T ASK CONSTABLE TOM IF 'E DONE DAT?
WELL... I... WHAT I... MEAN IS...
I'M SORRY, MAURICE. THAT WAS RATHER RUDE OF ME... IT WAS PROBABLY ONE OF THE SLED DOGS THAT DID IT. LET'S GET A SHOVEL AND SOME PAPER AND WE'LL CLEAN IT UP, EH..?
...OK..
DR. ROGERS BEGINS TO LEAVE THE ROOM....
WHAT THE...
DAT'S DA ONE I'M DID!

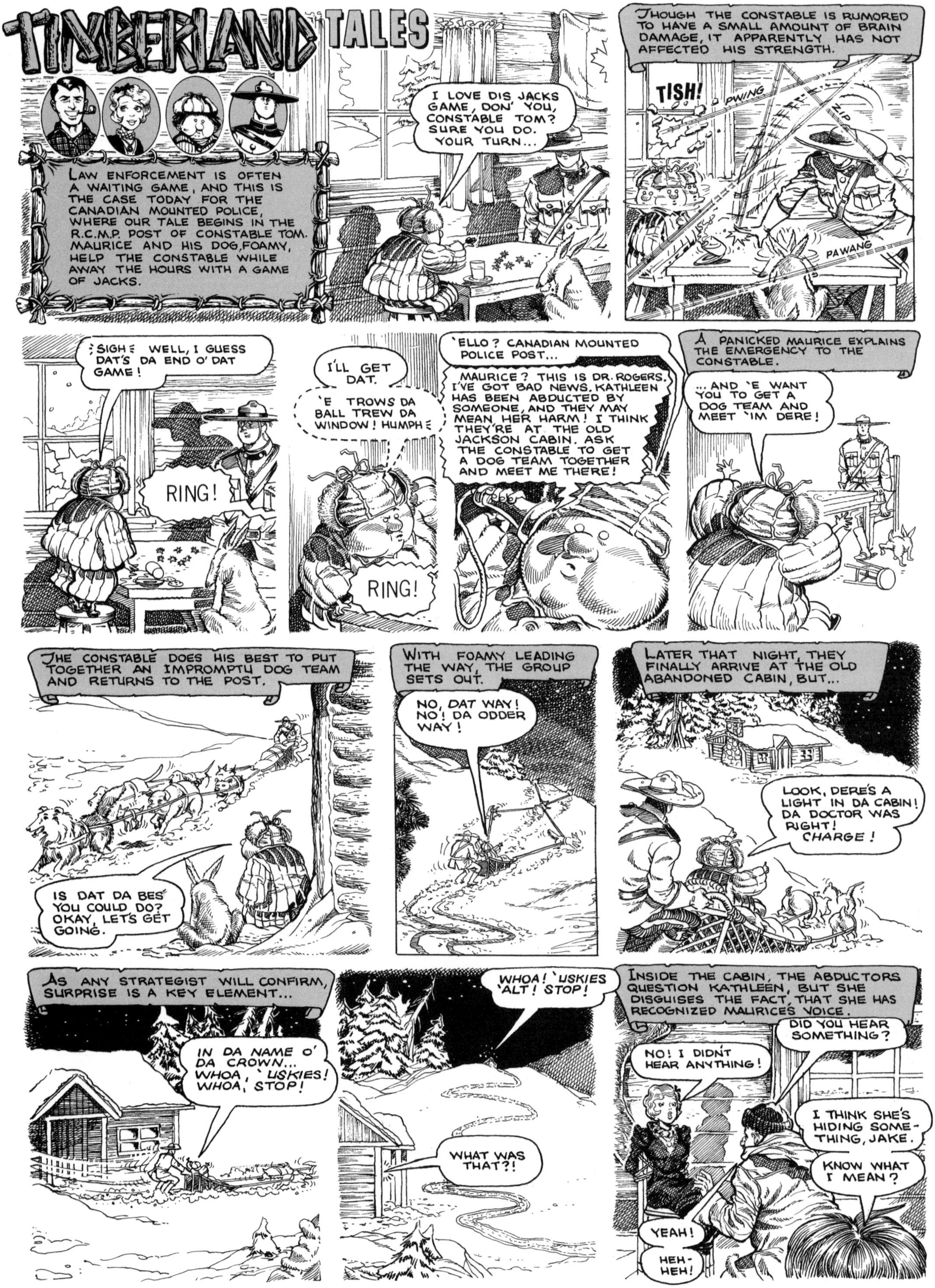
TIMBERLAND TALES
LAW ENFORCEMENT IS OFTEN A WAITING GAME, AND THIS IS THE CASE TODAY FOR THE CANADIAN MOUNTED POLICE, WHERE OUR TALE BEGINS IN THE R.C.M.P. POST OF CONSTABLE TOM. MAURICE AND HIS DOG, FOAMY, HELP THE CONSTABLE WHILE AWAY THE HOURS WITH A GAME OF JACKS.
I LOVE DIS JACKS GAME, DON' YOU, CONSTABLE TOM? SURE YOU DO. YOUR TURN...
THOUGH THE CONSTABLE IS RUMORED TO HAVE A SMALL AMOUNT OF BRAIN DAMAGE, IT APPARENTLY HAS NOT AFFECTED HIS STRENGTH.
TISH!
PWING
ZIP
PAWANG
SIGH WELL, I GUESS DAT'S DA END O' DAT GAME!
RING!
I'LL GET DAT.
'E TROWS DA BALL TREW DA WINDOW! HUMPH
RING!
'ELLO? CANADIAN MOUNTED POLICE POST...
MAURICE? THIS IS DR. ROGERS. I'VE GOT BAD NEWS. KATHLEEN HAS BEEN ABDUCTED BY SOMEONE, AND THEY MAY MEAN HER HARM! I THINK THEY'RE AT THE OLD JACKSON CABIN. ASK THE CONSTABLE TO GET A DOG TEAM TOGETHER AND MEET ME THERE!
A PANICKED MAURICE EXPLAINS THE EMERGENCY TO THE CONSTABLE.
...AND 'E WANT YOU TO GET A DOG TEAM AND MEET 'IM DERE!
THE CONSTABLE DOES HIS BEST TO PUT TOGETHER AN IMPROMPTU DOG TEAM AND RETURNS TO THE POST.
IS DAT DA BES' YOU COULD DO? OKAY, LET'S GET GOING.
WITH FOAMY LEADING THE WAY, THE GROUP SETS OUT.
NO, DAT WAY! NO! DA ODDER WAY!
LATER THAT NIGHT, THEY FINALLY ARRIVE AT THE OLD ABANDONED CABIN, BUT...
LOOK, DERE'S A LIGHT IN DA CABIN! DA DOCTOR WAS RIGHT! CHARGE!
AS ANY STRATEGIST WILL CONFIRM, SURPRISE IS A KEY ELEMENT...
IN DA NAME O' DA CROWN... WHOA, 'USKIES! WHOA, STOP!
WHOA! 'USKIES 'ALT! STOP!
WHAT WAS THAT?!
INSIDE THE CABIN, THE ABDUCTORS QUESTION KATHLEEN, BUT SHE DISGUISES THE FACT THAT SHE HAS RECOGNIZED MAURICE'S VOICE.
DID YOU HEAR SOMETHING?
NO! I DIDN'T HEAR ANYTHING!
I THINK SHE'S HIDING SOME-THING, JAKE.
KNOW WHAT I MEAN?
YEAH!
HEH-HEH!

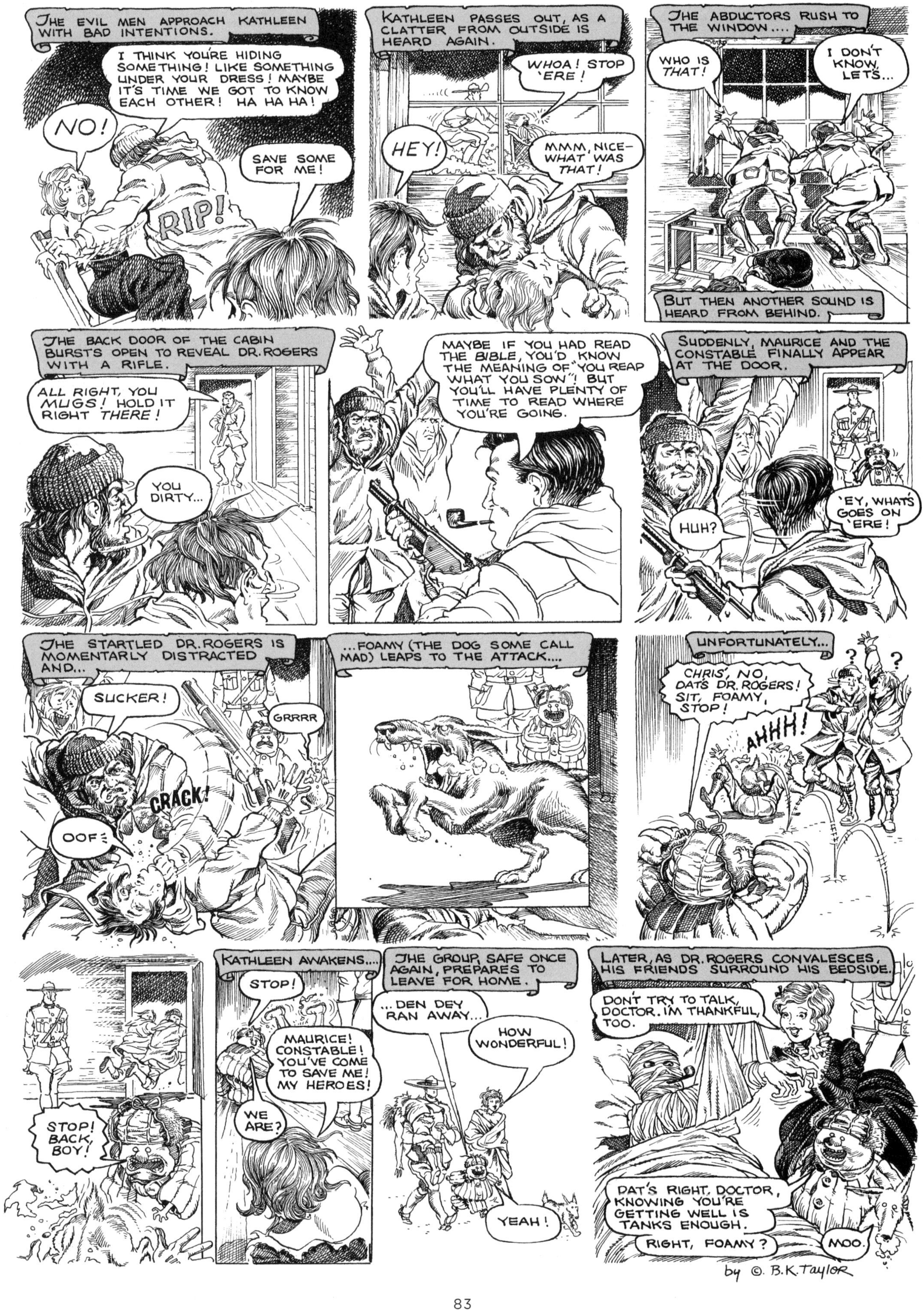

THE EVIL MEN APPROACH KATHLEEN WITH BAD INTENTIONS.
I THINK YOU'RE HIDING SOMETHING! LIKE SOMETHING UNDER YOUR DRESS! MAYBE IT'S TIME WE GOT TO KNOW EACH OTHER! HA HA HA!
NO!
RIP!
SAVE SOME FOR ME!
KATHLEEN PASSES OUT, AS A CLATTER FROM OUTSIDE IS HEARD AGAIN.
WHOA! STOP 'ERE!
HEY!
MMM, NICE- WHAT WAS THAT!
THE ABDUCTORS RUSH TO THE WINDOW....
WHO IS THAT!
I DON'T KNOW, LETS...
BUT THEN ANOTHER SOUND IS HEARD FROM BEHIND.
THE BACK DOOR OF THE CABIN BURSTS OPEN TO REVEAL DR. ROGERS WITH A RIFLE.
ALL RIGHT, YOU MUGS! HOLD IT RIGHT THERE!
YOU DIRTY...
MAYBE IF YOU HAD READ THE BIBLE, YOU'D KNOW THE MEANING OF "YOU REAP WHAT YOU SOW"! BUT YOU'LL HAVE PLENTY OF TIME TO READ WHERE YOU'RE GOING.
SUDDENLY, MAURICE AND THE CONSTABLE FINALLY APPEAR AT THE DOOR.
HUH?
'EY, WHAT'S GOES ON 'ERE!
THE STARTLED DR. ROGERS IS MOMENTARILY DISTRACTED AND...
SUCKER!
GRRRR
CRACK!
OOF
...FOAMY (THE DOG SOME CALL MAD) LEAPS TO THE ATTACK....
UNFORTUNATELY...
CHRIS', NO, DATS DR. ROGERS! SIT, FOAMY, STOP!
AHHH!
STOP! BACK, BOY!
KATHLEEN AWAKENS....
STOP!
MAURICE! CONSTABLE! YOU'VE COME TO SAVE ME! MY HEROES!
WE ARE?
THE GROUP, SAFE ONCE AGAIN, PREPARES TO LEAVE FOR HOME.
... DEN DEY RAN AWAY...
HOW WONDERFUL!
YEAH!
LATER, AS DR. ROGERS CONVALESCES, HIS FRIENDS SURROUND HIS BEDSIDE.
DON'T TRY TO TALK, DOCTOR. I'M THANKFUL, TOO.
DAT'S RIGHT, DOCTOR, KNOWING YOU'RE GETTING WELL IS TANKS ENOUGH.
RIGHT, FOAMY?
MOO.
by ©. B.K. Taylor

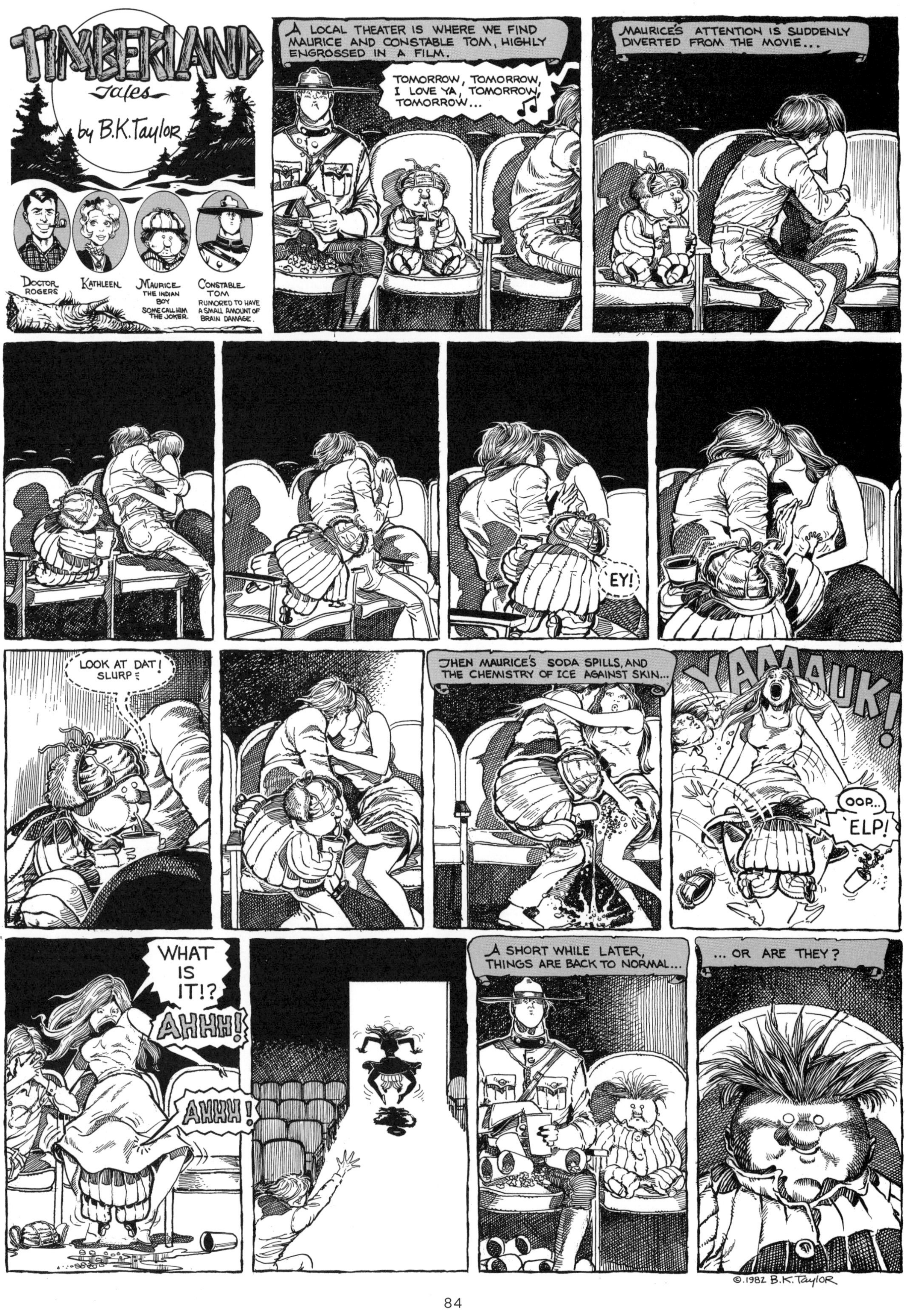
TIMBERLAND
Tales
by B.K. Taylor
DOCTOR ROGERS
KATHLEEN
MAURICE THE INDIAN BOY SOME CALL HIM THE JOKER.
CONSTABLE TOM RUMORED TO HAVE A SMALL AMOUNT OF BRAIN DAMAGE.
A LOCAL THEATER IS WHERE WE FIND MAURICE AND CONSTABLE TOM, HIGHLY ENGROSSED IN A FILM.
TOMORROW, TOMORROW, I LOVE YA, TOMORROW, TOMORROW...
MAURICE'S ATTENTION IS SUDDENLY DIVERTED FROM THE MOVIE...
EY!
LOOK AT DAT! SLURP
THEN MAURICE'S SODA SPILLS, AND THE CHEMISTRY OF ICE AGAINST SKIN...
YAAAAUK!
OOP...
ELP!
WHAT IS IT!?
AHHH!
AHHH!
A SHORT WHILE LATER, THINGS ARE BACK TO NORMAL...
... OR ARE THEY?
©.1982 B.K. TAYLOR

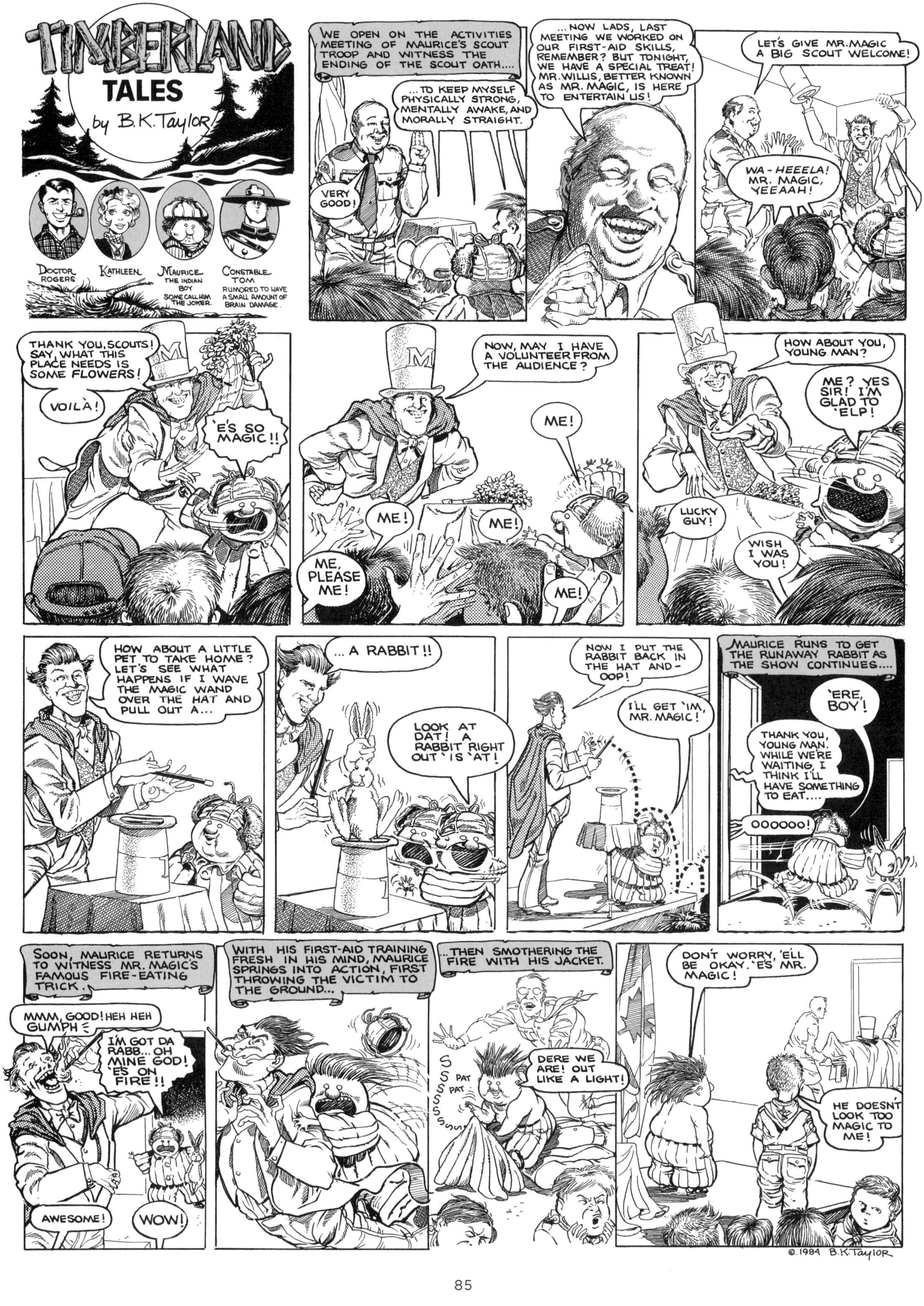
TIMBERLAND TALES
by B.K.Taylor
DOCTOR ROGERS
KATHLEEN
MAURICE THE INDIAN BOY SOME CALL HIM THE JOKER.
CONSTABLE TOM RUMORED TO HAVE A SMALL AMOUNT OF BRAIN DAMAGE.
WE OPEN ON THE ACTIVITIES MEETING OF MAURICE'S SCOUT TROOP AND WITNESS THE ENDING OF THE SCOUT OATH....
...TO KEEP MYSELF PHYSICALLY STRONG, MENTALLY AWAKE, AND MORALLY STRAIGHT.
VERY GOOD!
...NOW LADS, LAST MEETING WE WORKED ON OUR FIRST-AID SKILLS, REMEMBER? BUT TONIGHT, WE HAVE A SPECIAL TREAT! MR. WILLIS, BETTER KNOWN AS MR. MAGIC, IS HERE TO ENTERTAIN US!
LET'S GIVE MR. MAGIC A BIG SCOUT WELCOME!
WA-HEEELA! MR. MAGIC, YEEAAH!
THANK YOU, SCOUTS! SAY, WHAT THIS PLACE NEEDS IS SOME FLOWERS!
VOILÀ!
'E'S SO MAGIC!!
NOW, MAY I HAVE A VOLUNTEER FROM THE AUDIENCE?
ME!
ME!
ME!
ME, PLEASE ME!
ME!
HOW ABOUT YOU, YOUNG MAN?
ME? YES SIR! I'M GLAD TO 'ELP!
LUCKY GUY!
WISH I WAS YOU!
HOW ABOUT A LITTLE PET TO TAKE HOME? LET'S SEE WHAT HAPPENS IF I WAVE THE MAGIC WAND OVER THE HAT AND PULL OUT A...
...A RABBIT!!
LOOK AT DAT! A RABBIT RIGHT OUT 'IS 'AT!
NOW I PUT THE RABBIT BACK IN THE HAT AND- OOP!
I'LL GET 'IM, MR. MAGIC!
MAURICE RUNS TO GET THE RUNAWAY RABBIT AS THE SHOW CONTINUES....
'ERE, BOY!
THANK YOU, YOUNG MAN. WHILE WE'RE WAITING, I THINK I'LL HAVE SOMETHING TO EAT....
OOOOOO!
SOON, MAURICE RETURNS TO WITNESS MR. MAGIC'S FAMOUS FIRE-EATING TRICK.
MMM, GOOD! HEH HEH GUMPH
I'M GOT DA RABB... OH MINE GOD! 'E'S ON FIRE!!
AWESOME!
WOW!
WITH HIS FIRST-AID TRAINING FRESH IN HIS MIND, MAURICE SPRINGS INTO ACTION, FIRST THROWING THE VICTIM TO THE GROUND...
...THEN SMOTHERING THE FIRE WITH HIS JACKET.
SSSSSSSS
PAT PAT
DERE WE ARE! OUT LIKE A LIGHT!
DON'T WORRY, 'ELL BE OKAY. 'E'S MR. MAGIC!
HE DOESN'T LOOK TOO MAGIC TO ME!
©.1984 B.K.Taylor

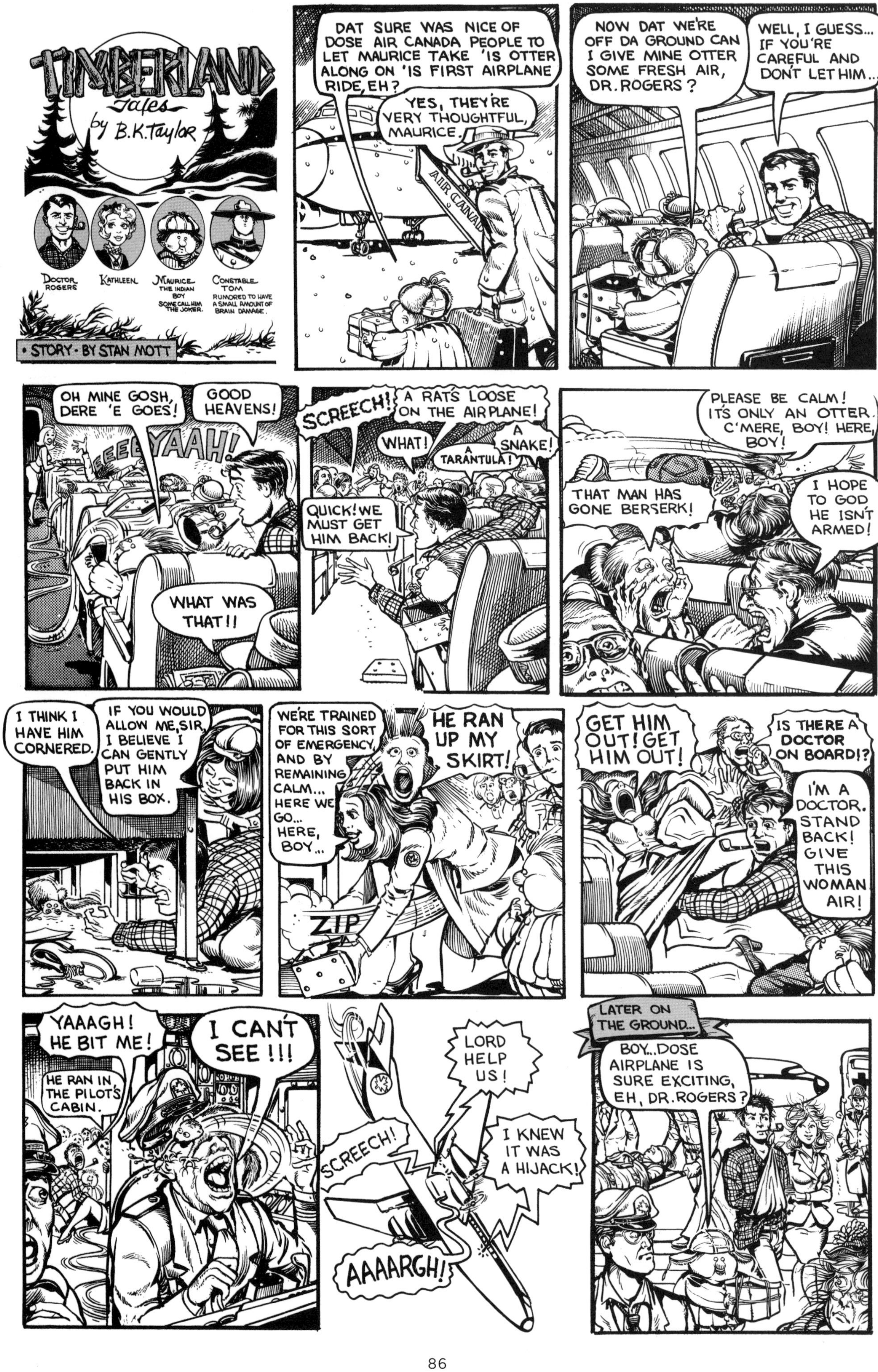
TIMBERLAND Tales
by B.K. Taylor
DOCTOR ROGERS
KATHLEEN
MAURICE THE INDIAN BOY SOME CALL HIM THE JOKER.
CONSTABLE TOM RUMORED TO HAVE A SMALL AMOUNT OF BRAIN DAMAGE.
• STORY • BY STAN MOTT
DAT SURE WAS NICE OF DOSE AIR CANADA PEOPLE TO LET MAURICE TAKE 'IS OTTER ALONG ON 'IS FIRST AIRPLANE RIDE, EH?
YES, THEY'RE VERY THOUGHTFUL, MAURICE.
AIR CANADA
NOW DAT WE'RE OFF DA GROUND CAN I GIVE MINE OTTER SOME FRESH AIR, DR. ROGERS?
WELL, I GUESS... IF YOU'RE CAREFUL AND DON'T LET HIM...
OH MINE GOSH, DERE 'E GOES!
GOOD HEAVENS!
EEEEYAAH!
WHAT WAS THAT!!
SCREECH!
A RAT'S LOOSE ON THE AIRPLANE!
WHAT!
A TARANTULA!
A SNAKE!
QUICK! WE MUST GET HIM BACK!
PLEASE BE CALM! IT'S ONLY AN OTTER. C'MERE, BOY! HERE, BOY!
THAT MAN HAS GONE BERSERK!
I HOPE TO GOD HE ISN'T ARMED!
I THINK I HAVE HIM CORNERED.
IF YOU WOULD ALLOW ME, SIR, I BELIEVE I CAN GENTLY PUT HIM BACK IN HIS BOX.
WE'RE TRAINED FOR THIS SORT OF EMERGENCY, AND BY REMAINING CALM... HERE WE GO... HERE, BOY...
HE RAN UP MY SKIRT!
ZIP
GET HIM OUT! GET HIM OUT!
IS THERE A DOCTOR ON BOARD!?
I'M A DOCTOR. STAND BACK! GIVE THIS WOMAN AIR!
YAAAGH! HE BIT ME!
I CAN'T SEE!!!
HE RAN IN THE PILOT'S CABIN.
LORD HELP US!
SCREECH!
I KNEW IT WAS A HIJACK!
AAAARGH!
LATER ON THE GROUND...
BOY... DOSE AIRPLANE IS SURE EXCITING, EH, DR. ROGERS?

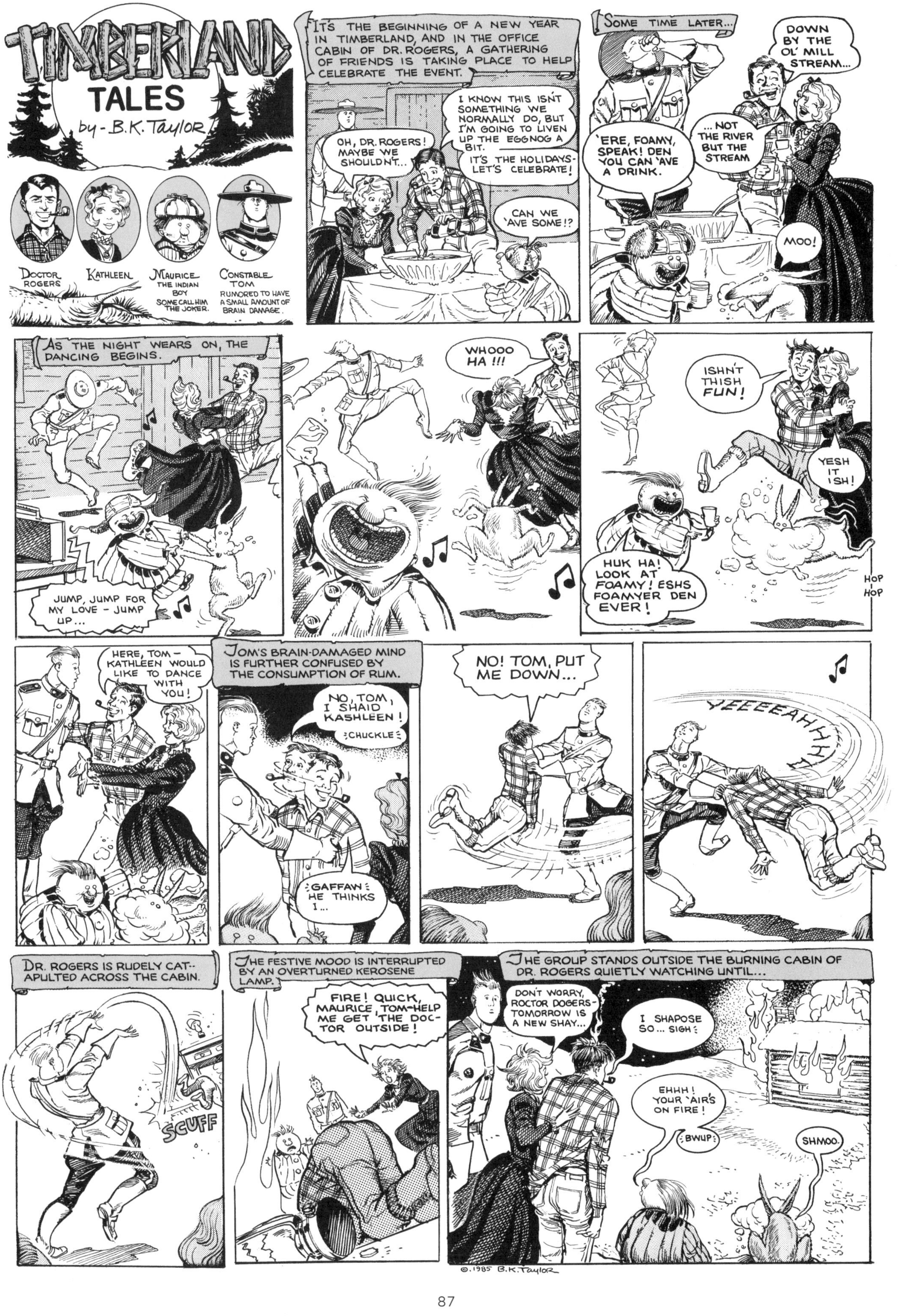
TIMBERLAND TALES
by - B.K. Taylor
Doctor Rogers
Kathleen
Maurice the Indian boy some call him the joker.
Constable Tom rumored to have a small amount of brain damage.
It's the beginning of a new year in Timberland, and in the office cabin of Dr. Rogers, a gathering of friends is taking place to help celebrate the event.
Oh, Dr. Rogers! Maybe we shouldn't...
I know this isn't something we normally do, but I'm going to liven up the eggnog a bit.
It's the holidays- let's celebrate!
Can we 'ave some!?
Some time later...
Down by the ol' mill stream...
...Not the river but the stream
'Ere, Foamy, speak! Den you can 'ave a drink.
Moo!
As the night wears on, the dancing begins.
Jump, jump for my love - jump up...
Whooo ha!!!
Ishn't thish fun!
Yesh it ish!
Huk ha! Look at Foamy! Eshs foamyer den ever!
Hop hop
Here, Tom - Kathleen would like to dance with you!
Tom's brain-damaged mind is further confused by the consumption of rum.
No, Tom, I shaid Kashleen!
Chuckle
Gaffaw he thinks I...
No! Tom, put me down...
Yeeeeahhhhh
Dr. Rogers is rudely cat-apulted across the cabin.
Scuff
The festive mood is interrupted by an overturned kerosene lamp.
Fire! Quick, Maurice, Tom-help me get the doctor outside!
The group stands outside the burning cabin of Dr. Rogers quietly watching until...
Don't worry, Roctor Dogers- tomorrow is a new shay...
I shapose so... sigh
Ehhh! Your 'air's on fire!
Bwup
Shmoo.
©. 1985 B.K. Taylor

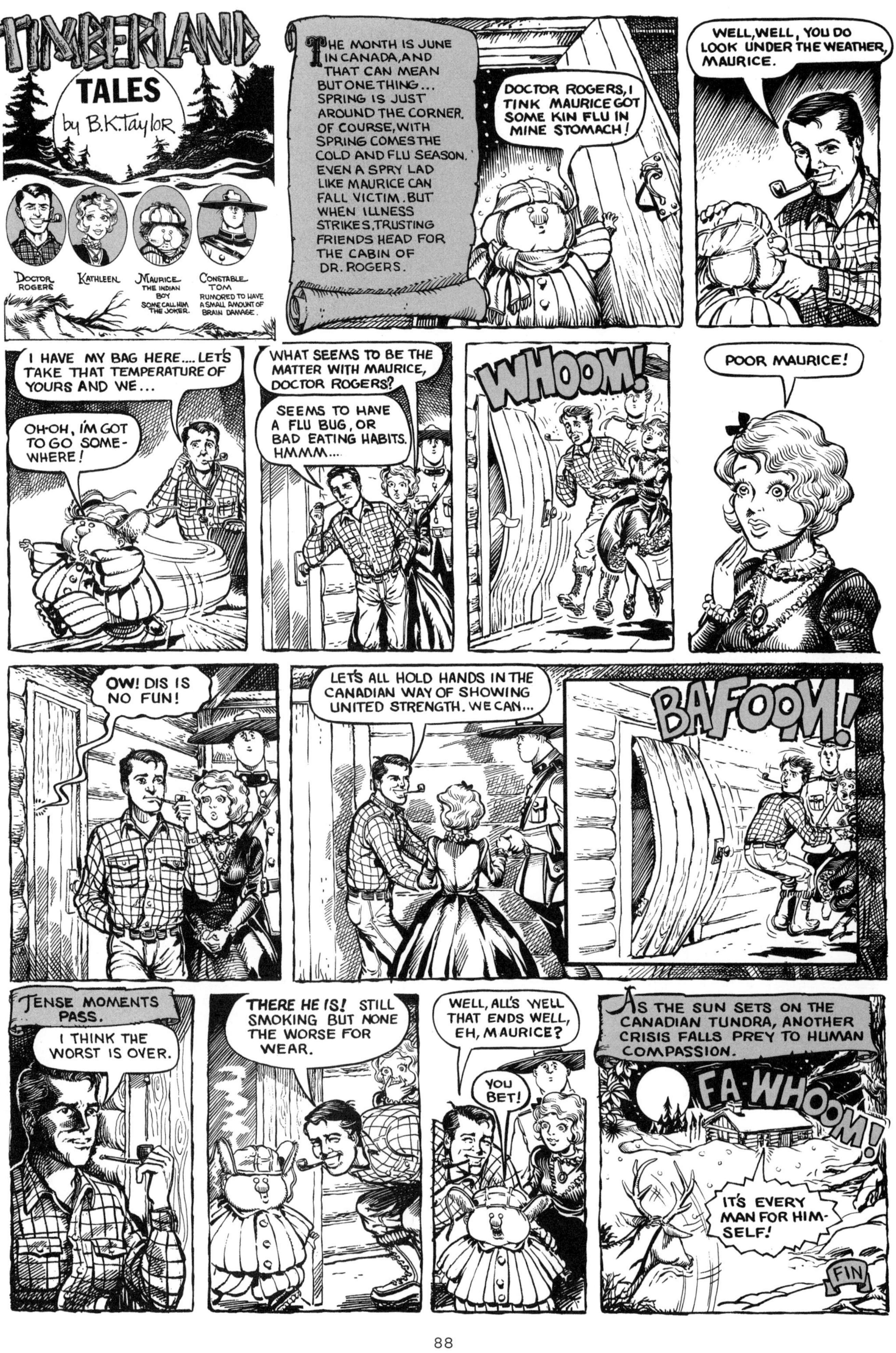
TIMBERLAND TALES
by B.K.Taylor
DOCTOR ROGERS
KATHLEEN
MAURICE THE INDIAN BOY SOME CALL HIM THE JOKER.
CONSTABLE TOM RUMORED TO HAVE A SMALL AMOUNT OF BRAIN DAMAGE.
THE MONTH IS JUNE IN CANADA, AND THAT CAN MEAN BUT ONE THING... SPRING IS JUST AROUND THE CORNER. OF COURSE, WITH SPRING COMES THE COLD AND FLU SEASON. EVEN A SPRY LAD LIKE MAURICE CAN FALL VICTIM. BUT WHEN ILLNESS STRIKES, TRUSTING FRIENDS HEAD FOR THE CABIN OF DR. ROGERS.
DOCTOR ROGERS, I TINK MAURICE GOT SOME KIN FLU IN MINE STOMACH!
WELL, WELL, YOU DO LOOK UNDER THE WEATHER, MAURICE.
I HAVE MY BAG HERE.... LET'S TAKE THAT TEMPERATURE OF YOURS AND WE...
OH-OH, I'M GOT TO GO SOME-WHERE!
WHAT SEEMS TO BE THE MATTER WITH MAURICE, DOCTOR ROGERS?
SEEMS TO HAVE A FLU BUG, OR BAD EATING HABITS. HMMM....
WHOOM!
POOR MAURICE!
OW! DIS IS NO FUN!
LET'S ALL HOLD HANDS IN THE CANADIAN WAY OF SHOWING UNITED STRENGTH. WE CAN...
BAFOOM!
TENSE MOMENTS PASS.
I THINK THE WORST IS OVER.
THERE HE IS! STILL SMOKING BUT NONE THE WORSE FOR WEAR.
WELL, ALL'S WELL THAT ENDS WELL, EH, MAURICE?
YOU BET!
AS THE SUN SETS ON THE CANADIAN TUNDRA, ANOTHER CRISIS FALLS PREY TO HUMAN COMPASSION.
FA-WHOOM!
IT'S EVERY MAN FOR HIM-SELF!
FIN

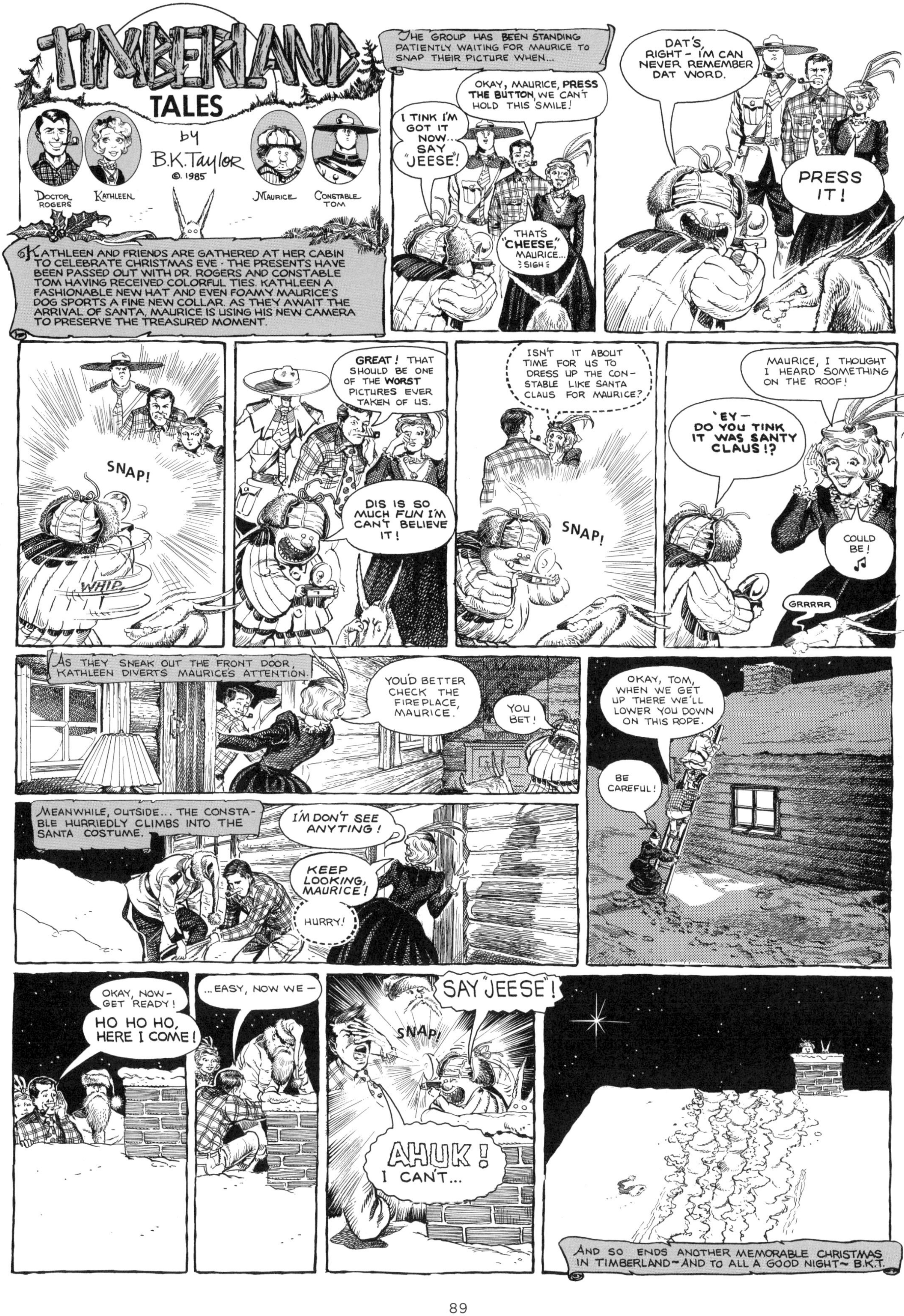

TIMBERLAND TALES
by B.K. Taylor
©. 1985
DOCTOR ROGERS
KATHLEEN
MAURICE
CONSTABLE TOM
KATHLEEN AND FRIENDS ARE GATHERED AT HER CABIN TO CELEBRATE CHRISTMAS EVE - THE PRESENTS HAVE BEEN PASSED OUT WITH DR. ROGERS AND CONSTABLE TOM HAVING RECEIVED COLORFUL TIES. KATHLEEN A FASHIONABLE NEW HAT AND EVEN FOAMY MAURICE'S DOG SPORTS A FINE NEW COLLAR. AS THEY AWAIT THE ARRIVAL OF SANTA, MAURICE IS USING HIS NEW CAMERA TO PRESERVE THE TREASURED MOMENT.
THE GROUP HAS BEEN STANDING PATIENTLY WAITING FOR MAURICE TO SNAP THEIR PICTURE WHEN...
OKAY, MAURICE, PRESS THE BUTTON, WE CAN'T HOLD THIS SMILE!
I TINK I'M GOT IT NOW... SAY "JEESE"!
THAT'S "CHEESE," MAURICE... SIGH
DAT'S RIGHT - I'M CAN NEVER REMEMBER DAT WORD.
PRESS IT!
SNAP!
WHIP
GREAT! THAT SHOULD BE ONE OF THE WORST PICTURES EVER TAKEN OF US.
DIS IS SO MUCH FUN I'M CAN'T BELIEVE IT!
ISN'T IT ABOUT TIME FOR US TO DRESS UP THE CON-STABLE LIKE SANTA CLAUS FOR MAURICE?
SNAP!
MAURICE, I THOUGHT I HEARD SOMETHING ON THE ROOF!
`EY - DO YOU TINK IT WAS SANTY CLAUS!?
COULD BE! ♪
GRRRRR
AS THEY SNEAK OUT THE FRONT DOOR, KATHLEEN DIVERTS MAURICE'S ATTENTION.
YOU'D BETTER CHECK THE FIREPLACE, MAURICE.
YOU BET!
OKAY, TOM, WHEN WE GET UP THERE WE'LL LOWER YOU DOWN ON THIS ROPE.
BE CAREFUL!
MEANWHILE, OUTSIDE... THE CONSTA-BLE HURRIEDLY CLIMBS INTO THE SANTA COSTUME.
I'M DON'T SEE ANYTING!
KEEP LOOKING, MAURICE!
HURRY!
OKAY, NOW - GET READY!
HO HO HO, HERE I COME!
...EASY, NOW WE -
SAY "JEESE"!
SNAP!
AHUK! I CAN'T...
AND SO ENDS ANOTHER MEMORABLE CHRISTMAS IN TIMBERLAND ~ AND TO ALL A GOOD NIGHT ~ B.K.T.

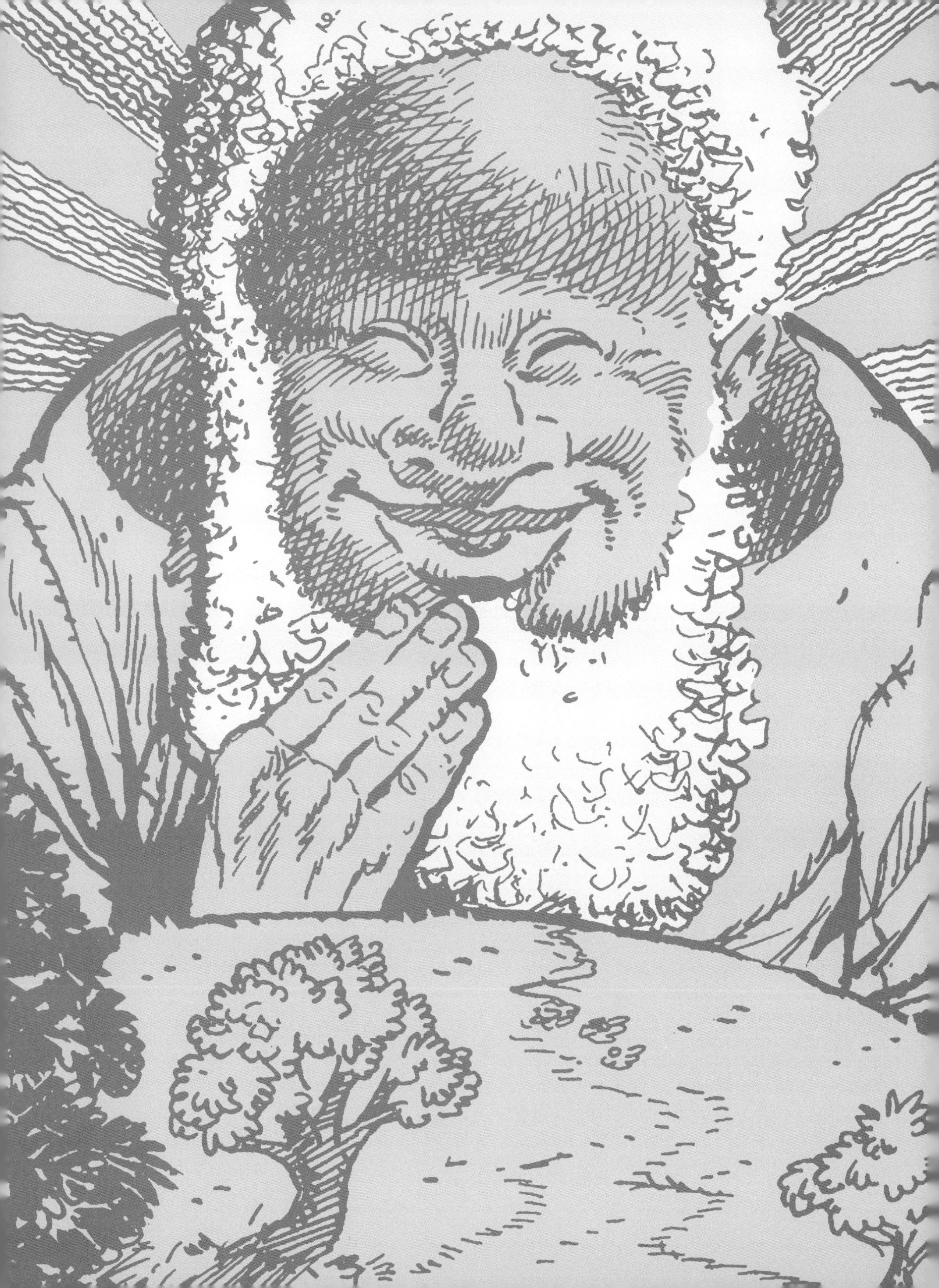

STORIES FROM

UNCLE KUNTA

Uncle Kunta was the third strip I created for *National Lampoon*. The stories are an unabashed satire of the classic Uncle Remus fables by Joel Chandler Harris. Uncle Remus would spin wonderful tales with charming anthropomorphized characters that amused and inspired the visiting children. However, Uncle Kunta is more like Norm Appleton in that he has a mischievous tongue-in-cheek edge and a devil-may-care attitude.

In each episode, Uncle Kunta tells one of his colorful stories to two neighboring white children, who listen in wide-eyed wonder to his slightly skewed renditions of historical and biblical tales. Certainly his perspectives put a unique slant on Creation, the Garden of Eden, and the meeting of Robinson Crusoe and Friday, among other classics.

Many have asked where the name Uncle Kunta came from. Actually, it was derived from Kunta Kinte, the main character in Alex Haley's 1976 novel, *Roots*, and its subsequent television miniseries. It seemed a perfect fit for this new character. And with a visual resemblance to Morgan Freeman ...

... how could you not like Uncle Kunta?

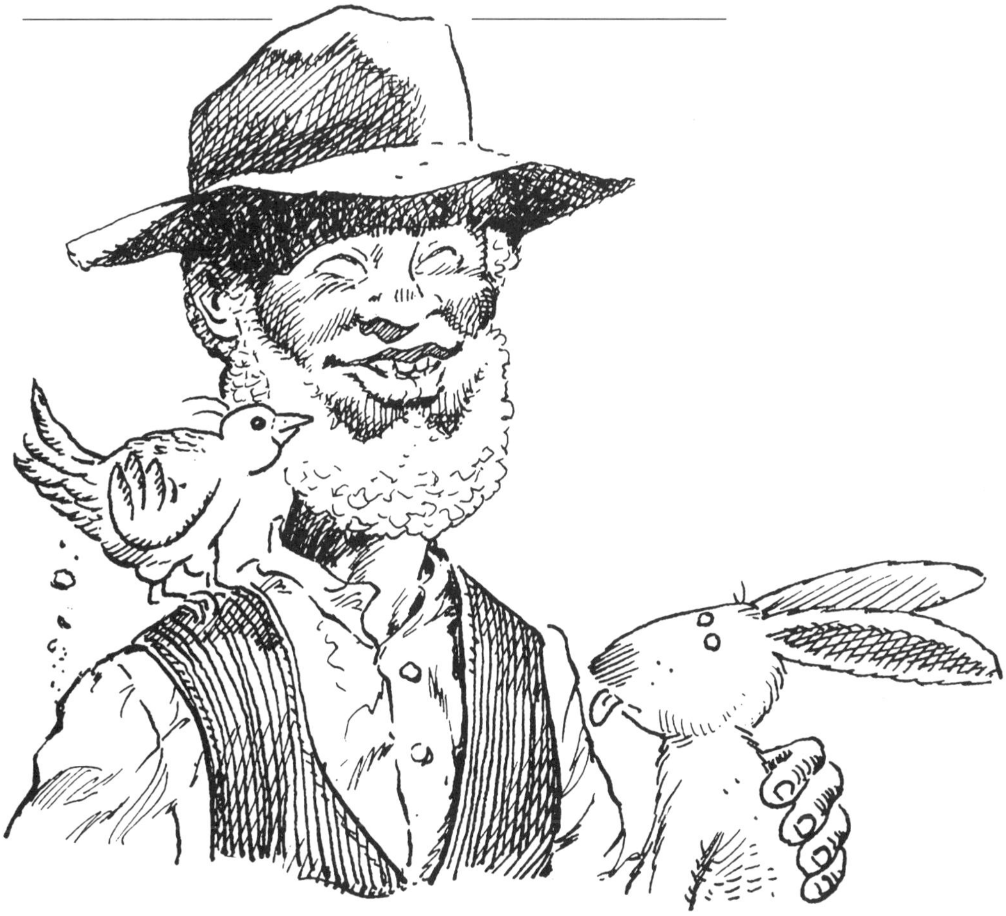

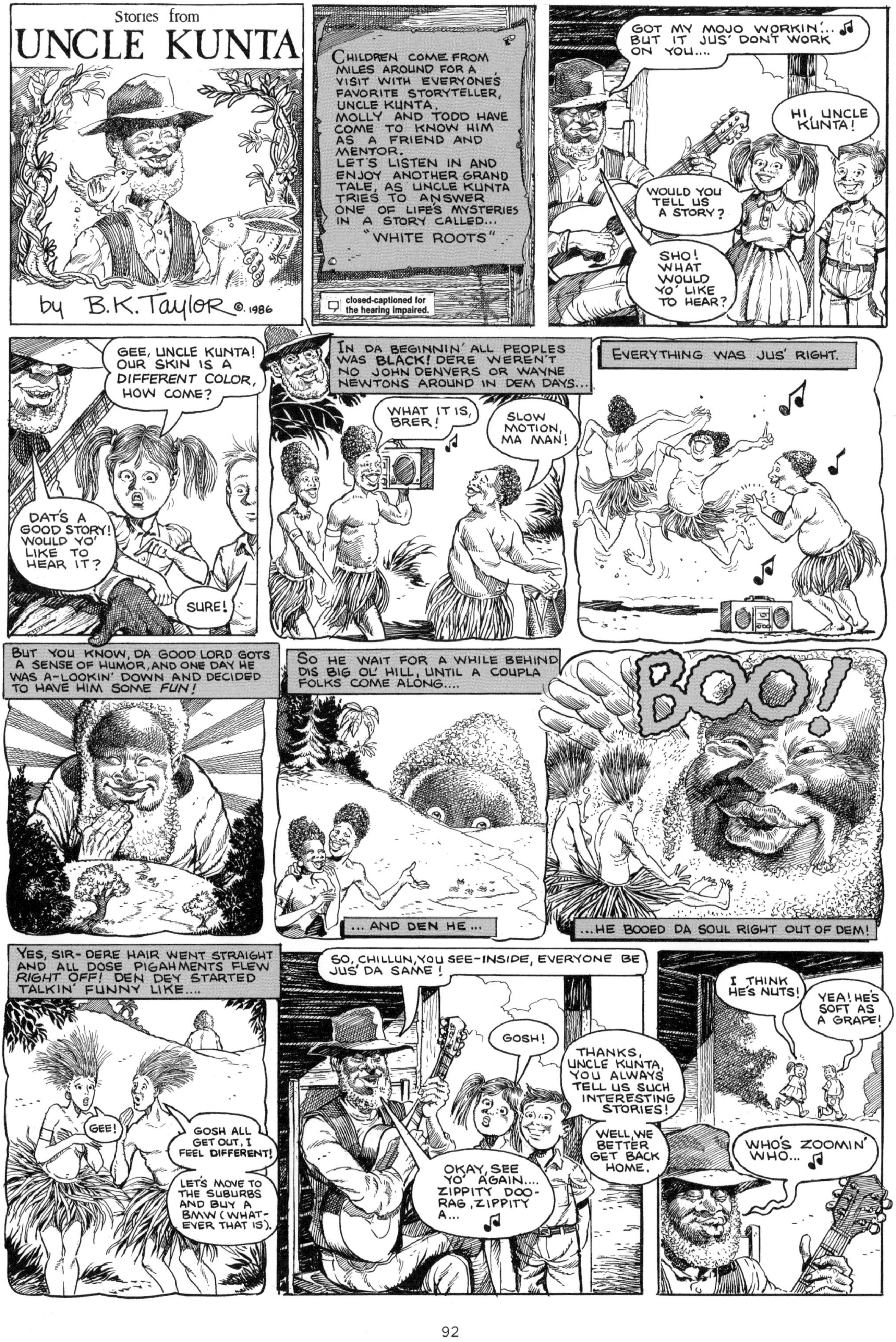

Stories from
UNCLE KUNTA
by B.K. Taylor ©. 1986
CHILDREN COME FROM MILES AROUND FOR A VISIT WITH EVERYONE'S FAVORITE STORYTELLER, UNCLE KUNTA. MOLLY AND TODD HAVE COME TO KNOW HIM AS A FRIEND AND MENTOR. LET'S LISTEN IN AND ENJOY ANOTHER GRAND TALE, AS UNCLE KUNTA TRIES TO ANSWER ONE OF LIFE'S MYSTERIES IN A STORY CALLED... "WHITE ROOTS"
closed-captioned for the hearing impaired.
GOT MY MOJO WORKIN'... BUT IT JUS' DONT WORK ON YOU....
HI, UNCLE KUNTA!
WOULD YOU TELL US A STORY?
SHO! WHAT WOULD YO' LIKE TO HEAR?
GEE, UNCLE KUNTA! OUR SKIN IS A DIFFERENT COLOR, HOW COME?
DAT'S A GOOD STORY! WOULD YO' LIKE TO HEAR IT?
SURE!
IN DA BEGINNIN' ALL PEOPLES WAS BLACK! DERE WEREN'T NO JOHN DENVERS OR WAYNE NEWTONS AROUND IN DEM DAYS...
WHAT IT IS, BRER!
SLOW MOTION, MA MAN!
EVERYTHING WAS JUS' RIGHT.
BUT YOU KNOW, DA GOOD LORD GOTS A SENSE OF HUMOR, AND ONE DAY HE WAS A-LOOKIN' DOWN AND DECIDED TO HAVE HIM SOME FUN!
SO HE WAIT FOR A WHILE BEHIND DIS BIG OL' HILL, UNTIL A COUPLA FOLKS COME ALONG....
... AND DEN HE ...
BOO!
...HE BOOED DA SOUL RIGHT OUT OF DEM!
YES, SIR- DERE HAIR WENT STRAIGHT AND ALL DOSE PIGAHMENTS FLEW RIGHT OFF! DEN DEY STARTED TALKIN' FUNNY LIKE....
GEE!
GOSH ALL GET OUT, I FEEL DIFFERENT!
LET'S MOVE TO THE SUBURBS AND BUY A BMW (WHAT-EVER THAT IS).
SO, CHILLUN, YOU SEE-INSIDE, EVERYONE BE JUS' DA SAME!
GOSH!
THANKS, UNCLE KUNTA, YOU ALWAYS TELL US SUCH INTERESTING STORIES!
WELL, WE BETTER GET BACK HOME.
OKAY, SEE YO' AGAIN.... ZIPPITY DOO-RAG, ZIPPITY A...
I THINK HE'S NUTS!
YEA! HE'S SOFT AS A GRAPE!
WHO'S ZOOMIN' WHO...

Stories from
UNCLE KUNTA

by B.K. Taylor © 1987

AT THE CABIN OF UNCLE KUNTA, MOLLY AND TODD WAIT IN ANTICIPATION AS THEIR FRIEND BEGINS ANOTHER CHAPTER OF HIS STORY ABOUT CREATION....

...YOU REMEMBER LAST TIME, GOD MADE DA WORLD IN SEVEN DAYS AND NIGHTS, AND DEN HIS BROTHER, DA DEVIL, MESS IT UP. WELL, HE START ALL OVER AGAIN, BUT THIS TIME WIT PEOPLE.

WOW!

DIS STORY START IN A PLACE CALLED DA GARDEN OF EDEN, AND GOD LOOK DOWN AT HIS FIRST TWO LITTLE PEOPLE CREATIONS AND HE SAY...

WHAT YOU THINK OF DIS FINE GARDEN I MADE FOR YOU, ADAM AND EVA?

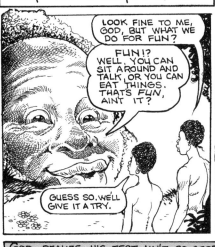

LOOK FINE TO ME, GOD, BUT WHAT WE DO FOR FUN?

FUN!? WELL, YOU CAN SIT AROUND AND TALK, OR YOU CAN EAT THINGS. THAT'S FUN, AIN'T IT?

GUESS SO. WE'LL GIVE IT A TRY.

...OH, BY DA WAY - YOU CAN EAT ANYTHING YOU WANT - CHITLINS, BARBEQUE... BUT DON'T EAT NO - UH...UM... ZUCCHINI! YEAH - NO ZUCCHINI! HEAR?

UH-HUH!

SEE, GOD WAS TESTIN' 'EM. SO HE GO AND CHANGE INTO A TREE TO SEE IF DEY BREAK HIS WORD.

DIS HAVIN' FUN AIN'T SO MUCH FUN - YOU WANT TO EAT SOME OF DEM ZUCCHINI?

EEEEOOO! NO WAY! I DON'T LIKE THEIR SMELL!

GOD REALIZE HIS TEST AIN'T SO GOOD CAUSE THEY DON'T WANT NO ZUCCHINI ANYHOW, SO HE CHANGE BACK TO HIS OWN SELF....

HEY, ADAM AND EVA - I CHANGE MY MIND - YOU CAN EAT ALL DA ZUCCHINI YOU WANT.

DON'T WANT NONE!

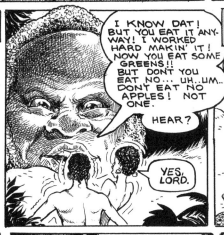

I KNOW DAT! BUT YOU EAT IT ANYWAY! I WORKED HARD MAKIN' IT! NOW YOU EAT SOME GREENS!! BUT DON'T YOU EAT NO... UH..UM.. DON'T EAT NO APPLES! NOT ONE. HEAR?

YES, LORD.

NOW GOD'S BROTHER, DA DEVIL, HE'S CHANGE HISSELF INTO A SNAKE, AND HE GONNA CAUSE SOME TROUBLE.

PSSST! HERE, YOU GUYS WANT AN APPLE?

CAN'T! GOD SAID WE CAN'T EAT NO APPLE.

SO DA DEVIL TEMPT DEM EVEN MORE.

LOOK, YOU EAT DIS APPLE AND I'LL GIVE YOU A JAMES BROWN ALBUM!

OOOWHEE! YOU SURE ARE A TEMPTER!

MOLLY, TODD!

AWW GEE, MOM'S CALLING US HOME. DID THEY EAT THE APPLE?

HEH-HEH! WELL, YOU COME BACK NEXT TIME AND I'LL TELLS YOU.

WE'LL BE BACK TOMORROW, UNCLE KUNTA. IT'S ALWAYS FUN AT YOUR CABIN, YOU'RE LIKE OUR REAL UNCLE!

YEAH RIGHT! OOO ♪ BIG BOSS MAN, CAN'T YOU HEAR ME WHEN I TALK...

KICK ME!

WHITE TRASH

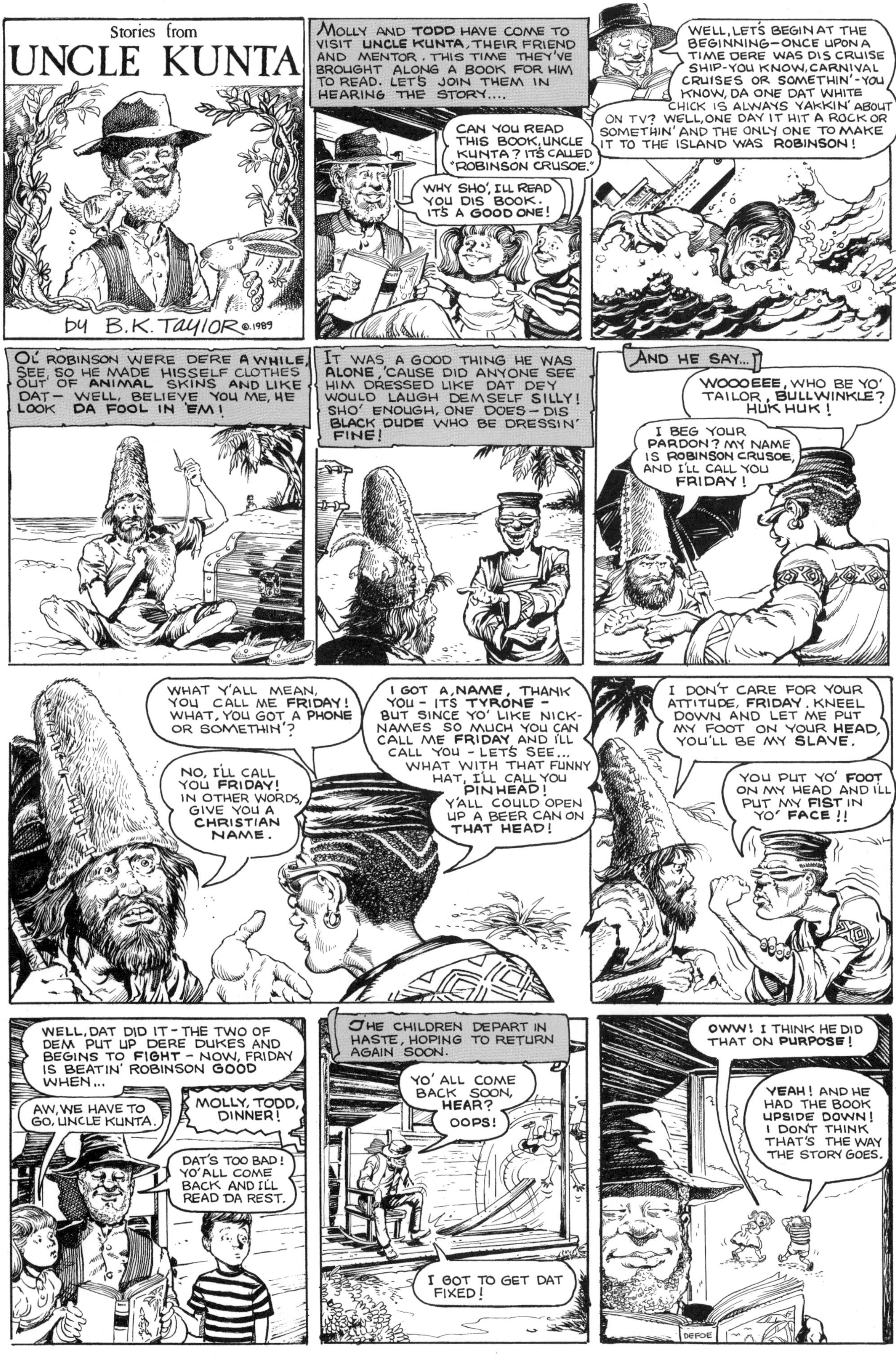

Stories from
UNCLE KUNTA
by B.K. TAYLOR ©1989
MOLLY AND TODD HAVE COME TO VISIT UNCLE KUNTA, THEIR FRIEND AND MENTOR. THIS TIME THEY'VE BROUGHT ALONG A BOOK FOR HIM TO READ. LET'S JOIN THEM IN HEARING THE STORY....
CAN YOU READ THIS BOOK, UNCLE KUNTA? IT'S CALLED "ROBINSON CRUSOE."
WHY SHO', I'LL READ YOU DIS BOOK. IT'S A GOOD ONE!
WELL, LET'S BEGIN AT THE BEGINNING—ONCE UPON A TIME DERE WAS DIS CRUISE SHIP-YOU KNOW, CARNIVAL CRUISES OR SOMETHIN'-YOU KNOW, DA ONE DAT WHITE CHICK IS ALWAYS YAKKIN' ABOUT ON TV? WELL, ONE DAY IT HIT A ROCK OR SOMETHIN' AND THE ONLY ONE TO MAKE IT TO THE ISLAND WAS ROBINSON!
OL' ROBINSON WERE DERE A WHILE, SEE, SO HE MADE HISSELF CLOTHES OUT OF ANIMAL SKINS AND LIKE DAT— WELL, BELIEVE YOU ME, HE LOOK DA FOOL IN 'EM!
IT WAS A GOOD THING HE WAS ALONE, 'CAUSE DID ANYONE SEE HIM DRESSED LIKE DAT DEY WOULD LAUGH DEMSELF SILLY! SHO' ENOUGH, ONE DOES—DIS BLACK DUDE WHO BE DRESSIN' FINE!
AND HE SAY...
WOOOEEE, WHO BE YO' TAILOR, BULLWINKLE? HUK HUK!
I BEG YOUR PARDON? MY NAME IS ROBINSON CRUSOE, AND I'LL CALL YOU FRIDAY!
WHAT Y'ALL MEAN, YOU CALL ME FRIDAY! WHAT, YOU GOT A PHONE OR SOMETHIN'?
NO, I'LL CALL YOU FRIDAY! IN OTHER WORDS, GIVE YOU A CHRISTIAN NAME.
I GOT A NAME, THANK YOU - ITS TYRONE - BUT SINCE YO' LIKE NICK-NAMES SO MUCH YOU CAN CALL ME FRIDAY AND I'LL CALL YOU - LET'S SEE... WHAT WITH THAT FUNNY HAT, I'LL CALL YOU PINHEAD! Y'ALL COULD OPEN UP A BEER CAN ON THAT HEAD!
I DON'T CARE FOR YOUR ATTITUDE, FRIDAY. KNEEL DOWN AND LET ME PUT MY FOOT ON YOUR HEAD, YOU'LL BE MY SLAVE.
YOU PUT YO' FOOT ON MY HEAD AND I'LL PUT MY FIST IN YO' FACE!!
WELL, DAT DID IT - THE TWO OF DEM PUT UP DERE DUKES AND BEGINS TO FIGHT - NOW, FRIDAY IS BEATIN' ROBINSON GOOD WHEN...
AW, WE HAVE TO GO, UNCLE KUNTA.
MOLLY, TODD, DINNER!
DAT'S TOO BAD! YO'ALL COME BACK AND I'LL READ DA REST.
THE CHILDREN DEPART IN HASTE, HOPING TO RETURN AGAIN SOON.
YO' ALL COME BACK SOON, HEAR? OOPS!
I GOT TO GET DAT FIXED!
OWW! I THINK HE DID THAT ON PURPOSE!
YEAH! AND HE HAD THE BOOK UPSIDE DOWN! I DON'T THINK THAT'S THE WAY THE STORY GOES.
DEFOE

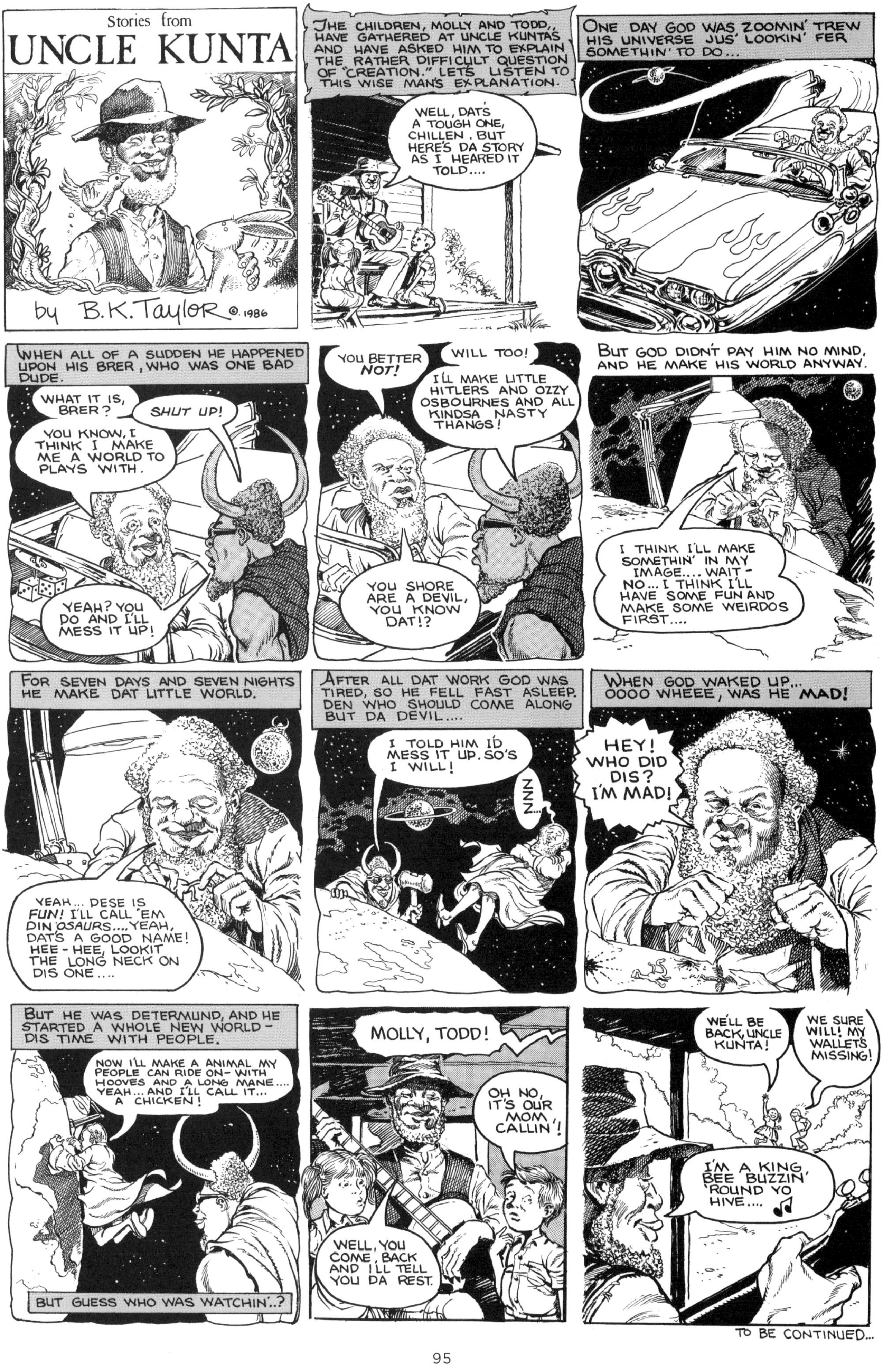
Stories from
UNCLE KUNTA
by B.K. Taylor ©. 1986
THE CHILDREN, MOLLY AND TODD, HAVE GATHERED AT UNCLE KUNTA'S AND HAVE ASKED HIM TO EXPLAIN THE RATHER DIFFICULT QUESTION OF "CREATION." LET'S LISTEN TO THIS WISE MAN'S EXPLANATION.
WELL, DAT'S A TOUGH ONE, CHILLEN. BUT HERE'S DA STORY AS I HEARED IT TOLD....
ONE DAY GOD WAS ZOOMIN' TREW HIS UNIVERSE JUS' LOOKIN' FER SOMETHIN' TO DO...
WHEN ALL OF A SUDDEN HE HAPPENED UPON HIS BRER, WHO WAS ONE BAD DUDE.
WHAT IT IS, BRER?
SHUT UP!
YOU KNOW, I THINK I MAKE ME A WORLD TO PLAYS WITH.
YEAH? YOU DO AND I'LL MESS IT UP!
YOU BETTER NOT!
WILL TOO!
I'LL MAKE LITTLE HITLERS AND OZZY OSBOURNES AND ALL KINDSA NASTY THANGS!
YOU SHORE ARE A DEVIL, YOU KNOW DAT!?
BUT GOD DIDN'T PAY HIM NO MIND, AND HE MAKE HIS WORLD ANYWAY.
I THINK I'LL MAKE SOMETHIN' IN MY IMAGE.... WAIT - NO... I THINK I'LL HAVE SOME FUN AND MAKE SOME WEIRDOS FIRST....
FOR SEVEN DAYS AND SEVEN NIGHTS HE MAKE DAT LITTLE WORLD.
YEAH... DESE IS FUN! I'LL CALL 'EM DIN'OSAURS....YEAH, DAT'S A GOOD NAME! HEE-HEE, LOOKIT THE LONG NECK ON DIS ONE....
AFTER ALL DAT WORK GOD WAS TIRED, SO HE FELL FAST ASLEEP. DEN WHO SHOULD COME ALONG BUT DA DEVIL....
I TOLD HIM I'D MESS IT UP. SO'S I WILL!
ZZZ...
WHEN GOD WAKED UP... OOOO WHEEE, WAS HE MAD!
HEY! WHO DID DIS? I'M MAD!
BUT HE WAS DETERMUND, AND HE STARTED A WHOLE NEW WORLD - DIS TIME WITH PEOPLE.
NOW I'LL MAKE A ANIMAL MY PEOPLE CAN RIDE ON- WITH HOOVES AND A LONG MANE.... YEAH... AND I'LL CALL IT... A CHICKEN!
BUT GUESS WHO WAS WATCHIN'..?
MOLLY, TODD!
OH NO, IT'S OUR MOM CALLIN'!
WELL, YOU COME BACK AND I'LL TELL YOU DA REST.
WE'LL BE BACK, UNCLE KUNTA!
WE SURE WILL! MY WALLET'S MISSING!
I'M A KING BEE BUZZIN' 'ROUND YO HIVE....
TO BE CONTINUED...

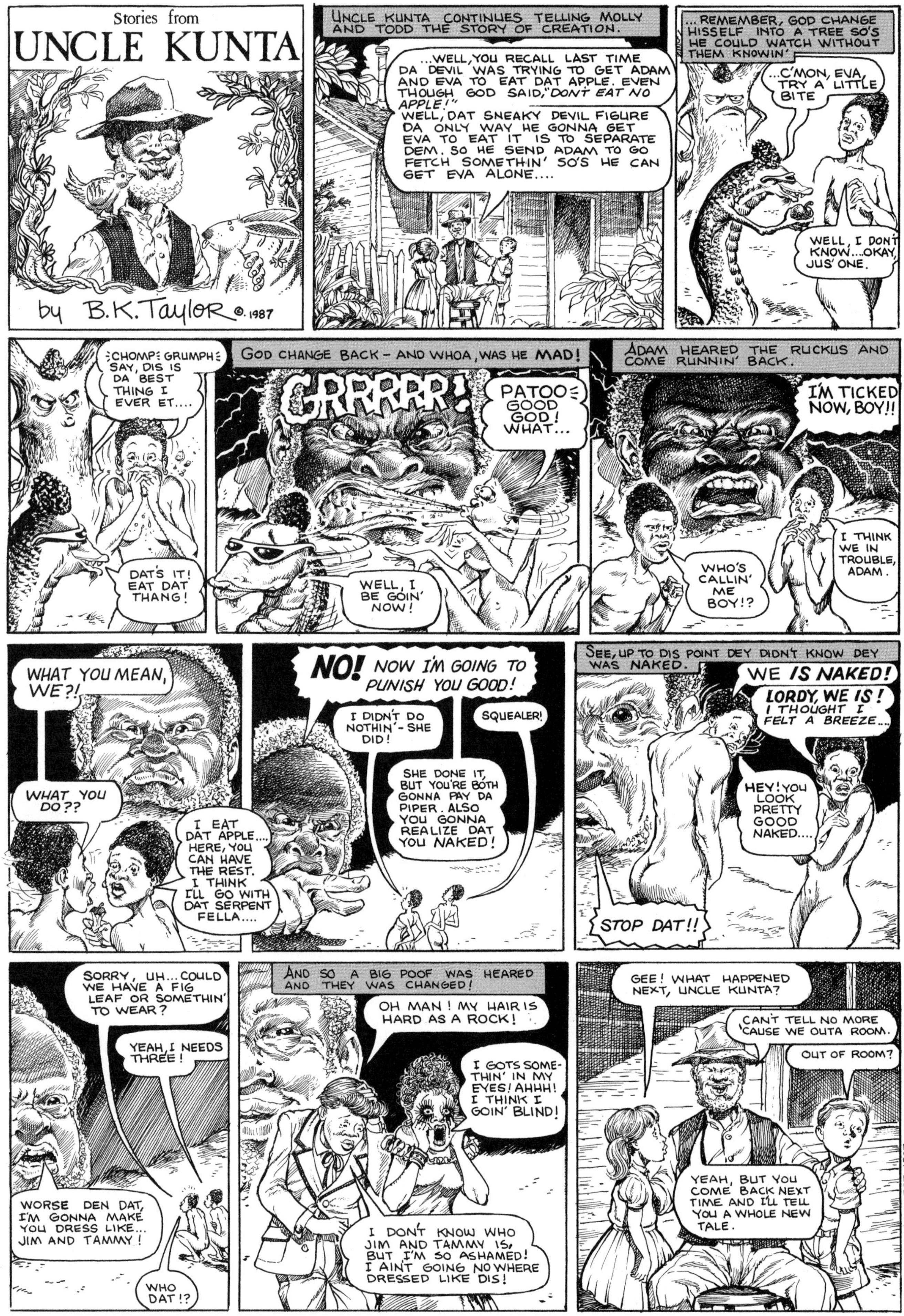

Stories from
UNCLE KUNTA
by B.K.Taylor ©.1987
UNCLE KUNTA CONTINUES TELLING MOLLY AND TODD THE STORY OF CREATION.
...WELL, YOU RECALL LAST TIME DA DEVIL WAS TRYING TO GET ADAM AND EVA TO EAT DAT APPLE. EVEN THOUGH GOD SAID, "DON'T EAT NO APPLE!"
WELL, DAT SNEAKY DEVIL FIGURE DA ONLY WAY HE GONNA GET EVA TO EAT IT IS TO SEPARATE DEM. SO HE SEND ADAM TO GO FETCH SOMETHIN' SO'S HE CAN GET EVA ALONE....
...REMEMBER, GOD CHANGE HISSELF INTO A TREE SO'S HE COULD WATCH WITHOUT THEM KNOWIN'
...C'MON, EVA, TRY A LITTLE BITE
WELL, I DON'T KNOW....OKAY, JUS' ONE.
CHOMP GRUMPH SAY, DIS IS DA BEST THING I EVER ET....
DAT'S IT! EAT DAT THANG!
GOD CHANGE BACK - AND WHOA, WAS HE MAD!
GRRRRR!
PATOO GOOD GOD! WHAT...
WELL, I BE GOIN' NOW!
ADAM HEARED THE RUCKUS AND COME RUNNIN' BACK.
I'M TICKED NOW, BOY!!
WHO'S CALLIN' ME BOY!?
I THINK WE IN TROUBLE, ADAM.
WHAT YOU MEAN, WE?!
WHAT YOU DO??
I EAT DAT APPLE.... HERE, YOU CAN HAVE THE REST. I THINK I'LL GO WITH DAT SERPENT FELLA....
NO! NOW I'M GOING TO PUNISH YOU GOOD!
I DIDN'T DO NOTHIN' - SHE DID!
SQUEALER!
SHE DONE IT, BUT YOU'RE BOTH GONNA PAY DA PIPER. ALSO YOU GONNA REALIZE DAT YOU NAKED!
SEE, UP TO DIS POINT DEY DIDN'T KNOW DEY WAS NAKED.
WE IS NAKED!
LORDY, WE IS! I THOUGHT I FELT A BREEZE....
HEY! YOU LOOK PRETTY GOOD NAKED....
STOP DAT!!
SORRY, UH... COULD WE HAVE A FIG LEAF OR SOMETHIN' TO WEAR?
YEAH, I NEEDS THREE!
WORSE DEN DAT, I'M GONNA MAKE YOU DRESS LIKE... JIM AND TAMMY!
WHO DAT!?
AND SO A BIG POOF WAS HEARED AND THEY WAS CHANGED!
OH MAN! MY HAIR IS HARD AS A ROCK!
I GOTS SOMETHIN' IN MY EYES! AHHH! I THINK I GOIN' BLIND!
I DON'T KNOW WHO JIM AND TAMMY IS, BUT I'M SO ASHAMED! I AIN'T GOING NO WHERE DRESSED LIKE DIS!
GEE! WHAT HAPPENED NEXT, UNCLE KUNTA?
CAN'T TELL NO MORE 'CAUSE WE OUTA ROOM.
OUT OF ROOM?
YEAH, BUT YOU COME BACK NEXT TIME AND I'LL TELL YOU A WHOLE NEW TALE.
KEYWEST 1987

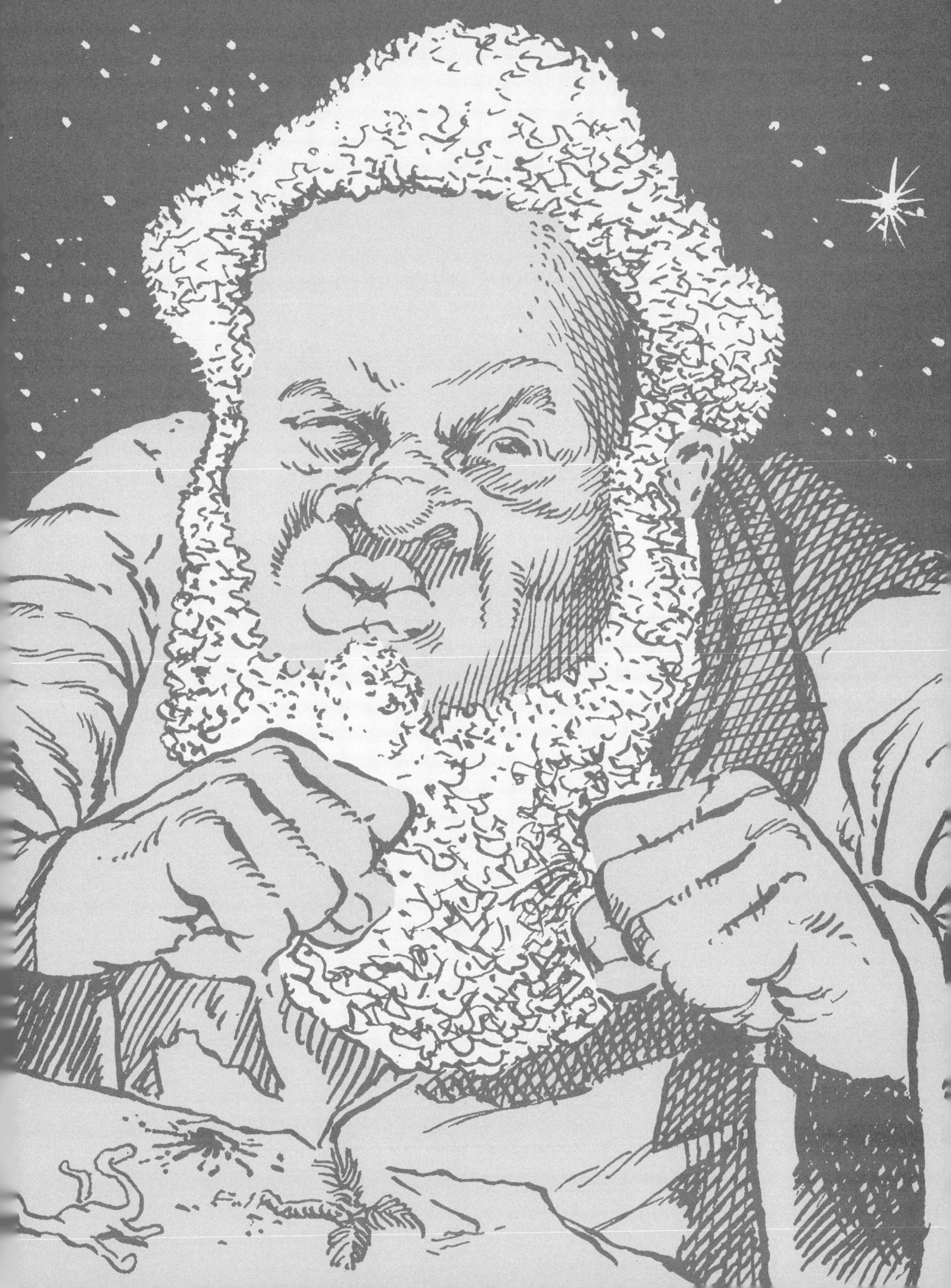

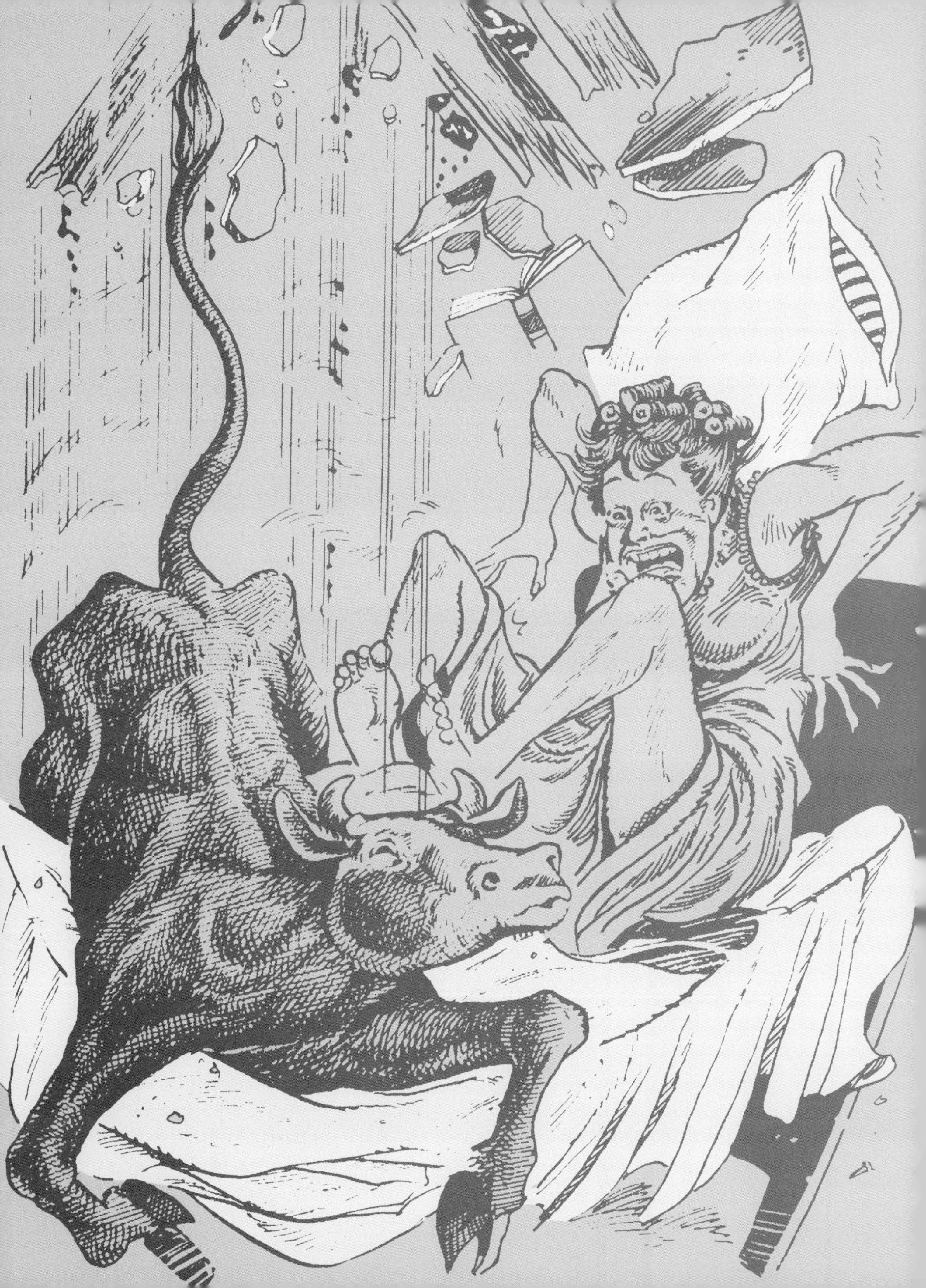

TRUTH IS STRANGER

LIFE AS WE KNOW IT

The True Facts section of *National Lampoon* was edited by John Bendel, who waded through stacks of submissions from readers and pored through magazines and newspapers from across the country for content worthy of the True Facts imprimatur. The result is proof that truth is stranger than fiction. No Hollywood writer could concoct some of the bizarre — but true! — situations you'll find on the following pages.

Because John provided me a script, I could concentrate on creating the best visual representations of these freakish events. Other artists worked on True Facts as well, and the feature became so popular that the *Lampoon* ultimately released a book collecting True Facts.

The Better You and Travel Tips sections were written by myself and Chato Hill (as will become quite obvious). Hopefully, you won't take any of these tips seriously. But if you do, please *a*) seek immediate help and *b*) send photos.

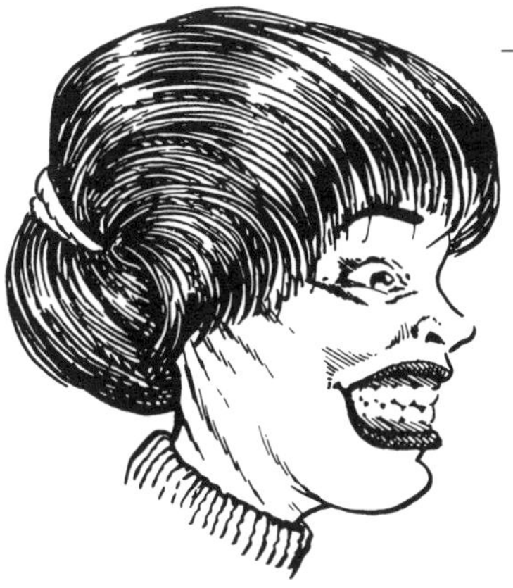

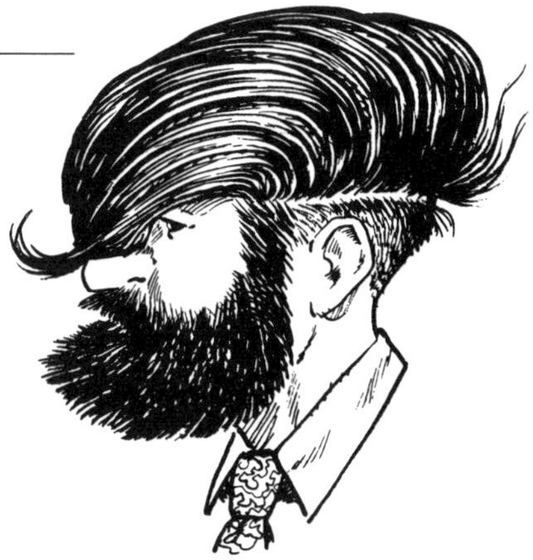

TRUE FACTS REPORTER

BY JOHN BENDEL • ILLUSTRATED BY B.K. TAYLOR

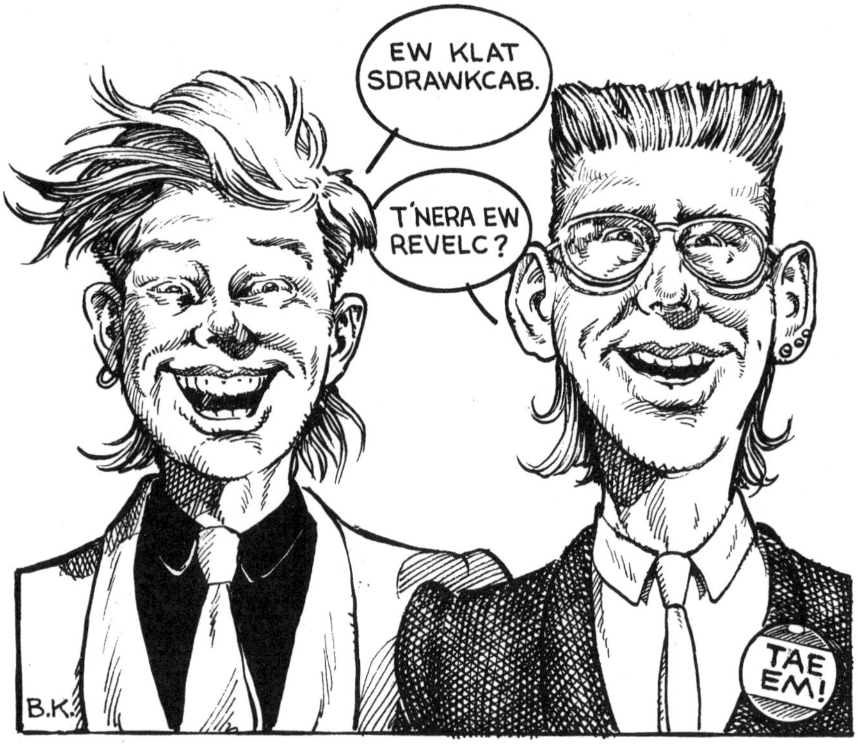
EW KLAT SDRAWKCAB.
T'NERA EW REVELC?
TAE EM!
B.K.

VOICES OF YOUNG AMERICA EDITION

America, besieged by competition around the world, looks to its new generation for leadership, excellence, and perfect attendance. We thought we'd take a look, too.

BACKWARDS INTO THE FUTURE

Your True Facts Reporter recently saw Richie Reisman and Adam Riback on a local TV show, talking backwards. We spoke by phone with Reisman and Riback, both seventeen, of Brooklyn, New York.

Reisman: Me and Darren Silverman started talking backwards in junior high. We were always looking for ways to make the girls laugh and talk behind their backs. So we started with simple things, like "kcid" was "dick." You know, words like that. Then in high school, Adam started talking backwards, too. Now all of us do it fluently.

True Facts Reporter: Fluently?

Reisman: Yltneulf.

TFR: I see.

Reisman: We started a club called the Backwards Club and people would pay to hear us talk backwards. We charged five dollars an hour for backwards-talking lessons. We want to have a battle with this guy David Feuer, who goes on the talk shows talking backwards. We're better than he is. We want to show the world who's the champ.

TFR: Have you challenged him?

Reisman: A couple of times, on local TV shows. But we haven't heard anything.

TFR: What do you do on TV?

Reisman: I'll like tell a story backwards while Adam or Darren translates for the audience. We want to start a trend. We want the world to talk backwards. Talking backwards really takes like a lot of intelligence. I want to be on television. I want to be in movies talking backwards.

TFR: What will you do on television or in the movies without a translator?

Reisman: So I'll need subtitles.

Riback: (*In the background*). Let me say something.

TFR: What would Adam like to say?

Riback: I just want to say, I think it's a good time to do something in this field. I mean, the average intelligent person couldn't talk backwards in a week. It would take some time. So I feel like now is a good time to start. Especially with this big Burger King commercial where one guy on a TV screen reaches across a couple of other TV screens trying to grab a hamburger. He brings back a Burger King label instead and when his friend reads it upside down he says "Regrub Gnik" instead of "Burger King." That commercial is a big breakthrough for talking backwards.

TFR: Big breakthrough?

Riback: Well, it's something. So I feel like now is a good time to do something in this field. We'd be cool, like totally.

TFR: But who would pay you to talk backwards?

Riback: That's a problem. If everybody did it, then nobody would want to pay us. My idea is to make up an actual language, because then we'd have something we could patent.

TFR: Can you patent a language?

Riback: I don't know.

TFR: Well, good luck to you.

Riback: Yeah, well, doog kcul ot uoy, oot.

FLAMING SHOES

At a Mobil gas station in New Jersey, two young attendants tussled near the garage. An older guy, maybe twenty, was stamping on the younger guy's foot. The younger guy's right shoe was on fire.

When the flames were finally stamped out, the two attendants went back to take care of the customers who were lined up. I got the young guy, who was about sixteen or so. Smiling languidly, obviously not burned, he ambled over, the merest trace of smoke rising from the toe of his heavy work shoe.

"Oh that," he said when I asked how his foot had caught on fire. "I light 'em every once in a while. It's fun." There's always a little bit of gas left in the pump nozzle, he explained. "All you have to do is shake a couple of drops onto the toe of your shoe and set it off."

"Isn't that dangerous?"

The young gas jockey shrugged. "I dunno, but it's handy," he said.

"Handy?"

"Yeah. This friend of mine works at a station out on Route 46, and it's hard to shut down at night, because people keep pulling up to the pumps. So if there's people at the pumps at closing time, he walks behind the building, sets his shoes on fire, then comes running out front with his feet blazing. It clears the place out in no time."

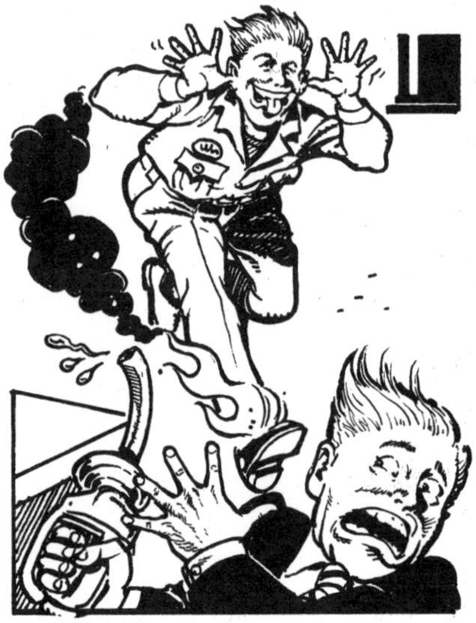

OPERATION 7-ELEVEN

Your True Facts Reporter recently interviewed a University of Missouri freshman about his high school extracurricular activities. He thought it best not to use his real name.

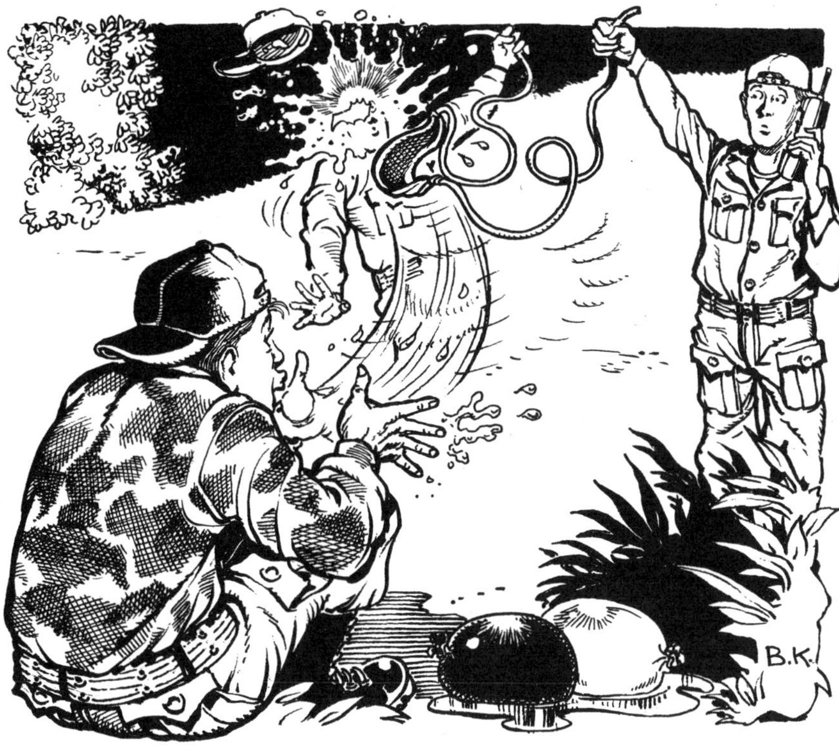
B.K.

There's only one 7-Eleven in our town, which is just west of Chicago. The owner would follow you around to make sure you weren't stuffing your pockets.

You'd come up to the cash register and he'd always ask, "You want Slurpee with that?" He was always calling the police on us, and, like, the police always made a production of it. They'd open everybody's trunk looking for beer. This went on all the time, and we weren't even doing anything!

We had this spiritual leader. We just called him Rob. So Rob says, "How's about a little noise distraction?"

We knew it meant war.

The 7-Eleven had a big industrial-size dumpster in a fenced-off area. So, one of us scaled the fence and put an M-80 in the dumpster and lit the fuse. We got in our cars and kept circling the area until "BANG!"

The sound was magnified by the empty dumpster. It was really loud. Even a local newspaper reporter came around, along with the cops. He interviewed the store owner. He told the reporter he thought it was a "racist, terrorist attack by some country." He wouldn't say which one. The thing is, he thought it was this major international plot against him.

This amused us and egged us on.

Rob got us a secret weapon, this thing called a Wanger. It's like a modern-day catapult. It had two long pieces of elastic surgical tubing attached to a pouch. It took three men to operate it.

One guy would stand with his right hand extended toward the sky, holding one end. Opposite him another guy would stand with his left arm extended, holding the other end. A third guy would pull the pouch back as much as four feet.

When he let it go?

Let's just say we could loft things.

The 7-Eleven is across the street from this home for retired priests, with huge grounds and lots of trees and stuff. You could get lost in there.

On the corner across from the 7-Eleven, they had built like a fifteen-foot landscaped mound. You could get behind it and not be seen from the street.

Rob had these really good two-way radios. We put one with the battery team, the guys who operated the Wanger behind the mound, and the other went with the spotters, who sat in a car across from the 7-Eleven, watching our shots.

The first couple of shots were always high and we'd hit the neon 7-Eleven sign, and the water would just spray onto the roof and the ground. Our real target was the big Plexiglas window. The balloon would come down, hit the wondow, and spray water. There would be this dull thud. That sound was the greatest. We knew we'd scored. People in the store knew. Everybody just knew.

We'd usually get off about twenty shots before the cops came. We would take off into the trees around the monastery and hide in the bushes.

Once in a while a cop would come across and shine his flashlight on the monastery grounds, but they didn't know what they were looking for.

Toward the end of the summer, we escalated the campaign. We switched from water balloons to mud balls. We just wanted to see those babies hit the window with a "whump," then ooze on down to the ground.

We had done this about three times and we were getting nervous. We knew it was driving the 7-Eleven owner out of his mind, but there hadn't been anything in the paper about it.

On our fourth mud-ball raid, we hit this guy's brand-new Chevy Blazer head-on with a real monster blob. He drove his Blazer over onto the monastery grounds and got us right in his headlights. We took off into the trees where he couldn't drive after us.

Hiding in the bushes in our camouflage outfits, we watched the guy drive away in his brand-new Blazer, dripping from a fresh mud bomb, but we knew the game was up.

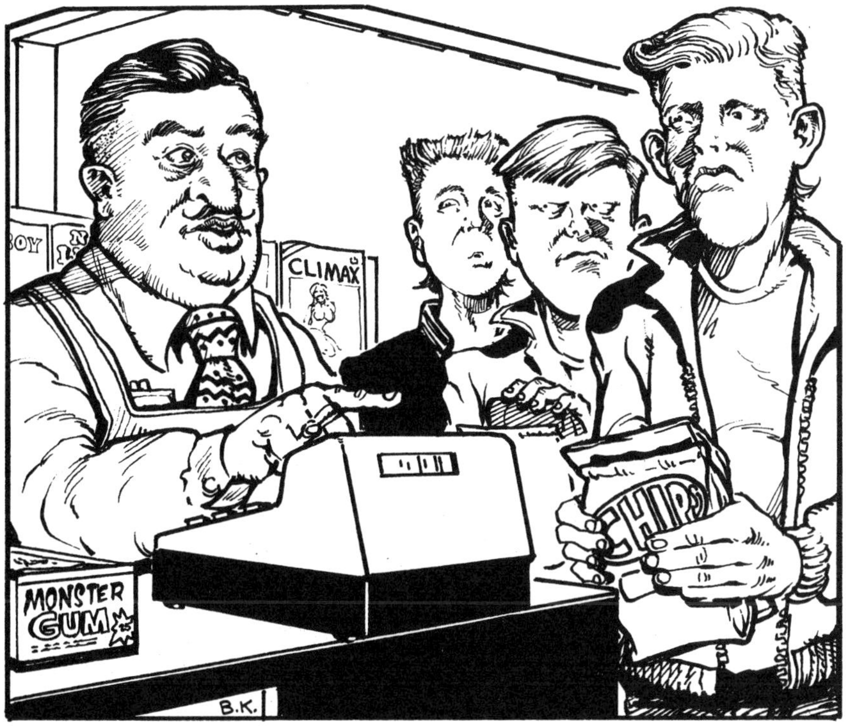
CLIMAX
MONSTER GUM
B.K.

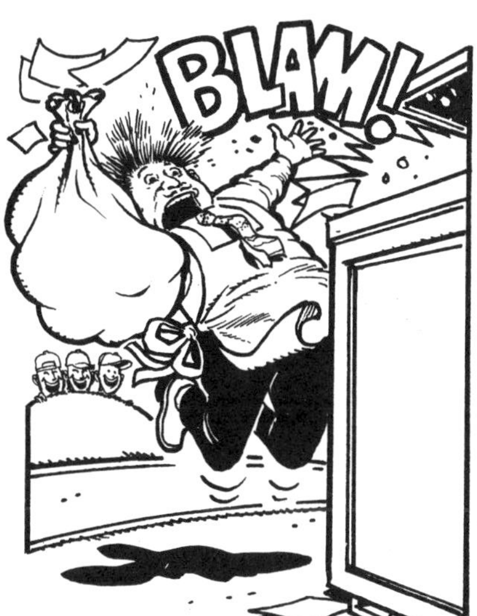
BLAM!

TRUE ANIMAL FACTS

ART BY B.K. TAYLOR

CUSTOMS PUTS BITE ON BIRD SMUGGLERS

Tony Escarciga has seen and heard of many methods — most of them inhuman — of smuggling exotic birds into the United States. But Escarciga chuckles when he recalls the woman who sedated a small parrot and tucked it in her bra while going through U.S. customs in Laredo, Texas.

"The only way we knew about it was the bird woke up and started biting her. She was jumping up and down and screaming and trying to get it out," said Escarciga, an animal health technician who works with the U.S. Department of Agriculture quarantine station in El Paso. *El Paso Times (Contributed by Richard Brandt)*

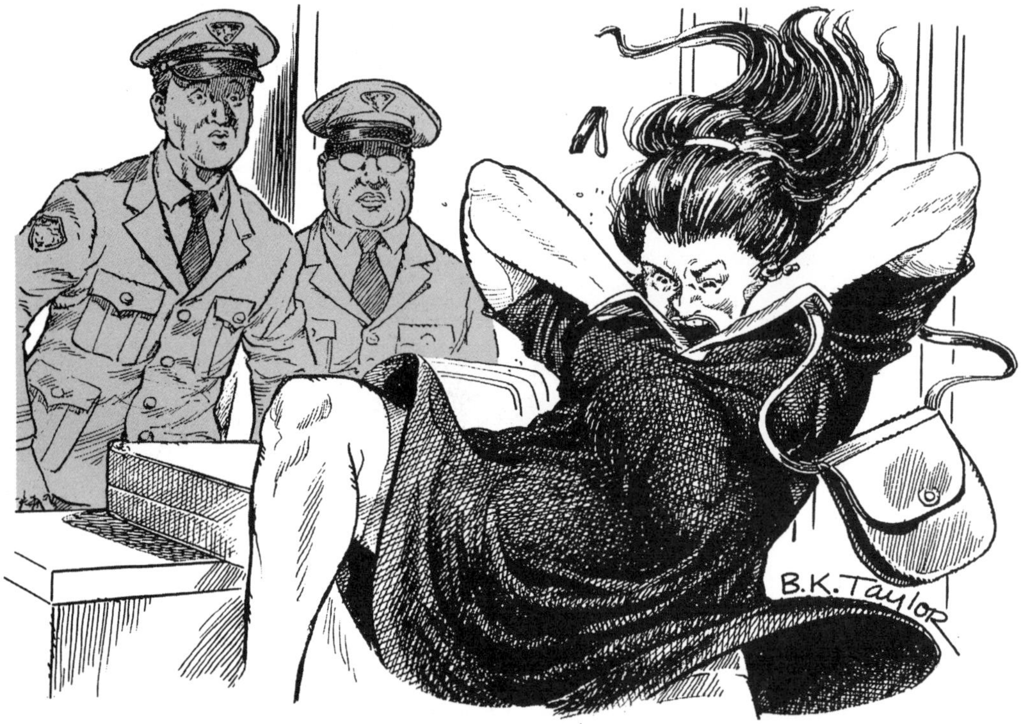
B.K.Taylor

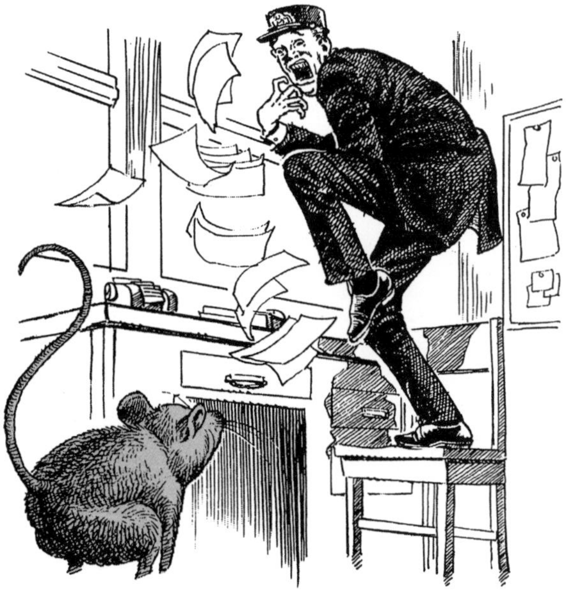

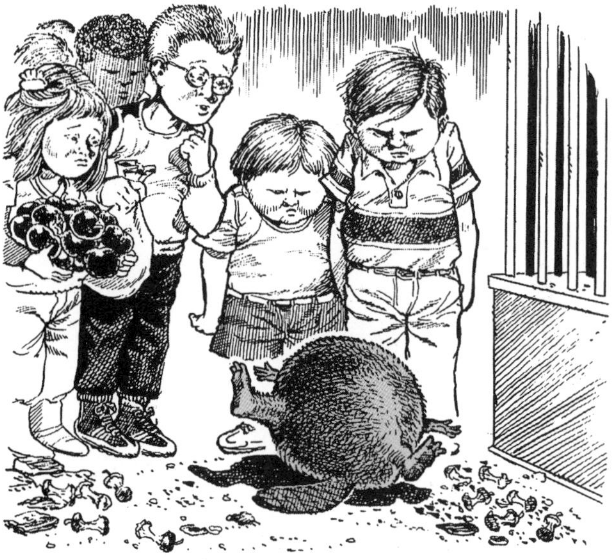

TRAIN DELAYED BECAUSE OF MICE IN TOWER

London (UPI) — Rush-hour morning trains ground to a halt in two southern English towns because the signal tower was taken over by mice and the fainthearted signalman fled.

Press reports said the sight of mice scampering among levers in the tower at Southbourne proved too much for the night signalman. He clocked out at 1 A.M., without leaving a note for his day replacement.

State-run British Rail is now looking for a new man who can cope with mice. "What we want is a well-qualified mouser," a spokesman said. *(Contributed by Robert Bourne)*

UNNAMED BEAVER BLOATS, DIES

Sixty-two children entered a "name-the-beaver" contest at a zoo at Bear Mountain, N.Y., but the event had to be canceled when the animal died. The eleven-week-old kit was the zoo's only specimen and had been pampered with its natural diet of aspen bark plus apples and sweet potatoes. The cause of death appeared to be a perforated stomach, stemming from overeating, director Jack Mead said. "You would think an animal would have enough sense to know when to stop," he added. Zoo officials hope to get two more beavers by next year and to reschedule the contest. (Cleveland) *Plain Dealer (contributed by Louis Gonzales)*

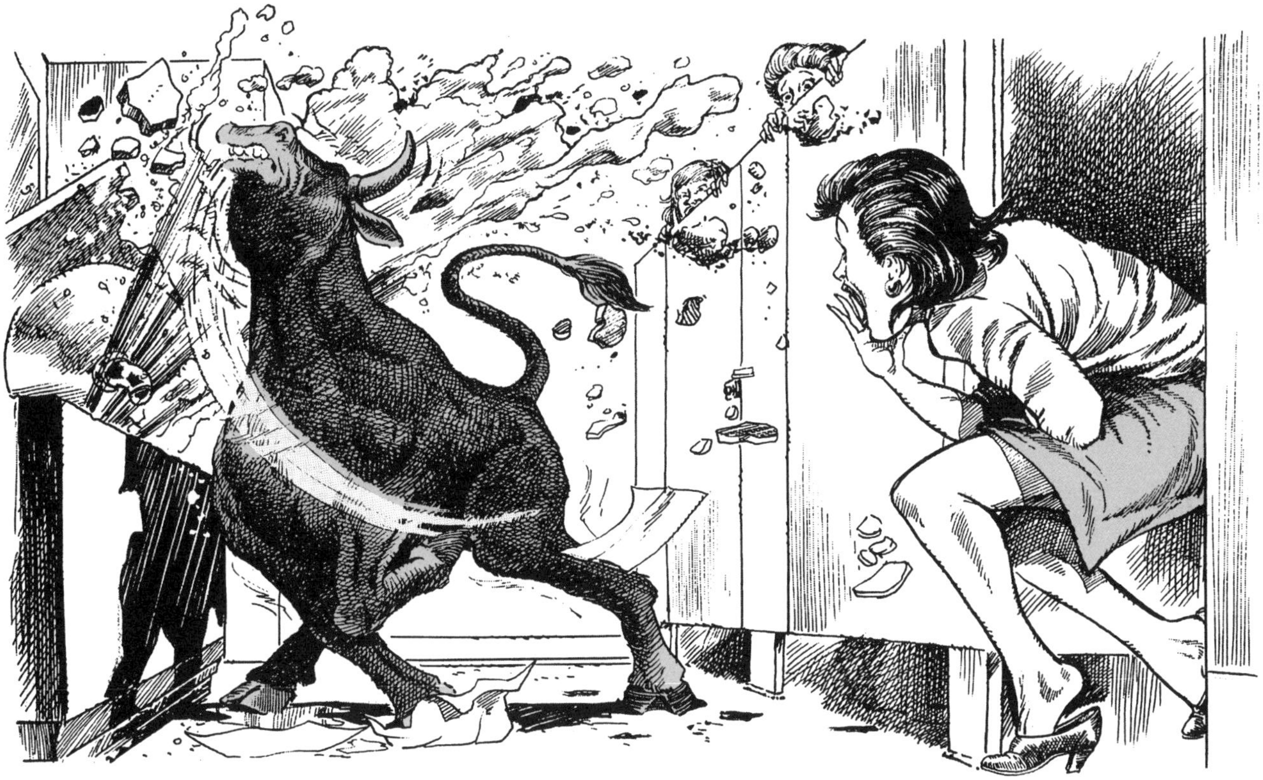

RAMPAGING BULL BARGES INTO WOMEN'S BIFFY

Minot, N.D. (AP) — An escaped rodeo bull barged into a women's rest room on the state fairgrounds, slightly injuring Barbara Deck of rural Harvey, N.D, forcing others to cower in stalls, and leaving water spraying from a smashed sink. It is estimated that the bull remained in the bathroom for five minutes.

"What we had was a wild bull. That's part of a bull's behavior. They're unpredictable," said Tracy Pearce, Miss Rodeo North Dakota. *Winnipeg Free Press (Contributed by David Rempel)*

JUDGE DISMISSES SUIT ON BEHALF OF DEAD MOSQUITOES

Glenwood Springs, Colo. (UPI) — District Judge J. E. DeVilbiss last week dismissed a lawsuit seeking damages on behalf of mosquitoes killed by a city spraying program. He ruled that plaintiff Paul Crawford had no standing in the case, had shown no personal harm, and that arguments by Crawford — a carpenter and poet — were "essentially cosmic." *Raleigh News and Observer (Contributed by Matt Corbett)*

HOUSE, POLICE REPORTED ATTACKED BY MONKEYS

Eighty enraged monkeys stormed a house and attacked two policemen who tried to rescue the occupants, *The Rand Daily Mail* of Johannesburg (South Africa) reported.

Kittie Lambrechts, of Durban, said that monkeys had pestered the family for more than a year. After catching a female and a baby in a trap, the monkeys descended on the house. "The whole troop went into a raging fury and attacked us," she said. "It was terrifying." *Baltimore Sun (Contributed by David Vernon Smith)*

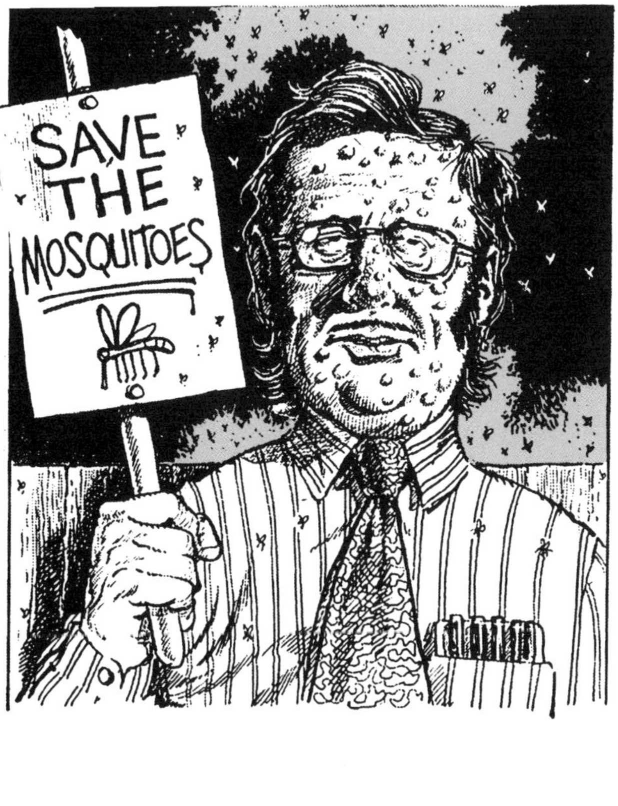
SAVE THE MOSQUITOES

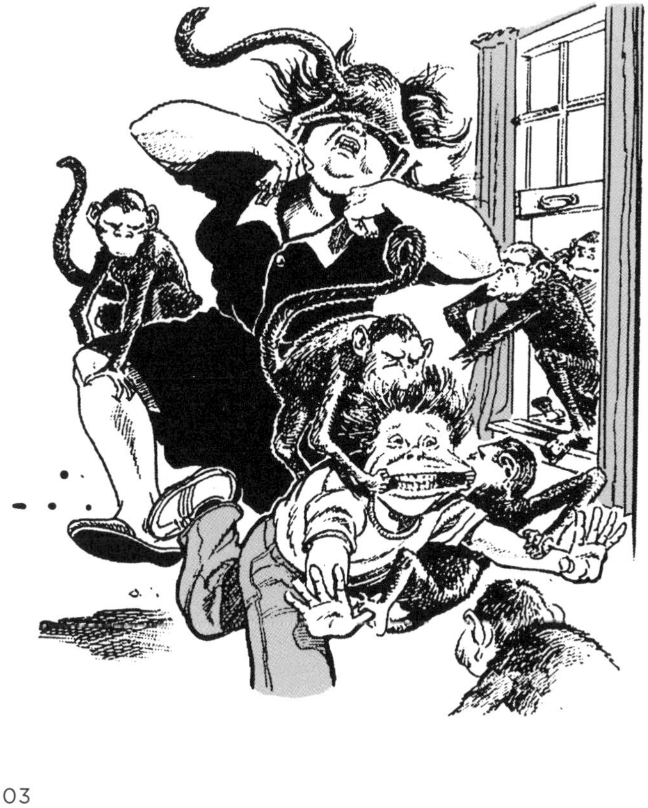

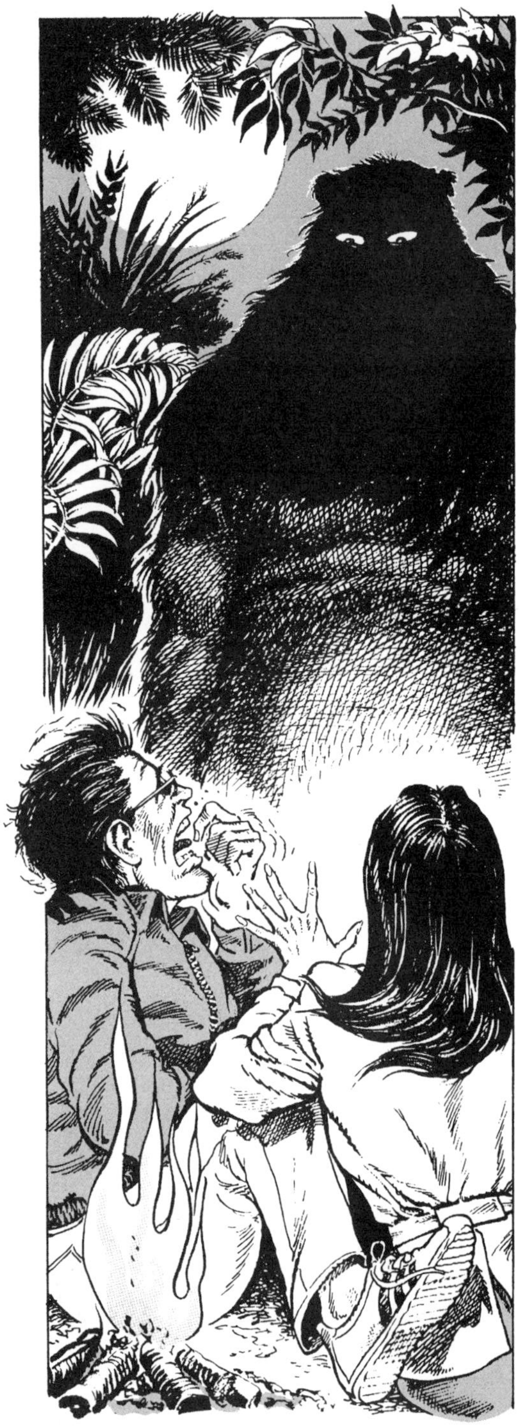

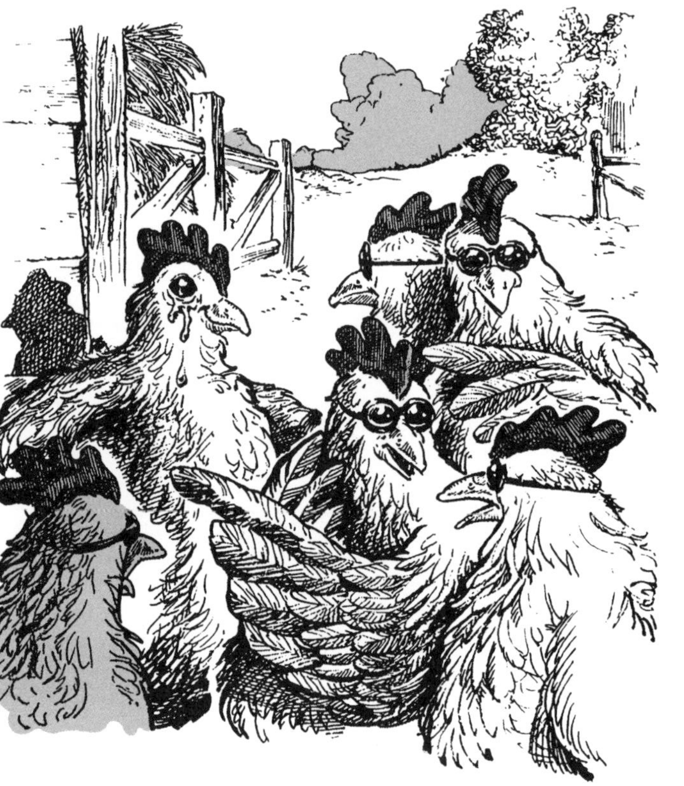

ROSIER DAYS AHEAD IN THE HENHOUSE

A Boston-based outfit is working to perfect red-tinted contact lenses to cut down on barnyard tension.

"It works," said Randall Wise of Animalens. "We don't know why but the lenses eliminate the hostility. They do not peck each other. They do not irritate the eyes and it doesn't hinder the chickens' sight. The biggest problem is trying to get them to stay in." *Boston Herald (Contributed by R. Hyman)*

HORDES OF HAMSTERS THREATENING BRITAIN

London (UPI) — Hundreds of renegade hamsters have invaded London suburbs, chewing through walls, floors, and ceilings, and raiding kitchens.

The hamsters also are apparently immune to poison. "They have survived one very harsh winter and have become a sort of superhamster," zoologist Sir Christopher Lever said. "Unless they are kept down they could infest the whole country." *(Contributed by Richard White)*

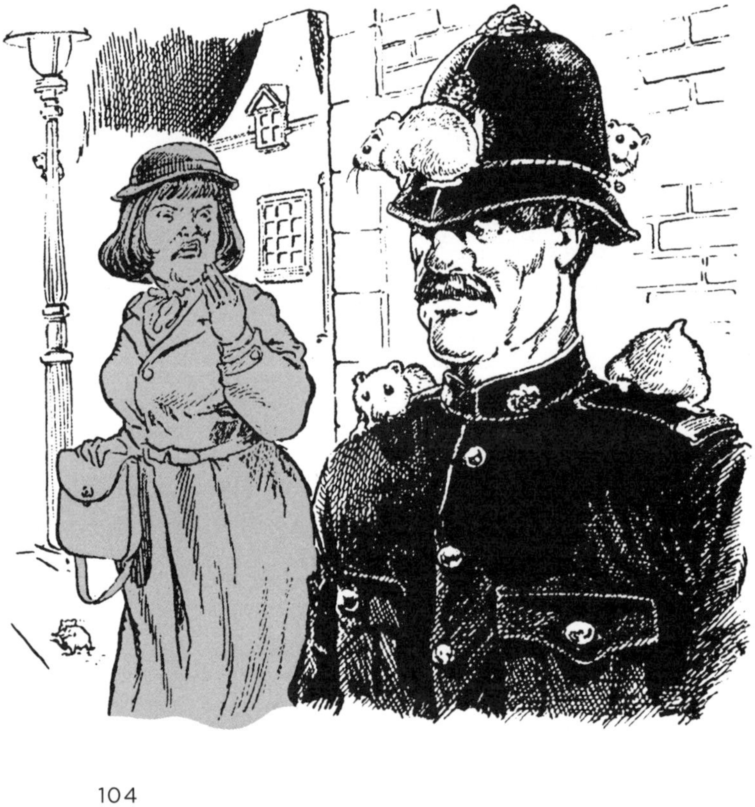

LIFE IN AMERICA

A bear-like creature attacked a campsite near Greenwater, Wash., and "ordered" the campers off the property, a couple has claimed. Greg and Stephanie McKay told Pierce County sheriff's deputies that an animal eight feet tall, ugly and smelly, with curly brown hair, attacked their tent Saturday. "You may think this sounds crazy, but the bear talked to us," Stephanie said. "It asked us what our names were and whether we had permission to use the campsite," she said. "We said we had gotten permission, but the bear told us to get off the property immediately. We ran like anything." While the couple gathered their belongings, the bear began throwing rocks at them, they said. Sheriff's Sgt. Terry Schmid said: "It could be a complete hoax, but... we're investigating." *Miami Herald (contributed by Fawn Chautinger)*

LOVE PIGS FALL ON CURIOUS VET

Tainan (Taiwan) — A pair of pigs weighing 330 kilograms fell on and injured a veterinarian as he helped them to mate, a local newspaper reported today. The accident occurred on Wednesday at a farm in Tainan, southern Taiwan, where Mr. Su Cheng-Jen had arranged the mating, the Chinese-language *China Daily News* reported. Farm workers had to remove the pigs before they could rescue Mr. Su. *AFP (contributed by Jhevek Carnelian)*

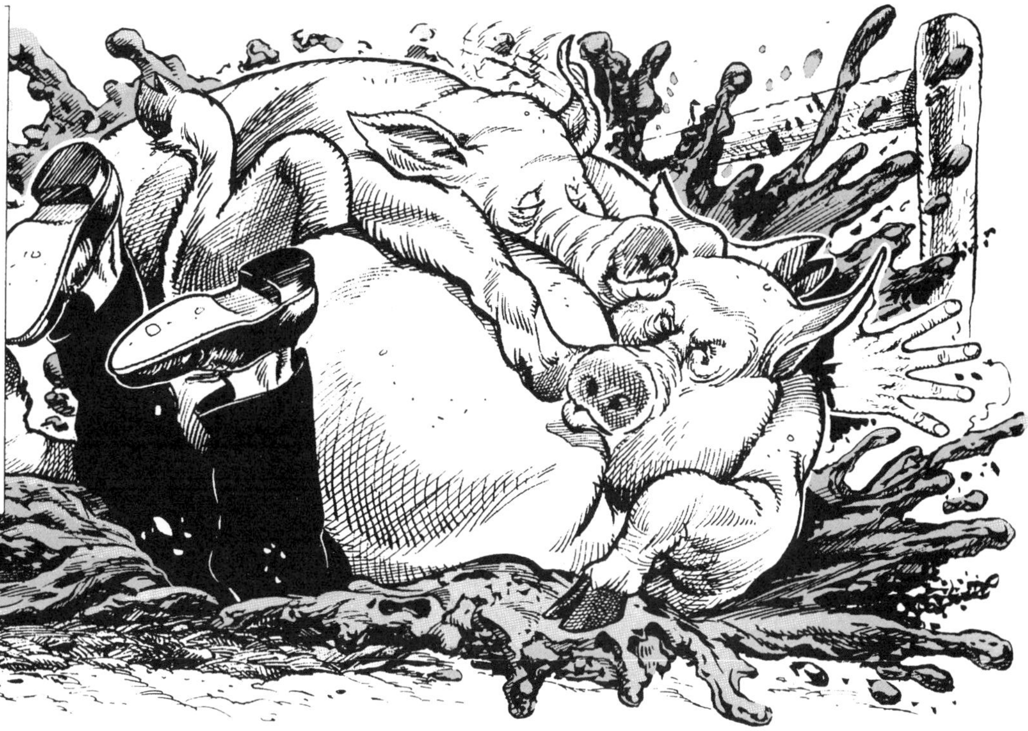

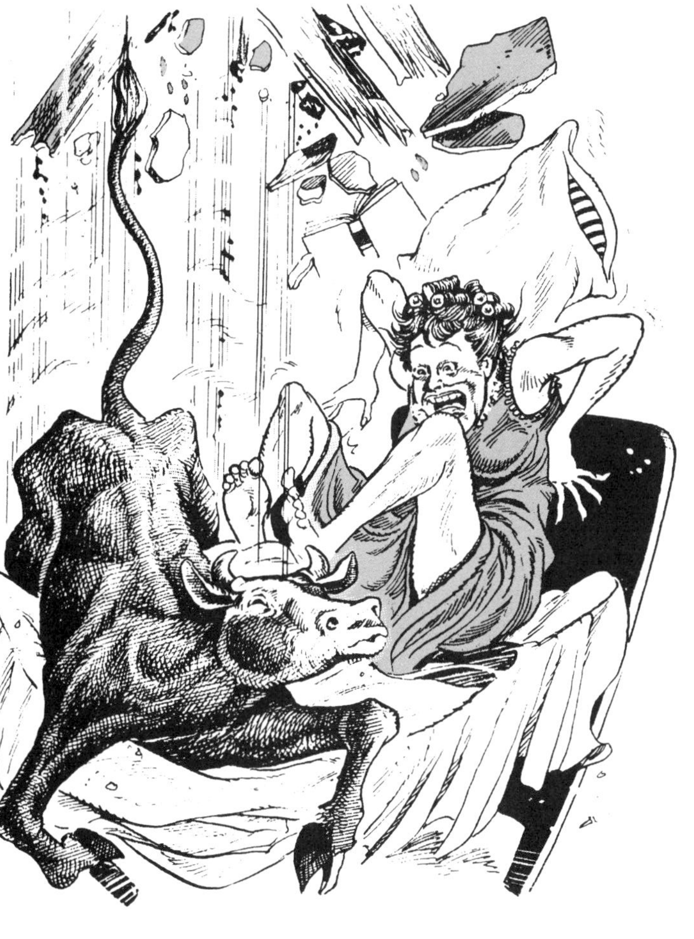

COW LANDS IN BEDROOM

Cape Town (AFP) — A terrified cow on the tiny British-ruled Atlantic island of Tristan da Cunha "came crashing through the roof" of a local woman's bedroom in the middle of a stormy night.

A local priest, Father John Pearson, said that the animal, evidently unhurt, "just lay there, stunned, before getting up and staggering through the kitchen and out of the front door." *Daily Yomiuri (Contributed by Joe Palermo)*

HAVE NO TRAFFIC WITH DARK HORSE

Kingman, Ariz. — Equestrienne Kathy Smith, thirty-four, got a ticket for failure to have a taillight on her horse. A sheriff's spokesman said that horses are considered "vehicles" and must be equipped with lights for nighttime riding to allow drivers to see them. (New York) *Daily News (contributed by Ray Laird)*

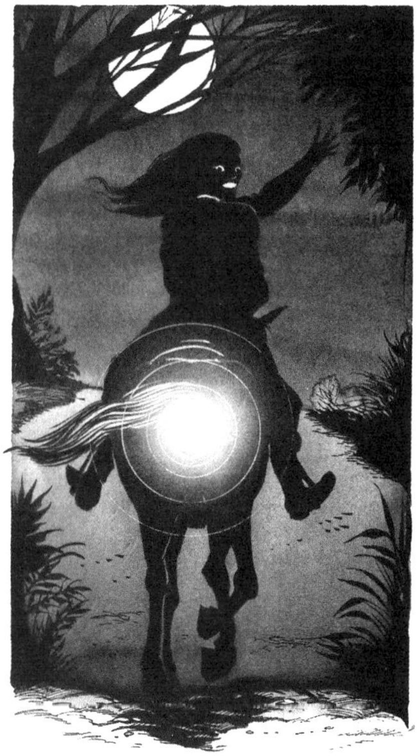

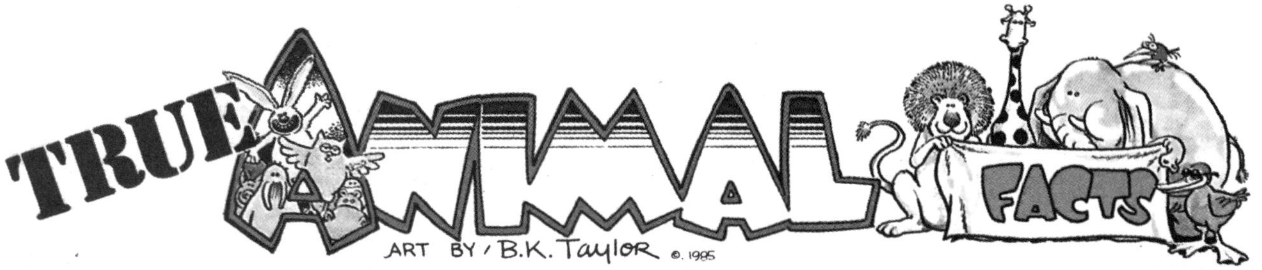
TRUE
ANIMAL
FACTS

ART BY / B.K. Taylor ©. 1985

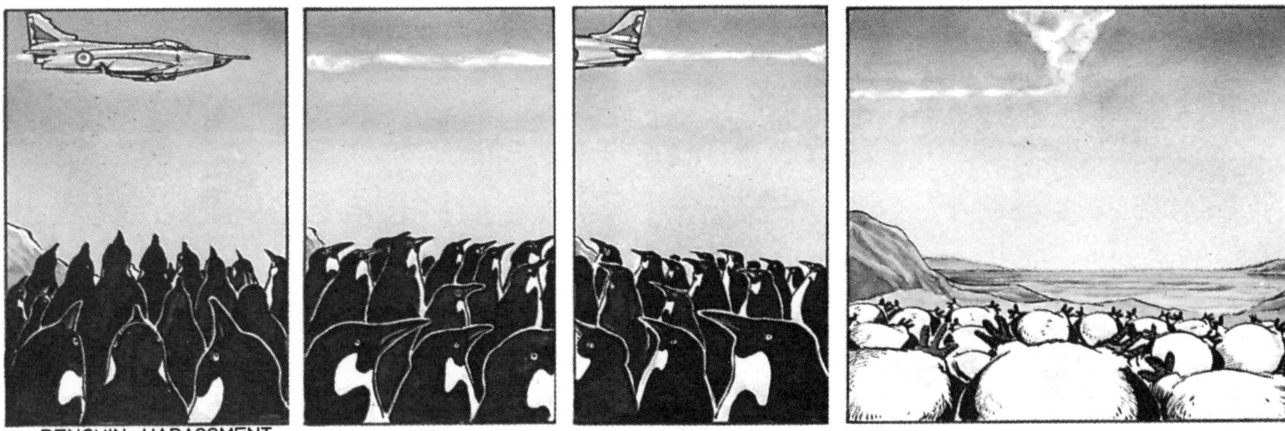

PENGUIN HARASSMENT

A MEXICAN NEWSPAPER REPORTS THAT BORED ROYAL AIR FORCE PILOTS STATIONED ON THE FALKLAND ISLANDS HAVE DEVISED WHAT THEY CONSIDER "A MARVELOUS NEW GAME." NOTING THAT THE LOCAL PENGUINS ARE FASCINATED BY AIRPLANES, THE PILOTS SEARCH OUT A BEACH WHERE THE BIRDS ARE GATHERED AND FLY SLOWLY ALONG IT AT THE WATER'S EDGE. PERHAPS TEN THOUSAND PENGUINS TURN THEIR HEADS IN UNISON WATCHING THE PLANES GO BY. AND WHEN THE PILOTS TURN AROUND AND FLY BACK, THE BIRDS TURN THEIR HEADS IN THE OPPOSITE DIRECTION - LIKE SPECTATORS AT A SLOW-MOTION TENNIS MATCH. THEN, THE PAPER REPORTS, "THE PILOTS FLY OUT TO SEA AND DIRECTLY TO THE PENGUIN COLONY AND OVERFLY IT. HEADS GO UP, UP, UP, AND THE TEN THOUSAND PENGUINS FALL OVER GENTLY ONTO THEIR BACKS."

SUBMITTED BY: LORRIE FERRIS & DAN CHURE / AUDUBON MAG.

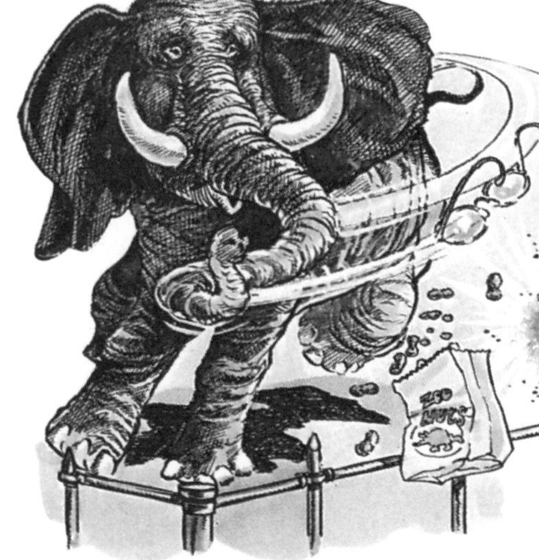
ZOO NUTS

ELEPHANT BEANS VISITOR

COCO, A BULL ELEPHANT AT THE COLUMBUS, OHIO, ZOO, THROWS A WICKED CHUNK OF CONCRETE. GLEN HONAKER, 36, IS LIVING PROOF. HONAKER RECEIVED A CUT HEAD FROM A BASE-BALL-SIZED PIECE OF CONCRETE TOSSED BY COCO. THE ELEPHANT APPARENTLY BECAME UPSET WITH A LAUGHING CROWD NEAR HIS PEN. "HE HATES VEHICLES," SAYS JACK HANNA, ZOO DIRECTOR. "HE'S BUSTED THREE WINDSHIELDS. WE USED TO TAKE A ZOO TRAIN PAST HIS PEN, BUT WE STOPPED LAST YEAR BECAUSE COCO THREW THINGS AT IT." HANNA SAYS THE ZOO WILL GIVE HONAKER A FREE PASS TO USE AFTER HE RECOVERS.

SUBMITTED BY:
FREDDY WAGUESPACK, JR.
USA TODAY

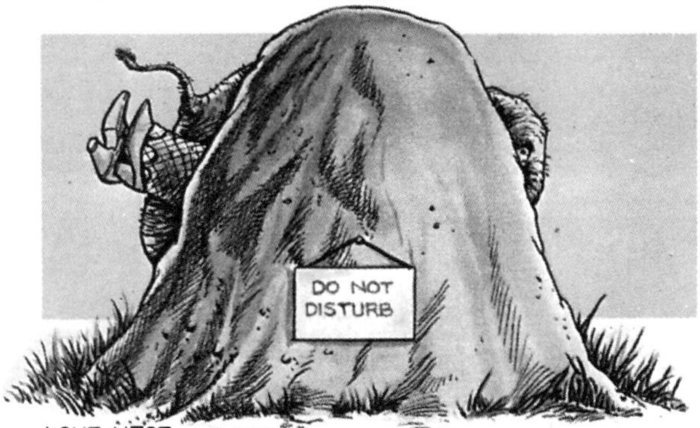
DO NOT DISTURB

LOVE NEST

IT'S DIFFICULT TO GET IN THE MOOD WITH A CROWD LOOKING ON, SO OFFICIALS AT THE OAKLAND, CALIF., ZOO ARE GOING TO BUILD THEIR ELEPHANTS A LOVE NEST. ZOO OFFICIALS HAVE ANNOUNCED THEY HAVE HIRED AN ARCHITECTURAL FIRM TO BUILD A NEW ELEPHANT ENVIRONMENT THAT IS CONDUCIVE TO MATING. "OUR IMMEDIATE GOAL IS TO DESIGN A SUITABLE AND COMFORTABLE ENCLOSURE FOR BREEDING ELEPHANTS," SAID GENERAL MANAGER WILLIAM MOTT, JR. THE NEW ELEPHANT HOME WILL GIVE THE ANIMALS SOME PRIVACY. THEIR CURRENT HOME IS AN OPEN PEN WITH A SMALL POOL AND CONCRETE SLAB THAT IS ALWAYS IN VIEW OF VISITORS. "JUST LIKE HUMANS, THEY REQUIRE PRIVACY. IN THE AFRICAN VELDT...THEY CAN GO AROUND BEHIND A HILL OR MOUNTAIN."

L.C. WEBER / GLOUCESTER CO. (N.J.) TIMES

GIANT LIZARD VISITS COURTROOM

THE APPEARANCE OF A GIANT MONITOR LIZARD IN A NAIROBI, KENYA, COURTROOM SO STUNNED SPECTATORS AND POLICE THAT 20 SUSPECTED CRIMINALS ESCAPED IN THE CONFUSION.

THE THREE-FOOT-LONG LIZARD CAUSED A STAMPEDE IN THE COURTROOM DURING WHICH ONE WOMAN WAS INJURED WHEN SHE FELL FROM A TABLE SHE HAD JUMPED ON TO ESCAPE THE CREATURE.

BY THE TIME THE LIZARD WAS BEATEN TO DEATH BY BAILIFFS, ALL THE SUSPECTS AWAITING TRIAL HAD DISAPPEARED. AFTER ISSUING WARRANTS FOR THEIR ARREST, MAGISTRATE FREDRICK MWAWASI SUGGESTED THAT THE COURTHOUSE BE DECLARED A NATIONAL PARK.

J.R. LEONARD
S.F. CHRONICLE

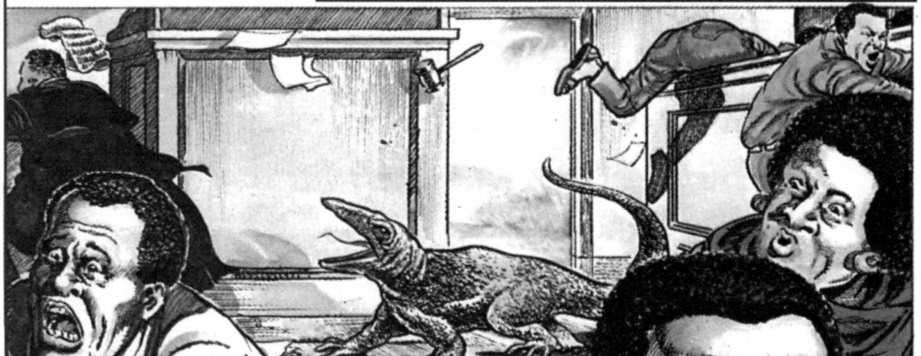

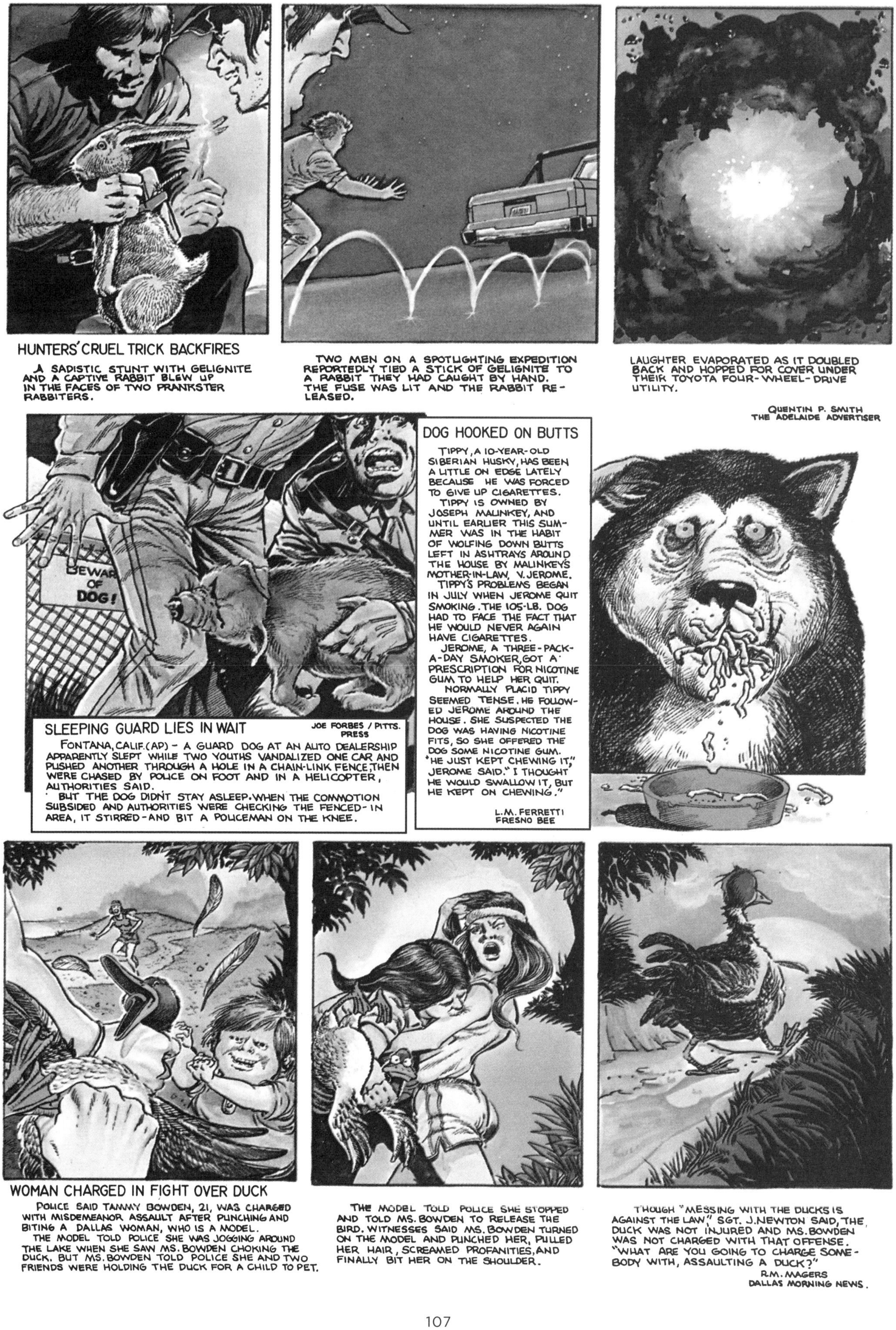
HUNTERS' CRUEL TRICK BACKFIRES
A SADISTIC STUNT WITH GELIGNITE AND A CAPTIVE RABBIT BLEW UP IN THE FACES OF TWO PRANKSTER RABBITERS.
TWO MEN ON A SPOTLIGHTING EXPEDITION REPORTEDLY TIED A STICK OF GELIGNITE TO A RABBIT THEY HAD CAUGHT BY HAND. THE FUSE WAS LIT AND THE RABBIT RELEASED.
LAUGHTER EVAPORATED AS IT DOUBLED BACK AND HOPPED FOR COVER UNDER THEIR TOYOTA FOUR-WHEEL-DRIVE UTILITY.
QUENTIN P. SMITH
THE ADELAIDE ADVERTISER
BEWARE OF DOG!
SLEEPING GUARD LIES IN WAIT
JOE FORBES / PITTS. PRESS
FONTANA, CALIF. (AP) - A GUARD DOG AT AN AUTO DEALERSHIP APPARENTLY SLEPT WHILE TWO YOUTHS VANDALIZED ONE CAR AND PUSHED ANOTHER THROUGH A HOLE IN A CHAIN-LINK FENCE, THEN WERE CHASED BY POLICE ON FOOT AND IN A HELICOPTER, AUTHORITIES SAID.
BUT THE DOG DIDN'T STAY ASLEEP. WHEN THE COMMOTION SUBSIDED AND AUTHORITIES WERE CHECKING THE FENCED-IN AREA, IT STIRRED - AND BIT A POLICEMAN ON THE KNEE.
DOG HOOKED ON BUTTS
TIPPY, A 10-YEAR-OLD SIBERIAN HUSKY, HAS BEEN A LITTLE ON EDGE LATELY BECAUSE HE WAS FORCED TO GIVE UP CIGARETTES.
TIPPY IS OWNED BY JOSEPH MALINKEY, AND UNTIL EARLIER THIS SUMMER WAS IN THE HABIT OF WOLFING DOWN BUTTS LEFT IN ASHTRAYS AROUND THE HOUSE BY MALINKEY'S MOTHER-IN-LAW, V. JEROME.
TIPPY'S PROBLEMS BEGAN IN JULY WHEN JEROME QUIT SMOKING. THE 105-LB. DOG HAD TO FACE THE FACT THAT HE WOULD NEVER AGAIN HAVE CIGARETTES.
JEROME, A THREE-PACK-A-DAY SMOKER, GOT A PRESCRIPTION FOR NICOTINE GUM TO HELP HER QUIT.
NORMALLY PLACID TIPPY SEEMED TENSE. HE FOLLOWED JEROME AROUND THE HOUSE. SHE SUSPECTED THE DOG WAS HAVING NICOTINE FITS, SO SHE OFFERED THE DOG SOME NICOTINE GUM.
"HE JUST KEPT CHEWING IT," JEROME SAID. "I THOUGHT HE WOULD SWALLOW IT, BUT HE KEPT ON CHEWING."
L.M. FERRETTI
FRESNO BEE
WOMAN CHARGED IN FIGHT OVER DUCK
POLICE SAID TAMMY BOWDEN, 21, WAS CHARGED WITH MISDEMEANOR ASSAULT AFTER PUNCHING AND BITING A DALLAS WOMAN, WHO IS A MODEL.
THE MODEL TOLD POLICE SHE WAS JOGGING AROUND THE LAKE WHEN SHE SAW MS. BOWDEN CHOKING THE DUCK. BUT MS. BOWDEN TOLD POLICE SHE AND TWO FRIENDS WERE HOLDING THE DUCK FOR A CHILD TO PET.
THE MODEL TOLD POLICE SHE STOPPED AND TOLD MS. BOWDEN TO RELEASE THE BIRD. WITNESSES SAID MS. BOWDEN TURNED ON THE MODEL AND PUNCHED HER, PULLED HER HAIR, SCREAMED PROFANITIES, AND FINALLY BIT HER ON THE SHOULDER.
THOUGH "MESSING WITH THE DUCKS IS AGAINST THE LAW," SGT. J. NEWTON SAID, THE DUCK WAS NOT INJURED AND MS. BOWDEN WAS NOT CHARGED WITH THAT OFFENSE.
"WHAT ARE YOU GOING TO CHARGE SOMEBODY WITH, ASSAULTING A DUCK?"
R.M. MAGERS
DALLAS MORNING NEWS.

HOT FLASHES

ILLUSTRATED BY B.K. TAYLOR

A Boston man opened a beer bottle with his teeth while "watching a tense baseball game," but the force of the compressed gas in the bottle fired the cap down his throat, where it lodged in his esophagus. The bottle cap was removed surgically. *Arizona Republic (Contributed by John M. Andresen)*

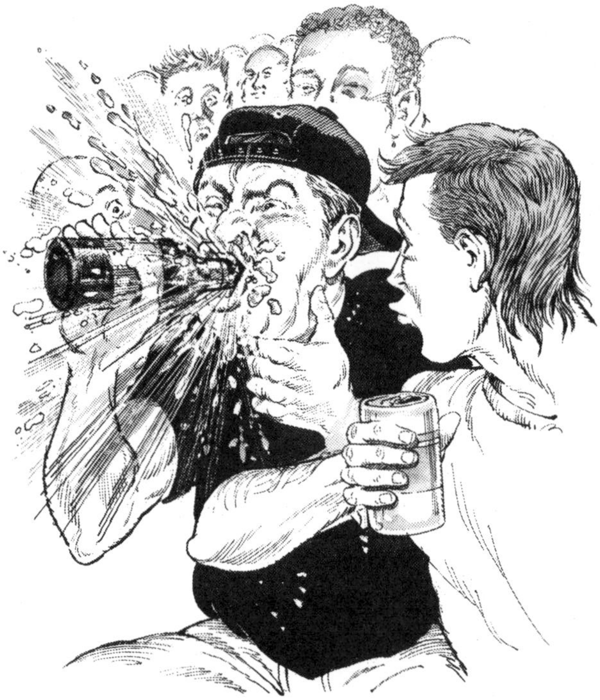

According to the *Wall Street Journal*, "Elvis sightings can now be collected and broadcast through use of a 900 telephone number." The Los Angeles–based system, created by Starbridge Communications, lets Elvis Presley fans record personal messages to the King. *(Contributed by Jeff Chutz)*

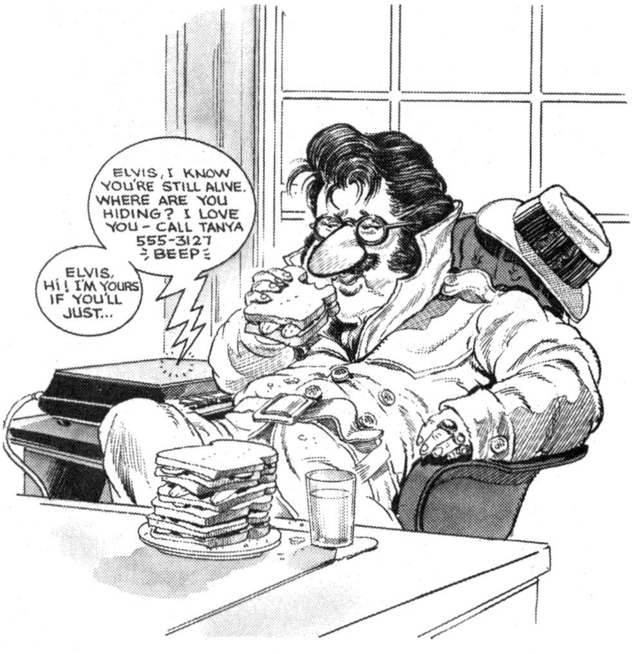
ELVIS, I KNOW YOU'RE STILL ALIVE. WHERE ARE YOU HIDING? I LOVE YOU - CALL TANYA 555-3127 BEEP
ELVIS, HI! I'M YOURS IF YOU'LL JUST...

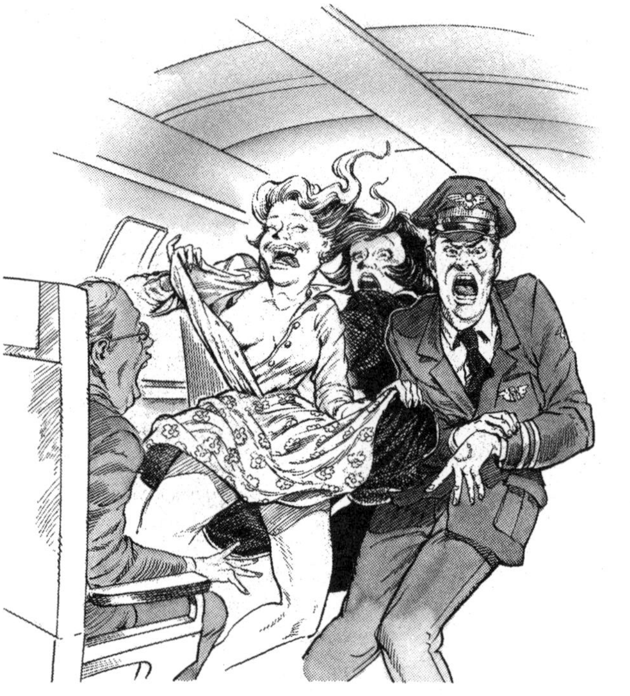

On a Northwest Airlines flight, a flight attendant saw a passenger "apparently intoxicated, sitting among men away from her assigned seat on the plane." As the attendant tried to escort her back to her seat, the passenger "used profanity and lifted her shirt to expose her breasts." When the copilot intervened, she allegedly bit him. *Detroit Free Press (Contributed by Nancy Lightbody)*

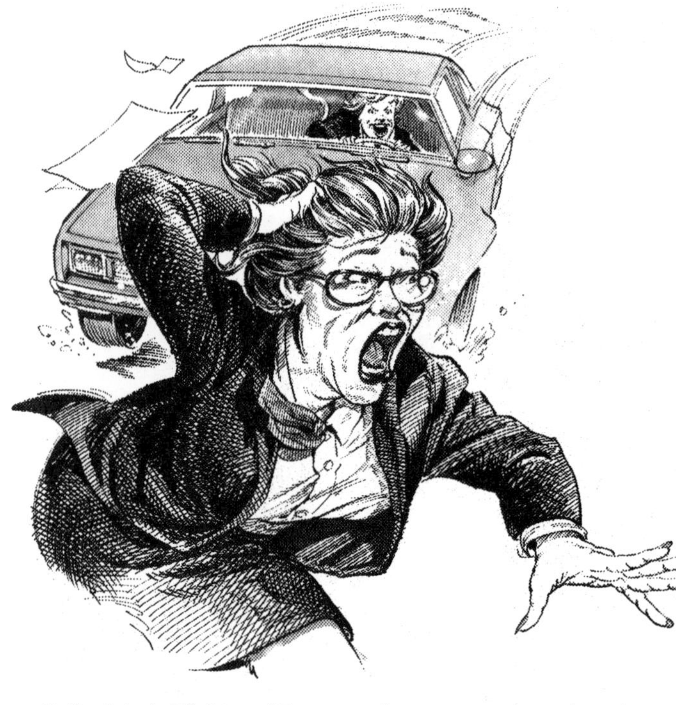

At the Ontario Ministry of Transportation, a woman drove through a traffic light during the test for her driver's license. The examiner asked the woman to return to the office, but, according to the Toronto *Globe & Mail*, "the applicant began shouting threats, driving erratically, and speeding down the wrong side of the road. When the examiner got out and started to walk to the office, the applicant tried to run her down in the parking lot. She failed her test." *(Contributed by R. B. Graham)*

TRAVEL TIPZ

WRITTEN AND ILLUSTRATED BY B.K. TAYLOR

Too many bags to check? That last one won't fit under the seat in front of you? Why not dress it up as a child under two, and let it sit on your lap?

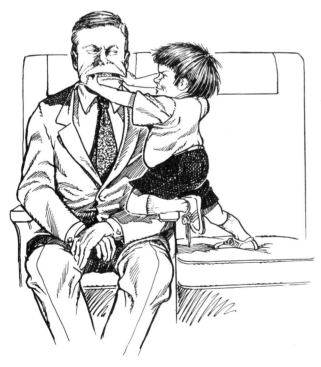

Do anything you can to *not* sit next to children. They become bored quickly and will soon be playing with your face. This has proven to be a severe hindrance to writing that sales speech you're delivering in Amarillo.

Avoid sitting next to people who are dead. They may not plague you with meaningless chatter like other passengers, but they probably won't have many new business leads either.

A BETTER YOU DEPT.

WRITTEN AND ILLUSTRATED BY B.K. TAYLOR

HOME IMPROVEMENT WITHOUT SURGERY

All right, a lot of you are saying, "No, I'm not going to risk surgery — is there another way?" The good news is, "Yes!" And in your own home! Utilizing a few simple tricks, you can obtain many of the results of plastic surgery. Though these may not be permanent, they can still give the appearance of a younger you.

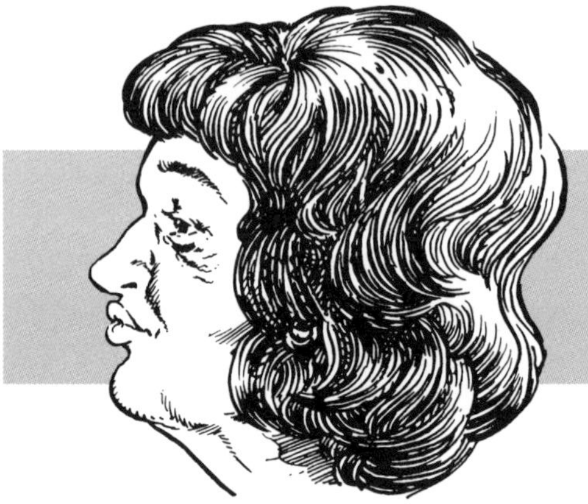

Here is a plain-looking woman with a sagging skin structure. Let's take her through a simple make-over as an example of the possibilities.

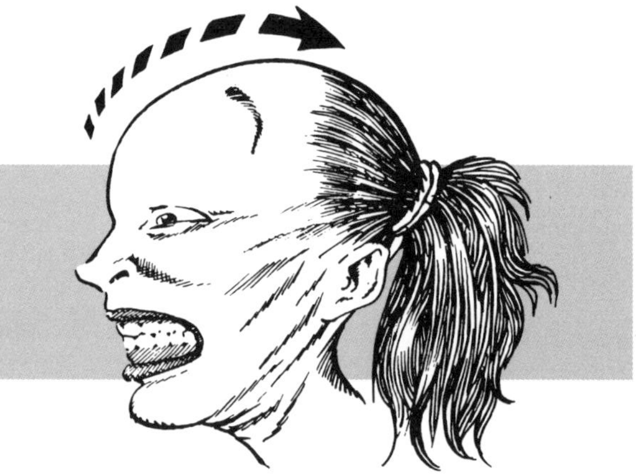

Drawing the hair back behind the head pulls the skin tight for a less sagging appearance. This does cause a small problem, however, in that the hair-line and eyebrows may appear slightly higher than is pleasing to the eye.

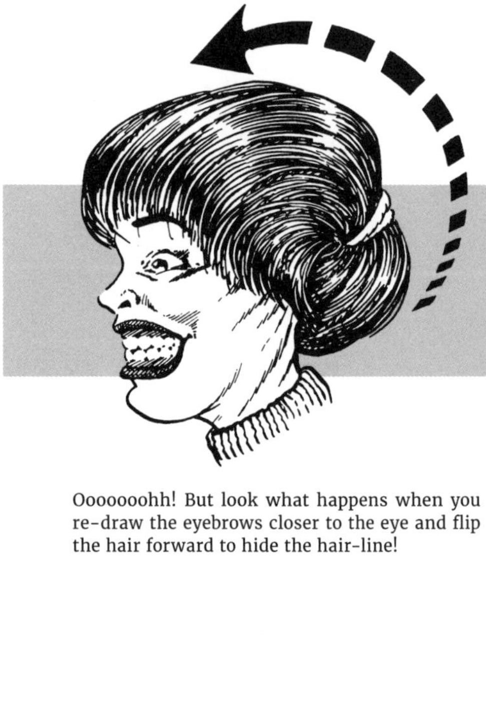

Ooooooohh! But look what happens when you re-draw the eyebrows closer to the eye and flip the hair forward to hide the hair-line!

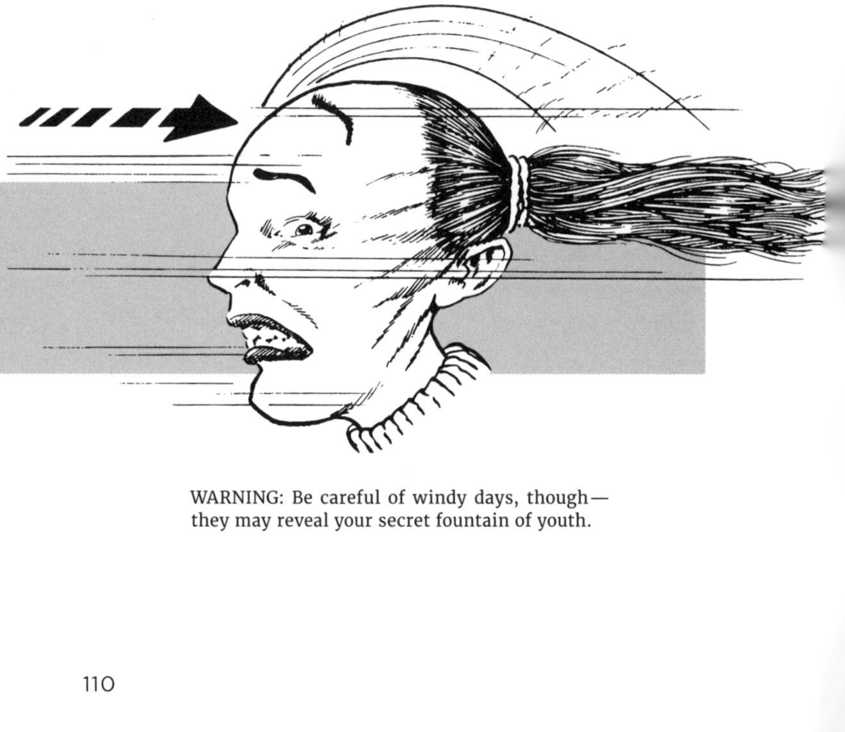

WARNING: Be careful of windy days, though—they may reveal your secret fountain of youth.

EASY FIXES

OVERWEIGHT

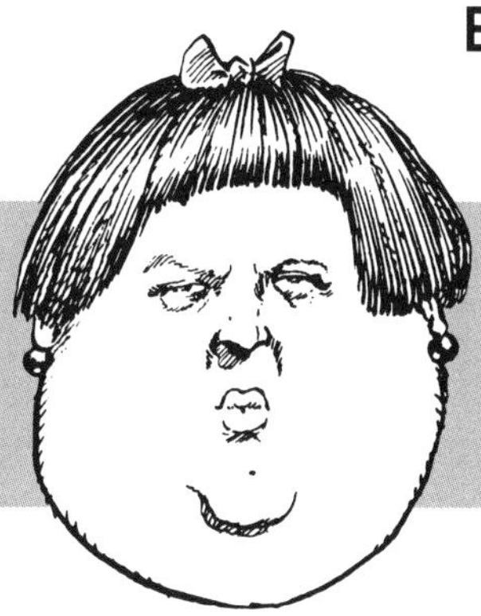

Note the hair is pushed too far back, framing the face and giving it a heavy appearance.

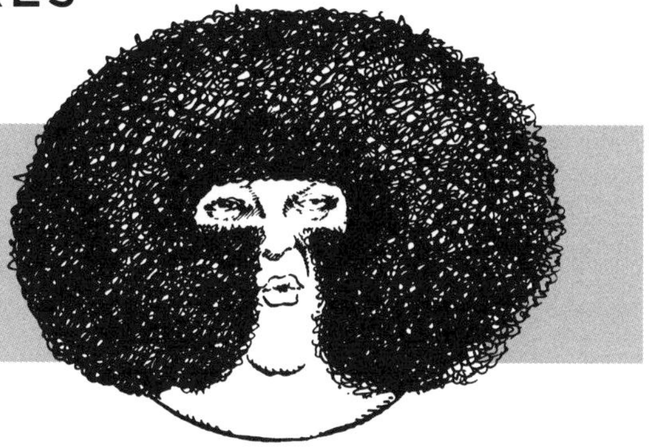

There we are!
Hey, Good-Looking!

UNDERWEIGHT

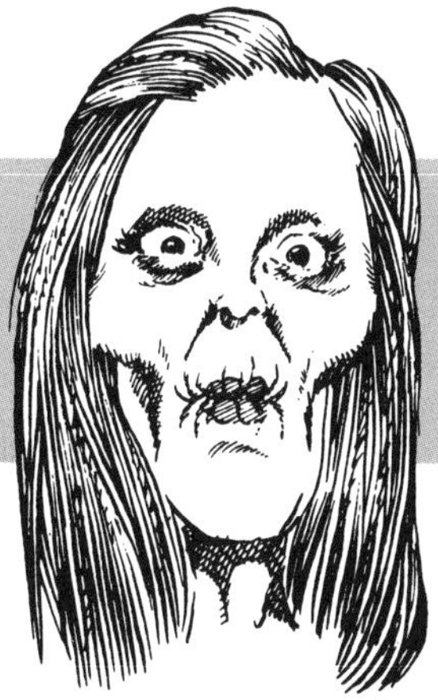

Does this person look thin to you? We think so. But don't despair if this is your image.

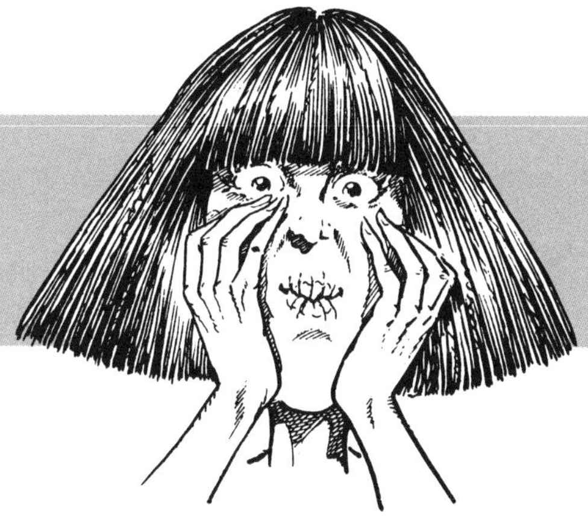

See what a new hairdo can do for that long, drawn look? Plus, keeping your hands over your face makes all the difference in the world. And, in time, if you faithfully keep your hands on your cheeks, everywhere, all the time, people will get used to seeing you this way. We must warn you, though, this method will impede your typing skills.

DOES YOUR NOSE SEEM TOO LARGE?

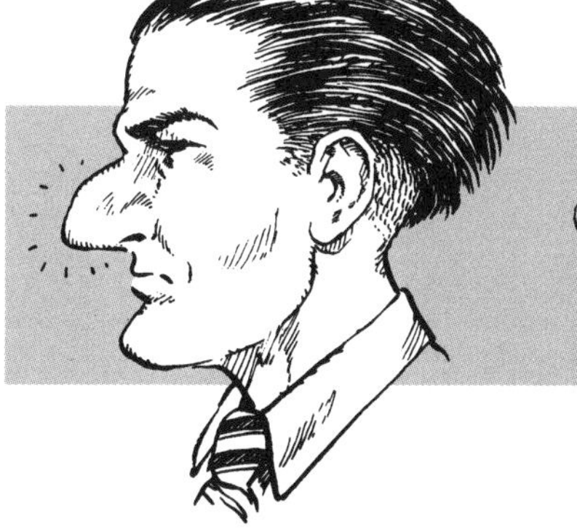

Notice how the prominent nose is accented by the hairstyle? This person is undoubtedly tainted with a moniker such as "Eagle Beak" or "Casaba Schnozz."

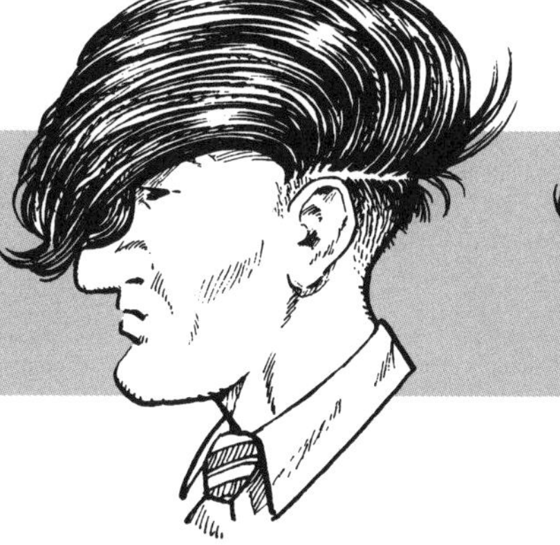

Now look. With the new "Be a Success" hairstyle, the nose is one of the last things people in the office will notice.

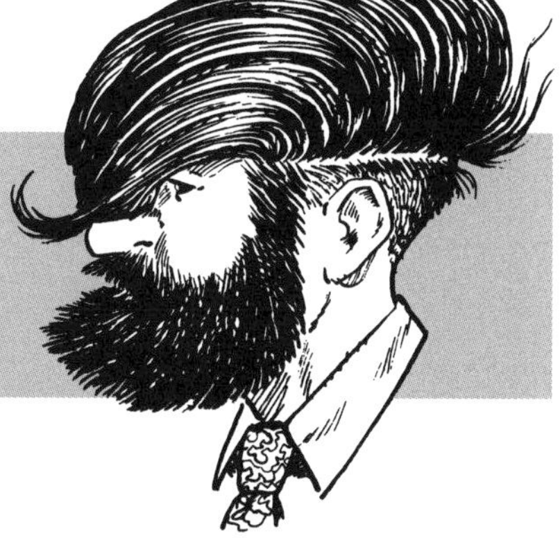

Add to this a moustache and beard and — *Voila!* — a large nose is a worry of the past!

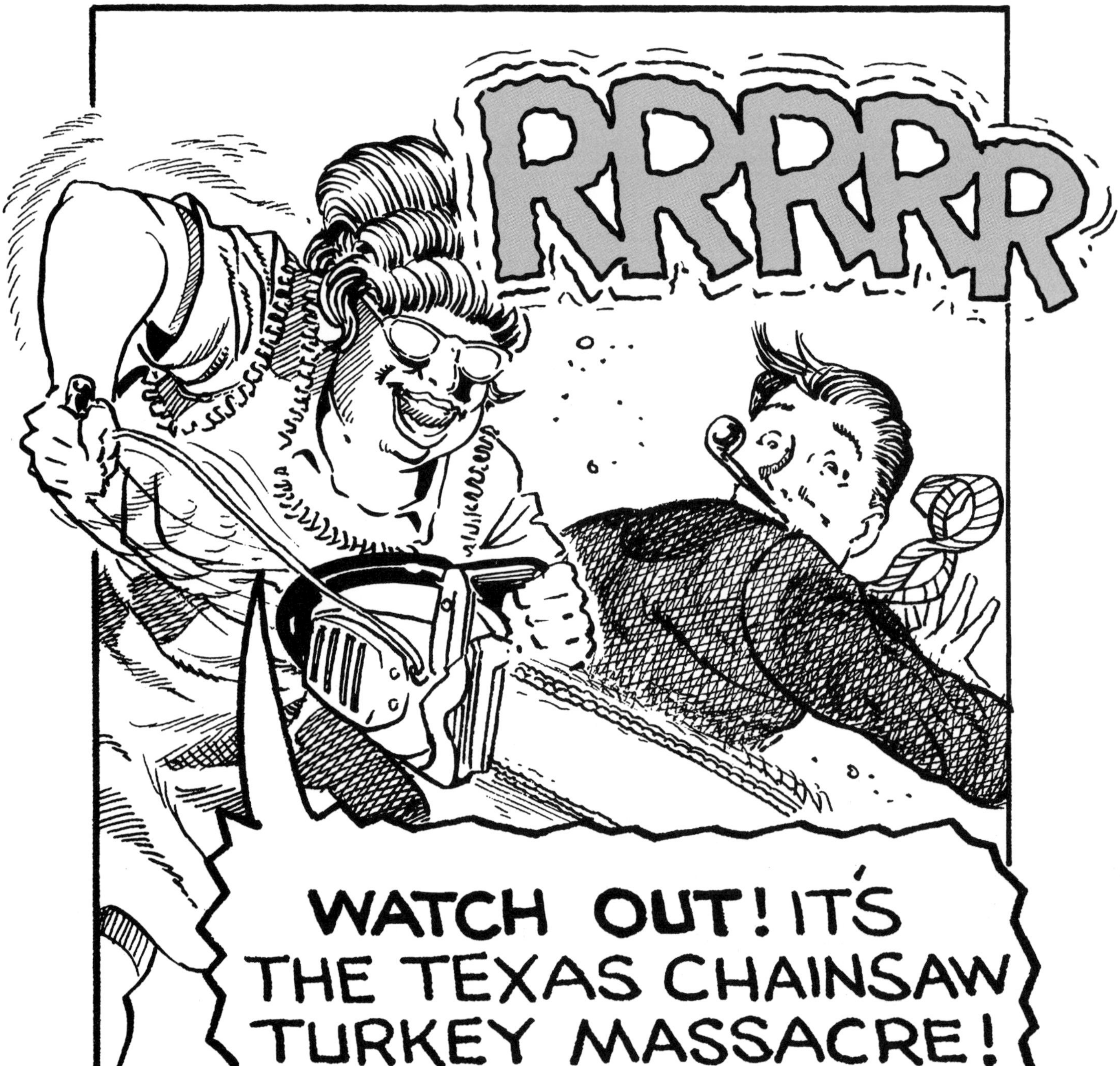
RRRRRR
WATCH OUT! IT'S THE TEXAS CHAINSAW TURKEY MASSACRE!

A LEGACY OF LUNACY

BACKWOЯD BY R.L. STINE

THERE IS SO MUCH LUNACY HERE. THE STAID family setting, a true Norman Rockwell milieu, can fool you at first into thinking you're about to experience some faded episodes of lost Americana, à la *Father Knows Best*. But father can't know best in the Appletons' house, because everything is tilted and twisted and just plain wrong.

As soon as Grandma and Grandpa come to visit, you know there's something terribly wrong in the Appleton household. It all looks like a familiar 1960s sitcom family scene. But Grandma comes prepared with a whoopee cushion and a ghastly pile of fake vomit for use at the dinner table. And what's up with the special greeting she has for her son, Norm Appleton? Granny does a mean karate lift, swings Norm over her shoulder, and heaves him headfirst down the basement stairs. Norm is nonplussed. The pipe never leaves his mouth. But the dazed look in his eyes makes you wonder exactly what he has been smoking in that pipe.

Grandma Appleton straps on her knee cymbals and knocks out an Aretha Franklin–worthy version of "Respect" on her accordion. Later, she attacks the "slightly" overcooked Thanksgiving turkey with a chainsaw.

As for the others in the family, Helen, Norm's wife, is a long-suffering good sport. It's as if Jane Wyatt or Barbara Billingsley or Harriet Nelson, the perfect TV wife, suddenly found herself in a horror movie. What should she do? Carry on, of course!

And Kathy and Bobby, the two blond and perfect kids? They mostly stare straight ahead, their faces tight with terror, eyes wide with alarm and disbelief.

You get the idea. B.K. isn't trying to portray the underside of suburban life here. He's not making a comment about life in America. He has given us this family of characters, respectable-looking people who are totally insane, who don't follow any civilized rules, who go berserk all the time, who will do anything — mainly because it's funny.

And yes, these strips — collected here for the first time from their long run in the *National Lampoon* humor magazine — are laugh-out-loud funny. B.K.'s wonderful artwork will make you start laughing even before you read the text.

But be warned: once you get to know the Appleton family, you may never think about family life the same way ever again.

As for *Timberland Tales*, that strip is a disgrace. It's a disgrace to Canada, a disgrace to the Mounties, a disgrace to every addled, brain-dead character in it. And because it's a total disgrace, I know you'll laugh your head off at that one, too.

Bob Taylor and I have been friends for many years. We are both devotees of the early years of *Mad* comics and *Mad* magazine. The zany but cynical humor influenced us both. And *Mad*'s meticulously hilarious artwork — by such brilliant illustrators as Will Elder, Jack Davis, and Wallace Wood — blew us away.

Bob continues that tradition with his art. I think you'll agree that you are looking at comics craftsmanship here that is seldom seen today. Controlled and out-of-control at the same time. It's quite a trick.

— *R.L. Stine*

ACKNOWLEDGEMENTS

Thank you (and my apologies) to loyal followers who wrote (and possibly never received a reply). In fact, you were my inspiration and the true motivation behind this long-overdue anthology.

My heartfelt thanks also to:

Gary Groth, **Mike Catron**, and **Justin Allan-Spencer** at Fantagraphics Books (and to the long-suffering production crew who had to eradicate Zipatone dots!).

Matty Simmons (Publisher and CEO 1970–1990) for founding the *National Lampoon* and being adventurous enough to make it all happen.

Evan Shapiro, new president of *National Lampoon*, for helping to make this happen and for resurrecting the *Lampoon* name.

Tim Allen, **R.L. Stine**, **Mike Judge**, and **Al Jean** for taking time to express your very generous comments.

Michael Gerber and *The American Bystander*, for spreading the news.

Melissa Turk at The Artists Network, art rep and guidance counselor.

Jane Stine at Parachute Press, for starting me out (*Dynamite*, *Hot Dog*, *Bananas* magazines), for your friendship, and for always knowing what worked.

Bob and **Gina Chapman** at Graphitti Designs, for many years of encouragement and friendship.

Denis Kitchen, fellow cartoonist, for prodding me to publish so many years ago.

Batton Lash and **Jackie Estrada**, for your friendship and guidance.

Harvey Kurtzman, **Jack Davis**, **Will Elder**, **Wallace Wood**, **Al Jaffee**, and **Arnold Roth**, for their influence during my formative years as a young lad.

Bob and **Ray** on CDs and tapes, who always made me laugh as I drew the strips.

Harry Borgman, fabulous artist, teacher, mentor, lifetime friend.

Jim Fox, best man, close friend, and artist extraordinaire, for our shared Detroit Lions commiseration and for the *Lampoon* "first attempt."

Bob Elnicky, for our many TV projects, your valued introductions (Jim Henson, Tim Allen), your friendship, and breakfast meetings pondering the mysteries of the world.

Brian McConnachie and **Sean Kelly**, for inviting me into the *National Lampoon* club.

Shary Flenniken, my *National Lampoon* buddy.

Dirk Gibson, producer at Inspired Entertainment (wanna make something of this?).

Birgit Kiel, cartoonist and writer, for your friendship and artistic eye.

Paula and **Dwayne**, for your friendship, encouragement, and desert sanctuary!

Mark Simonson, of *Mark's Very Large Lampoon Site*, for keeping it real.

Julie Simmons, for dreaming with me and helping champion the Appletons' cause.

Glenn Barr, artist, friend, and early studiomate.

Chato Hill, co-writer on our first humor book, *Make It Big in Business*, and all-around funny guy.

Rick Groffsky, legal eagle (you shoulda been a P.I.), confidante, and long-time pal.

Bob Schwartz, humor author and friend (let's do more books!).

Randall Diehl, friend and fellow artist, who sent me the amazing A.B. Frost book.

Paul Burke, Stabur Publishing (what's next?).

Tex Ragsdale, studiomate at Stunt Pilot Productions (we had a lot of fun!).

Hilary McCourt Bald, for being the target of my Canadian satire.

Helen and **Norm**, because you're Helen and Norm.

Cari and **Lauren**, my daughters, who somehow managed to remain innocent and relatively unscathed by the entire lurid *National Lampoon* process (and later married guys we actually like).

And last, but certainly not least, thank you to my wife and soulmate, **Kathy**, who had to suffer through fielding endless gag ideas and proofing text on each strip, as well as my inevitable and anguished question, "... but is it funny enough?" And who always (*usually*) laughed at my abstract humor.

ABOUT THE AUTHOR

B.K. Taylor grew up in Royal Oak, Michigan, the son of commercial artist Robert Grant Taylor (known for illustrating such works as Motown's *The Supremes Greatest Hits* album). While attending the College for Creative Studies in Detroit (and being reprimanded for drawing fruit flies over his still-life fruit bowls), B.K. began illustrating and writing for various satirical publications. Taylor also began work on the long-running *Odd Rods* bubblegum card series.

While performing and puppeteering on a local children's television show, a producer referred him to Jim Henson. Taylor collaborated with Henson for several years on Muppet design, creating the original Dr. Teeth character (the first-ever Muppet with teeth!) for the Muppet band, and the design of Digit and the band for NBC's *The Jim Henson Hour.* His work with Henson also led to several projects for Sesame Street television, books, and magazines.

Around that time, Taylor visited the *National Lampoon* offices in New York and pitched the original concept for *The Appletons.* It initially appeared in 1975 in *National Lampoon Presents The Very Large Book of Comical Funnies.* Reader popularity led to a second concept, and *Timberland Tales* was born. The *Lampoon* began running the two strips alternately, later joined by *Uncle Kunta* — and the rest is part of *Lampoon* history!

During this same period, Taylor began a long-standing association illustrating for Scholastic Publishing. He was approached by editor R.L. Stine to collaborate on *Nickelodeon Magazine* and television. He also illustrated several humor books with Stine, prior to R.L.'s staggering popularity with the *Goosebumps* and *Fear Street* book series.

An introduction to fellow Michigander Tim Allen, who was an avid reader of the *Lampoon* (and *The Appletons* in particular), led to a writing stint on the first three seasons of ABC's *Home Improvement* in 1991. Later, Taylor created character and concept designs for Walt Disney feature animations — a pivotal "dream come true" period all-around!

Over the years, B.K. Taylor's *Lampoon* strips have created an extensive reader following, opening many doors in his career, which he finds both gratifying and humbling. Seeing all the strips finally compiled in one volume, Taylor feels a special affinity for this strange cast of characters and the opportunities they helped bring about. This long-awaited collection is the final result.

Taylor is currently partnering with Inspired Entertainment on concept development for various television animation projects.

For my wife, Kathy (the real Kathleen of the North).
And my daughters, Cari and Lauren,
who will see the contents for the very first time.

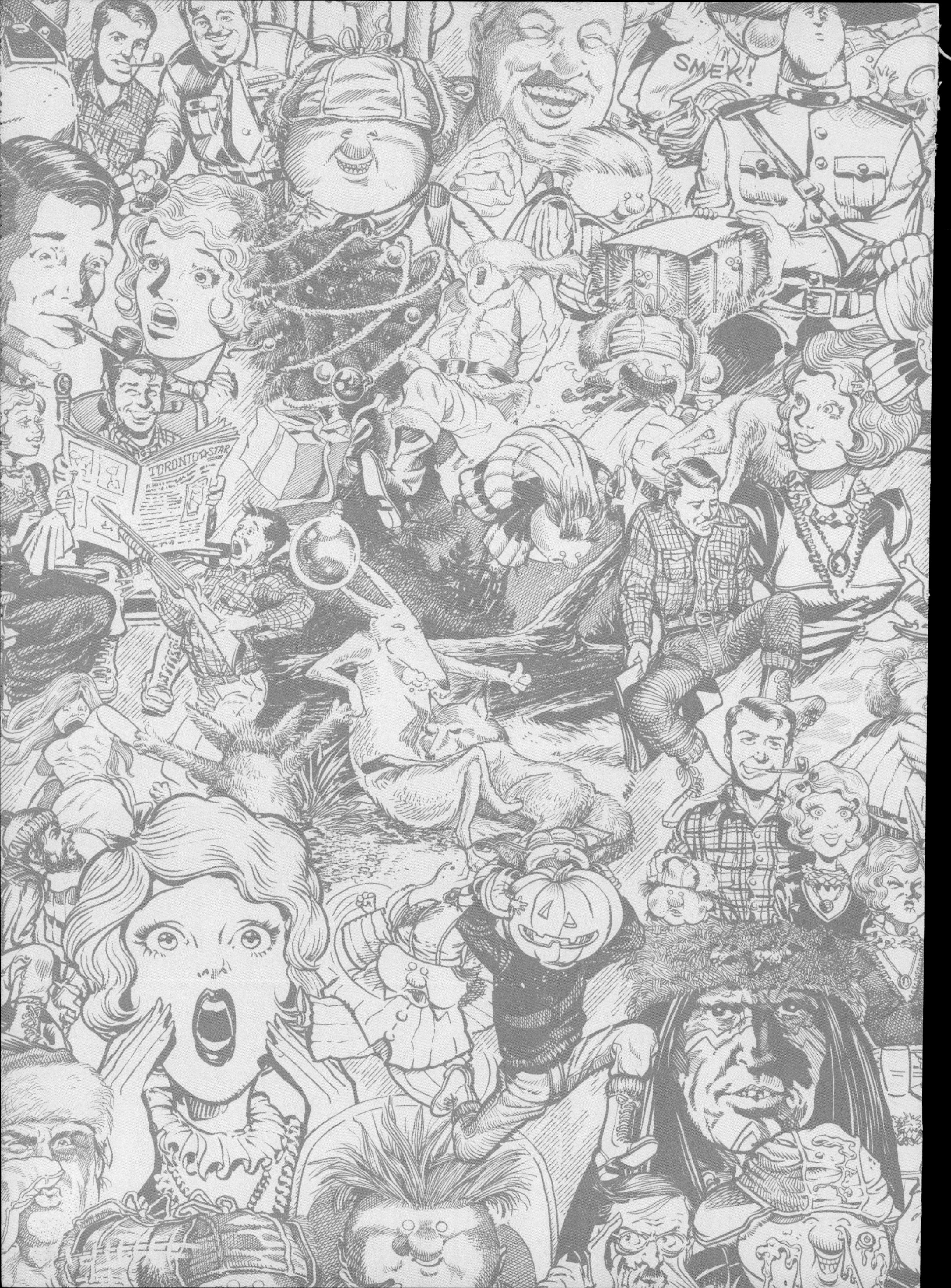
SMEK!
TORONTO STAR